ROUTLEDGE LIBRARY E
JOSEPH STALIN

Volume 1

THE REAL STALIN

THE REAL STALIN

YVES DELBARS

Routledge
Taylor & Francis Group

LONDON AND NEW YORK

First published in French in 1951
First published in English in 1953 by George Allen & Unwin Ltd

This edition first published in 2017
by Routledge
2 Park Square, Milton Park, Abingdon, Oxon OX14 4RN

and by Routledge
711 Third Avenue, New York, NY 10017

Routledge is an imprint of the Taylor & Francis Group, an informa business

British Library Cataloguing in Publication Data
A catalogue record for this book is available from the British Library

ISBN: 978-0-415-79299-8 (Set)
ISBN: 978-1-315-19466-0 (Set) (ebk)
ISBN: 978-1-138-70383-4 (Volume 1) (hbk)
ISBN: 978-1-138-70384-1 (Volume 1) (pbk)
ISBN: 978-1-315-20298-3 (Volume 1) (ebk)

Publisher's Note
The publisher has gone to great lengths to ensure the quality of this reprint but
points out that some imperfections in the original copies may be apparent.

Disclaimer
The publisher has made every effort to trace copyright holders and would welcome
correspondence from those they have been unable to trace.

THE
REAL
STALIN

Yves Delbars

TRANSLATED FROM THE FRENCH BY BERNARD MIALL

George Allen & Unwin Ltd
RUSKIN HOUSE · MUSEUM STREET · LONDON

Translated from
LE VRAI STALINE
Je Sors, Paris, 1951

PRINTED IN GREAT BRITAIN
in 12 *point Bembo type,*
BY WILLIAM BRENDON AND SON, LTD.
THE MAYFLOWER PRESS (LATE OF PLYMOUTH)
AT BUSHEY MILL LANE
WATFORD, HERTS

PREFACE

Stalin is one of those individuals who hold the keys of the modern world. A man who wields such an influence decade after decade is inevitably stamped with the seal of an exceptional destiny. Stalin is endowed with the gift of following the lines of historical development so closely that he seems to have been served by exceptional circumstances. Yet this is a psychological illusion; he has been favoured, not by chance, but by a nexus of individual qualities. Yet it is precisely as an individual that Stalin is so little known or understood. The veil of mystery that enshrouds him is not easily pierced, and the judgements and appreciations which have been formed of him have been singularly contradictory.

Although he is regarded, in principle, as the omnipotent ruler of the U.S.S.R., he is hardly ever held personally responsible for the misunderstandings between the West and the East. Truman, Churchill, and other Western statesmen often isolate him, in a fashion, from the other rulers of the U.S.S.R., whose attitude and whose actions they agree in condemning. This fact is due to a great complexity of reasons, the chief of which is the fact that the real Stalin is already disappearing behind the legendary figure, which was engendered and fashioned in accordance with preconceived ideas.

Propaganda—emitted by radio and the cinema, by the tongue and the pen—has finally created a sort of global landscape in which a Stalin—who for some is a baleful demon, and for others the angel of an Earthly Paradise—bestrides an immense country.

It has, therefore, become difficult to distinguish the features of the real man, who is neither a symbol, nor a being endowed with superhuman intelligence, nor the personification of the spirit of evil.

Moreover, the personal—or, to be more exact, the private element—is obscured by the monstrous publicity which has gathered about his name. His quasi-deification is a political measure from which all personal egocentrism is excluded. Soviet history, with

v

the potent means of propaganda at the disposal of the modern State, has endeavoured to modify the story of the first thirty years of the U.S.S.R., and of the period of revolutionary activity which preceded them, by eliminating a number of personages, by charging others with all the sins in creation, and by presenting a travesty of the actual facts.

The comparatively modest part played by Stalin when the U.S.S.R. was coming into existence has thus been amplified, while many episodes of his progress towards power which cannot be recalled without a shudder are simply eliminated. On the other hand, those authors who are hostile to him seek to accuse him of all the failures of the system, and all its crimes; while refusing to recognize his influence over international politics.

Before the official legend has finally submerged his actual personality in a pseudo-historical fog, we shall endeavour to depict it in the pages of this book—the outcome of ten years of constant observation, which has enabled us, on many occasions, to foresee and explain certain of his actions, as no one else has explained and foreseen them. This documentation we have constantly completed and amplified by investigations, contacts, and carefully verified items of evidence, while chance has sometimes come to our assistance.

If we study, intensively, the memoirs and the records of those who bear witness to the life of Stalin and to the infancy and adolescence of the Soviet system, and the opinions of its countless enemies, one preliminary fact forces itself on our attention. This man, who has emerged from the people, and who seemed, for a long while, to be without extensive influence, whose academic culture is comparatively restricted, and who never gave evidence of any great intellectual vigour, is an individual endowed with a kind of psychological radar. Only a peculiar genius could have enabled this Georgian, born on the Russian frontier, to follow and control the main psychological currents of the 160 million inhabitants of the U.S.S.R., and to establish a workable compromise between the revolutionary ideology of which he is the protagonist, and the national continuity which always, in the end, rises to the surface.

In a time of social upheaval, revolution, and warfare, other men of exceptional powers—men like Roosevelt and Churchill—have exerted a great influence over the scales of world-equilibrium. But they have acted as representatives of a well-defined social and economic order, and have operated within a long-established framework. Others, like Mussolini and Hitler, incapable of reconciling their unruly imaginations and inordinate pretensions with the realities of national life, have left behind them nothing but disorder and useless destruction.

History has entrusted Stalin with a special task, a task for which he has assumed full responsibility, and in whose defence he has fought with fierce determination. It is to close, in the U.S.S.R.—by the methods of Stalinism, a variant of the Marxist and Leninist doctrines—an epoch which for more than a century has been dominated by the world offensive of Socialism against the traditional order.

A representative of the Georgian minority, who has finally installed himself at the head of the Russian State, and of the ethnical groups which have gathered about it, he has retained many of the peculiarities of his native land. Thus, in tracing the course of his life, and his progress toward power, and analysing the part he is now playing in international politics, it is essential that we should speak of the country that shaped his childhood and youth. For in the course of its history Georgia, of which the modern world has taken little heed, has presented many striking analogies with certain ideological and material aspects of the régime of which one of her sons is now the chief support.

We must attempt to give an impartial description, based upon numerous data, many of which have not hitherto been revealed to the public, nor analysed.

We shall endeavour, then, to describe Stalin as he really is, resolutely discarding the lazy solution of the all too famous 'veil of mystery,' and refusing to surrender to the lure of legend, but also assessing at their true value the judgements inspired by hatred or ignorance.

We shall show him as he is in his strength and weakness, in the versatility of his dogmatic theories, in the patient subtlety of his tactics, in the pitiless enforcement of his decisions, in his skill in attributing to others the responsibility for the cruellest measures, in his gift for focusing the irresistible aspirations of the Russian masses, and his capacity for avoiding the peril of being swept away by the tides.

There existed a certain lacuna, and this gap we hope we have filled; at least in part. In so doing we have taken into account neither the sympathies of certain readers, nor the phobias of others, nor the reactions which this book may evoke in the pro-Stalinist or the anti-Stalinist. We ourselves have refrained from expressing any judgements, in order to confine ourselves to a strict objectivity.

Y.D.

CONTENTS

	PREFACE	page v
I	*Prologue*	11
II	*The Youth of Joseph Stalin*	18
III	*The Seminary at Tiflis*	24
IV	*Professional Revolutionary*	30
V	*Imprisonment and Deportation*	37
VI	*Escape*	42
VII	*The Birth of 'Stalin'*	48
VIII	*Further Imprisonment and Life Abroad*	56
IX	*St. Petersburg, 1913–17*	66
X	*The First Revolution and the Struggle for Power*	73
XI	*Lenin as Stalin's Teacher*	78
XII	*Trotzky in the Foreground: Difficult Days*	86
XIII	*The Congress of Unification*	92
XIV	*The Bolshevik Coup*	95
XV	*Revolution and Civil War*	102
XVI	*Second Marriage: War with Poland*	112
XVII	*Stalin becomes Party Secretary*	116
XVIII	*Lenin's Testament, and the Conquest of Power*	122
XIX	*The End of the Triumvirate*	131
XX	*The Secret of Stalin's Ascent to Power*	136
XXI	*The New Dogma*	140
XXII	*Stalin and the Politburo*	147
XXIII	*The Struggle against the Right*	157
XXIV	*Collectivization: the First Five-Year Plan*	161
XXV	*The Great Purge Approaches*	167
XXVI	*Extermination of the Opposition: the First Phase*	172
XXVII	*Extermination of the Opposition: the Second Phase*	181

XXVIII	*The Apotheosis of Stalin*	189
XXIX	*Stalin and Foreign Politics*	195
XXX	*Diplomatic General Post*	204
XXXI	*Towards Munich*	210
XXXII	*Munich*	222
XXXIII	*The Russo-German Treaties*	233
XXXIV	*The War and Communism*	246
XXXV	*Unconverted Diplomacy*	256
XXXVI	*The Russo-German Struggle for the Balkans*	261
XXXVII	*Molotov in Berlin*	267
XXXVIII	*Towards a Russo-German War*	275
XXXIX	*Industrial Preparation: The Pact with Japan*	284
XL	*Stalin is Taken by Surprise*	289
XLI	*Stalin Organizes his Work in Time of War*	301
XLII	*The Battles of Moscow: Contacts with the Allies*	308
XLIII	*The New Command*	315
XLIV	*Stalingrad*	321
XLV	*Tentatives in Direction of a Separate Peace*	334
XLVI	*Stalin and Roosevelt: Teheran*	338
XLVII	*Between Teheran and Yalta*	354
XLVIII	*Yalta*	365
XLIX	*Between Yalta and Potsdam*	379
L	*Potsdam*	390
LI	*The Atomic Age and the Cold War*	396
LII	*The U.S.S.R. and Stalin as Time has Changed Them*	408
	BIBLIOGRAPHY	419
	INDEX	423

PUBLISHER'S NOTE

Since this book has been translated from the French, the French transliteration of Russian names has been retained with only one or two obvious exceptions. It may even be claimed that these French forms are phonetically more correct than their generally accepted English equivalents, but they are in every case always recognizable.

CHAPTER I

PROLOGUE

Jossif Vissarionovitch Djugachvili-Stalin was born at Gori, in Georgia, a small Transcaucasian country. He is greatly attached to it, and he is fond of drawing parallels between its individual history and the events of world-history.

It is a territory of something less than 30,000 square miles, bounded on the south-east by the Chirvan, on the south by Armenia, on the north by Ossetia and Western Caucasia, on the north-east by Daghestan, and on the west by the Turkish districts of Asia Minor. A very ancient country, it makes its appearance in history at the very dawn of the civilizations of the Near East. From this point of view it is contemporary with the great Semitic and Hamitic empires; but it did not lie across the route of the Egyptian or Assyrian armies, as the land of Palestine would lie at a later period. It is to this fact that it owes the circumstance that it was able to preserve its peculiar character even in our own epoch. It is an insular territory. These facts must be taken into account if we wish to understand the development of the Georgian mentality, all of whose characteristics we shall find in Stalin.

Thanks to early relations between Georgia and the land of the Pharaohs, the roots of Georgian culture were nourished by the culture of Egypt. The famous *Instructions* of Ammen-Em-Phta to his son, Oussor-Te-Sen I, introduced into Georgia by Papi-Sineh, are at the base of the ancient literature of Georgia.

The Georgian kings governed their country by crushing the revolts of their vassals in the germ, and by practising the 'preventive execution' of those whose disloyal whispers were heard by those about the throne.

From time to time they 'purged' their generals and their ministers; as King Pharnavaz purged them, inspired by the example of his neighbours, the kings of Persia.

When the army of Alexander the Great made its appearance on the Silk Route, in order to reach India by way of Persia, one of the generals of this army conquered Georgia. But this foreign domination was shaken off by the same King Pharnavaz. Later on Georgia allied herself with King Mithridates VI—'the Great'—antiquity's greatest connoisseur in poisons. The Georgian court also was contaminated by this passion for the study of poisons. A very potent soporific—*kerdag*—was employed in the royal palace, where several kings passed from life to death in their sleep.

In the year 65 B.C. Pompey, the conqueror of Mithridates, subjected Georgia likewise. But this little country refused to assimilate either the civilization of the Great Republic, or its religion, or its manners.

In the eleventh century the kings of Georgia became the allies of the Byzantine court. The arts and manners of Byzantium were introduced into the country by George IV (A.D. 1019). At this time the small but ambitious Georgian court became a replica of the court of 'the second Rome'—Byzantium. An Arab traveller, Ibn Melek, has left us a picturesque description of the Georgian court:

'I have seen the king of this country in the great hall of his palace. He was tall and handsome, his countenance radiant with intelligence and beauty. Clad in purple and gold, he was seated on a golden throne, his courtiers standing around him.

'A great mechanical lion, like that of the Emperor of Byzantium, roared, rolled its eyes, and lashed its flanks with its tail. A metallic panther—an animal sacred to the Georgians—turned its head, being placed on the opposite side of the throne. . . .

'I prostrated myself as the etiquette of the court required. When I rose the king and his throne, lifted into the air by a mysterious mechanism, overlooked the hall; the crown, of pure gold, was glittering on the king's head. One could have likened it to a blazing sun. . . .

'Then sundry persons entered the hall: poets, musicians, and men of science. They recited verses, they played upon long curving harps. The men of science showed us great charts which represented the stars, the sun and the moon.

'The king gave ear to them. Often he made a sign; then all were silent, and he alone spoke. I understood that he was giving instructions to these musicians, poets, and men of science; they listened to him, prostrating themselves. . . .'

If a Western traveller were able to attend a session of the Academy of Science of the U.S.S.R., with Stalin in the chair, his description would certainly be less picturesque. But one has only to read the first page of *Izvestia*, or see the Sovietic film of the Battle of Stalingrad, or of Berlin, to be impressed by the psychological analogy.

In the age of Genghis Khan and Tamerlane (the thirteenth and fourteenth centuries) Georgia, like her neighbours, was traversed by the Mongolian and Turkish hordes. A Tatar general, Makrou, the nephew of Batou, entered the capital. In the great square of the city was erected—a sinister symbol of the Mongol conquest—a 'pyramid of heads,' with the head of the Georgian king at the summit.

The occupation was of brief duration, thanks to a courageous revolt. The princes who had taken refuge in the mountains formed an alliance with the populations dwelling on the frontiers of Georgia: the Ossetes, Lazes, Mingrelians and Lesghians. An offensive delivered by the mountaineers drove the Mongol detachments out of the country, which became once more independent.

At the beginning of the sixteenth century the Ossetes came down from the mountains to pillage the countryside. The Ossetes were an Indo-Caucasian people, like the Georgians, who had long mingled their blood with that of the Mongolized tribes coming from Tatar Azerbeidjan. They installed themselves in great strength in the region of Gori, and the pure Georgian type disappeared. The rude, vigorous features of the Ossetian mountaineers replaced the beautiful, regular and melancholy features of the Georgians, the handsomest of the Caucasian peoples.

Another ethnical event followed the penetration of the Ossetes. A group of immigrants made its way across the mountains and plains of Iran. It was not very numerous, but it was composed of active individuals: artisans, traders and soldiers. These immigrants came from the island of 'Dju,' in the Gulf of Cambay, and they included a number of Marranos—Portuguese Jews who practised the rites of their religion in secret.

In the dialect of the populations of this region the word 'Djuga,' which signified the natives of the island of Dju, acquired the signification of 'Israelite.' Some three centuries later, on the occasion of a census of the people, when proper names were given to those in-habitants of Georgia who were not of noble family, the descendants of the people of Dju became known as Djugachvili (in Georgian, 'the sons of Dju').

It is practically impossible to estimate the proportions of the blood of the Lisbon *marranos*, the galley-slaves from Porto and Vinho, the Georgians, the Ossetes, and the Mongoloid tribes of Tatar Azerbeidjan in the veins of the clan of the 'Djugachvili.'

From the sixteenth century Moscow asserted its claim to the political and religious heritage of Byzantium. Muscovy was the only Orthodox state to retain its sovereignty, and on Muscovy was incum-bent the task of defending the Christian faith against the infidels, and liberating the Orthodox peoples. Among these peoples were the Orthodox Georgians.

In the second half of the sixteenth century the paths followed by the destinies of the Russians and the Georgians began to coincide. The troops of Tsar Ivan the Terrible (Ivan IV) descended the Volga, to conquer first Kazan, and then Astrakhan, the centre of a Tatar kingdom of the same name: an event whose historical importance was manifest four centuries later, when a Djugachvili, born in Gori, installed himself in Moscow as the ruler of the Russian people, bearing the name of Stalin.

When one of the earliest expeditions arrived at Derbent, in the reign of Tsar Feodor, the son of Ivan the Terrible, the Cossacks found there an embassy of five persons, led by a Georgian prince, Amilakhvari,[1] the feudal Prince of Gori. This embassy begged that it might proceed to Moscow, there to implore the Tsar's protection against the Persians. A second mission came to Moscow during the reign of Boris Godounov. But it was not until the reign of Peter the Great that Russia seriously turned her attention upon the Caucasus. When in 1721 the great Tsar had ended the war against Sweden by the Treaty of Nystad he again turned southwards.

On the 3 September, 1723, the Shah signed a treaty of alliance with the Tsar: the Treaty of Derbent. By this treaty Persia ceded to Russia the regions of Derbent and Baku, and the provinces of Ghilan, Mazanderan and Astrabad, and in it the Shah recognized—though

---

[1]Ancestor of the hero, of Bir-Hakeim.

somewhat vaguely—a sort of common Russo-Persian protectorate over Georgia.

In 1783 Heraclius II recognized the Russian suzerainty over his country. A firm and lasting bond was established. In 1799 King George XII signed a treaty with the Tsar Paul I, by which Georgia recognized the right of Russia to represent Georgian interests abroad. The country became an autonomous province of the Russian Empire.

In 1801 the Tsar Alexander annexed the country outright, annulling its autonomy, despite the protests of the nobles. The reigning Georgian dynasty became the dynasty of 'the Most Serene Georgian princes of the Russian Empire.' Every Georgian born henceforth enjoyed the same rights in Russia as any other Russian subject: a situation analogous to that of the Corsicans in France after 1768.

The Caucasians have always been a turbulent folk. The Georgians are no exception to the rule. A year after the conclusion of the Treaty of Gulistan the first revolt against the Russians broke out. It was followed by another outbreak in 1820, and in 1828 yet another revolt drenched a great part of the country in blood.

In 1832, in accordance with the traditions of the post-revolutionary period, the entire Georgian people rose, and an army of liberation was formed. The Ossetes, led by their prince, Koussiki, took part in the revolution. After a general Caucasian revolt, led by the Iman Chamil, had been effectively suppressed, in the mountains the 'Abreks'—half brigands, half revolutionaries—continued to attack the Russian troops, the Tsar's officials, and even the Armenian merchants and the State treasuries. They enjoyed the sympathies of the local clergy.

The youth of Georgia, nourished on the religious and warlike songs collected in the eighteenth century by the Patriarch Anton, passionately followed the exploits of the 'Abreks,' their attacks upon the troops, and the pillage of the treasuries, which had become traditional. The 'Abreks' were regarded as heroes, liberators, friends of the people.

One day Prince Galitzin, Viceroy of the Caucasus, paid a visit to Gori. The cathedral choir executed a few religious chants. The director of the choir, the Orthodox almoner Mardalian, wanted the viceroy to hear one of his best choristers.

This was a pupil of the local theological college, who had won a deserved reputation by his voice, a true and supple alto. The boy was nine years of age. His name was Jossif Djugachvili, and he was the son of a bootmaker.

The Viceroy, wishing to thank the young singer, beckoned to him and gave him some sweets. 'You will become a greater singer,' he told Djugachvili.

'I don't want to,' the future dictator of Soviet Russia replied. 'I want to become an Abrek!'

Twenty-five years later Djugachvili, who in the meantime had passed by a whole series of different names, adopted, finally, the name of Stalin. He had been exiled to Siberia. The Abreks were still in the mountains. Their leader was a certain Zelim-Khan, a sort of mountain Cartouche.

Lenin was living in Switzerland. One day he was asked his opinion of Stalin. He replied, with a mischievous wink of his Tatar eyes: 'Stalin is Zelim-Khan after studying Karl Marx's "Capital".'

The *sobriquet* was never forgotten.

Ascending the course of the Aioli, a stream which flows into the Koura at Gori, we find, a few miles from the town, a large mountain village, bearing the fantastic name of Didi-Lilo.

In 1850 a bootmaker, Ivan Djugachvili, opened his shop in Didi-Lilo. When the Russian Government required all the inhabitants of Georgia to provide themselves with passports[1] the Djugachvilis of Didi-Lilo were described, by reason of their possession of a vineyard, as a family of peasants. This gave rise, at a later period, to the legend that Stalin was of peasant origin.

Ivan Djugachvili, who married a Gori woman, a member of the Bakhtadzé family, continued to carry on the trade of his ancestors. But he was a notable drinker. Thanks to his vineyard, he was able to drink a wine of his own vintage, the famous Georgian wine, light and tart, which is drunk at all hours of the day.

In the year which saw his establishment at Didi-Lilo, a son was born to Ivan. He was baptized Vissarion—Bezo in Georgian—in the little parish church. In the bootmaker's shop he followed his father; the trade had become a family tradition. In 1861–63, when the serfs were liberated, Ivan became a free artisan. He no longer had to pay a

[1] An 'internal passport' very similar to an identity card.

personal due to Prince Amilakhvari, but his material position was not much improved.

Vissarion had a different character. Despite his poverty, his was a turbulent nature; it was as though the blood of his adventurous forbears gave him no rest. He took part in every local affray.

On 2 May, 1874, Vissarion-Bezo made the acquaintance of Catherine Guéorguicona Guéladzé, a handsome girl with hair black as jet, and the regular features of a pure-blooded Georgian. One could see already that once she had passed her first youth her face would remind one of the austere Byzantine ikons in which the Holy Virgin is represented as the Mater Dolorosa, the protectress of all sufferers.

The two children of Vissarion and Catherine lived only a few months. When she was expecting the birth of her third child she would often say: 'My third child—I am certain he will be a boy, like the first two—will be a priest or a monk. His whole life will be devoted to serving God, and I hope I shall one day see him become the exarch (patriarch) of our holy Orthodox Georgian Church. Then I shall die at peace and happy. . . .'

The pious Kéké's wish was granted after a fashion, but not quite in the manner which she had anticipated.

The third son was born on the 21 December, 1879. He did not become the head of the Georgian Church, which numbers two million believers. But he was to become the living god of another and a far more widespread religion, which seeks to extend its rule over nearly 800 millions of human beings, in many countries, and which claims to be a universal Church, beside which all other religions would play but a secondary and often negligible part. And the road by which it would come to power was to be drenched with blood.

B

CHAPTER II

THE YOUTH OF JOSEPH STALIN

A T this time Gori, where the son of Vissarion Djugachvili
was born, was only a small town of 7,500 inhabitants. The
centre of a department, it boasted a sub-prefect, a theological college, a boys' school, a primary school for girls,
a cathedral, and four churches, in one of which were celebrated the
rites of the Armenian Catholics.

The cottage in which Stalin first saw the light of day has but one
living-room. Its rent was one and a half roubles. This room is a little
over twelve feet square. It opens into a small kitchen. The floor is of
brick. One very small window admits a little light. But the landscape
which this window reveals has a wild beauty of its own.

Mount Kasbek rises into the heavens, its two summits gleaming
with snow. In fine weather one can see, in the distance, the majestic
outline of Elbruz, and the range of mountains which divide Georgia
into two parts. In the spring the fruit trees cover the slopes of the
hills with blossoms. The air is cool and bracing. It is laden with the
fragrance of the mountain flowers, above all of the Caucasian
lavender, the *Kouratchi*, which is reputed to possess miraculous tonic
properties.

The furniture of the room was more than modest: it contained a
hard, narrow couch, known as a *tachta*, covered with a *tchilopa*—a
straw mat, a Kirvan carpet, with an Oriental pattern, and a *mutaki*—
a parti-coloured cushion; a simple table, two stools, and a *gingodani*—
a sort of chest, in which the Georgians keep their bread. On the wall
was an ivory crucifix—which Catherine inherited from her grandmother, who died the year she was married. This was the only object
of any value possessed by the family; it was the work of a well-known
artist, the Armenian Anastasius Koliantz.

Other articles of Russian origin completed the scanty furnishing.
Of these the first was a samovar, which the bootmaker bought one day
from a wounded soldier. It represented the first introduction of

18

Russian customs into the household in which Stalin was born. There was also a sewing-machine which Catherine was able to buy on the instalment system. With the help of this machine she hoped to pay at least part of the expenses of the education of the son whom she was expecting.

Life was not easy for Kéké. Sosso, like the two brothers whom he never knew, was born a sickly child. His left arm was shorter than the right, and he could move it only with difficulty. The second and third toes of each foot were joined together. Tormented by the dread of seeing him share the fate of her first two children, Catherine was ready to make any sacrifice to increase his chances of survival. She worked as charwoman in the houses of the wealthier inhabitants of Gori, and her sewing-machine might be heard until late into the night.

At eleven months little Sosso began to walk. His first tongue, which he spoke until his eighth year, was Georgian; but a fortunate chance enabled him to learn to pronounce the Russian language. The guttural Georgian language is spoken with great rapidity, and those Georgians who have not learned Russian from their earliest childhood have great difficulty in pronouncing Russian words correctly. It so happened, however, that one of Sosso's playmates was a Russian boy, son of the inspector of the theological college. Boutilsky was a native of Vologda, in Southern Russia, who spoke both Russian and Georgian. Sosso, who had a good ear, soon picked up the Slav intonations.

An unruly child, he was often corrected by his father. Once he and his Russian playfellow had a stone-throwing contest, in the course of which they killed some of their neighbour's chickens. For this they had to pay, in compensation, the fabulous sum of forty kopecks—approximately tenpence. On another occasion they broke a neighbour's window. Sosso uttered a violent oath; a Russian expression, whose meaning the child could not possibly have understood. But his father understood it, having heard it on the lips of Russian soldiers, and Sosso, despite his mother's intervention, was severely punished.

The pious teaching of his mother and the awakening of a fervent Georgian nationalism were the two chief influences by which the boy's mind and character were formed. Kapanadzé, a playmate who had once lent him a book—*The Knight in the Panther's Skin*, by the Georgian poet Chota Roustaveli—took him one day to see his grandfather, who had taken part in the great revolt of 1832. This grandfather, then an old man of eighty-five, had spent twenty years in the terrible prison of the Tiflis fortress. He was almost deaf, and all but blind. He sat up in bed and looked little Sosso in the eyes. 'Do you want to learn of all the harm that has been done to our unhappy country? Would you like to hear how our little nation fought against an immense empire? Listen to me! . . .'

This encounter with the old Kapanadzé made an ineffaceable impression on the boy. Instead of playing ball, he and his contemporaries 'played at soldiers.' Fifteen to twenty boys enacted 'the war against Russia.' They were divided into two groups: Sosso was usually the Georgian leader. He was not only a plucky lad; he was cunning, and in these early battles he would lie in ambush, seeking to entrap or surprise the enemy.

When he was approaching his tenth year his mother decided that he must prepare for the entrance examination of the theological college at Gori. His teacher was a Ukrainian; Riabko, a student at the university of Kharkov, had been deported to the Caucasus, after the assassination of Prince Kropotkin, a cousin of the illustrious 'founder' of anarchism.

Early in 1890 there occurred one of those little incidents that play their part in shaping a child's character. It impressed itself on the memory of those who witnessed it; Stalin himself never forgot it, and with the passage of years it acquired a symbolic significance.

He was working, one day, in his father's workshop, and chattering to a fellow student, young Katochvili. Bezo Djugachvili, his father, was busy at his bench over an urgent order: the boots of the young Prince Amilakhavari, who would be calling for them about seven. At twelve o'clock the prince appeared. He dismounted from his horse, picked up his boots, and turned to Sosso:

'Here, youngster, hold my horse while I get into the saddle—and here are five kopecks for you!' And he threw the boy a copper coin. 'Never,' said Katochvili afterwards, 'have I seen such a look of black hatred in Sosso's eyes. His features were distorted with rage. He was breathing quickly; it was evident that he found it unbearable to be treated in such a way while I was present.' Amilakhvari had been gone for some time before he cooled down. In sudden rage he spat on the coin, and shaking his fist at the old castle of the Amilakhvari princes he uttered one of the frightful Russian oaths, and added:

'B— and b— him! You see, Noé, there are swine among the Georgians too! When we've settled accounts with the Russians we mustn't forget to deal with them!'

'Later on,' added Katochvili, 'I understood that he had just had a revelation of the real nature of social injustice.'

Sosso's father died at the age of thirty-eight. He was buried in the little Gori cemetery, in the section set aside for the poor. Catherine put up a little headstone, which remained until 1912, when the cemetery was secularized.

In the autumn of 1890 Sosso passed the entrance examination of the theological college. He headed the list. This meant that he could enter the college as an external student, while he was awarded a bursary of three and a half roubles a month.

The theological college at Gori (*doukovnoié outchilichtché*) prepared students for the theological seminary. Its general scholastic programme was very much that of the five lower classes of the Russian public schools of the period. It comprised Latin. There were special classes for the catechism, the dogmas of the Orthodox religion, the liturgy, the elements of logic, and the Greek language; and there was an optional class for the Hebrew language, which was taught very thoroughly in many of the seminaries, including that of Tiflis. Teaching was given in Russian, but on three days in the week a professor of the Georgian language gave lessons to those pupils whose parents wished them to study Georgian.

At eleven years of age Sosso was a cheerful, rowdy urchin, who took part in all the games of his schoolfellows, especially the ball games; and he was passionately fond of singing. He was rather short in stature, but strong and broad-shouldered. His thick hair fell over his eyes, so that you might have thought he had a low forehead; but when he swept it back you saw that he had a good forehead and finely chiselled temples. His ears were small and set close to his head; his lips were thin, and his nose was straight. His eyes were very bright. They were large, but they were not jet black like the eyes of the Georgians. He had inherited from his Ossetian forefathers their straight nose and their brown eyes—eyes of a chestnut brown, with dilated pupils, the iris being speckled like the skin of a mountain trout. His movements were quick and accurate. He was fond of dancing, and his feet, always very badly shod, sped nimbly over the dusty paving of the Gori market-place when the popular dances were held there.

In 1892 he gave his mother great happiness. At a solemn mass, in celebration of the anniversary of the Emperor Alexander III, Sosso sang the solo chants before the sub-prefect and the notables of the city. Kéké listened to her son with tears in her eyes; already she saw her dream half realized. She could no longer doubt that her son would enter the Church, and would one day become a great dignitary.

Little Sosso's voice rang out under the vaulted roof of the cathedral, as the worshippers besought God to grant long life and happiness to the Tsar, the Tsarina, and the little Grand Duke Nicholas, the future Tsar Nicholas II. This Nicholas was to be the last of the Russian Emperors; and in 1918 he was executed by the order of the Central Committee of the Bolshevik Party, of which Sosso, who had then become Stalin, was a member.

Sosso had read and re-read a romance whose hero, a mountaineer, was called Koba. One day he and his playmates undertook an expedition into the mountains—that is, the hill behind the castle.

'Listen to me!' he cried. 'I'm no longer Sosso; from now on my name is Koba! Yes, Koba! I shall follow in Koba's footsteps. I devote myself to the struggle for the liberation of our people, so that Georgia may be free and happy! I'll sacrifice my life to the cause if need be. Do you understand? Will you march beside me?'

'Yes!' cried the boys to their self-appointed leader.

'Hurrah for Brdzola!' cried Sosso-Koba.

'Hurrah for Brdzola!' the others responded.

In the spring of this year, 1894, Sosso completed his studies in the Gori school. He passed out first, with honours.

At the end of August, furnished with a certificate bearing the signature of the headmaster, and carrying a cloth satchel, he left Gori for Tiflis, some forty to fifty miles distant. On the 1 September,

1894, he was admitted to the seminary as a boarder. There he remained for five years; and today the walls of the ancient college are adorned by a commemorative tablet, on which one may read:

'Here, in the ancient seminary of Tiflis, Comrade Stalin studied, from the 1st September, 1894, to the 29th July, 1899.'

CHAPTER III

THE SEMINARY AT TIFLIS

NIGHT was already falling when Sosso and his future comrades entered the seminary. They went into the office, where the *smotritel* (registrar) Mokareli entered their names on a list after verifying their passports and credentials. Before the usher showed them the way to the dormitory he handed Sosso a document on which it was stated that Joseph Djugachvili, 'having taken the first place in his studies at the theological college of Gori, will now receive the benefit of a complete scholarship, including clothes, footwear and books.'

There being no university in Tiflis, the seminary took the place of a university. The course of studies lasted for six years, the student passing through four general and two special classes. The programme of the first four classes was equivalent to the course for the school certificate in the Russian schools. In the two upper classes the student received a religious and classical education, and on passing out he could enter the Theological Academy of St. Petersburg.

This was a period when liberal and revolutionary ideas were floating in the air. The younger generation had assimilated these ideas. The students, of all nationalities, took part in the clandestine activities of the different political parties and the various clubs. The seminary pupils, of whom 85 per cent were Georgians, regarded themselves as the vanguard of the student politicians of Tiflis. In Russia the university students were among the leaders of the revolutionary movement. The seminary students aspired to play the same part in Tiflis, and to assume the leadership of the national movement of liberation.

It was inevitable that Sosso, transplanted into this environment and breathing this atmosphere, should have been enlisted by his seniors, who had discarded the cassock even before they had begun to wear it, and had thrown themselves into the national Georgian revolutionary movement.

24

But the psychological conversion of the young student was not effected overnight. He was not yet ready to enter into open rebellion against the Emperor of all the Russias, 'crowned by God.' His mother's teaching held him back, and the Christian faith. Before he could become a revolutionist he must break these bonds; and this he could not do at a moment's notice. His mind was yet insufficiently mature.

As always, he was reading a great deal. In Tiflis he could get all the books he wanted, whether Russian or Georgian. He read everything that came into his hands; often surreptitiously, and even during his classes, assisted by the surprising ease with which he assimilated the official instruction.

One day he came across a Russian translation of the principal volumes of Balzac's *Comédie Humaine*. He read them in a kind of ecstasy which recalled the religious trances of his childhood. When he had become the all-powerful leader of the Communist Party of Russia, and generalissimo of the armies, he would often quote, in his speeches, from the few pages of the *Comédie Humaine* which had taught him, in the dawn of life, 'the whole gamut of the human passions.' The works of Balzac were always, for him, his favourite text-books of human psychology.

The time had come when a sudden shock would free him from the constraint of his childhood beliefs.

One day his comrade Kurdiani gave him a copy of a weekly paper and a pamphlet. The paper was an old copy of the Moscow *Telescope*, dating from 1836. The pamphlet was a privately produced edition of the catechism of the Mouravieff brothers, which in 1825 had served as propaganda to encourage Tchougourieff's regiment to revolt.

Sosso began by studying the catechism. Some words of the poet Rybeieff—one of the conspirators of the Petersburg plot of 1825, who was hanged with other Decembrists in 1826—were printed on the first page: 'It is by means of such works that one can influence the mind of the people.' Then followed a series of questions and responses:

'Was the autocracy established by God?—God in His goodness cannot have established an evil thing. An evil power cannot emanate

from God.—Does God love the Tsars?—No! They are accursed by
God, as oppressors of the people and because God loves men. He
who would learn God's judgement concerning the Tsars has only to
read the eighth chapter of the First Book of Samuel.—What does the
sacred law command the Russian people and the Russian army to
do?—To repent of their prolonged servitude, to arm themselves
against tyranny and impiety, to swear that for all men there shall be
on earth, and in the heavens, but one God: Jesus Christ.'

Sosso read this new catechism with attention. It corresponded, in
a conventional form, to what he had become accustomed in the
seminary, with his personal tendencies. It seemed to him that it was
logical, and that it revealed the true meaning of a religion, far more
clearly than the official catechism of Philaretus which he had
learned in the seminary and the theological college.

The old number of the *Telescope*, now yellow with age, impressed
him even more deeply. On the first page was an article by Tchaadaieff
entitled: 'Letter on the Philosophy of History.'

The letter began with three words of the Paternoster: *adveniat
regnum tuum*. They represented the entire philosophy and the whole
religion of the author: *The realization of the Kingdom of God must
come not only in heaven but also on earth. During the earthly life of
humanity a religious society should set itself up, a Church, which would be
none other than the Kingdom of God, in which all men would be free and
equal before fate. According to Tchaadaieff this is the real aim of
Christianity.*

Thus, almost a century before the advent of the Christian
Socialists, the author expounded a theory to which Fate attracted
Sosso's attention at the moment which was decisive for his spiritual
orientation. Tchaadaieff believed in the particular and universal
destiny of Russia as distinct from that of Europe and Byzantium.
He was convinced that the salvation of the country depended on a
fresh revelation, for which men were waiting; a revelation of the
religious and social principles of the Church conceived as the Kingdom of God on earth: principles which were comprised in the teaching of Christ, but had somehow been misunderstood or disregarded
by men.

Sosso pondered these theories day and night. He began to feel
that in his case the mission of the priesthood might perhaps be re-

placed by a different mission. But the real nature of this mission had not yet become apparent. Mouravieff had supplied him with negative arguments. Tchaadaieff offered him constructive ideas, and suggested a task of enormous scope, though as yet these suggestions were indefinite. . . .

Meanwhile his character began to acquire consistency. He became hard and obstinate, as his father had been; as were all the men of the Djugachvili clan, with their complex heredity, bequeathed by generations which had been unduly tested; but he was also patient and enduring, like all mountaineers. But under the influence of his mother and the teaching of the theological college he submitted to the discipline established by the catechism and by his teachers. This internal discipline helped to produce firmness of character, and to give him great self-control; it also developed a prudence which in the course of years took the form of taciturnity. He was reserved, but affable, though many of those who came into closest contact with him already described him as crafty.

Already he was unable to see how he could reconcile his duties as a priest with the things which were nearest to his heart—which had possessed his imagination, and had led him to adopt the name of Koba. He was still too young to find a solution of his difficulties. It was, indeed, to be a long while before he did find it.

He was sixteen years of age. He continued to read books by the dozen. But the 'Orthodox Catechism' of the Mouravieffs and Tchaadaieff's 'Commentaries on the Philosophy of History' had imprinted themselves upon his mind.

Towards the close of the year 1895 it seemed that he had found a solution. It was not yet definitive; but it gave his philosophy and his actions a definite orientation. This was the moment when Fate, having shaped the mind and the character of the man she had singled out, launched him upon the strange current that inspires and guides and supports the exceptional destiny. Sosso concluded that the rôle of priest was incompatible with his dream of fighting by every means for Georgia and social equality. He would join the great social-revolutionary movement which was shaking the foundations of the vast Russian Empire.

There is one point which distinguishes him from other revolutionaries, and which explains the peculiarities of his evolution. It enabled him to escape the inflexible setting of the Marxist doctrines, which the other revolutionaries obeyed so rigidly. He knew the Orthodox Church, and did not fear it as did Lenin, Trotzky, and the rest, in whose eyes it was a dangerous enemy which must be attacked without respite.

In the struggle upon which he was entering he would make admirable use of the patience and the cunning of his mountaineer ancestors, and like them he would excel in preparing ambushes, as he had done in his childhood on the hillside above Gori.

But through all the vicissitudes of his life the philosophical notions which he had acquired in 1895 would always determine the moral motives of his general behaviour, which would often reveal a disconcerting cruelty.

At the age of seventeen, Sosso impressed the beholder by his appearance of strength. He was not tall, but he was thickset. He held himself always very erect. His hair was still thick, but he swept it back without a parting, after the fashion of the Russian nihilists. His eyes were a little darker; his eyebrows were thick, and slightly lifted by a muscular contraction. The lachrymal sinuses were almost non-existent. This perhaps explains why no one ever saw Sosso, or Koba, or Stalin weep.

For Stalin, the hour for action had struck. Through Sylvester Djibladzé, a seminarist who had been expelled for striking a professor, Sosso made the acquaintance of a certain Sasha Tsouloukidzé, who was five years his senior. It was Sasha, one of the propagandists of Marxism in the Caucasus, who represented the link between the young revolutionary aspirant and the growing movement.

Tsouloukidzé gave Stalin a few popular pamphlets on Marxism; a summary of *Das Kapital*, published by Paramonov, at Rostov; a German book on the philosophy of Feuerbach; and Burchener's *Kraft und Stoff*; together with manuscript translations and a Russo-German dictionary.

In 1896 Sosso established the first Marxist group, of which he was the leader. It was a clandestine club, known as Brdzola (Fight), and consisted of eighteen seminarists. They all adopted pseudonyms; Sosso chose the pseudonym of Koba, in memory of his childish ambitions. The club was really a sort of secret revolutionary school, in which the seminarists discussed the clandestine books and pamphlets which Koba introduced, and debated the questions which he proposed. When their differences of opinion could not be reconciled Koba would settle the matter, relying on the authority conferred upon him by his rôle of leader. It became a veritable secret organization, and Koba led it with iron discipline and with the prudence that is one of his most prominent characteristics. His taste for conspiracy was increasing.

It was time to bid the reverend fathers farewell.

He asked for three days' leave, so that he could go home to Gori, to see his mother, who was ill. He found her convalescent. Old Father Boudou had been looking after her, and she was preparing to go out for the first time after having kept to her room for more than three months.

Koba did not dare to confess the real object of his visit, which was to announce his decision to leave the seminary. But he spoke of it to Boudou. Boudou had written to the Rector, asking him to arrange for Sosso's departure without attracting any special attention.

In 1899 Sosso left the seminary. But he did not enter the university. His future course was already laid down. It was that of the revolutionist. It was to lead him to the forefront of the historical stage.

CHAPTER IV

PROFESSIONAL REVOLUTIONARY

ON the 29 July, 1899, the doors of the seminary closed behind Sosso. An engineer in the railway workshops, Laptakinsky, obtained for him the post of 'calculator' in the Tiflis Observatory. Lodgings were provided in an adjacent building. Now he could proceed to action.

A number of Georgians had decided to initiate a movement against Tsarism, grouping themselves round the journal *Kvali* (The Furrow). The moderates favoured a cultural propaganda by means of small clubs, like that which Koba had managed at the seminary.

Koba, without hesitation, joined the partisans of direct action. He had not left his club merely to manage another similar organization. His temperament, his vocation, his faith in his special mission, his philosophy, on which Tchaadaieff had left his imprint, all steered him in the direction of radical action, and urged him to join the partisans of the latter.

But even among the extremists there was no unanimity. Some wanted to begin operations by means of strikes. They preferred to confine their activities to purely economic claims, in order not to alarm the masses. Others, who contemptuously called them 'the economists,' called for immediate revolutionary action. Their leaders were Tsouloukidzé and Kotschkoveli, both friends of Koba's.

Stalin became a follower of Lenin, who had conceived a notion very simple in itself, but extremely effective. He had decided to graft the theoretical socialism of Marx on to the labour movement, which since 1883 had manifested itself in Russia by a series of strikes, riots, and conflicts with the police. This movement was directed by the more prominent and better educated of the workers, and also by the groups of intellectuals known as 'Papalists.' These latter, although Socialists, flatly refused to adopt Marx's philosophy of historical materialism. Lenin was looking a long way ahead. He was not interested merely in questions of wages, social insurance, and the welfare of the workers. What he wanted was a social upheaval.

Koba agreed to support this policy without a moment's hesitation. Nothing could have suited his combative temperament better. The fusion between the *abrek* and Social Democracy was effected. At the same time, his capacities as organizer found immediate application. It would be necessary to print pamphlets and to establish clandestine presses. Koba undertook this task.

He decided to keep his post as calculator in the Observatory. For that matter, he liked the work. In a confidential conversation with his friend Kapanadzé he one day admitted that if he had not chosen the career of a professional revolutionist he would have remained for a long while to come at the Observatory. He loved the science of astronomy. His interest in his work at the Observatory is reflected in the secret correspondence of the Party. In this he indicates his comrades by terms borrowed from astronomy. Tsouloukidzé is called Saturn; Ketschkoyeli is Mars; Kapanadzé, Mercury.

The year 1900 marked a fresh stage in his apprenticeship as a professional revolutionist. A synthesis was effected between his hope of a 'special mission' and the facts of the revolutionary situation. A personal emissary of Lenin's arrived in Tiflis, Victor Kournatovsky. He was a great friend of Lenin's. Lenin himself, having completed his term of Siberian exile, had gone abroad. He had recently founded the revolutionary journal, *Iskra* (The Spark). It was Kournatovsky's task to ensure the distribution of this journal in the Caucasus.

Much later—in 1924—when the ex-Koba, now Stalin, began his ascent toward supreme power, he explained, in an address to the pupils of the Military College in the Kremlin, how he had first become a revolutionist, and why, when it became necessary to choose a successor to Lenin, he decided to present himself as a candidate.

'This meeting with Comrade Kournatovsky, Lenin's delegate,' he explained, 'convinced me that in Lenin we had an exceptional man. He was not, in my opinion, a mere party leader. He was the creator of the Party, whose intimate nature and pressing needs only he understood. Even at this time he seemed to me to stand head and shoulders above his contemporaries—Plekhanov, Markov, Axelrod. Compared with them, Lenin was a *mountain eagle* who pointed out to the Party the unexplored paths of the Russian revolutionary movement.'

Kournatovsky expounded Lenin's point of view: 'What is needed is a *political* revolution. We must not base any vain hopes on the economic struggle. Even strikes cannot produce lasting results. The Tsarist power must be overthrown and the Tsarist system destroyed. Only the labouring masses of the cities—the proletariat—can do this. The arena of history lies open before them, and there, in the future, they will have to play a leading part.'

But if the movement was to triumph it would be necessary to create *a special organization of professional revolutionists*, capable of ensuring the vigour, the permanence, and the pre-eminence of the political conflict.

'*The Revolution needs not amateurs, but technicians, specialists, to whom it will give directions. They will belong to the Revolution, and the Revolution will pay them.*'

Koba experienced a true revelation; now everything was clear to him. By determining the function of the professional revolutionists, Lenin posited them exactly, in their social function, as paid agents of the working class, who can devote themselves entirely to the Revolution. In Lenin's definition Koba perceived a fresh definition of the 'special mission' of which he had always dreamed, and which was to be like that of the priest of a new Church, supported by his superiors and his parishioners. He thought that these professional revolutionists ought to take vows: of poverty, of total sacrifice, of complete and hierarchic submission to an inflexible spiritual discipline—vows of renunciation of all individual interests, the better to carry out the orders of a supreme organ, which would guide and command the new order.

One point was as yet unexplained: How were the means to be provided for running this revolutionary machine? But it was not for nothing that Koba had become an *abrek*. He soon found the answer which the ordinary Social Democrats had never had the courage to give: the costs of the revolution must be defrayed by the 'class enemy.' They would be taken from the enemy by force.

The other great event of the year 1901 was the labour demonstration organized by the Party for the 1 May. Kournatovsky was to have organized it, but he was arrested a month earlier. On the same night the police had entered the Observatory in search of Koba, who had been compromised by the denunciation of an employé in the railway workshops, who hoped to purchase his freedom by 'coming clean.' Koba succeeded in escaping. He slipped through a skylight which gave on to the roof of the Observatory, and there he remained for more than an hour. Then, changing his address, he took refuge in the Rue Mikhailovskaia.

The police captain Zavarzine gave orders that Joseph Djugachvili was to be found and interrogated as to his part in fomenting the strike in the railway workshops, in co-operation with a certain Michel Kalinin, a locksmith by trade.[1]

Koba took refuge for some days with Allilouev, but it was already known that the workman's flat was under observation. He had to find other quarters—especially as his friend's wife had just given birth to a child.[2] He was given an address which would offer a safe refuge—No. 17 in the 'Street of the Nobles.' A young journalist, Leon Rosenfeld, was living there: good-looking, a woman-hunter, and very popular, Rosenfeld had no great difficulty in concealing Koba. He found lodgings for him in the apartments of an elderly woman, Catherine Svanidzé, who had living with her a niece of the same name—Kéké (Catherine), a girl of eighteen, who was to become Stalin's first wife.

From daybreak on the 1 May various groups of armed men, many of them in Caucasian costume, equipped with daggers and cartridge-belts, began to move about the city. One of these groups, some 200 strong, was brought from Gori by Prince Mdivani. It included a number of horsemen, of whom Stalin was one. The chief of the Tiflis police and five subordinate officers harangued the crowd, requesting it to disperse; the Viceroy wished to avoid bloodshed. Koba, who was leading the group, ordered it to continue its march. It did so, singing revolutionary songs.

The police fired a salvo into the air. The crowd hesitated. Petrossian urged it on. Then, at a sign from Koba, it broke into the Dead March of the Russian revolutionists:

[1]The future President of the U.S.S.R.
[2]Nadyida, the future Stalin's second wife.

C

'You fell as victims of the fight that had to be,
And of your boundless love for all oppressed . . .'

For the first time in history, a Russian hymn of revolution was
chanted by a Caucasian crowd, led by the Georgian Koba-Djugachvili, a disciple of the Great-Russian Ulianov-Tulin-Lenin. In so
doing the revolutionary Caucasus confessed itself to be an integral
part of Russia. Koba's separatism had accepted the stamp of the
Social Democratic mould.

About mid-day the Cossacks charged the crowd with cracking
whips and levelled lances. But long before this Koba had left the
field, establishing his headquarters in Arabalian's *doukhan*.[1] Mokadzé
and Kikichvili served him as liaison officers. Half an hour later the
crowd had dispersed. Koba's first attempt at 'direct action' passed off
without bloodshed. But henceforth he was a man 'on the run,' a
fugitive from the police, who redoubled their efforts to arrest him.

Koba could not take refuge in his mother's house, since that
would be the first place where the police would look for him. So his
friend Sosso Aremachvili, a local schoolmaster, found him a hiding-
place. In one of the small mountain hamlets a cousin, Kikinadzé,
owned a vineyard and a garden; and in the garden there was a hut.
There were only seven houses in the hamlet, which was about an
hour's walk from Gori. Here the future Stalin installed himself, disguised as a vine-dresser.

Gori was an old-fashioned town whose inhabitants had no great
love of formalities or official regulations. The *ispravnik*[2]—the head of
the local police—had received orders from the Tiflis police to discover Koba's whereabouts. The local police called on poor Kéké,
who replied that her son was not at home, and that she was quite
ignorant of his actual whereabouts. The *ispravnik*, accepting her
statement, wrote to Tiflis to the effect that *the search for the criminal
malefactor Joseph Djugachvili in the neighbourhood of Gori had been un-
availing*.

One day Koba saw Sosso Aremachvili climbing up the hill in the
company of a stranger: a tall man with strong features and a little

[1]Caucasian public-house.
[2]The functions of the *ispravnik* are approximately those of a French *sous-préfet*.

goatee; he carried a walking-stick of kizil wood. The stranger introduced himself: 'I am Leonid Krassin, representing the newspaper
Iskra, and Lenin, in the Caucasus.' Kournatovsky having been arrested, Krassin had taken his place.

He spoke with admiration of Koba's organization of the Tiflis
demonstration. The *Iskra* had published a full report of the incident.
Everyone regarded it as a great victory.

'Lenin knows,' said Krassin, 'that it was you who directed the
whole affair. You will meet him one day. For the moment you must
remain here, in the Caucasus. You are more useful here than you
would be abroad. Lenin has already baptized you the *Tehoudierni
gronzine*—the 'miraculous Georgian.' You will be co-opted by the
Party committee in Tiflis, and you will direct the underground
activities. By August the police will have begun to forget you. However, you won't remain in Tiflis very long; you will go to Batoum,
where there's plenty to be done.'

Returning to Tiflis, the scene of his first revolutionary exploit,
Koba found a lodging in the house of a schoolmaster, André
Iablokov, who lived in the suburb of Artatchali. Beginning as an
apprentice, working with improvised means, he was to become,
despite the numerical poverty of his effectives, one of the most
efficient of the modern leaders of the revolutionary movement.

On his arrival in Tiflis Koba was co-opted by the Party committee and was placed in charge of the revolutionary propaganda.

He had suddenly become a personality; and, what was more, he
was now one of the *professional revolutionaries* of whom Lenin had
spoken.

Russia, that vast country, was then in the throes of a social and
political fever. From the Baltic to the steppes of Central Asia, from
the White Sea to the Caucasus, history was being made. The whole
country was resounding like an anvil to the blows of the revolutionary hammer. But in some regions the workers' organizations were
unwilling to follow the advice of the Party representatives. The
workers distrusted the *baritchis* (the 'young gentry'), even when the
latter were the bearers of Party mandates.

There was even a violent altercation between Koba and his life-
long friend Djibladzé. The violence of the dispute, and of Koba's

language, provoked a demand for his exclusion from the Party, and he was summoned before a 'court of honour.' Before this court, Koba was intractable.

'Friendship,' he said, 'counts for nothing when the Party and its interests are at stake. I am extremely fond of Sylvester, and I am ready to offer him my personal apologies. But whenever he adopts an attitude that is contrary to the interests of the Party I shall oppose him with the same violence, the same energy. The absolute refusal to compromise is the most effective weapon in the revolutionary conflict. People may say that I'm rude and offensive; it's all one to me. I shall continue to fight all those who threaten to destroy the Party.'

Thus, in 1901, Koba defined the principles which were to guide Stalin during the great purge of 1936–37, when he showed himself pitiless and inhuman even toward his dearest friends if these had 'sinned' against the interests of the Party as he understood them.

The 'court of honour' passed a vote of censure on Koba. But Lenin's representative approved his behaviour and decided to expedite the departure of the 'miraculous Georgian' for Batoum, where he could direct the work of propaganda and act as secretary of the local Committee.

So, at the age of twenty-two, Koba became one of the leaders of the Party.

CHAPTER V

IMPRISONMENT AND DEPORTATION

O N the 30 November a certain Kandeliaki, a member of the local Social-Democratic organization, met Koba, coming from Tiflis, in the Batoum railway-station. He led him to a small attic room in a modest working-class house in the suburb of Rtchala. The owner of the house was a petty official in the P.T.T. Koba introduced himself as Khoundadzé, an accountant.

Losing no time, he embarked upon the most feverish activity. His first care was to create a militant organization of unique character, which would amalgamate the workers' clubs of different nationalities. This he accomplished on New Year's Eve, 1901–02.

Under the pretext of celebrating the New Year, and thereby misleading the police spies, the comrades met at the house of a fellow-worker, Gogoberidzé. Some of the guests shouted and sang and drank the local wine, while the leaders discussed serious matters, and by 4 a.m. the general lines of the common organization had been laid down.

One of its first objectives was to establish a secret printing-press, from which pamphlets in the Georgian, Armenian, Turkish, and Russian languages could be issued. Unfortunately, Koba had not the necessary capital at his disposal.

On the following night there was a burglary at the establishment of the wealthy Armenian printer, Magaliantz. The burglars carried away a number of cases of type. Koba was able to set up his secret press.

In March, on the arrest of a number of strikers, he organized a monster manifestation and proclaimed a general strike. On the following day a large number of workers assembled outside the Governor's palace. In the words of the Public Prosecutor, Lomadzé: 'A numerous crowd, composed of working-men, preceded by their ringleaders, marched in ordered ranks, singing songs of a seditious

37

character (among others, the *Marseillaise*). The crowd shouted and whistled and threatened the police. The affair ended in bloodshed.'

In his memoirs, Arakhvelidzé, one of the members of the Committee, relates how Koba 'was with us all the time, the real leader of the strike committee which organized the manifestation. He was in the midst of the crowd. When our comrade Kandaladzé was wounded in the hand by a bullet he carried him off and saw him to his house.'

Lenin, in Munich, commenting on the happenings in Batoum, wrote as follows: 'Koba has once again done a good job. The consciousness of the revolutionary masses is awaking. A good day for us!'

On the day following the funeral of the victims the police went over to the offensive.

The Social-Democratic Committee of Batoum was accustomed to hold its meetings in the cottage of a certain locksmith, Stepan Malenkov,[1] on the outskirts of the city. This was a sort of wooden shack, standing in a kitchen-garden, where the locksmith grew melons, and had planted a few vines. Here there was a meeting on the 5 April, 1902. It was a camouflaged assembly; the guests sang the songs in vogue, and were refreshed with fruit and wine. Then, in the evening, they proceeded to the serious business of the meeting.

Koba had barely finished a speech when Malenkov's son, who was keeping watch, cried: 'Papa, the police!' A detachment of police, under the command of Captain Lavrov, entered the garden and surrounded the shack. Escape was impossible.

They were marched off to various police stations. Koba, arrested for the first time, betrayed no sign of emotion. He was capable of perfect self-control under circumstances infinitely more serious. On the following day Lavrov subjected the prisoners to a preliminary interrogation. In accordance with their general custom, the police addressed the intellectuals politely. Koba had no papers on him, either genuine or spurious. When he was questioned as to his domicile, he replied: 'I have no fixed domicile. I sleep where I can find shelter; sometimes in the open air in one of the squares.'

[1]A distant relative of George Malenkov, the present secretary of the Communist Party of Russia.

For a police officer, Lavrov was not an especially ferocious man:[1]
'I know who you are; it's no use playing the goat with me. You are
Joseph Djugachvili, known as Koba, the secretary of the Party com-
mittee. . . .'

On the 10 April Koba was transferred to the Batoum prison. The
order of detention drawn up by the police and presented to the
warden of the Kvotov prison contained the following details:

'Joseph Djugachvili. Aged 23 years. Born at Gori. Ex-pupil of the
Tiflis seminary. Expelled for unruly behaviour.[2] Inhabitant of
Batoum without fixed domicile. No profession. Means of liveli-
hood: unknown.'

That was all. The police knew nothing beyond what their
prisoner had chosen to tell them. On the front page of the dossier
Lavrov wrote, 'No proof of participation in the demonstration of
9 March. No ground for prosecution in this connection.'

On the second page was written: 'According to statements made
by informers Joseph Djugachvili is one of the leaders of the local
Party committee, liable to administrative sanction.'

As a matter of routine, Koba's dossier was submitted to a special
council in the Ministry for the Interior in St. Petersburg. This
council, which was composed of four high officials of the Ministry
for the Interior and the Ministry of Justice, was authorized to sentence a prisoner, on the evidence of his dossier alone, to 'deportation
and compulsory residence.'

Meanwhile, Koba was under confinement in the Louloua jail.
There he remained until October 1903. His name was then inscribed
on a list of criminals sentenced to enforced residence in Eastern
Siberia. This list included the most prominent members of the
Social-Democratic Party of the Caucasus: Koba, Kournatovski,
Djibladzé and Kotchkoveli.

In the meantime events were occurring abroad which were to
have a decisive influence on the future revolution, and on Koba's
career.

Lenin was editing his *Iskra* in London, where he passed under the

---

[1]After the revolution of 1917 he applied to Stalin, then in the Commissariat of
Nationalities, for a letter of recommendation. He wanted to enlist in the Tcheka as
a technical specialist. Thanks to Stalin's recommendation, he was accepted.

[2]It is not known from what source Lavrov obtained this incorrect information.

name of Dr. Richter. He was preparing to control and direct the revolution of the masses, which in Russia, according to him, was already 'in the air.' It was therefore necessary to create a centralized Party. He believed that this imminent Russian revolution would inevitably follow the traditional and chaotic lines of those terrible Russian risings which the great poet Pushkin had described as 'frightful upheavals, pitiless and senseless.' Lenin wanted such risings to be 'pitiless' indeed, but endowed with a 'Marxist sense.' That is, they must be steered with an iron hand toward the goal appointed by the order of professional revolutionists.

He did not want the Social-Democratic Party of Russia to become an organization of officials, like the Social-Democrats of Germany, or an association of humanists, like the Latin Socialist Parties of the period. He wanted 'to incite the peasant mob against the landowners, to shake the foundations of the Empire, to provoke disorder and anarchy, to disorganize the apparatus of State, to paralyse the economy of the nation, its railways and its shipping, to incite an armed conflict, a fight to the death, pitiless toward all, in order to destroy first the autocracy and then capitalism.'

In recalling this period Lenin was fond of comparing himself with one of Tolstoy's characters: 'A man was crouching there, making clumsy gestures; from a distance one would have taken him to be a madman, but on approaching him one saw that he was whetting a knife on the curbstone.'

Thus, Lenin was whetting his knife: he was forwarding letters and general instructions with a view to bringing the greatest possible number of his partisans to the Congress. And Koba, though still a prisoner, was elected a member of the Pan-Caucasian Committee. His reputation was made.

On the 30 July, 1903, the famous Congress was to have met in Brussels, at the headquarters of the Co-operative Societies. But the Belgian police intervened, and the delegates made for London.

The meetings which took place in London were to determine the entire orientation of the Russian revolution. Discussions were extremely lively, and often violent. Lenin insisted on the importance of an absolute centralization, and endeavoured to enforce an inflexible discipline, claiming sovereign powers for his Central Committee.

'The Central Committee,' he said, 'is a clenched fist. It is its duty to *strike at any member whomsoever of the Party for the least failure of discipline, the least deviation in the execution of the programme and obedience to the statutes. The local organizations must submit to it without grumbling and without any notion of resistance, which would be a crime. . . .'*

This definition was to shape and control the history of the U.S.S.R. Thirty years later Stalin was to execute his comrades in arms for 'deviations' and 'notions of resistance to the Central Committee.' These comrades, convicted of their 'crime against their Order of Professional Revolutionists,' accepted their fate, consenting to figure as 'counter-revolutionaries' so that they might not discredit the 'Order' by the spectacle of the execution of a genuine revolutionist. *Here, perhaps, we have the chief explanation of their behaviour, which was incomprehensible to all those who did not happen to find themselves within the terrible magic circle which was traced, in 1903, by the paranoiac genius of Lenin.*

Lenin requested that only those should be accepted as members of the Party who *had actively collaborated with one of the groups.* The moderates considered that membership should be granted to 'one who accepts the Party programme and pays the subscriptions.'

Lenin got his way—thanks to a majority of one vote. It was a near thing.

'We are the *bolchinstvo*!' he cried. 'We are the *bolcheviki.* . . .'

The new word was born. It made its entry into History, and in reply to a letter which Tuponidzé secretly delivered to him in his prison Stalin exclaimed, 'Our whole organization will give the utmost support to the Bolsheviks.'

On the 26 October, 1903, Koba was exiled. The village of Novaia-Ouda, in the district of Balagan, in the government of Irkutsk, Eastern Siberia, was given as his place of compulsory residence for the next three years. He reached the village on the 27 November, but he did not remain there for very long.

CHAPTER VI

ESCAPE

THE village of Novaia-Ouda was a wretched hamlet, lost amidst the snows, some 300 miles to the north of Irkutsk. It numbered only 150 inhabitants, of whom fifteen were exiles in 'compulsory residence.' The representative of authority was an *ouriadnik*—a corporal of the gendarmerie.

He had been given special instructions regarding Koba: '*Joseph Djugachvili, surname Koba, is to be closely watched. Any danger of or attempt at evasion must be reported immediately to Balagan.*'[1]

The exiles enjoyed absolute liberty within the district of Balagan, an area equal to that of several counties. They could do very much as they liked; they could hunt, or fish in the brooks and rivers, and could even buy horses and hounds if their means permitted. This held good for all those who were exiled to Siberia; a fact which has not prevented the revolutionary propagandists from spreading throughout the world the most horrible tales of the 'terrible Siberia' of the Imperial régime.

A few days after Koba's arrival a police lieutenant came from Balagan on a tour of inspection, to see for himself what the exiles were doing. Together with the *ouriadnik* he called at Koba's residence. This was a log cabin, a classic *izba*, on the edge of a forest of pine and fir trees. Koba was not at home. History has recorded the following dialogue:

'The pocky devil—perhaps he's escaped!'

'Pocky?' the *ouriadnik* inquired.

'Yes, so he's called in our records. He's been known as "the pocky one" since the day he was arrested; his face is marked by smallpox.'

It was while he was at Novaia-Ouda that Koba received a personal letter from Lenin. In 1924, in the course of one of his famous

[1]The administrative capital of the district.

conversations with the pupils of the Military Academy in the Kremlin, Koba, now Stalin, referred to this letter.

'I first became directly acquainted with Comrade Lenin in 1903. It's true, it was only by correspondence. But it made an indelible impression on me, an impression that never left me during my work in the Party.

'At the time I was an exile at Novaia-Ouda. Thanks to a special channel, I received this letter from Comrade Lenin at the end of the year 1903. It was simply worded, but it had a deep meaning. It contained a bold and fearless criticism of the doings of our Party, and it outlined a remarkably clear and definite plan as regards our activities in the immediate future.

'Lenin alone had a way of treating the most complicated subjects with perfect simplicity and lucidity, and yet so concisely and so boldly that every phrase was like a pistol-shot. . . .

'I shall never forgive myself for having burned that letter—as I burned many others; it was the custom among the illegal militants. . . . That was the beginning of my direct relations with Lenin.'

Having read Lenin's letter, Koba felt that he could remain at Novaia-Ouda no longer. In Russia, the pace of events was constantly accelerating. The Tsarist Empire was at odds with Japan. War was expected to break out at any moment. Such situations facilitate the spread of revolutionary doctrines and favour revolutionary activity.

It was a comparatively simple matter to leave a place of compulsory residence. But in order to reach Irkutsk it was necessary to make a journey of more than 300 miles, in the depth of winter, when the temperature of Eastern Siberia often falls to 50 degrees below zero.[1] The refugee would need a false passport,[2] for on the Siberian trains the police always inspect the travellers' papers.

At Irkutsk, Koba applied to a certain Kolotov, a sympathizer with the Social-Democratic movement. Ten days later, he became possessed of a passport in the name of David Nijeradzé. The holder of this passport had died more than two years earlier: a Georgian; by trade, a dealer in carpets. Like most Caucasians, Koba knew something about carpets.

[1]The lowest temperature registered at the 'cold pole'—at Verkoiansk—is −65°. This 'cold pole' is far to the north of Irkutsk.
[2]A 'passport for the interior.'

The story of this first escape, and of its failure, is told by Allilouev, who took notes of Koba's own description of his experiences after his return to Tiflis:

'Comrade Stalin left Novaia-Ouda on Christmas Eve, during the night of 24 December. He thought that on this particular evening everybody, and in particular the *ouriadnik*, would be too much occupied in celebrating the Christmas festival to think of other things.

'He decided to walk the thirty versts (about twenty miles) to Makarovka, a fairly large village, from which a friend of his would drive him by sledge as far as Balagan. From Balagan another friend would drive him to Irkutsk.'

The road from Novaia-Ouda to Makarovka ran through a ravine, then, climbing on to a tableland, it crossed a section of the *taïga*[1] before reaching the outskirts of the village. The ravine was safe enough, except that a solitary wolf might sometimes venture into it. The *taïga* was not so safe; there the wolves hunted in packs; the winter was cold, and they were fierce and famishing. There was always a risk of encountering a Siberian bear: a very dangerous animal when the cold drives him from his den, in which he usually sleeps all the winter. Comrade Stalin was armed with a sporting rifle which had been lent to him by the local grocer.

'He was wearing valenki[2] and a touloupe,[3] but the cold was intense; a man accustomed to a milder climate would find it hard to endure. He pushed on with difficulty, gasping for breath. Despite his ear-muffs, his ears began to freeze. But his nose suffered most. Comrade Stalin felt that he was in danger of being frozen to death. Nevertheless, he struggled on courageously, and descended into the ravine. A few wolves were prowling round him, but they fled at his first shot. When he emerged from the ravine a whole pack, ten at least, attacked him. He succeeded in driving them off, but he felt that his feet were growing numb. . . . There was nothing for it but to go back; to retrace the ten or twelve miles which he had already covered with such difficulty. . . .'

This check compelled Koba to modify his plan. On the 5 January, 1904—on the eve of the Day of Kings—Twelfth Night—he escaped

[1]Polar steppe country, with stretches of Arctic woodland and marsh.
[2]Felt boots.
[3]A sheepskin cloak.

once more, but not on foot. The *ouriadnik* was lying in a drunken sleep when a sledge carrying Koba—now David Nijeradzé—set off briskly in a southerly direction.

On the 1 February, 1904, he reached Tiflis, where he went immediately to the house of Rosenfeld, who had received the pseudonym of Kamenev. Rosenfeld found him a room in the house of a friend of his, one Molotchkov. Then, without wasting time, Koba began to make preparations for an insurrection.

Koba-Nijeradzé could no longer work openly at spreading propaganda; he was too well known in Tiflis. On the Committee he had seven colleagues. Most of the older revolutionaries were still in exile, in Siberia. The leader of the movement was the young Leo Rosenfeld, who had finally adopted the pseudonym of Kamenev. But it was becoming the fashion to use Christian names or nicknames. Kamenev was known as Lieva, while his secret nickname was Krassavitchik (the handsome). Koba had become David, while in his secret reports to Lenin he signed himself 'Bars' (Leopard)—a name borrowed from his favourite Georgian legend.

The first defeats suffered in the war against Japan produced a great impression in Russia, where this distant campaign was not altogether popular. The government's inability to wage war in a satisfactory manner alienated its remaining sympathizers. The educated classes, the intelligentsia, were steadily turning against it. The general movement toward liberation became accentuated, including ever wider circles of society. The whole nation, with the *élite* at its head, was longing for a liberal régime, and was prepared to win it by a political revolution.

The prevailing tendencies were inspired and directed by a genuine idealism, but the would-be liberals had no experience of political regimentation.

On the other hand, Lenin's little group of professional revolutionists had very different aspirations. Despite the small number of his partisans, the 'crazy genius' installed in Switzerland was dreaming of serving the future revolution which would overthrow the existing system and clap the nation into a strait-jacket, so that he could impose his own ideas upon it. Among his few faithful disciples there was one devoted man who was ready for anything: Koba-Nijeradzé.

Lenin learned from Kamenev that the Caucasian Committee was still staunchly faithful to him, thanks to the firm and revolutionary attitude of the 'Leopard.' 'This miraculous Georgian!' cried Lenin, once more, in astonishment.

He would never forget Koba's fidelity. During the Civil War, when Trotzky, leader of the Red Army, wished to summon Stalin before the military tribunal which had just sentenced the old Bolshevik Panteliev, an army commander, to death for failing to carry out an order, Lenin declared: 'I will never allow my miraculous Georgian to be dragged before a court martial!'

On the 22 June, 1904, the marriage of Joseph Djugachvili and Catherine Svanidzé was recorded in the register of the ancient church of Gori. In July, Koba left for Baku, in order to make preparations for settling down there; the police were drawing their nets too closely around Tiflis. He returned to Tiflis for a few weeks in September, where he presented a report to the Pan-Caucasian Committee. Then, in December, he and his wife set out for Baku.

Before settling there, Koba-Nijeradzé acquired a passport in the name of Joseph Ivanovitch, accountant, born at Sevastopol in the year 1880. A room had been rented for him in a house in 'Grand Duke Street,' opposite the chemist's shop kept by a Russianized Pole, Vishinsky.[1]

The working-class population of Baku was in a state of effervescence. A strike committee, of which 'Ivanovitch' was the secretary, was very restive.

In the smoky city of Baku, where everything smelt of petroleum, Koba-Joseph Ivanovitch wrote and published inflammatory articles. He attacked the Liberals, who, for him, were enemies as dangerous as the Tsarist police.

Now, at the age of twenty-six, Sosso-Koba-David-Ivanovitch was at the height of his powers. His literary style had gained in strength and simplicity. Unlike Lenin's, it did not need to be explained and interpreted before the masses could understand his words.

New newspapers were founded in order to further the Bolshevik propaganda: *The New Life, The New Times, Our Life, The Times.*

[1] The father of the present Foreign Minister of the U.S.S.R.

In all these journals Koba supported Lenin's ideas as to the hegemony of the proletariat in the revolution. He called for a general armed insurrection, and announced a new phase, for which he was making detailed preparations. It was to be a *revolutionary dictatorship*; and it would be realized by the order of professional revolutionists in the interests of the workers and the peasants.

The Third Party Congress met in London, in April 1905. For personal reasons, Koba was not present. His wife, who had given birth to a son, Jacob, was seriously ill. And in Baku he was desperately busy as a propagandist.

CHAPTER VII

THE BIRTH OF 'STALIN'

Koba's *apologia* for violent methods was becoming more and more urgent, and Lenin, in the distance, was full of praise for his Caucasian disciple. The titles of Koba's articles were becoming more and more inflammatory—'Armed Insurrection is our tactics!'—'Reaction is intensified!'—'On the brink of decision!'—'Off with the masks!'—'No quarter for the traitors and their protectors!'

In his *Iskra* Lenin devoted a whole page to praises of Koba's article, 'What's to be Done?'—from which he quoted extensively.

He added: 'This is a remarkable sample of the true revolutionary tactics. But in order to realize it the leader must himself be hard as granite, and he must not lay down his arms during the compromise.'

This article was published in 1905.

The Russian revolution was continuing its advance. The peasants were rebelling. The sailors of the *Potemkin* mutinied. The garrisons of Tiflis, Vladivostock, Samarkand, Komsk, Soukhoum, Warsaw, Kiev, Poltava, and Kharkov poured into the streets, bearing red flags. The fortresses of Kronstadt and Sebastopol hoisted the standard of insurrection. On the 19 September the printers of Moscow came out on strike, and this strike became general. St. Petersburg followed suit. The railway workers joined in. The postal and telegraph services ceased to function.

The first Soviets of working-class deputies were formed. The president of the Soviet of St. Petersburg was a Menshevik, the advocate Khroustalev-Nossar. He was presently succeeded by Trotzky. The Moscow Soviet was in the hands of the Bolsheviks.

Koba was still in Baku. Lenin, from Geneva, wrote to him insisting that 'he must immediately launch an armed revolt.' It would seem that in Geneva he was not fully informed as to the activities of his lieutenant. For some weeks past the bodies of policemen had been found in the streets of Tiflis and Baku, killed by shots fired by persons unknown, for Koba had broadcast the instructions received from Lenin:

'The armed detachments of the Party must without delay complete their military education by engaging in immediate operations. Some must see to the instant execution of informers, the destruction by means of bombs of a police station, while others will attack a bank, in order to confiscate the funds required for the future insurrection. . . . Let each detachment do something, if only to kill a few policemen.'

On the 17 October Tsar Nicholas II yielded to the advice of his minister Witte, and granted a constitution, with a Parliament—the Duma. He promised agrarian reforms also, various political liberties, and a comprehensive amnesty. But this did not suit Lenin or his party. They wanted to continue their revolutionary activities, and to bring about a social upheaval on the lines of the theories which they had so often expounded.

At Tammersfors, in Finland, Koba-Ivanovitch and Lenin met for the first time. In 1924 Stalin described their interview:

'I met Comrade Lenin for the first time in December 1905, at the Bolshevik Conference of Tammersfors in Finland. I was looking to see the mountain eagle of our fatherland, a great man; great not only in the political sense, but physically; a tall, big man; for in my youthful enthusiasm I imagined him a giant, a man of martial bearing. What was not my disappointment when I saw a most ordinary-looking person, rather shorter than myself—and I am only of medium stature—a man absolutely indistinguishable in any respect whatsoever from the ordinary run of mortals!'

In recording these first impressions, Stalin seemed to be hinting at a subconscious feeling that a day would come when he would find himself in the place of this leader.

But the youthful Koba-Ivanovitch would not allow himself to be subjugated even by the prestige of Lenin. He severely criticized a 'hybrid proposal of Krassin's.' He protested against the 'Machiavellian tactics of intellectuals crazy for popularity,' and demanded an effective boycott of the Duma.

The result was a *coup de théâtre*. Lenin suddenly gave way to his

D

young disciple, declaring publicly that he would accept Koba's advice.

In this connection, in 1920, during the private celebration of Lenin's fiftieth birthday, in the presence of Lenin himself, and Trotzky, Stalin related: "I remember that Comrade Lenin, this Titan, has twice confessed himself mistaken. The first time was in Finland, in December 1905, at the Pan-Russian conference of Bolsheviks, on the occasion of the boycott of the Duma convoked by Witte. . . . Seeing that he was mistaken, he agreed to support the proposition of the Caucasian delegation. We were stupefied. It was like an electric shock. We gave Lenin a terrific ovation. . . .'

We shall perceive, in the following chapters, the historic importance of this statement of Stalin's, made before Lenin himself, in the presence of all the members of the Politburo and the Central Committee, which had assembled in honour of Lenin's birthday. It prepared the way for the nomination of Stalin, two years later, for the post of Secretary-General of the Communist Party. *Without the previous agreement of Lenin the allusion to his hesitation could not have been made.*

Lenin found that the young Caucasian delegate, whom he knew as a dynamic agitator, was also a strategist of the revolutionary movement. The two men were now directly in touch. Undeterred by the intense cold, they strolled through the streets of Tammersfors, exchanging ideas. The two men travelled together from Tammersfors to St. Petersburg.

During the return journey to St. Petersburg, Lenin said: 'One will have to choose a more impressive pseudonym than Ivanovitch; that is too impersonal.'

Teniani, who was present during the conversation, observed: 'We all call him Koba.'

Lenin smiled. 'That sounds rather queer, in Russian. Comrade Ivanovitch is hard as steel. Why not call him 'Stalin,' the man of steel?'

At the moment, the two Caucasians were not impressed. The Russian words aroused no automatic response in their minds. Some years were to pass before Ivanovitch, on a second invitation from Lenin, became Stalin.

In January 1906 Koba was again in Baku. The Russian Revolution was quieting down. The Liberals had great hopes of the new Constitution, and were busily preparing for the elections to the Duma. Only the extremists—the Bolsheviks, Anarchists and Maximalists[1]—remained faithful to the policy of the immediate conquest of power and the formation of a dictatorial republic of workers and peasants.

The Unification Congress at Stockholm in April 1908 ended in the victory of the Mensheviks. The elected Central Committee contained six Mensheviks, as against three Bolsheviks. But the three had no intention of giving way to the six. The union of the parties was not destined to endure.

Koba returned once more to Baku. There he was in his element. While others were making fine speeches, he devoted himself to forming a vast organization of the most backward workers of the petroleum industry—the Persians and Azerbeidjans. But this was not enough for him. In a report to the Ministry of the Interior, the head of the Caucasian police, Chirinkin, wrote as follows:

'A special system is in force in the Government of Koutaïss. There the revolutionaries have disarmed the police; they have seized the railway; they themselves sell the tickets and maintain order. I am no longer in receipt of any reports from this region. The police have been withdrawn to Tiflis. The official couriers are held up and searched by the revolutionaries. The position is positively impossible. The Governor is suffering from nervous exhaustion. I shall try to send you further details by post, or if that is impossible, by special courier.'

This police officer was not aware that the secret dictator of the Koutaïss district was none other than Koba, who had brought a large detachment of *abreks* into this region, and had disarmed the gendarmes, together with their commander, Captain Mabelski.

But these episodes were only the last convulsive efforts of the revolution. Everywhere the forces of order were gaining the upper hand. Lenin himself was in hiding in Finland, at Kuokalla, not far from St. Petersburg. There Koba met and formed a friendship with Klementi Voroshilov, the head of the Bolshevik organization of

[1] A radical fraction of the Socialists, often confounded, abroad, with the Bolsheviks.

Lovgansk. When travelling, he now carried a new passport. He had
become Boudou Besochvili.

The year 1907 was a tragic one for Koba. His first wife was
attacked by pleurisy, and before long she had succumbed to a gal-
loping consumption.

One of Koba's college friends, Iremachvili, was among his occasional visitors. He has written of the last hours of the young wife.
A fellow-countryman, a native of Gori, and a distant relative, he was
none the less a political enemy of Koba's; but among the Georgians
the clan spirit takes precedence of political quarrels.

While his visitor was watching over the dying woman, Koba
drafted a letter to Lenin. It throws some light on the characters of
the two men.

'You ask me, what were the reasons of our failure. One has no
need of a minute analysis in order to understand the causes of our
defeat! The workers had no weapons, or they had too few. . . .
Otherwise, in the Caucasus I could have guaranteed such an insurrection as the government of St. Petersburg could not have
quashed so readily. . . . But our forces must be armed, must be given
rifles, revolvers, bombs, and dynamite.'

Koba's letter was the typical manual of the complete revolutionary Bolshevik. Lenin was delighted with it; he found it clear and
concise, 'worthy of a captain of the Revolution.' He showed it to
the members of the Central Committee, in which Rykov was sitting.
Rykov's opinion was: 'The writer will be a very useful man in time
of revolution. But I should be afraid to work with him.'

Rykov was right. In 1937 the execution squad was to prove to
this lieutenant of Stalin's that it was as dangerous to work on his side
as to fight in the ranks of his adversaries.

On the 10 April, 1907, Sosso's first wife died, after partaking of
the sacraments of the Church. When her friends and relatives came
to bid her farewell, Sosso told them: 'I promised Kéké she should
be buried in accordance with the Orthodox rites. I shall keep my
promise.'

Iremachvili was present at the funeral service. He has left us a
sober and dramatic account of the occasion. ' . . . When the modest
procession had reached the gate of the cemetery, Koba gripped my

hand, and pointed to the bier, saying: "She was the one creature who softened my stony heart. She is dead, and with her have died any feelings of tenderness I had for humanity." Laying his hand on his heart, he said, "There's an emptiness there now, an unspeakable emptiness." '

This might appear too melodramatic to be an expression of genuine feeling. But Koba's seminary training had taught him to employ figures of speech which might seem a little too literary, and flavoured with a romanticism which was not always in the best of taste.

Shortly after the death of his wife, Koba received a letter from Lenin. It was rather pessimistic in tone, for the writer found himself unsupported in the Party Committee. His oldest friends had deserted him. Trotzky spoke of him in the most injurious terms: 'An intriguer, a professional exploiter of the ignorance of the labouring masses; a liar; an indefatigable forger of documents. . . .'

Lenin wrote that he was quite of Sosso's opinion. They must have weapons, and at all costs the spirit of insurrection must be revived. But there was another immediate requirement: 'Revolution is war. But war means money. Gold, according to Napoleon, is the sinews of war. What do you think?'

Between the 12 and the 19 May, 1907, the Fifth Party Congress was held in London. Koba-Besochvili arrived with six Caucasian delegates. In the secret committee on which he sat with Lenin and Krassin, both resolutely in favour of 'expropriations,' the question of a *coup de main* was discussed.

On the 13 May he met for the first time the man who for decades to come was to be his most persistent personal rival. A speaker ascended the improvised platform. Of medium stature, he had a sharply cut profile and an aquiline nose; his hair was brushed back from his forehead; his mouth was wide and sensual, his chin pointed. There was something in him of the Biblical prophet and of Mephistopheles. He had a trick of constantly wiping his pince-nez. Obviously anxious to make an impression, he did not speak until he saw that the last members had taken their places.

'Who is that?' Koba asked his neighbour, Chaoumian.

'Don't you know him? It's Comrade Trotzky, the best speaker in the Party, the author of the theory of permanent revolution. . . .'

Koba made no reply. He was not greatly impressed by the tricks of eloquence, but he noted attentively the impression which this eloquence produced upon the audience.

'What do you think of him?' Chaoumian asked him presently. 'A dangerous man,' replied the Georgian. 'A stump orator who understands the Marxist theory and comes to us in order to make sure of an audience. He's one of those fellows who would be witty at the expense of their own fathers.'[1]

That evening, in the secret committee, Krassin proposed 'a stroke of business.' This was, to levy a forced contribution from the treasury of Tiflis, which often moved sums of money amounting to one or two millions of roubles. Sosso was entrusted with the execution of the affair. He was given a sum of 5,000 roubles by way of preparatory expenses. By the end of May he was back in Baku. There, in co-operation with Petrossian, he settled the details of the operation. He himself would take charge of it. He was now to be known as David Tchijikov, born at Vladivostok on the 6 January, 1881.

On the 12 June, 1907, at 6.45 a.m., the armoured lorry of the Tiflis treasury, escorted by eighteen Cossacks, was suddenly attacked. Ten members of the escort were killed or wounded. A satchel containing 341,000 roubles in 500 rouble notes was stolen; but they were all of one series—AM62900—so that they could not be negotiated in Russia after so sensational an affair. There were also various bonds and debentures: Treasury bonds of the Agricultural Bank, stocks and railway shares, which could not be negotiated in Russia.

For some time the booty was concealed in a recess of the dome of the Tiflis Observatory. Then Petrossian undertook the task of getting the notes and shares smuggled out of the country.

In Paris, Lenin entrusted Wallakh-Litvinov, alias Finkelstein, nicknamed Papacha, with the disposal of the booty. But Litvinov was arrested; and the records of the Paris police contain evidence of the complicity in the Tiflis affair of the future Foreign Secretary of the U.S.S.R.

The repercussions of the affair were widespread. Liberal opinion was scandalized. The Mensheviks were horrified. No one would

[1] A Russian proverb.

admit that a political party could adopt methods worthy of gangsters. The world had not yet experienced the trials of the second world war, during which the German occupation and the surrender of local authorities created peculiar conditions which might justify unusual activities. Lenin had gained nothing, and in the eyes of the Liberals he was completely discredited.

As for Koba, he had once again to adopt a new identity. He became Oganess Vartanovitch Totomiantz, accountant, born in 1880 at Erivan.

CHAPTER VIII

FURTHER IMPRISONMENT AND LIFE ABROAD

KOBA was becoming more widely known among the working-class population of Baku. The chief of the Tiflis police, Chirinkin, the captain of gendarmes, Karvazine, the colonel of gendarmes, Martynov, and the chief of the Baku police, Gourov, were beginning to feel worried by the activities of the mysterious Totomiantz, who could always fall back on his alibi as accountant in the petroleum offices at Mantachev.

In accordance with the general practice of the police all the world over, two informers, Goglidzé and Agabekov, were instructed by Karvazine to obtain evidence of the 'subversive activity' of Totomiantz and to establish his real identity.

On the 15 March, 1908, Karvazine reported that Totomiantz was none other than Joseph Djugachvili, for whom the police had been searching. On the 25 March Djugachvili was arrested and sent to the Baku jail, a prison with a bad reputation. Karvazine's report to Colonel Martynov contained the following information: 'Djaparidzé (Aliocha) is replacing Djugachvili at the head of the Baku Bolsheviks, as the other leader, Chaoumian (Stiopa) was arrested a week before Totomiantz-Djugachvili.'

After Sosso Djugachvili had been briefly questioned, Karvazine, like a good, conscientious official, wrote on his dossier, before sending him off to prison: 'Very dangerous. According to the police he is a leader of the first rank. However, there is no material proof of his subversive activity. Forward the dossier to the Special Council of the Ministry of the Interior.'

The Tsar's police were certainly conscientious. Membership of the 'subversive' party was punished by terms of penal servitude, of anything up to twenty years. But they sorrowfully admitted that Djugachvili's membership of the Bolshevik Party 'had not been proven.'

56

Djugachvili remained in the Baïlov prison in Baku for six months. On the 20 September, 1908, he was informed of the decision of the Special Council. He was sentenced to two years' enforced residence at Soloytchegodsk, in the Government of Vologda. The Council had really been lenient in dealing with Koba. The second sentence was far less severe than the first.

The town of Solvytchegodsk is in European Russia. It lies far to the north, but is within easy reach of Moscow. It has some 22,000 inhabitants. Books and newspapers reach it punctually, and since the Tsar's police allowed the exiles a monthly pension of ten roubles fifty kopeks, while a minor official who had a family to support earned no more than fifteen roubles, the revolutionaries were able to live very comfortably. The Tsar whom they were trying to overthrow was actually paying them a salary !

The colony of exiles comprised Social Democrats, Bolsheviks, Mensheviks, Revolutionary Socialists, Anarchists, Maximalists, and Populists. Their tongues were never still. Their more or less clandestine meetings degenerated into interminable theoretical discussions which occasionally ended in bloodshed. Djugachvili soon became one of the notables of this colony of Tsarist pensioners. He founded a club of Esperantists, and astonished the inhabitants of the town by talking Esperanto in the street.

His police dossier contains an entry under the heading, *Conduct*: 'Coarse and brutal. Disrespectful to the authorities. Quarrels with the townsfolk. Suggested the Governor of Vologda should transfer him to the village of Krioukouka.' Fifteen years later, Lenin, in his 'testament,' made the same complaint of Stalin; he was 'excessively coarse and brutal.'

On the 24 June, 1909, Koba was on the move again, under the bogus name of Mouradiantz. He spent a couple of days in Moscow, where a Party comrade gave him shelter; this was Lialin, an engineer employed in a textile factory. On the 28 June he took train for Baku. He returned to the black city, despite the danger of making his appearance where he was known as 'the white wolf.' But anything was preferable to allowing the Mensheviks to triumph.

The Bolshevik organization in Baku was for all practical purposes dispersed. Nearly all the leading men had been arrested, and the treasury was empty. The organization could be reconstituted only by hard and continuous work; but the bogus Mouradiantz would have to be careful. The risk of being recaptured by the police was very great.

His method of replenishing the treasury was not very original. It has been employed by the secret organizations of every country: by the Irish, the Italians, the Chinese, the Greeks. But the 'weakly' members who constituted the majority of the Party did not approve of this method.

Lists were made of shopkeepers, bankers, and industrialists, and they were invited—quite politely—to 'subscribe.' If the 'class enemy' refused to subscribe, and complained to the police, the political racketeers and commandos got to work, and the offender was severely punished. Such operations were facilitated by the fact that there was an outbreak of crime throughout the Caucasus, in which the criminals in common law vied in expropriatory zeal with those who regarded themselves as the apostles of a noble cause.

Three months later the Party treasury was in possession of adequate funds. The printing-press was set up and numbers of tracts and pamphlets were issued. But Lenin was not the only person to appreciate the secret activities of Koba. A new police officer, a certain Galimbatovsky, had arrived in Baku, to cope with the Bolsheviks, whose doings were beginning to disturb the Okhrana. One of his chief detectives, Lieutenant Mosslov, was especially entrusted with the task of tracking down 'the conductor of the clandestine orchestra.'

On the 23 March, 1910, Koba was arrested. Galimbatovsky tried to make him speak. He did not succeed. Perhaps the Tsar's police had not at their disposal the means which nowadays elicit the famous 'spontaneous' confessions for which Moscow is notorious. Their technique was still primitive.

They showed Koba his dossier, with a suggested inscription: 'In view of Djugachvili's persistent participation, and his two escapes, I propose to subject him to the extreme penalty. . . .'

Koba smiled and shrugged his shoulders. The extreme penalty was not so terribly alarming. It consisted of a maximum of five years' deportation to Siberia and enforced residence in some remote locality.

The police officer decided to send Koba back to the Baïlov

prison until the Special Council should take some fresh decision.

During this second term of detention in Baku, Koba drew some attention to himself by his peculiar actions. He was on very easy terms with the ordinary criminals. He joined in their games, advised them if they consulted him, and wrote their letters for them. The Revolutionary Socialists in the prison were scandalized. His attitude was due to a principle which he had borrowed from Lenin, who had decided that "the social debris of capitalist society, the criminals in common law, would play an important part in the social revolution. These 'ragged' fellows[1] were combative by nature; they could be utilized in the first phase of the revolution as a battering-ram, in order to ensure the radical destruction of the mechanism of the State, for which they cherished a profound hatred.

Trotzky, who criticized Stalin for this 'strange and abnormal characteristic,' mentions a curious incident in his biography of Lenin: '. . . During the civil war, when certain sections of the army, above all the cavalry, let themselves go, and were guilty of acts of violence and indecency [Trotzky might have said frankly, of rape and pillage), Lenin said: "Why not send them to Stalin? He knows how to talk to such fellows. . . ." '

The Special Council of the Ministry for the Interior was extremely moderate in its treatment of Koba. It decided to send him back to the same place of enforced residence from which he had escaped, considering, no doubt, that the six months in prison would constitute a sufficient punishment. On the 20 September, 1910, Koba left for Solvytchegodsk in company with fifteen other prisoners. They arrived at their destination on the 1 October.

There all was as usual. Nothing had changed: there were the same discussions, the same meetings, the same disputes. But Koba no longer wished to take part in this 'battle of mice.' He was in postal communication with Lenin, and wrote to him regularly, telling him what was happening in 'this Russia strangled by Stolypin's necktie.' He was beginning to show a new tendency. He wrote to foreign correspondents as a member of the central illegal committee of Russia, and his words of advice were often like words of command. He began to feel a certain hostility toward the Bolsheviks who were living peacefully abroad, and who wanted, from their distant places

[1]*Lumpenproletariat:* the ragged proletariat. The definition is that of Karl Marx.

of refuge, to issue orders to the soldiers of the Revolution. This time Lenin saw that the letters of the Caucasian revolutionist were no longer letters of advice: their tone was new to him, despite their deference.

One day he said to Zinoviev: 'I like this man: he's full of energy, full of decision, ready to go to extremes in the revolution. But sometimes I find him enigmatic. What is he thinking with those yellow eyes of his?'[1]

But Koba was becoming less enigmatic. In a letter to a 'Comrade Simon' dated the 31 December, 1910, and sent to a foreign address, he wrote, taking the date as a pretext:

'Comrade Simon, I received your letter yesterday, thanks to our comrades. Warmest greetings to Lenin, Kamenev, and the rest. I am glad to get their letters, though sometimes I find them too academic. It seems to me that the peaceful atmosphere in which you are living yonder prevents you from realizing the approach of a new tempest which is gathering here. I don't venture to compare my modest personality with the men who have kindled the spark.[2] But I have already had experience of a good few conflagrations here. . . . I am practically the only one of our group[3] who is actually concerned with the conflagration. People must listen to what I say.'

This was not the first time that Koba, writing directly to Lenin, had suggested himself as candidate for the leadership of the illegal Bolshevik Party. The 'Old Man' became uneasy. He was neither vain nor arrogant, but he was convinced, with all the tenacity of a man possessed by fixed ideas, that no one but himself could quite understand his doctrine and his tactics—the only true doctrine, the only true tactics—and he was anxious to learn what Koba actually intended.

Accordingly, he advised Koba to escape once again: 'You are tired,' he wrote. 'Try the open air.'

Koba was to be released on the 31 July, 1911, unless the Special Commission should prolong his period of enforced residence. Without waiting for this date, on the 1 July, 1911, Koba once again

---

[1]The expression gave rise to a legend in the course of Zinoviev's tussle with Stalin. Wishing to wound his adversary, Zinoviev paraphrased Lenin's expression, pretending that what he had really said was: 'This man with his beastly yellow eyes.'
[2]An allusion to *Iskra*—'the Spark.'
[3]The secret Central Bolshevik Committee for Russia.

secretly departed from his place of enforced residence. This time he had a passport in the name of Lado Doumbadzé, born at Koutaïss on the 12 January, 1880. This was his third escape. By the 20 July he had reached the capital.

He was at last at the centre of the political life of the great empire, and in permanent contact with the Bolshevik members of the Duma. He was now at the actual summit of the Party. Lenin, imprisoned within his rectilinear meditations, and the obstinate logic of the paranoiac, was psychologically self-sufficing. If he had been transported to a desert island his brain would have continued to function in the same fashion. Koba, on the contrary, had his two feet solidly planted on the ground. Without human contacts, without his clandestine life and its activities, he would have been absolutely at a loss.

His letters continued to lay stress upon the opposition between the theoreticians who were living far withdrawn from the heat of the arena, and the revolutionaries who were 'on the spot.' On the 5 August he said, in a long letter:

'The emigration isn't everything; it isn't even the main thing. The main thing is the organization of the work in Russia, among our friends. Your group (the Lenin-Plekhanov group) is alive, because it is solidly based on the unity of conceptions in respect of the means of regenerating the Party. But precisely because they are only a group, and not a fusion of groups, the Bolsheviks must have their own organization, a secret, powerful and independent organization, even with fellow-travellers like Plekhanov. This organization ought to be here and not abroad. There the Mensheviks are beginning to open their mouths, embarrassing us with their conferences and their "unification" meetings. . . .'

Before the 'Old Man' could give him his advice he had convoked seventy-five militants at Viborg, in Finland, only thirty-five miles from St. Petersburg. But a great disappointment awaited them. Colonel Martynov, transferred from Baku to St. Petersburg, had received warning of the conference. At the same time one of his spies, Kolpov, gave him a valuable piece of information: a Bolshevik leader, who had been organizing the conference, was hiding in Allilouev's flat. Three detectives, in turn, kept the flat under observation.

Allilouev, an experienced conspirator, soon realized what was afoot. One day, on returning to the flat, he found Stalin and another Georgian conversing in their native language. 'Comrade Koba, be prudent! The 'tecs are at the door !' he said.

'And then?' he replied: 'I am Lado Doumbadzé. We are discussing business. What the deuce !—you're becoming a timid, Philistine little bourgeois ! You'll be afraid of your own shadow soon !'

But on the 9 September, 1911, at the terminus of one Finland railway, when Koba was about to take train for Viborg, he was arrested and confronted with the Okhrana.

Martynov recognized him immediately: 'Good day, my friend. We said goodbye at Baku; we meet again in St. Petersburg. What are you doing here? Who authorized you to come here? Why are you masquerading as Lado Doumbadzé?'

Koba did not reply. Experience had taught him that silence is a virtue. Martynov sent him to the Kriesty prison. His dossier was forwarded to the Minister for the Interior. But chance and destiny were in Koba's favour, and their instrument, on this occasion, was the police. The Governor of Vologda neglected to inform St. Petersburg that Koba had departed before his official release. The note which he despatched mentioned that the man in question 'had completed his term of enforced residence.'

Consequently the Special Council found Koba guilty only of leaving the Government of Vologda without permission. The offence was not a serious one, and the Council, disregarding the innumerable notes of the secret police, confined itself to sentencing him to deportation to Vologda. It was therefore impossible for him to take part in the Prague Conference, convoked by Lenin on the 5 January. Yet this conference was to play a part of capital importance in the history of Bolshevism. It declared that 'the adversaries' of clandestine activities were 'enemies of the working class,' and decided to constitute, as quickly as possible, an illegal Bolshevik organization, in Russia, which would be independent of the other fractions. Further, it would elect a Central Committee and organize a head office. The absent are often in the wrong; but Koba was co-opted upon Lenin's proposal.

The new clandestine Politburo, appointed by the Central Committee at the instance of Lenin, was composed of Koba, Ordjonikidzé, Spandarian and Golochtchekin. Kalinin and Sverdlov were deputy-members.

In May 1912, Koba, who had meanwhile become Papadjanian, came to St. Petersburg as director of the legal Bolshevik journals, *Pravda* and *Zviezda*. He was not a good journalist. His style was often reminiscent of the seminary; but he chose his subjects cleverly.

Presently the Petersburg police observed that the Bolshevik journals were becoming more and more aggressive. A rapid inquiry revealed the presence of a new editor-in-chief, who was living in hiding. On the 28 April, 1912, the detectives of the Okhrana arrested Koba-Papadjanian opposite No. 11, Gorokhovaia Street.[1] By chance he was passing the very lair of those who were seeking him.

Koba spent more than two months in the 'Kresty' prison. The Okhrana was becoming weary of his repeated escapes. This time, it suggested to the Special Council that he might be sent beyond the Arctic Circle. On the 2 July, 1912, Koba was deported for four years to Western Siberia, to the north of the province of Tomsk, in the district of Naryma, a region of forests and lakes and marshes. He spent some time in the village of Kolpatchevo, where he found other Bolshevik leaders; then he was sent farther north, to the village of Khmarovka.

But he was soon moved on. On the 1 September, 1912, he left the village, embarked on the river steamer *Moukha*, and, on reaching the railway, took the train for Tomsk. Thence, with papers in the name of Stepan Papadopoulos, born at Taganrog in 1879, and once more an accountant, he set out for St. Petersburg. This time he did not pass through Baku. The Caucasian period of his life was over. By the 12 September he was in the capital, where the elections for the Duma were approaching. His new papers were of doubtful quality, so that he led a clandestine existence.

The elections gave seven seats to the Mensheviks and six to the Bolsheviks. The former were all intellectuals, the latter, working men. The Mensheviks began to agitate for the union of the working class, but the Bolsheviks were immune to their propaganda. It was at this moment that Lenin, who wanted to elucidate the situation and

[1]The future seat of the Tcheka.

realize the exact position of his party, sent for Koba; and on the 22 December Koba-Papadopoulos left Russia.

On the 25 December Koba was in Austria, at Poronino, with Lenin. He arrived just in time; for on the 25 a conference was opened, in the course of which Lenin intended to give his disciples their final instructions. The conference sat for five days. It included Lenin, Krupskaia (Lenin's wife), Zinoviev, the three Bolshevik deputies of the Duma, Petrovsky, Badoviev and Malinovsky, the spy of the Okhrana, Lobov, Miedviedev, Troyanosky[1] (a gunner lieutenant), his wife, Rozmirovitch, and a Bolshevik from Moscow, Polietaiev.

The meetings were held in a wooden bungalow in which the Lenins were living; Krupskaia busied herself in the kitchen.

Koba had not much to say at the Conference. He still felt ill at ease there; most of the other Bolsheviks were better speakers than he, and he felt it more prudent to avoid oratorical encounters. As for Malinovsky, he did not like him or trust him; he had a criminal record before joining the Party.

On the evening of the 31 December the Party members rested from their labours in order to celebrate the New Year. The Russian revolutionaries never fail to observe the 'Night of Saint Sylvester.' Their New Year feast was a modest one. Koba, who like many Caucasians was fond of cooking, helped Krupskaia and Rozmirovitch. He prepared a ragout of Caucasian mutton, with a spiced sauce. On learning that he was the cook, Lenin said, smiling: 'You are a cook who will always prepare spicy dishes!'

Did he remember this, eleven years later, when he said of Stalin, in his 'political testament': 'He is a good cook, but I am afraid his dishes will be too strongly spiced'?

After the Conference, Lenin spent some time with Koba. They went for walks together in the hills; they went into Zakopani to buy newspapers. Lenin was fond of cycling and tried to persuade Koba to ride a bicycle. But after several falls and a damaged leg, Koba concluded that he was not suited to this form of exercise.

Lenin drank no alcohol; but one day, when Kamenev was visiting Poronino, the 'Old Man' arranged a little party, at which he

[1]The future Soviet Ambassador to the U.S.A.

tried to make Koba drunk. Koba drank copiously, but remained perfectly lucid, and kept his temper when Lenin began to tease him. Then, while Kamenev, a little the worse for drink, began to pay court to the Polish housekeeper, Koba played chess with Lenin. The game ended in a draw.

'You are really made of steel!' said Lenin. 'The drink hasn't affected your nerves!' After a pause, he added: 'I've already recommended you to adopt a pseudonym. Henceforth the articles you write for our press are to be signed Stalin!'

Koba wrote dozens of such articles. Lenin edited them. He found them in full agreement with his own ideas of tactics. One day he said: 'I suggest that you should write an essay on Marxism and the problem of nationalism. You are a Caucasian. With you, in the Caucasus, there are twenty-three different nations. You ought to be the very man to analyse this problem.'

Stalin spent three weeks in Vienna, where he lived with Troyanovsky, and worked with Bukharin, who, being a good German scholar, translated some of the work of the Austrian Social-Democrats, Karl Renner and Bauer. By the beginning of February 1913 the essay was ready.

Stalin gave it to Lenin, who expressed his lively appreciation: 'Excellent!' he said. 'Your essay will be the best thing written on the Marxist aspect of the national problem!' Even Trotzky, though he was Stalin's enemy, praised his work.[1]

On the 15 February Stalin received an alarming letter from St. Petersburg. The police had arrested Sverdlov, who had replaced him as editor of *Pravda*. There were eight candidates, for the editor-in-chief of *Pravda* was in effect the leader of the Bolshevik 'underground' in Russia. Lenin's choice was soon made. He needed a man who would not leave the beaten track. Stalin, the pupil whose measure he had taken, was the man for *Pravda*. In nominating him, Lenin did not measure the energy he was releasing.

---

[1]See Trotsky's autobiography.

E

CHAPTER IX

ST. PETERSBURG, 1913-17

O N the 24 February Stalin was in St. Petersburg. He had to find suitable quarters. One of his friends, the Bolshevik Vazov, gave him the address of a certain Viatcheslav Skriabin, a student in the Polytechnic.

Stalin remained with the Skriabins for about a month. Young Viatcheslav was then twenty-two years of age. Well versed in the theory of economics, he was an indefatigable worker, a little slow and stubborn, but punctual and methodical. After a series of nocturnal discussions, interrupted by games of chess, Stalin decided to make young Skriabin his adjutant, and appointed him secretary to the editor of *Pravda*. This was the beginning of the career of the future Molotov.

Skriabin worked in the editorial office, where Stalin did not venture to appear. The young secretary brought to the office the articles written by Stalin, and in general acted as *homme de liaison*. The work proceeded smoothly; from the very first the two men appeared to constitute an ideal partnership.

About the middle of March Lenin wrote to Stalin: 'I congratulate you warmly on your success. The improvement of the paper is obvious and most important; it is to be hoped that this will continue, provided we don't have too much bad luck.'

These congratulations were in effect addressed not only to Stalin, but to the future Molotov, whose very existence was as yet unknown to Lenin.

In 1913 the Russians, apart from a very small group, were hardly aware of the existence of the Bolsheviks. Nobody took very seriously 'the elucubrations of a few half-insane criminals who were preaching sheer absurdities.' By a strange paradox, it was this attitude toward 'the Bolshevik virus' that was one of the principal factors that later favoured the Bolsheviks' seizure of power !

From Poronino, Lenin attentively followed all the manifestations of the labour movement in the capital—for St. Petersburg was the real centre of the working-class movement—recording and classifying all the data which would enable him to 'feel the pulse of the proletariat.'

In the meantime the police were again closing in upon Stalin. Chance favoured their plans. On the 22 March, 1913, they received information to the effect that the musical evening at the Kalachnikov Exchange, for the benefit of the workers' insurance funds, was actually organized by the Bolshevik Committee of St. Petersburg, and that the secret leaders of the Party would be present.

On the very day of the concert Bielietzky, the chief of the St. Petersburg police, was completing a report on the activities of the underground workers. 'The most energetic element,' he wrote, 'the most vigorous, the most capable of carrying on an unwearying struggle, consists of the men grouped about Lenin. Cells, clubs, and Bolshevik organizations are springing up in all the cities. The Central Committee is regularly convoked. A personal representative of Lenin's, a certain Djugachvili, is now present in the capital. It is he who is responsible for the publication of *Pravda*, and he is directing the activities of the secret clubs.'

Joukovsky, a spy, assured the police that all the 'cream' of the Party would be present at the musical evening, and a captain of the gendarmerie, Orlov, was entrusted with a special mission: 'to search for and arrest the criminal Joseph Djugachvili, who had escaped from deportation in the region of Naryma.'

When the police entered the hall Stalin was conversing with Skriabin, Samirlov, Gronov, and the wife of the conductor Barsky. 'Clear out quickly!' Skriabin warned him. 'Those are policemen.'

Mme. Barsky led Stalin to the cloakroom, wrapped him in her cloak, drew the hood over his head, and sent him down the stairs leading from the stage door. Since returning to St. Petersburg Stalin had shaved off his moustache; but his cheeks were those of a man who has a thick beard. The attention of the sergeant, Ivan Stepanovitch Loiko, was drawn to the curious walk of this woman who was in such a hurry to leave the hall. He lifted the hood, and the 'fugitive' was discovered.

This time things looked very serious for Stalin. The Department of Police had decided to take stronger measures against so slippery a customer. There were limits to what the Minister for the Interior could do in such a case; but he instructed his representatives on the Special Council to sentence Joseph Koba-Djugachvili to four years' deportation to the region of Turukhansk, in the province of the Yenisei, on the river of the same name, in Northern Siberia. He left St. Petersburg on the 22 April, 1913.

On the 6 June, 1913, Stalin reached the village of Kostino. Its north latitude was 66.45 degrees so that it lay on the Arctic Circle. This isolated spot had been selected as the destination of such exiles as were regarded as representing a danger to the Tsarist régime —amongst them Stalin's predecessor in the editorial chair of *Pravda*, Jacob Sverdlov.

This was the beginning of a monotonous existence. Thanks to Ivan Makarov, newspapers arrived from time to time. Letters and telegrams were sent on from the village of Monastyrskiré. As always, there were interminable discussions on political, economic and philo-sophical themes. But Stalin was not particularly sociable; he 'kept himself to himself.' He was entirely preoccupied with the idea of a fresh escape.

The Governor of the province of Yeniseisk gave orders, after the police had intercepted a letter, that Stalin should be transferred farther north, to the village of Kureika, on the 6th degree north latitude, beyond the Arctic Circle.

At Kureika, Stalin settled down in company with Sverdlov, in a room provided by a hunter of squirrels and sables, Khvatov by name. An adjacent room was inhabited by the hunter; a third room sheltered the chief of the local police, an Ossetian,[1] Kibirov by name. Ten days later they were joined by a second group of exiles: Kar-ganov, Spandarian,[2] with his wife, and a criminal in common law, Khvilia, a hired murderer, deported from Odessa.

Life was even more monotonous here than it had been at Kostino. Mme. Spandarian has left a description of the room in which he was living.

[1]The Ossetians, as we have seen, were a Caucasian tribe, whose blood flowed in the veins of Djugachvili himself.

[2]A member of the Central Committee of the Bolshevik Party, like Stalin and Sverdlov.

'It was a fairly large room, but badly lit. Everything was in disorder: the table was covered with books and great bundles of newspapers; in one corner, hanging on a cord, were various traps, fishing-lines, and the like, which Stalin himself had made. . . .'

In August 1914, on the outbreak of war, Stalin found himself almost alone. Only the Armenian Spandarian remained at Kureika; but he, a victim of phthisis, died at the beginning of 1916. As a general rule the Caucasians, natives of a warm, southern climate, found it difficult to endure the Arctic cold. Stalin, however, was never ill at Kureika. He spent much time in the open air, practising physical exercises and learning to ski. In summer he bathed a great deal, and paddled a canoe when he organized a hunting or fishing expedition. Someone sent him a book on *yogi*, then the fashion among the Russian intellectuals, and he practised 'Hindu breathing' to strengthen his lungs.

He resumed his reading, and in 1915 he was able to send Allilouev a new manscript, which was to make the second volume of his study of the problem of nationalities; and he asked Allilouev to send this on to Lenin. But he was obliged to abandon all hope of escape. The country was at war. The possibilities of an underground existence were now practically nil. Papers were inspected everywhere; on the roads and on board the trains military documents had to be produced.

In the autumn of 1915 Lenin, who was living in Switzerland, wrote a letter to the emigré Karpinsky, whose contents were somewhat surprising.

'I want to ask a great favour of you,' he wrote. 'Try to discover what precisely is the real name of Comrade Koba-Stalin. It seems to me that it is something like Diega? . . . We have all forgotten it; and it is very important. . . .'

Lenin was then preparing his famous 'Theses,' and his 'Manifesto' to the Party and the working class. In 1916 Lenin's theses were transmitted by way of Monastyrskiré to the Bolshevik exiles. Their cynicism and violence alarmed the other Bolshevik leaders, who felt that Lenin had gone altogether too far.

'We are not naive pacifists, and we are not sighing for peace,' wrote the Bolshevik apostle. 'To preach peace at the present time is a piece of stupidity and a mistake, above all after the treachery of such scum as Guerde, Plekhanov, Vandervelde and Kautsky.[1] It would be the lamentation of a timid and bewildered *petit bourgeois*. We must still be revolutionaries, even in a country at war. Our *mot d'ordre* is plain: let us transform the imperialist war which the scoundrels of Germany and the *Entente* have forced on the peoples into a civil war, a war of liberation. Let us preach the class conflict in the armies—let us call for armed insurrection against the imperialist butchers.

'The refusal to serve in the army, strike action against war, etc. . . . dear to the hearts of some pacific fools, are useless save as the propaganda of circus clowns. The timid and cowardly dream of a struggle without weapons against an armed *bourgeoisie* is mere stupidity. The suppression of capitalism without a pitiless civil war is a Utopia of crétins. . . . Revolutionary cells and groups must be formed in all the armies.

'We shall say to the soldiers: "They have put guns into your hands, and quick-firing rifles. Take them, and don't listen to the snivelling sentimentalists who are afraid of conflict. There are still too many things on this earth which have to be destroyed by steel and fire, too many scoundrels to be shot down like dogs." '

The Bolshevik leaders in exile, though they were accustomed to Lenin's style, felt that this was really past human understanding. His latest writings seemed the work of a madman, a sadist who wanted to take advantage of a war in order to provoke an orgy of pitiless and senseless carnage which would drown the world in seas of blood. They, on principle, were pacifists; he justified the very notion of war by the simple addition of an adjective: *civil*.

Stalin was the only one of the exiles to agree with his leader. For him, violence was the only means of conflict; blood was 'the fuel of History.' The essential thing was to arrive at the resolution which would drag the whole country into the whirlpool which the Order of professional revolutionaries would have to tame by enforcing a blind obedience upon the masses. But as a preliminary the masses must be liberated, set free from 'the chains of slavery and obedience.'

While the latest words of the 'Old Man' were still being discussed, Stalin wrote to him: 'Greetings to you, dear Ilyitch—my warmest, warmest greetings! I have read your thesis and your mani-

[1]The Second International accepted the principle of a patriotic attitude.

festo. They are admirable! One is conscious of a breath of fresh air—
a revolutionary breeze that refreshes the soul.[1] We must get to work
as quickly as possible: one can't remain with folded arms. . . .'

Thus Stalin, with the soul of a Caucasian *abrek*, 'a Zelim-Khan
who had read Marx's *Capitalism*,' accepted and supported, without
hesitation, the inhuman logic of his leader, Lenin. He was supported
by another Caucasian, Spandarian, then dying of phthisis, and hating
the whole world.

'The "Old Man" has gone crazy,' one Lazarev, a recent arrival,
declared. 'He is nervous, violent, intolerable.'

Stalin rose to his feet: 'The "Old Man" is right. Robert Grimm
and Rakovsky are just what he said. And so are you, Lazarev. . . .'

The result was a free fight, and an officer of the local police had
to separate the squabbling Leninists.

Stalin had thus made up his mind to follow Lenin. He saw no
possibility of reaching a position where the seizure of power would
be practicable, save through the ruins of a vast conflagration. And
the imperialist war gave him a chance to kindle such a blaze.

Let the liberal revolution come—one would soon find a way of
putting it into harness! That was what the professional revolutionaries were for.

In March 1916 Stalin was called before a recruiting board. He
was discharged as unfit for service. In November 1916 he had been
called up again at Krassnoiarsk, where he arrived the 23 January. On
the 25 February, having assumed yet another identity—that of Piotr
Galkine, born at Koutaïss in 1873—thinking it better to add a few
years to his age in time of war—he took refuge in Atchiansk.

At this moment the revolution broke out: the Tsarist régime
foundered.

For the majority of Russian citizens, the next step would be to
realize the aspirations of a comprehensive liberalism. A very
delirium of liberty had seized upon the people. Interminable speeches
were delivered; endless processions marched behind the Red Flag;
the troops took part in all these demonstrations, and in the rural
districts the peasants began to burn down the houses of the great
landowners and take possession of the soil. In their reaction against

[1]Stalin was still employing the inflated style of the seminary.

the fallen government the majority of the population, forgetting all prudence, rebelled against any manifestation of real authority. People must no longer be given orders; they must be moved only by persuasion.

For Lenin, this was the time to profit by the tornado which was sweeping the Empire—the time to let loose upon the country, and perhaps upon the world, the calamities of which he had established the terrifying code—the code which Stalin would help him to enforce. But Stalin had certain ideas of his own; his secret thoughts were not always in conformity with those of the 'Old Man.'

On the 8(21) March Joseph Djugachvili-Stalin left for St. Petersburg. For the first time in eighteen years he was travelling under his own name. His underground life was over. A past master in the arts of conspiracy, he had perfect control of his nervous reactions; his heart was long hardened; he was essentially incapable of pity; his patience was inexhaustible, and he knew what taciturnity and cunning could accomplish. He was truly 'the man of steel.' His apprenticeship as statesman and ruler was about to begin.

CHAPTER X

THE FIRST REVOLUTION AND THE STRUGGLE FOR POWER

EARLY on the morning of the 13(26) March, 1917, Stalin and his companions, among whom was Kamenev, arrived in St. Petersburg. Their journey had been a protracted triumph. The Central Committee of the Bolshevik Party welcomed them at the terminus. It was represented by the working man Chliapnikov, one day to be First Councillor of the U.S.S.R. Embassy in Paris, the semi-intellectual Zaloutzky, and Viatcheslav Skriabin-Molotov, student in the economic faculty of the Polytechnic Institute of St. Petersburg.

Stalin and his comrades adopted a prudent attitude. They were still undecided. Chliapnikov welcomed them with a speech: 'The Revolution has already taken a first step toward the final victory of the working class. The *bourgeoisie* and its lackeys in the provisional government, the hideous imperialists, like Miliukov,[1] are trying to continue their course of brigandage. But the proletarian masses will not suffer this! Greetings to you, comrades, who come from Siberia to bring us a revolutionary leadership!'

The new arrivals were greatly embarrassed. They knew nothing as to the proportions of the conflicting forces. They did not even know that the country was sinking into anarchy. Prince Lvov's Government had been obliged to discharge the whole of the Imperial police and to replace them by a militia recruited anyhow and officered by men without experience, unable to fight the ordinary criminals released from all the gaols.

The Soviet of army and working-class deputies, led by the Georgian Menshevik Tcheidzé, constituted a powerful opposition to the Government, so that events began to take the shape of a social revolution. In the army, Tcheidzé imposed a decree that suppressed

[1]Minister for Foreign Affairs and leader of the Constitutional Democrats, he had contributed to the overthrow of the Tsarist régime. In Paris he edited *Les Dernières Nouvelles*.

the disciplinary powers of the officers, which were henceforth exercised by committees elected by the soldiers themselves.

At Kronstadt, the naval citadel, crowned by the huge dome of the largest modern cathedral in Russia,[1] the sailors of the Baltic fleet, having killed the commandant of the fortress, threw such officers as they disliked into the furnaces, or the sea, and as revolutionary Bolsheviks confronted the Provisional Government with a force with which it was obliged to negotiate.

'Molotov explained,' said Stalin, afterwards, 'that the ideal of a provisional revolutionary government could easily be realized: it would suffice to proclaim that the Petrograd Soviet was the government to which the government of Prince Lvov would hand over its powers. Thus the aim of the revolution would be completely realized.'

Stalin was not of this opinion. He thought it was far too soon for such action, and that the Bolsheviks themselves were neither sufficiently powerful nor adequately organized to take control. At the close of his conversation, he declared that the Russian Central Committee had been reorganized. It would consist henceforth of Chliapnikov, Kamenev, Sverdlov, Molotov and Stalin himself, until a Pan-Russian Conference of the Bolshevik Party was convoked. As for Lenin, his advice would be asked when he returned.

In Lenin's absence the leadership of the Bolshevik Party might devolve upon Stalin and Kamenev. But Kamenev hoped to neutralize Stalin's influence by the presence of Sverdlov.

In Molotov, *Pravda*, the central organ of the Bolshevik Party, had a devoted collaborator; but some discussions arose between him and Stalin. The young student was very definitely 'of the Left'; he even tried to provoke a *pronunciamento*. On his initiative the Viborg Committee adopted a motion demanding 'the immediate dismissal of the comrades from Siberia who have displaced the Petrograd comrades.'

This provoked an explanation which had a decisive result as regards the relations between Stalin and Molotov. 'Viatcheslav Mikhailovitch,' said Stalin, 'a choice must be made. One can't sit on two chairs at once. You are a member of the Central Provisional Committee. You must calm down these comrades from the Viborg-

[1] Work of the famous architect of Imperial Russia, Basil Kossiakov.

skaia Storona. We are both going to their meeting. You are still young, and you don't understand the necessity of discipline in the Party. But all we of the old guard, the old, pre-revolutionary Bolsheviks, have to lead the crowd; we must not allow it to lead us. I propose an eternal alliance. Do you agree?'[1]

Molotov agreed. Henceforth he would always be at Stalin's side.

The two associates began their preparations for the Pan-Russian Conference of the Party. The most important point at the moment was to decide who should present the political report. As a rule, it was presented by the leader of the Party himself. But Lenin had not yet returned from exile. Someone must be chosen to take his place. Kamenev seemed to be the most likely candidate; but Molotov was in favour of Stalin. The Georgian was duly elected. This fact is important. It destroys the legend of the mysterious and miraculous ascent of an unknown stranger, almost an intruder in the ranks of the Party.

His political report was of enormous historical interest. It shows that at this stage Stalin was firmly opposed to the seizure of power by the Bolsheviks. He thought it was much too soon for such a step, and he even proposed to support the provisional government of Prince Lvov. He was already inclined to hesitate before serious decisions.

The official reports of this supplementary Sixth Conference of March 1917 have disappeared from circulation. Apart from the copies preserved in the archives of the Politburo, there is at present one copy in a foreign country:[2] 'Power is divided equally between two organs, neither of which possesses absolute power,' Stalin begins. 'The Soviet[3] has taken upon itself the initiative of revolutionary transformations; it is the revolutionary leader of the insurgent people, the organ which controls the provisional *bourgeois* government. ...'

'It is not fitting,' Stalin continued, 'that we should now force events. We must not undertake to accelerate the process of divorce

---

[1] It was Molotov himself who related this incident, at a private gathering in 1929, on the occasion of Stalin's fiftieth birthday, at which members of the Politburo and the Orgburo were present. Not until 1944 did serious differences develop between the two men.

[2] I owe my heartfelt thanks to the owner of one of these copies, a refugee, who has allowed me to consult it.

[3] This refers to the Soviet of soldiers and workers of Petrograd, which had assumed control of all governmental action. It contained a majority of Mensheviks, and contributed largely to the undermining of all legal authority.

between the Soviet and the strata of the petty and middle *bourgeoisie*. We ought to take our time, to wait until the peasantry is definitely tired of the war and can no longer resist its ardent desire to seize the land.

'It must be explained to the masses, as clearly as possible, that the only source of the power and authority of the provisional government is the will of the people, to which it is bound to be completely obedient. The provisional government must be supported only in so far as it undertakes to satisfy the claims of the working class and the revolutionary peasantry. If the government declares that it is incapable of satisfying them, the revolutionary democracy can only withdraw its support and replace it by the provisional revolutionary government. . . .'

Thus Stalin was clearly opposed to the Bolshevik *coup d'état*. He was in favour of evolution within the framework of revolution.

His report met with violent criticism from the Radicals of the Party. On the following day, in the assembly of the presidents of the local Soviets, Steklov-Nakhamkes presented a secret report on the counter-revolutionary measures prepared by the provisional government, and the assembly strongly condemned Stalin's formula of conditional support.

Stalin showed that he was capable of yielding ground when advisable. He abandoned the formula of 'conditional support' which was favoured by Martov's Mensheviks. But he maintained the basic principle of his idea. 'One should neither accelerate nor anticipate disagreements with the parties from which we are divided only by divergencies of a secondary order. The essential thing is to seek for allies, for fellow-travellers. There is no life in a party where there are no disagreements.[1] We shall manage to settle petty disagreements within the party. . . .'

Kamenev supported Stalin; Sverdlov, on the other hand, sided with the Radicals. The members of the Petrograd Committee, under the leadership of Molotov, accepted Stalin's standpoint. His proposal, extremely moderate for a professional revolutionary of the Bolshevik Party, had every prospect of being accepted.

In this event the Bolshevik Party would remain *within* the Soviet,

---

[1] If Beria had ever wished to find arguments justifying the capital punishment of Stalin, he had only to refer to the proceedings of this Conference.

side by side with the Menshevik internationalists and the revolutionary Socialists of the Left, and would not take up its position *outside* the Soviet, in order to lead the masses who wanted to impose their will on the Provisional Government and on the Soviet, operating *from the outside*.

The entire development of the Russian revolution was determined at this crucial moment. But Stalin did not remain the provisional leader of the Party and of the Central Committee; for on the 2 August, 1917, Lenin himself gave the extremist party another orientation.

The conference was obliged to interrupt its labours, in accordance with a telegram from Stockholm. Sent by Ganietzky, it enumerated Lenin's requirements. It announced, also, that Lenin, together with about thirty of his supporters, was crossing Germany and Sweden on his way to Russia. Lenin ordered his disciples 'to undertake neither consultation nor fusion with the other parties and to await his arrival in Petrograd to work out a general party line.'

The telegram was greeted with bewildered amazement. 'How can he travel across Germany?' cried Kamenev. 'If only he doesn't compromise us by doing so!'

Stalin said nothing. But the 'Old Man's' telegram was equivalent to an order, and Kamenev, at the head of a party delegation, proceeded to meet him at Tammerfors, in Finland.

The die was cast. Lenin took the reins. The Russian revolution would now follow the dramatic route which the crazy genius had traced for it. In the meantime Koba-Stalin, the indomitable terrorist, was showing an aspect of his character which is one of his trump cards. He refused to rush blindly onwards.

Lenin's journey through Germany in a sealed carriage was facilitated by the Germans, who were convinced that they were sending to Russia a cargo of dynamite which, even if it did not annihilate the entire mechanism of government, would at least destroy an important part of the war machine. The news of the revolution had reached Lenin in Zurich, where he was living in the Spiegelgasse—like Robespierre, in the house of a cabinet-maker. He had but one thought: to go as quickly as possible to Petrograd, the centre of the revolution.

CHAPTER XI

LENIN AS STALIN'S TEACHER

IN the train between Tammerfors and Helsinki, on the 15 April, Lenin asked Kamenev: 'And my miraculous Georgian? How is he doing? He's the sort of man we want!'

The future director-in-chief of the Sovietic cinema, Chioumiatzky, who was present during this conversation, made it, in 1930, the subject of a film.

As they approached Petrograd, Lenin, always prudent, began to grow uneasy. 'Are you sure they won't arrest me in the station, when we get there?' he asked Kamenev.

'On the contrary,' Kamenev replied, 'they'll receive you with honours! Koba has made preparations for your reception. . . .'

And indeed, when the train entered the Finnish railway station searchlights were sweeping the sky. On the platform was a disorderly gathering of soldiers, sailors, and working men. The Red Flag was flying everywhere, adorned with revolutionary inscriptions. The bands were playing the *Marseillaise* and the *Internationale*. In the front were two Georgians, side by side: Tehkheidzé (a Menshevik, President of the Petrograd Soviet) and Stalin. The Georgian period of Russian history had already begun. The little country annexed by Alexander I was taking its revenge.

Tchkheidzé saluted Lenin 'in the name of Revolutionary Democracy.' He expressed the hope that Lenin would take his place beside them all 'to defend the revolution against all attacks from without and within.'

Stalin greeted the 'Old Man' in the name of the Bolshevik Party.

In his reply, Lenin immediately defined his own point of view. With angry vehemence, he declared: 'The war of the imperialist bandits is the beginning of civil war throughout Europe; the dawn of the universal social revolution has appeared . . . Germany is in a state of effervescence. The Russian revolution is moving toward a new epoch. . . . The old shirt of Social Democracy, rotten and unsavoury, must be cast into the dustbin of history. Long live the Social Revolution!'

Tchkheidzé withdrew, in some bewilderment; but the crowd shouted with enthusiasm. The tidal wave of revolution had brought to the surface all the confused sentiments of the masses, and among them the secular resentment of the poor and the desire to have done with war. Stalin gave a sign, and in a moment Lenin was lifted by dozens of hands and borne in triumph on men's shoulders. He was carried toward an armoured car which the Bolshevik Party had managed to procure. At every cross-roads the car stopped, and Lenin harangued the crowd, which as yet understood nothing of his vehement exhortations, but applauded at a venture, as it was accustomed to do.

Stalin tried to restrain Lenin's transports: 'Vladimir Ilyitch, you are tired! They are waiting for your report to the Conference. We'll begin by voting a motion. . . .'

Lenin refused to listen to him: 'Break off the Conference! We shall convoke another at the end of April. I must make the Party aware of the situation in Europe. You have all become provincials! Convoke the Central Committee! Immediately! And convoke the editorial staff of *Pravda*!'

On the evening of the 3 April the Central Committee met at the general headquarters of the Bolshevik Party, the private house of the dancer Kchesinskaia, once the mistress of the Tsar Nicholas II. The house was requisitioned for the use of the Party by a troop of sailors from the Baltic fleet. Stalin presided over the assembly. Prudent and undecided, he tried to allay the effect of Lenin's words. But Lenin resolutely returned to the attack.

'Contemporary Socialism is the enemy of the international proletariat! The very name of Socialism has been defiled by the treason of its leaders. We have nothing in common with it. It is impossible to purge it; we must cast it aside as one casts a dirty clout. We must put on a clean shirt and call ourselves the Communist Party. . . .'

Kamenev glanced at Stalin, shrugging his shoulders. But Stalin was imperturbable. He waited, refusing to give any indication of his actual position. The proposition was put to the vote. All, with the exception of Lenin, decided to retain the title of the Social-Democratic Bolshevik Party. It was more than a year before Lenin's 'professional revolutionaries' consented to describe themselves as Communists.

Lenin, who had been making speeches ever since his arrival, ended by losing his voice. Stalin and Kamenev took him to the house of his elder sister, Anna Elizarov, where a bed awaited him. But Lenin was indefatigable: 'I am not going to rest,' he said, 'until I have completed the theses which I am going to present to the Central Committee tomorrow. Convoke a plenary session for to-morrow. You have disappointed me. . . .'

Stalin made no reply. Nor had he anything to say when Kamenev exclaimed, in the street: 'The "Old Man" has certainly gone crazy! He'll end by isolating us in the heart of the Soviet!'

Stalin continued to hold his tongue. He did not agree with his master. But his sixth sense, which guided him with the certainty of radar, convinced him of the practical strength of Lenin's argument. He felt that Lenin's exhortations would exert a decisive influence in the whirlwind that was sweeping onward the tens of millions of human beings who were sick of the terrible war, and liberated from all constraint by the revolutionary anarchy which had already shattered almost all the restraints of authority.

On the 4(17) April, 1917, the plenary assembly of the Central Committee, joined by the Petrograd Committee and the staff of *Pravda*, heard Lenin expound his principles, the famous theses of the 4 April, which have contributed to change the course of history. At the moment they seemed so utterly absurd that very few people took them seriously.

They were expressed in lapidary formulae:

The immediate termination of the imperialist war of brigand-age.

Refusal to give any support to the mercenary Provisional Government.[1]

All power to the Soviets.

Immediate expropriation of the soil which would be restored to the peasants by the local Soviets.

Immediate nationalization of the banks.

Absolute control of the national production by the Soviets.

[1]It must be recalled that the Provisional Government was composed of Liberals who refused any measures of constraint.

There were yet other theses, even more revolutionary: Lenin saw, with the clairvoyance of a man possessed, a clairvoyance that never failed him, the goal which he was seeking to reach. He had decided once and for all that a conjuncture so favourable to his plans would never occur again, and he resolved to stake his all. In his inhuman cynicism he shrank from no means that would serve his end.

Stalin, who distrusted sudden and violent solutions, did not openly oppose Lenin: 'We will publish these theses in *Pravda* as the personal principles of Comrade Lenin.'

With this Lenin agreed.

On his departure, Lenin made a proposal to Stalin: 'Koba, I propose to form an alliance with you. I need a man of action like you, with your experience, your courage, your way of handling underground groups of armed men. Kamenev, Zinoviev, Rykov, Noguin, Federov, Miliukov, Bubnov, are merely "academicians." . . . The Provisional Government must be overthrown, and we shall overthrow it when the masses are with us! And that I guarantee they will be very soon! We are promising them all they can ask of a triumphant revolution. Come, Koba, do you agree?'

Stalin looked Lenin in the face, without replying, but according to Angarsky his gaze was full of 'understanding comradeship.' Lenin pushed his shabby grey cap over his ears, went up to Stalin and clapped him on the shoulder.[1] The alliance was sealed.

That evening Stalin dined with Kamenev, who tried to warn him against the adventurous proposals of 'the Old Man.'

'I should like to warn you that you are running a great risk. You will pay the cost of an adventure which the 'Old Man' wants to undertake. Let him act alone; he will soon realize his isolation and calm down. If you help him he will go to any lengths, and then we shall be for it!'

'What do you expect me to do *dans cette galère*?' Stalin answered. 'I became a professional revolutionary in order to act, not in order to chatter; and the moment has arrived. . . .'

The Seventh Pan-Russian Conference of the Bolshevik Party opened on the 24 April. The delegates represented 80,000 members of the Party; which was not bad for a revolutionary party which had

---

[1]Angarsky, who was present, records this conversation in his memoirs.

F

barely emerged from underground. This time it was Lenin himself who presented the political report, repeating his theses of the 4 April and adding a paragraph on 'the necessity of creating an International of the revolutionary parties.' Some of the leaders present—Rykov, Dzerjinski, Bubnov—and militants like Angarsky, attempted. to form a moderate fraction under the leadership of Kamenev.

Lenin behaved like a devil in holy water. Stalin supported him, without making any great show of his support, and without indulging in long perorations. Lenin, despite his prolonged absence from the country, knew his Russia. He knew, also, that the promise of the immediate distribution of all the land expropriated from the landowners and the State would bring all the peasants over to his side, for they would not be greatly interested in whatever the Socialist programme might propose to do in the cities.

In commenting upon the attitude of Stalin at these decisive moments, Trotzky, his implacable enemy, wrote: 'Stalin deserted his allies of the day before. He replied to Kamenev; he expounded his disagreement with his Tiflis friend. He backed Lenin to the utmost.'

When writing thus, Trotzky was as yet unaware that Stalin was already bound to Lenin by an alliance concluded the day before. He did not realize that Stalin, from being a hesitating moderate, had in fact become as great an extremist as Lenin. With his innate sense of reality, Stalin knew that in the general confusion, when the spontaneous demobilization of the army had set in, and when all men's passions were unleashed, only those could win who were ready for the extremest measures.

The Central Committee was composed of Lenin, Stalin, Zinoviev, Kamenev, Milioutin, Noguin, Sverdlov, Smilga, and Fédorov. Deputy members were Theodorovitch, Bubnov, Glébov, Avilov and Pravdin. Despite his disagreement with Kamenev, Lenin insisted on the latter's nomination. He felt that Kamenev's opposition would always be friendly: he admired Lenin to such a degree that he even adopted his intonations, and copied the Master's handwriting. Early in May the Central Committee appointed its first political bureau, the Politburo which was to become the Vatican of Communist thought.

In respect of these first members of the Committee, Trotzky

justly observed: 'Of the members of the Central Committee elected at the Seventh Pan-Russian Conference of the Bolshevik Party, only Sverdlov and Lenin managed to die in time. All the rest—with the exception, of course, of Stalin himself—as well as the four delegate members, fell out of favour, were officially shot, or mysteriously disappeared. . . .'

Trotzky wrote the truth. Since the days of the great French Revolution it has often been said that 'revolution devours its own children.' The Russian Revolution was no exception to this historic rule. The militant, in order to escape, had to follow all the zigzags of the historical developments, and sometimes be ahead of them. This was what Stalin did.

Lenin applied himself above all to what he called direct propaganda. From the balcony of the Kchessinska Palace he harangued the crowds. His speeches were primitive, appealing to the most immediate instincts of the soldiers and peasants, and of the turbid magma formed by the masses of a country in a state of ebullition. Day after day he exclaimed: 'Loot what has been looted! . . . Peace to the cabins, war upon the palaces! . . . The defence of the native land means the defence of the capitalists of one country against the capitalists of another.'

Stalin was often present when Lenin was speaking. He was undergoing a fresh apprenticeship: he was learning to know the Russian crowd, with which he had been only imperfectly acquainted. In the Caucasus the peasants, to be sure, were poor, but they had the mentality of landowners, and their aspirations were definitely those of the *petits bourgeois*. Here he saw a vast crowd vibrating with excitement, drinking—as though it were buttermilk—appeals to overthrow what was established, to expropriate the possessions of others. Lenin was showing the masses an easy and immediate way of enriching themselves.

Stalin himself has written of his revolutionary apprenticeship:[1] 'I well remember the year 1917, when, after many peregrinations through prisons and places of exile, I was entrusted by the Party with certain work in Leningrad. There, in the midst of the Russian workers, finding myself in the immediate neighbourhood of the

[1]See his article in No. 136, year 1926, of *Pravda*.

great teacher of the proletarians of all countries—Comrade Lenin—in the turmoil of the great battles of the proletariat and the *bourgeoisie*, while the Imperialist war was running its course, I learnt for the first time what it was to be the leader of the great party of the working class. . . . It was under Lenin's guidance that I became a true artisan of the revolution.'

Krupskaia was often present at these conversations, of which she took notes. In one of them she says: 'One day Stalin asked Ilyitch: "Do you believe in all sincerity, Vladimir Ilyitch, that capitalist society is already definitely condemned?"

' "You haven't read Napoleon's reflections, Comrade Koba. He wrote: 'The cannon has destroyed the feudal system: ink will destroy modern society.' You see, Napoleon lived before Marx, or instead of *modern society* he would have said *capitalist society*." '

One day Krupskaia noted down some phrases of a conversation concerning Clausewitz, which was to be productive of great results:

' "Read Clausewitz," said Ilyitch. He gave Stalin the copy of Clausewitz's work on war and strategy which he had brought from Switzerland, and in which he had made a number of marginal notes. He showed Comrade Stalin a passage which he had underlined, and a note which he had written on the margin. *War constitutes a part of a whole. This whole is politics. . . . One cannot conquer a great civilized European country save with the assistance of internal disturbances!* . . . I say, logically reversing this, that politics is war waged by other means.[1] . . . Now, Koba, you understand my present tactics!'

Stalin understood. There might be something almost maniacal in the 'Old Man's' attachment to rigid formulae, to which he gave literal obedience. But the crowd responded to these formulae, which affected it, in their primitive rigidity, more powerfully than the phrases of the 'reasonable' opportunists.

One day Lenin sent for Stalin and Zinoviev. He had news for them: Trotzky was coming. Zinoviev did not conceal his displeasure at the news. He was afraid that Trotzky would replace him as Lenin's first lieutenant. Stalin showed no such concern. He did not like Trotzky; he had already placed him in the category of 'chattering Talmudists.' Yet the organization of the intellectuals of the Left

[1] If Lenin were living today he might have said: 'The cold war. . . .'

comprised with Trotzky many tried Marxists. They were not to be disdained as allies.

After the meeting Zinoviev spoke to Stalin privately. He was trying, then, to form an alliance against Trotzky. Stalin, in accordance with his usual tactics, appeared to show little interest.

Lenin's personal secretary, Stassova, who was present during their conversation, has described it: 'Comrade Stalin smiled. "You are afraid Trotzky will supplant you? Apply to Kamenev. He'll stick up for you. He detests Trotzky."

'But on the following day Trotzky presented himself at the Politburo and the office of *Pravda*. He began with an arrogant declaration: "I am ready to enter the Bolshevik Party. But in order to secure the adhesion of the intellectuals of the Left I must find arguments which will overcome their opposition."

' "You are already thinking of offering positions on the editorial board and on the Central Committee!" Zinoviev retorted.

'The discussion was becoming heated, when Lenin made a sign to Stalin, who understood him. "I don't think it is necessary," he said, "to discuss this and that. When Comrade Trotzky has assured us that he is ready to join us with his political friends, we will consider the matter again."

'Alone with Stalin, Lenin thanked him. "You'll see that Trotzky will form part of a common team, and he will be very useful to us."

' "I only advise him not to tread on my toes." Lenin gazed at him attentively.'

CHAPTER XII

TROTZKY IN THE FOREGROUND: DIFFICULT DAYS

I N this summer of 1917 Trotzky in turn received his 'third revolutionary baptism.' He took up his position in the political foreground of Petrograd, at the side of Lenin. Behind them, in the shadow, at the heart of the Party and its Politburo, Koba-Djugachvili Stalin was hard at work.

It was not long before he had his first great quarrel with Trotzky. At the National Conference of Military Groups convoked by Stalin in order to obtain support for the activity of his secret Military Committee, Trotzky made a vehement speech, inciting the troops to an immediate insurrection: 'This Bonaparte of a Kerensky will summon you presently to an offensive against the German Army. Refuse to march! Thrust your bayonets into the earth! It is for your conference to decide!'

Stalin had no wish that the existence of his secret Military Committee should be revealed before the fitting moment. He interrupted Trotzky: 'If I did not know who you are I should take you for an *agent provocateur* of the Provisional Government. Are you trying to provoke the dissolution of our organization?'

On the 3 June, 1917, the first Pan-Russian Congress of the Soviets inaugurated its sessions. Of the 1,050 delegates only 106 were Bolsheviks; but they represented the two capitals and the industrial centres.

While the Congress was sitting, Kerensky began to make preparations for a great offensive against the German armies. He hoped a military success would enable him to deal with the defeatists. He was guilty, however, of a great error of judgment, which he shared with all the Liberal patriots, for whom the continuation of the war was an absolute necessity, and who regarded the Bolshevik movement as a mere German-paid manœuvre.

As soon as the news of the preparations for an offensive became known the Bolshevik Party redoubled its activities. Stalin selected from his secret military committee a group of propagandists whom he sent to the front, while the Bolsheviks of the Pan-Russian Congress of the Soviets summoned Kerensky to appear before them and explain his attitude in respect of the 'imperialist adventure' for which he was making preparations.

The majority of the Congress approved of Kerensky's action, but in practice their approval was of no service to him, since the Soviets were encouraging mass desertion and the final destruction of all military discipline. Meanwhile Lenin instructed Stalin and Sverdlov to organize demonstrations, while taking measures to ensure that soldiers taking part in them should not carry arms. Prudence was essential.

On the 2 July, at the conference of the Bolsheviks of Petrograd, Stalin represented the Central Committee and the Politburo. The situation was tense. The workers of the Viborg region voted resolutions demanding the immediate seizure of power by the Soviets.

Pestovsky, the future ambassador of the U.S.S.R. to Mexico, has left us a record of the occasion: '. . . Suddenly two machine-gunners appeared. They were two representatives of the Bolshevik military organization of a regiment. They wished to be heard immediately; and they were. "Our regiment," they said, "has decided to go into the streets tomorrow, arms in hand. We have had enough of the imperialistic bloodshed. We have had enough of the Provisional Government.[1] Yesterday Trotzky came to speak to us, and we soldiers say that only he is a true revolutionary, and that the Bolsheviks too are traitors." The two machine-gunners withdrew, uttering threats as they did so.'

On the following day the intended manifestation took place: the Anarchists, with Assine at their head, were the leaders of the crowd. The streets were invaded by soldiers armed to the teeth. They carried placards on which were inscribed the slogans of Lenin and Trotzky.

Despite the impotence of Kerensky and the Provisional Government, the Liberal forces reacted, awakening to the actual state of affairs. As though by a miracle, their resistance was organized. Troops recalled from the environs of Petrograd entered the capital.

[1]They were really simply repeating Lenin's slogans.

The Cossacks charged with levelled lances. The pupils of the military colleges poured into the streets to fight the demonstrators. The armed bands who were already—to quote Lenin—'looting what had been looted,' began to disperse. A show of energy, and the masses, excited by the Bolshevik propagandists, were seized with panic and fled before the phantom of resuscitated order.

Lenin himself was alarmed. He convoked an emergency session of the Central Committee and the Politburo. He wanted to ensure that the Bolshevik Party should not be held responsible for the riot.

Stalin was sent post-haste to the Central Executive Committee, which had emerged from the Pan-Russian Congress of Soviets of the 3 June, 1917, and which ever since had posed as the active controller of the Provisional Government. The most influential members of the Committee were Georgians: Tchkheidzé and Tserétéli. Lenin hoped that the solidarity of the Georgian 'kunaks'[1] would facilitate the task of his lieutenant.

The riot of the 3 July, 1917, coincided with a serious defeat of the Russian Army. The end of Kerensky's offensive was what might have been foreseen. The Russian Army had practically ceased to exist. The troops refused to advance and occupy German positions which in many places had been pulverized by the Russian artillery. Their officers, abandoned by their men, formed themselves into detachments of riflemen and occupied the enemy trenches. On some sections of the front they were accompanied by nurses from the hospital trains who took to arms. But this state of affairs could not continue, and it was an easy matter for the Germans to recapture their old fortified positions.

The moderate press of Petrograd took this opportunity openly to accuse the Bolsheviks of treachery. Lenin's journey across Germany in his famous sealed carriage seemed at the time to furnish irrefutable proof of this treachery. No one had yet understood that Lenin was not working for the Germans, but that he had made use of them as he would have made use of anyone.

Under these conditions Stalin's task was not an easy one. In 1926 he himself described his experiences: '. . . In my quality of member of the Central Executive Committee I went to the Taurid Palace. I

[1]In Georgian: friends.

asked the Committee to entrust me with a mission to the sailors in occupation of the Peter and Paul fortress.[1] I was given, as an assistant, the Menshevik Bogdanov. . . . They told me that the commandant of the insurgent troops, Sub-lieutenant Kozmine, had made all preparations to fight. I asked that Kozmine should hear what I had to say. "Tell him that I have come as representative of the Central Executive Committee." . . . I knew that Kozmine, who was a member of our secret committee, would understand that I had come above all as a representative of our Party.'

Kozmine allowed himself to be convinced, and Bogdanov hastened to inform them in the Taurid Palace that 'thanks to Stalin all is in order again.' The leaders of the Soviet even proposed to vote a motion expressing their gratitude to Stalin. Lenin also congratulated him warmly. The Bolshevik Party was cleared of all responsibility for the riot of 3 July.

But the supporters of order had suddenly awakened from their lethargy. On all sides sanctions against the Bolsheviks were demanded. The very word 'Bolshevik' became, in ordinary conversation, an insult, a term by which one indicated a brutal and unscrupulous person, eager for rape or pillage.

But Kerensky's Government remained unaware of the existence of the secret Military Committee over which Stalin was presiding. It knew nothing of the Committee's aims or its secret circulars. Of the militant Bolsheviks, the Provisional Government was acquainted only with those who arrived in the sealed carriage with Lenin, Zinoviev, Trotzky, and a few personalities of secondary importance. Thus, the Second Bureau issued a warrant of arrest against Kamenev, who had not played any part in the affair of 3 July.

The very existence of the Politburo was unknown to the intelligence service of the armies.   Stalin and Sverdlov were not involved in the enquiry into the riot of 3 July ordered by General Polovtzev, the commandant of the military district of Petrograd. It is true that except during the brief period of the riot his authority was purely nominal. He could not give orders even to his own orderly.

Stalin spent much time in the Taurid Palace, among the Mensheviks and the moderate Revolutionary Socialists, lobbying them

---

[1]Stalin is trying to create confusion between the Central Executive Committee of the Soviets and the Bolshevik Politburo.

in the name of the Bolshevik Party against 'the bourgeois rabble and the reactionary press.'

This press was extremely active, and full of good intentions, but it published nothing but insignificant facts. The lack of information concerning the real intentions of the Bolsheviks, their plans, their ideas, and their leaders, compelled the newspapers to fall back on scandalous and dubious reports, hinting at espionage and treason. Kerensky, with his usual irresponsibility, based on these reports an accusation of high treason.

Lenin and his disciples were fortunate. Their speeches, delivered in time of war, were enough to justify summary judgement and execution. But Kerensky, being, as he said, unwilling to 'infringe the liberty of speech,' instructed the Ministry of Justice to investigate a vague and complicated affair relating to the commercial operations of Ganietzky and the proceedings of the Zimmerwald Conference.

Trotzky says, in his biography of Stalin: 'The dread of the inevitable summary execution was anchored more firmly in Stalin's head than in the minds of the others. Such an outcome would have been entirely in correspondence with his own character.'

Trotzky was right. If Stalin, in July 1917, had been in Kerensky's place Lenin's life would have ended seven years before it actually did.

Lenin, in company with Stalin, made for Sestrorietzk, where they took refuge with the platelayer Emelianov, who lodged them in a shed near the station of Razliv, a railway halt of local importance.

Stalin returned to Petrograd to fetch Zinoviev. Lenin went to Finland, where a group of moderate Finnish Social-Democrats (among whom was Tanner, who negotiated peace with Stalin in 1939-40) found him a hiding-place. Stalin travelled to and fro between Petrograd and the fugitive leader, carrying letters and receiving his instructions.

At Allilouev's, in his little room, Stalin was extremely busy. For the time being Lenin, Zinoviev, Kamenev and Trotzky were not in the foreground. Stalin and Sverdlov, at the Politburo, were in charge of current affairs. From Finland, Lenin was writing constantly, giving Stalin advice and instructions, and sending him articles for the press.

Young Nadiejda Alliloueva—she was then seventeen—gave 'Uncle Joseph' a great deal of assistance. She was well educated, intelligent, and interested in social questions. She was familiar with the life of her father's Party comrades, whom she saw passing through his little rooms. She was proud to know that she had sheltered in her room 'the great Lenin,' and she was now ready to become the future companion of Koba-Stalin.

The Caucasian often teased the girl, who was twenty-one years his junior. But Allilouev's visitors put their own interpretation on the glances exchanged by Nadiejda and 'Uncle Joseph.'

Ordjonikdzé, in his outright fashion, spoke to Father Allilouev one day: 'You just notice how your Nadia is showing off before Sosso! You'll have to marry them!'

CHAPTER XIII

THE CONGRESS OF UNIFICATION

O F this period Stalin wrote, analysing the situation: 'The victory of the *bourgeois* counter-revolution on the inauspicious days of the 3 and 4 July is unstable. As long as the war continues, as long as the economic disorder persists, as long as the peasants have not obtained the land, crises will occur inevitably; the masses will over and over again surge into the streets, and more or less decisive engagements will be fought. We have suffered a defeat, because we were carried away by the masses *against our will*. This means that the mechanism of our party is not yet sufficiently powerful to direct the movement. What we need now is a breathing-space;[1] time to renew our propaganda, and to create a network of propagandists and agitators who will direct the movement by directing its revolutionary dynamism. Above all we must increase our influence over the military units at the front. . . . Before long there will be decisive battles. The peaceful period of the revolution is ended.'

Stalin was now something more than a professional revolutionary; he was becoming a true leader of the masses, capable of comprehensive judgements, analyses, and syntheses, and of drawing valuable conclusions from passing events. After the Petrograd conference, he convoked yet another conference on the 21 and 22 July. The Conference was followed by the Sixth Congress of the Bolshevik Party, the first since the revolution. Lenin, who could not attend it, had insisted on its convocation. In a message conveyed to Stalin by Ordjonikidzé, he had said: 'The Congress must be convoked. Kerensky will not dare to dissolve it.' And on the 26 July it assembled in the suburb of Viborg. On the 29th it was transferred to a schoolhouse near the Narva gate, where it sat until the 3 August.

In this Sixth Congress Stalin, without much previous reflection, gave a definition of the general aim of the Bolshevik doctrine: '*The*

[1]Lenin makes use of this phrase to explain the peace of Brest-Litovsk.

possibility is not excluded that Russia may be the very country which will open up the path for Socialism. We must reject the obsolete notion that only Europe can show us the way.

'*There is a dogmatic Marxism and a creative Marxism. I take my stand with the latter.*'[1]

The Sixth Congress ended with the adhesion of Trotzky's intellectuals of the Left. To the strains of the *Internationale* the reunion of the 'Congress of Unification' was baptized. Trotzky himself was not there; he and Kamenev were still in prison, charged with high treason. But both were presently released.

The New Central Committee comprised twenty-one members and ten supplementary delegates:

Lenin	Ouritzky	Lomov
Zinoviev	Miliutin	Joffé
Trotzky	Berzine	Stassova
Kamenev	Bubnov	Iakovlev
Stalin	Dzerjinsky	Djaparidzé
Noguin	Krestinsky	Kissel
Kollontai	Muralov	Préobrajensky
Sverdlov	Smilga	Skrypnik
Rykov	Sokolnikov	Piatakov
Bukharin	Chaoumian	Brioukhanov
Artem		

This was the Great General Staff of the Bolshevik Party, which was to direct the revolution of October. Of this General Staff the only survivor today is Stalin.

Lenin, Dzerjinsky, Sverdlov, Brioukhanov, Noguin, Kissel, Stassova and Iakovlev died natural deaths. Trotzky was assassinated in Mexico City. Ourtizky was assassinated by a student, a Social Revolutionary. Artem was killed in a railway accident.

Zinoviev, Rykov, Bukharin, Miliutin, Berzin, Bubnov, Krestinsky, Muralov, Smilga, Lomov, Préobrajensky and Piatakov were executed; Kamenev also, according to an official report, was eventually executed.

[1]Proceedings of the 6th Congress of the Bolshevik Party. Russian edition, pp. 233-4.

Joffé and Skrypnik committed suicide. Sokolnikov died in prison, at Yakutsk.

Chaoumian and Djaparidzé were sentenced to death by a court under the presidency of the Revolutionary Socialist Fountikov, a subordinate of the famous Captain Tigg-Johns of the Intelligence Service. Kollontai died recently.

CHAPTER XIV

THE BOLSHEVIK COUP

On the 5 August, Kamenev was liberated. He was opposed to the policy of an insurrection. Stalin was almost inclined to agree with him, but he could not believe that the head of the Provisional Government, unstable though it was, would surrender power without a fight.

Kerensky felt that power was slipping from his control. On the 12 August he convoked a State Conference. The deputies of the four bygone Dumas, the representatives of the Zemstvos, the Co-operatives, and many other moderate organizations, proposed to form 'a barrage against the extremists.' But Kerensky was unable to consolidate this opposition. His only gestures were those which emphasized his oratorical periods.

The Bolsheviks were not invited to the Conference. Stalin went to Moscow, to organize a strike of protest. He failed. The Conference ended with the success of the Provisional Government. But its success was merely academic. Kerensky was incapable of action.

Stalin, on returning to Petrograd, listened to what Kamenev had to tell him. It was obvious that the masses were beginning to weary of the orgy of propaganda. The soldiers, too, were becoming indifferent; they would prefer to remain neutral in the event of a decisive battle between Kerensky and the Bolsheviks.

Stalin thought that Lenin's tactics would lead to a conflict in which the Bolshevik Party would risk its very existence. Obviously Kerensky was not a dangerous adversary, so that the projected insurrection had a good chance of success. Nevertheless, as always, at the last moment Stalin hesitated. He was not fond of clear-cut decisions; he would have preferred to take his time.

On the 18 August he had a long conversation with the revolutionary Socialist Gotz, one of the moderate leaders of the Soviet.

'Kerensky is too ambitious to surrender the power into the hands of a general and admit his own incapacity,' he said.

Stalin was full of honeyed words. The revolutionary Socialist Ratner, who overheard the conversation, wrote of it: 'Stalin spoke to Gotz in the most friendly manner. He tapped him on the shoulder, saying: "Between us socialists an agreement is always possible. The Bolsheviks don't want to set up a dictatorship of their party. . . ." '

Stalin was right. On the 25 August General Kornilov began his adventure. Circumstances turned it into a sinister farce. Kerensky had ordered General Kornilov to send some reliable divisions to Petrograd. Among them was the famous 'savage' division, composed of natives of the Caucasus.

Kornilov knew nothing about politics, but he had with him a few improvised political advisers. He decided to proclaim his own dictatorship, to dissolve the Soviet, to arrest its leaders, and to re-establish the power of the Committee of the Duma, which was, as a matter of fact, the only legal power, but which had lost all authority.

On the 27 August Kerensky, who did not know what to do with the power in his hands, but none the less clung to it, proclaimed that Kornilov was 'a traitor to the nation,' and declared that he had never ordered troops to be sent to the capital. He delivered a harangue which contained a pathetic prayer to the Soviet, imploring it to 'save the Nation and Liberty,' and called upon it to take up arms! The moderates, even more alarmed, made the same demand . . . of the Bolsheviks!

On the 21 August the Germans had taken Riga. Krymov committed suicide. Kornilov and his staff allowed themselves to be arrested by General Alexeiev. Kerensky was jubilant—but his rejoicing was of brief duration. The mobilization against the generals had placed at the disposal of the Bolsheviks tens of thousands of demobilized soldiers, who drifted into the capital, fearing only one thing: the restoration of order.

On the 31 August the Petrograd Soviet adopted a resolution proposed by Lenin's party. Stalin had been hard at work . . . but Kerensky had helped him.

The Moderates were still proposing collaboration with the Provisional Government, but their proposal was rejected by 519 votes against 414, sixty-four members abstaining. The President, Tchkheidzé, resigned. The path was open for the insurrection. On the 6 September, 1917, the examining magistrate released Trotzky, who was elected president of the Petrograd Soviet.

A new red star had arisen, beside that of Lenin, in the firmament of the Russian Revolution. Stalin, who had undertaken the ungrateful task of preparation, found himself eclipsed. Another was to pluck the fruit of his labours. He had never liked Trotzky. But from this moment he was full of resentment—that terrible rancour of the mountain-dweller, accustomed to the methods of the pitiless Caucasian vendetta, who will wait his time with the patience of the hunter, watching his prey from the cover of a rock.

A prudent tactician, Stalin looked for allies against Trotzky. He found one in Zinoviev, who was afraid of being supplanted. Another was Kamenev, who, although he was Trotzky's brother-in-law, was opposed to him, since he sincerely believed 'in the necessity of uniting all the Socialist parties in a homogeneous government and ending the revolution by the establishment of a Socialist and pacifist State.'

Stalin now published in the *Proletarian*, whose editor he was, an article by Zinoviev, directed against Trotzky: 'We must face the truth. There is now in Petrograd a situation which would favour the occurrence of an insurrection like that of the Paris Commune in 1871. . . .'

Zinoviev was aiming at Trotzky, who had proclaimed himself 'leader of the Commune.' But Lenin felt that this was an indirect attack upon himself. He sent an angry article from Finland—but Stalin held it back for a week.

While Trotzky continued his frantic manœuvres, Stalin took refuge in the commissions of the Central Committee and the Politburo, which dealt only with questions of secondary importance; including discussions as to the location of a printing-press.

The moderates of the Central Executive Committee of the Soviet, supported by the Revolutionary Socialists of the Left, decided at this moment to convoke a Democratic Conference, which was to establish a real collaboration between the Provisional Government and the Committee. The Conference opened on the 14 September. That same day Lenin despatched two letters: 'The Bolsheviks must assume power' and 'Marxism and Insurrection.' He was categorical:

G

there must be an insurrection in the regiments and the factories; the members of the Government and of the Democratic Conference must be arrested. The Party must seize power.

But when the decisive moment arrived the disagreement between Lenin's disciples was only aggravated. Stalin, as usual, thought it best to mark time. He proposed to refer the discussion to a later date, so that there would be time to consult the more important of the Party organizations in the provinces.

By subtle manœuvring he supported Kamenev, struck a blow at Trotzky, and retained his position on the democratic front of the Party. He knew that the provincial organizations, more moderate than the 'Commune of Petrograd,' would reject Lenin's proposals. His proposal was accepted. Lenin was obliged to hold his hand. The opinions of the provinces would be communicated to the Central Committee in five days' time.

On the day of the decisive meeting Stalin was not present. But he had taken his precautions, and to prove that he was a 'hundred per cent Leninist' he published an article in which he said: 'The reptilian hiss of the counter-revolution is heard more and more loudly. From its lair the hideous hydra of reaction threatens with its poisoned sting. It will strike, and hide itself anew in its dark retreat. But the popular masses will one day find it and tear out its fangs. This will be the end of the base fraud, the falsification, the hideous persecution, the bacchanal of lies and calumnies of the Kerensky Government.'

At the meeting of the 127 Bolsheviks of the fraction of the 'Pre-Parliament,' Stalin demolished the whole of Lenin's and Trotzky's arguments, while seeming to support them: 'Comrades,' he said,[1] 'I am, of course, all for Comrade Lenin, who is not here, and who is in favour of the boycott. But what has just been said is not at all what I understood from Comrade Lenin when I went to see him in his place of refuge. Comrade Lenin says he is in favour of the boycott of the Pre-Parliament, *but that in his absence he cannot exactly appreciate the situation, and that you must therefore take it upon yourselves to decide, having full knowledge of the matter. . . .'*

Finally, Kamenev prevailed over the Trotzky-Stalin coalition, with seventy-seven votes against only fifty. This was the only time

[1] A pamphlet by Yaroslavsky, withdrawn from circulation in the U.S.S.R.

when Trotzky and Stalin acted together; but in reality Stalin had attached himself to Trotzky in order to attempt his overthrow.

From Finland, Lenin, losing patience, and fearing that he might have to go without his insurrection, sent Krupskaia to Stalin, with orders to convoke the Central Committee without delay. He himself would attend the meeting. The decisive moment had arrived: he was ready to risk everything—in order to gain everything.

'Ilyitch wanted to arrive made up, rouged and painted and wearing a wig,' Stalin related, on the occasion of Lenin's anniversary in 1920. 'I was to accompany him to Petrograd. . . .

'Vladimir Ilyitch scolded us: "I ought to be totally unrecognizable," he said.

'We found a make-up artist, a Finn, a Social Democrat of the Left; he was a hairdresser and wig-maker. But in Finland the wigs are blond or red. We had to choose a red wig for Ilyitch. The make-up artist also trimmed his beard short and clipped his eyebrows. Having put on his dark glasses, Ilyitch accompanied us to Petrograd. After the meeting he returned to Finland.'[1]

At this decisive meeting of the Bolsheviks Dzerjinsky proposed to form a bureau in control of the insurrection, consisting of Lenin, Trotzky, Kamenev, Zinoviev, Sokolnikov, Bubnov and Stalin. This was the famous 'Bureau of the Seven.' Lenin then proposed the creation of a revolutionary military centre composed of Stalin, Sverdlov, Bubnov, Ouritzky, and Dzerjinsky. Stalin contrived to ensure that Trotzky should not be a member.

On the 11 October Zinoviev and Kamenev published, in Gorki's paper—the organ of the 'Menshevik-Leftists'—a letter opposing any attempt at insurrection. On hearing of this, Lenin decided to proclaim the authors of the article as traitors and deserters.

Stalin and Sverdlov convoked the Central Committee for the 20 October, but on the eve of the meeting Stalin published another article, in which he stated that notwithstanding the bitterness of Comrade Lenin's tone, 'we have all the same ideas.' In the Central Committee he proposed a resolution blaming Kamenev and Zinoviev, but in terms more moderate than Lenin's.

Observing the prevailing indecision, Trotzky, unwilling to lose

[1]These details were given by the Revolutionary Socialist Fabrikant, who died in Paris in 1933.

his advantage, decided to act. He set up a 'Revolutionary Military Committee,' and proposed its fusion with the clandestine Revolutionary Military Centre of which Stalin had been in charge for some weeks past, thus making Stalin a subordinate. The Caucasian retorted that it was the Centre, and not the Committee which would have to direct the insurrection. It was an organ of the Party, and would have to take precedence of the Committee, which was merely an emanation of the Petrograd Soviet.

On the 24 October the Central Committee of the Bolshevik Party proclaimed the state of insurrection. The garrison of Petrograd, under the nominal command of General Bagratioun and Colonel Polkolnikov, decided to maintain neutrality. However, as though in derision, on the previous evening the Pre-Parliament had advised the commander of the garrison *not to make use of force in the event of insurrection* (sic!).

The Provisional Government was sinking into obscurity. The 60,000 officers, practically demobilized, who were then in the capital, did not even consider the possibility of reaction, since they detested Kerensky, and felt that to support him would be like clinging to a rotten branch.

The Bolsheviks encountered no obstacles. They had only to issue commands by telephone in order to take possession of the Ministries. On the evening of the 6 November detachments of the members of Trotzky's Committee and Stalin's Centre occupied, without encountering the least resistance, the post and telegraph offices, the bridges over the Neva, the railway stations and depôts, and the State Bank. They knocked upon doors, and the doors opened; they went in and made themselves at home, without meeting with the slightest opposition.

A few of Kerensky's Ministers assembled in the Winter Palace under the ephemeral protection of a hundred female soldiers and officer-pupils. Stalin's Centre sent thither some hundreds of Red Guards, and Trotzky's Centre despatched some Kronstadt sailors. These latter quietly advanced across the great square before the Palace, while in the streets two hundred yards away, and in the Millionaïa, the soldiers of the 1st Regiment of the Guard manifested their 'neutrality' by promenading with women to the music of their band.

About 6 o'clock in the evening the cruiser *Aurore* ascended the Neva and fired a salvo at the Winter Palace, the shells falling some hundreds of yards from the target. When one of these shells was picked up it was found to be covered with rust. Towards midnight the sub-lieutenant Antonov-Ovseenko[1] finished 'cleaning up' the Palace, the last refuge of the Provisional Government. By 2 o'clock in the morning of 8 November all was over. The 'insurrection' had taken place. It had its victims—a few killed and wounded—about eighty—among the officer-cadets, and some dozens of women soldiers raped by the victors.

Having left Petrograd at the beginning of the insurrection, Kerensky proposed to retake the capital on the following day with a few hundreds of General Krassnov's Cossacks. At Gatchina, some eighteen miles from the capital, Krassnov was obliged to surrender, almost before the struggle for power had begun, and to sign an armistice with the sailor Dybenko.[2] Afraid of falling into the hands of Dybenko, who had promised to shoot him at sight, Kerensky disguised himself as a hospital nurse and left Gatchina in a hospital train.

The Bolsheviks were in power. In order to achieve that position they had only to overcome the dissensions which had arisen within their own ranks. They were stupefied and at a loss. For a long while to come the swashbucklers of yesterday were prudent and fearful. The revolutionaries had now to learn how to govern a country. They had to create an apparatus of power in the place of that which had disappeared, and they did not in the least know how to set about it.

[1]Future Ambassador to Prague and Consul-General of the U.S.S.R. in Barcelona during the Spanish Civil War. Shot in 1938.

[2]Future commandant of the Military District of the Volga, who was shot by Iéjov as one of the 'obscene vipers.'

CHAPTER XV

REVOLUTION AND CIVIL WAR

THUS, the Bolsheviks were installed in power. Their *coup de main* had cost less blood than the March Revolution. The apparatus of State no longer existed, and the great majority of the public looked on almost with amusement at the rise of a party which numbered only 240,000 adherents among the 140 million inhabitants of Russia, and which no one could take seriously.

By the following day Lenin and his group encountered only a passive resistance.

The Municipal Council of Petrograd joined forces with the Executive Committee of the old Soviet, the Provisional Council of the Republic, the controlling committees of all the other parties of the Left, and the General Union of railway workers.

These formed a 'Committee of Safety of the Nation and the Revolution,' which formally requested the citizens to disregard Lenin's orders, and constituted itself a shadow government which would govern the country until the Constituent Assembly was in being.

Lenin also had no effective power at his disposal. He depended on the complete political insolvency of 99 per cent of the population. On the injunction of the Committee of Safety, the *employés* of the administration, the State Bank, and the other banks, went on strike. Everyone adopted an attitude of *laissez faire*, under the illusory belief that 'order would soon be restored, they wouldn't tolerate this caricature of power for very long.'

But as the mysterious 'they' existed only in the imagination of those who were accustomed to find the authorities on the watch for signs of disorder, nothing was done; and the Bolsheviks, surprised and disconcerted by their victory, which they had not anticipated, were able, unhindered, to embark on their apprenticeship as organizers of the State.

Lenin thought himself so powerless that one of his first official pledges was the undertaking that he would do nothing to prevent the elections to the Constituent Assembly proposed by Kerensky, and even that he would convoke 'this Constituent Assembly which would determine the future structure of the Russian State.'

This period of Stalin's life is the most difficult to recapture. His adversaries, and his detractors, like Trotzky, give accounts which are entirely subjective, dictated by their desire to represent him under the worst aspect, as a person entirely without intellectual capacity. At the same time, the documents on which they base their accounts are very far from complete, since the greater part of their archives were lost or destroyed during their peregrinations.

On the other hand, the official legend, which bears only a remote resemblance to the reality, has completely falsified all the historical data, and destroyed the great majority of the documents, which do not lend themselves to the glorification of Stalin.

His activities, at the time under consideration, are hidden in obscurity; and even his official biographers are obliged to pass over this period lightly, having nothing of importance to tell us about him; so that they resort to the subterfuge so commonly applied in such cases, of accusing the more prominent personalities of all the sins in creation. Those who occupied positions of greater importance than Stalin's become traitors to the revolution, plotting against the Soviet régime, just as they were represented later on at the time of the famous 'purges.'

It took years of research and study, and also a certain amount of luck, in respect of encountering the few survivors of Stalin's immediate entourage, before we could clearly establish the nature of his activities at this time, having first discarded the more recent additions to the legend, and the assertions inspired by the hatred of his enemies; hatred increased by the fact that they themselves were finally eliminated by Stalin.

We are, therefore, able to define the nature of his activities without at the same time rewriting the history of the U.S.S.R., but confining ourselves to speaking of essential events.

On the morrow of the insurrection Stalin, accompanied by the sailor Dybenko, presented himself at the transmitting station of the radio service in order to broadcast a message from Lenin. In this message Lenin prudently explained the insurrection in his own fashion, as a manœuvre of the Bolsheviks to make sure of the elections to an organ which in the last resort would have to decide the laws of the Constitution. Neither Lenin nor Stalin was as yet very confident; though Lenin told his disciple: 'The seizure of power was easier than the gesture of taking up a pen.'

On the evening of the 8 November one of the halls of the Smolny Institute,[1] in which the Bolshevik Soviet and the Central Committee of the Party had established themselves, presented a somewhat unusual aspect: Lenin, Trotzky, Sverdlov and Stalin, after the fatigues of a most exhausting day, were lying on the floor, on what looked like a large red velvet bedspread. This was the old curtain of the little Smolny Theatre. It was embroidered with two-headed eagles. A fire was burning in the grate.

'What a touching spectacle!' cried Lenin in his bantering manner. The four artisans of the Socialist Revolution, resting before the fire, with weapons in their hands. . . .'

Despite the infernal din that filled the whole building, the quartet fell asleep. But at midnight they were aroused. The delegates of the Pan-Russian Congress of Soviets,[2] warned by the Mensheviks, demanded that Lenin should come and explain the aims of his conspiracy. Lenin, who had a cold, could not speak from the tribune. He sent Trotzky, the mainspring of the *coup d'état*. Stalin and Sverdlov accompanied the orator.

While Trotzky was addressing the Congress, Stalin got to work in the lobbies. His previous contacts had enabled him to make many acquaintances, and he was less handicapped than Trotzky, who had openly placed himself at the head of the *coup d'état*.

The Congress ended by approving of the insurrection. The Revolutionary Socialist and Menshevik fractions left the hall in token of protest, as they could not—in Martov's words—'sanction the crime against the Revolution.' This was characteristic of the period. People sanctioned or condemned a policy or action in words; no one resorted to action.

---

[1]Originally a boarding-school for the daughters of nobles; now the headquarters of the Bolsheviks, who were often described as 'the Smolny people.'

[2]This was the Soviet which had been sitting since the March Revolution in the Taurid Palace. For a long while the majority was Revolutionary Socialist and Menshevik.

On the 10 November Lenin assembled the quartet of the Polit-buro. Zinoviev and Kamenev, who had been opposed to the in-surrection, hastened to make their apologies; but Lenin, prepared for fresh divagations on their part, did not yet consent to their reinstate-ment.

On Stalin's suggestion the term 'People's Commissars' was chosen for the new government's members. Lenin became President and Trotzky became People's Commissar for Foreign Affairs. As for Stalin, he was assigned the less prominent function of People's Com-missar for the Nationalities.

During the following day Stalin began to organize his depart-ment. His secretary to the Commissariat, Pestkovsky, has left detailed notes on this subject.

'I met Comrade Stalin in one of the corridors at the Smolny. He seemed in a great hurry.

' "Ah, good day, Pestkovsky. I've a proposal to make to you. I have just been appointed People's Commissar for the Nationalities. I've got to organize my department. Be my secretary-general."

' "By all means. But where is your commissariat?"

'Comrade Stalin went to the Bureau of the Council of the People's Commissaries, and returned a few minutes later with a mandate signed by Lenin.

' "I found there was a room in the right wing of the Smolny, near the chapel. It was dark and malodorous. It contained only a table and two chairs. I took a sheet of paper, and I wrote: 'People's Commissariat for the Affairs of the Nationalities.' "

'That evening Stalin returned, accompanied by a shorthand-typist, Nadiejda Alliloueva. But they had no money.'

Pestkovsky went to see Trotzky, whose Secretary-General had only 15,000 roubles left in the safe, out of the 50,000 they had found there.

The career of Djugachvili-Koba-Stalin, the statesman, had begun with the 3,000 roubles at his disposal.

Lenin preferred always to consult one of his 'quartet.' But Trotzky presently left for Brest-Litovsk, in order to take charge of the peace negotiations. Sverdlov was often busied with the countless affairs of the Central Executive Committee of the Party, so that Stalin was the man whom Lenin consulted most frequently.

During the first weeks of the Bolsheviks' exercise of power two tendencies were to be noted among their leaders. These tendencies indicated that there were serious differences of temperament, of intellectual character, and of past experiences in the representatives of the two groups.

Trotzky, carried away by his own superb eloquence, wanted to proceed immediately from the Bolshevik *coup d'état* in Russia to world revolution.

He dragged out the negotiations at Brest-Litovsk in the hope that the German proletariat would overthrow the Kaiser, the real obstacle to peace. In the beginning Lenin and Stalin took the same point of view; but they soon saw that the German proletariat was not ready to play the part which Trotzky was eager to allot to it. As Radek has noted in his memoirs, Lenin tried to restrain Trotzky, to induce him to abandon the hope of becoming the leader of the world proletariat in a state of revolution. But he himself was embarrassed by the enormous popularity of Trotzky, as the inspiring spirit of the October revolution.

The Germans were amused. The Russian troops, remaining in the trenches, spent their time peaceably enough, drinking, playing the accordion, dancing with women, and abandoning or selling their weapons. So when Trotzky arrived in Petrograd, there was a lively altercation between him and Lenin.

On the 18 February, 1918, the German High Command informed the Soviet Government that the armistice would be terminated on the 18 February, at noon. The situation of the new régime was critical. Lenin understood that they must at all costs obtain a 'breathing-space.' He was convinced that Germany would be defeated, and he looked forward to attracting 'the imperialism of the *Entente*' with the aid of the German proletariat.

During this critical period Stalin had little to say. He was continuing his apprenticeship. The Lenin of that period was still and above all a revolutionist who had suddenly become the head of the State. As yet he had not the authority of a ruler, and Stalin, the realist, drew his own conclusions.

Stalin continued to function as Commissar for the Nationalities. He was also appointed member of the Revolutionary Council of

War. The Pan-Russian Congress had decided to call itself the Communist Congress. Zinoviev and Kamenev had been reinstated. Krestinsky had joined the Congress as First Secretary of the Central Committee. The Politburo was thus composed of Lenin, Trotzky, Stalin, Sverdlov, Kamenev, Zinoviev and Krestinsky. It was now faced with civil war.

The war began with a series of sporadic revolts. The Politburo decided to organize a new army—the Red Army. It appointed Trotzky People's Commissar for Defence and President of the Supreme Council of War, of which Stalin was a member. The seat of the Government was transferred from Petrograd to Moscow.

In the new capital the new ministries did not know where to establish themselves. The Commissariat of the People for the Nationalities found itself literally in the street, or rather on the platform of the railway station, where Alliloueva had unloaded the files of *The Life of the Nationalities*, a journal edited by Stalin.

During this curious and probably unique period of history the Government which could have concluded the peace was existing on the border of a country that paid hardly any attention to it. But the moment any direct action against the Government was taken anywhere forces arose immediately, though whence no one knew, which neutralized the revolt and then disappeared. They were not actuated by their sympathy with Lenin's Government, but by their dread of a return to the system which had been abolished.

Several days went by, and Stalin and his department were still without a roof. At last they were housed in eight different buildings. Then, one day, he came to a decision. Pestkovsky tells the story:

'Comrade Stalin said: "We must find premises large enough to provide accommodation for everybody. They were giving us the Grand Siberian Hotel, but the Superior Council of the National Economy has taken possession of it.'

' "I shall not give way," Stalin announced. "Tell Alliloueva to type a number of leaflets saying: *These offices are occupied by the Commissariat of the Nationalities*, and take some drawing-pins with you."

'So Stalin and I set out in a cab for the Siberian Hotel. It was growing dark. The principal entrance was closed. A notice was tacked to the door, bearing the inscription: *These premises are occupied by the Superior Council of National Economy*. Comrade Stalin removed the notice and put ours in its place. Then he said: "Now we must get inside and stick up our placards. Otherwise we have no authority. . . ."

'It was not easy. After a long search we found a service staircase. There was no electric light. I struck a match and we went up to the second floor, where we came out into a long narrow corridor with doors opening into the offices; and there we placed our improvised placards. We had to return the way we came, but I had no more matches. We went forward in absolute darkness. Comrade Stalin tripped up and fell to the ground floor at the risk of breaking his neck. Fortunately he got off with a few scratches on the right cheek. On the following day, when the Council was in session, Comrade Lenin questioned him as to the origin of these scratches. He replied: "It's the beginning of the civil war between the Commissariats of the People." '

The actual Civil War, which was then being waged, gave Stalin an opportunity for further activity. Central Russia was in need of bread, and the treaty with the Germans had deprived it of more than a quarter of its crops. Western Siberia and the region of the Volga were occupied by the Whites. There was nothing available but the grain of the Northern Caucasus and Kuban. Now, however, the new 'Extraordinary Commission for the struggle against counter-revolution, sabotage, banditry, speculation and peculation,' of which Dzerjinsky was president—it was known by the abbreviated title of the 'Tcheka'—was beginning to take action.

On the 28 May, 1918, Stalin was appointed to a new task. The situation in the capital and the industrial districts of the Centre was critical. In Petrograd the workers were receiving only fifty grammes of bread per diem and those of Moscow seventy-five grammes, while the Toula ration was only thirty grammes. As for the *bourgeois*, they received a few handfuls of oats and a salt herring once every five or six days.

Stalin left Moscow with an armed detachment which he had recruited among the workers. On the 6 June this detachment, accompanied by two armoured trains, arrived in Tsaritzin.

On the 18 June, 1918, Stalin telegraphed to Lenin: *Chliapnikov left Kuban, organized despatch grain: Am forming new Tenth Army with Vorochilov. The Whites preparing an attack. We shall defend the city.*

The loss of Tsaritzin would be deadly blow cutting us off from petrol and corn; Krassnov's Cossacks might effect junction with Koltchak.[1] Send reinforcements.

The reference is to the remnants of the Tenth 'Revolutionary' Army of Vorochilov, which returned from the Ukraine after fighting the German cavalry near Bataisk.

Lenin read the telegram during a session of the Politburo. Trotzky protested: 'We have already got Ordjonikidzé and Okolov at Tsaritzin. They can remain with Vorochilov. Stalin ought to go to Kuban to organize the commissariat.'

The Commissar for War seemed to feel instinctively that the prolongation of Stalin's sojourn in Tsaritzin and his intervention in military questions would be an intrusion of which one could not foresee the consequences.

Meanwhile the Cossacks of the Don had broken the Tsaritzin front. The city was practically encircled. Its garrison was sufficiently strong to repulse attacks; the real danger came from the Revolutionary Socialists and the Mensheviks, who were influencing the workers inside the city. It was at this moment that Stalin manifested for the first time the full extent of his ability as a civil war leader. It was then, too, that there was formed around him a group which would follow him in his future ascent to power, and which was known as 'The Tsaritzin Group.' Its more prominent members were Vorochilov, Timochenko, future Marshal of the U.S.S.R., and Iéjov, who was to effect the greatest 'purges' known to history.

An order of the Supreme War Committee, signed by Trotzky, states: 'Comrade Stalin is appointed Commander-in-Chief of all the armed forces of the Southern Front. He has the right to restore order, to proceed to general or partial mobilizations, to refer to military tribunals all persons guilty of disorder or indiscipline, to convoke or dissolve local defence committees, and to organize an adequate command after expelling all persons guilty of insubordination.'

Stalin returned to Moscow on the 22 November, 1918. After

[1]Admiral, ex-commander of the Black Sea fleet; became leader of the White Movement in Siberia; recognized by the Allies as the Russian ruler. Was finally surrendered by General Janin, tried, and shot.

much discussion, on the 1 December he entered the new Defence Committee, composed of Lenin, Trotzky, Stalin, Sverdlov, and Krassin. Lenin was president of the Committee; Trotzky and Stalin were vice-presidents.

This was a setback for Trotzky, who nevertheless continued to perorate and place himself in the foreground, while Stalin, in comparative silence, reinforced his position. He had need of tried and reliable friends, like Vorochilov, and his experience of men enabled him to choose them with infallible assurance.

After carrying out several missions in the South, Stalin returned once more to Moscow. 'I am profoundly convinced,' he wrote, 'that no change in the situation could be produced by my presence on the south-eastern front.'

In reality he had very different motives for returning to Moscow. Trotzky was becoming more and more influential. President of the Revolutionary War Committee, he was tactfully controlled by Lenin, who saw him as the future 'Commander-in-Chief of the World Red Army,' Stalin did not feel equal to continuing an open conflict which might end in his defeat. Several times Trotzky tried to accuse him of incapacity and insubordination. The Bolshevik leaders were actuated by personal motives, each regarding himself as the only person fitted for the supreme command. For them, the development of the Revolution was identical with the confirmation of their own place in the Sovietic State. Those who did not share this profound conviction were one by one eliminated. This conviction was the principal reason for the implacable harshness which they displayed whenever they thought they were in personal danger— for a threat to their persons endangered their work. The transposition was complete; and it is surprising that the psycho-analysts have not drawn attention to it, instead of accepting such simplified explanations as 'the impenetrable mystery of the Kremlin' and 'the spiritual atrocity of the Bolsheviks.'

In Moscow, Stalin could defend himself more effectively than at the periphery. He could also find allies who would act behind the scenes in all the departments of the governmental machine.

He had hardly returned when *Pravda*, the organ of the Central Committee of the Party, published a couple of articles aimed against Trotzky. The first of these, signed by Stalin himself, sought to minimize the part played by Trotzky in the revolution of October. The second criticized his military achievements. Before attending to the creation of his own legend, he attacked the legend of Trotzky's achievements.

Having launched these two attacks upon Trotzky, Stalin took advantage of the Eighth Pan-Russian Congress of the Communist Party (19-23 March, 1919) to foment a military opposition against his enemy. This was directed by an old Bolshevik, Smirnov, once a colonel in the Imperial artillery, and a leader in the Moscow insurrection of November 1917.

A new Politburo was elected. It consisted of Lenin, Trotzky, Stalin, Zinoviev, Kamenev, Krestinsky, Stassova, Serebriakov, Sokolnikov, Bukharin and Dzerjinski. Stalin, moreover, was given a new appointment. While retaining his post as People's Commissar for the Nationalities, he became Commissar for State Control. He would thus be brought into direct contact with all the administrative cog-wheels of the State. This enabled him to accelerate his education as a governmental expert and to multiply his personal relations.

CHAPTER XVI

SECOND MARRIAGE : WAR WITH POLAND

ON the 23 March, 1919, Stalin installed himself in his second post. On the following day he celebrated his marriage to Nadiejda Alliloueva at the Moscow registry office. The witnesses were: for the bride, her brother-in-law Redenss, a Polish Communist and a prominent member of the Tcheka, and for Stalin, Abel Iénukidzé, his friend and companion in exile, now secretary of the Central Executive Committee.[1]

For his dwelling, he chose a small house which had once been inhabited by members of the domestic household of the Tsars. It stood within the precincts of the Kremlin, near the gate of entry. It was a yellowish-grey building, approached by a flight of steps. It consisted of one large room and a kitchen on the ground floor; there were two rooms upstairs. The military commandant of the Kremlin, a friend of Stalin's, found a few rather dilapidated pieces of furniture for him.

Stalin was hard at work, and Alliloueva was often absent. She had friends living in the old Kutnaia Palace, now 'the Palace of the Red Sailors.' Four young women were living there, employees of the Central Committee of the Communist Party: Lera Roubtzova,[2] Rosa Oulitzkaia, Ida Volodarskaia and Moussia Ignatieva. They often arranged evening parties, attended by officials of the Central Committee and students: Malenkov,[3] Sousslov, Popov, Mikhailov, Toustoukha,[4] Gricha Kanner,[4] Mekhliss, Poskrebychev,[5] Borodaievsky, Leipa, and the younger Sverdlov. This was the famous 'political salon of the Red Sailors,' from which Soviet leaders were recruited.

[1]Alliloueva committed suicide after a friend of hers had been killed in his office by the great 'expurgator' Iéjov. Iénoukidzé also was executed.
[2]She afterwards married Malenkov.
[3]Present Secretary of the Communist Party.
[4]Both future members of Stalin's Secretariat.
[5]Now at the head of Stalin's personal secretariat.

Stalin, though older than the rest, was a frequent visitor, followed by his inseparable Pestkovsky. Malenkov was an excellent performer on the balalaïka, and Stalin would sometimes sing to his accompaniment.

Early in May the Soviet Government suddenly became aware that it was threatened. On the 14 May the White General Rodzianko, in pursuance of orders received from Yudenitch, who at Helsingfors had set up a Government of North-Western Russia, broke the front of the Seventh Sovietic Army, occupied Pskov and Iambourg, and began to advance in the direction of Petrograd. Already he was approaching Gatchina and Tsarskoie Selo.[1] The garrisons defending the outskirts of the capital went over to his side.

On the 15 May Lenin proposed to send Stalin to Petrograd, with unlimited powers, for Zinoviev had fled in alarm. Stalin arrived in Petrograd on 26 May. There was reason to fear a revolt on the part of the fleet, but the two Sovietic battleships remained neutral, and the citadel of Kronstadt gave no sign of activity.

This struggle for Petrograd had very little resemblance to an organized battle. The Whites had been able to muster only a few thousand troops, imperfectly armed. With this handful of volunteers they attempted to seize the capital, where more than 300,000 well-armed workers were ready for street fighting.

There was, however, a total lack of cohesion between the leaders of the Red organizations. The orders which came from Moscow were signed by Trotzky, but in reality, no one was in command—or rather, everybody was attempting to act as commander. There was a relapse to the archi-demagogic period of Kerensky, when the officers were elected by the soldiers, while military orders were revised by the company cooks.

Consequently, Stalin's task was not so much to effect the strategical organization of the battle—for at the moment it would have been ridiculous to speak of any sort of strategy—as to impose a minimum of co-ordination between the countless committees and commissaries, all of whom were acting in a state of indescribable disorder.

Recalling his own terrorist activities, Stalin did not hesitate to adopt the most summary measures. He arrived in his armoured train;

[1]Now Dietskoe Selo, 'the Children's Village.'

H

it consisted of a locomotive and four carriages. A military tribunal was installed; its president was a Ukrainian sailor, Zozoula, and the prosecutor was an Ekaterinoslav bookbinder, Epstein. The sentences of the Court were executed immediately by a Kronstadt sailor, an enormous brute over 6 ft. 6 in. in height, girt with cartridge-belts charged with machine-gun ammunition, and followed everywhere by two women secretaries, who had graduated from a brothel.

Stalin described the situation as 'conflagration in a brothel.' But it was enough to introduce a co-ordinating principle into this disorder, and the crushing numerical superiority of the Reds made short work of the handful of Whites. It was Stalin who won the Battle of Petrograd; but he won it as an *abrek* not as a general. On his return to Moscow he was welcomed as a triumphant conqueror.

The defeat of Denikin in the South coincided with an attack delivered by the Poles. The situation was worse than confused. The Civil War and the Sovieto-Polish War were raging over a vast territory, where Ukrainian and Cossack hetmans were clashing with enormous bands of organized pillagers. At the moment when the South-Western front was preparing to receive the main thrust of Pilsudski's armies, Wrangel, who had succeeded to Denikin, made a sortie in force from the Crimea in the direction of Donietz. In the beginning of May 1921 the Poles entered Kiev. The Politburo thereupon organized a new command of the Western front, confiding it to Tukhatchevsky, while Frunzé was especially entrusted with the struggle against Wrangel. Pilsudski ventured too far east, believing in the general revolt of the Ukrainians which had been promised by Petlura.

Lenin felt that the time had come 'to feel the pulse of the world revolution with the bayonet.'

At this moment Stalin, who was in the South, was entering upon a course of action which had the most serious results, but in respect of which his actual motives were far from absolutely clear. His enemies offered one explanation; his supporters none. His enemies concluded that he was anxious to thwart the activities of Trotzky and Tukhatchevsky, and to deprive them of the unparalleled prestige which they would win by a victory at the gates of Warsaw.

While the armies of the West were thrusting towards Warsaw,

abandoning their supply columns, Budienny's cavalry, with Stalin as chief commissar, had defeated the Polish hussars, and captured Stanislavov and Tarnopol, and was approaching Lvov, instead of running to the aid of the main forces, which were absurdly small—about 45,000 only. Tukhatchevsky was defeated by the Polish reserves, employed in accordance with the instructions of General Weygand. The Russians fled in disorder. Their retirement soon became a rout—all the more readily, inasmuch as their organization had but little resemblance to that of a real army. This defeat compelled the Southern armies to withdraw, and Russia signed the disastrous Treaty of Riga.

For a long while after this the friends and supporters of Trotzky and Tukhatchevsky blamed Stalin for failing to support the main attack upon the Polish capital, and for undertaking an independent operation towards the South-West. History may one day settle the dispute.

In November 1920 Frunzé and Blucher forced the passes of the Crimea and liquidated the remnants of the White armies. The Civil War was over. Stalin finally returned to Moscow. A new era was beginning for the U.S.S.R., with the organization of the Soviet State and the economic renaissance of the country. While actively co-operating in these labours, Stalin was plotting the track of his patient ascent toward supreme power.

CHAPTER XVII

STALIN BECOMES PARTY SECRETARY

'EARLY in January 1921,' says Pestkovsky, 'I was present, in Stalin's house, at a conversation between him and Comrade Lenin. Vladimir Ilyitch declared: "I propose a coalition to defend my theses in the Party. You, in *Pravda*, will see to the polemical articles, and you will go into the provinces to represent me before the local organizations. In these discussions we shall no longer be speaking as members of the Politburo; we shall defend our theses as simple members of the Party, and I am asking you to act as my personal assistant in all this."

' "Now, they are all on Trotzky's side; Preobrajensky and Serebriakov are open about it; Krestinsky is supporting him on the sly, as his manner is. I can't put any confidence in them."

' "Agreed," said Comrade Stalin; and they shook hands.'

A few days later Stalin published in *Pravda* an article on 'Our Differences.' For in the face of the terrible trials which the country was facing, the Soviet leaders were in disagreement.

Lenin had already spoken of the dangers of the situation in December 1920, during a session of the Politburo. The discontented peasants were unwilling to sow their fields. Two or three bad harvests might result in a famine which would destroy half the population. Certain members of the Central Committee of the Party, such as the engineer Krassin, had the courage to demand the complete abolition of all State control, with economic liberty for the peasants, and the granting of concessions to foreign capitalists in exchange for very large loans which would be applied to the re-equipment of industry and to the saving of millions of peasants from starvation.

But Lenin was unwilling to surrender to the foreign capitalists and the *petits bourgeois* of Russia. The situation continued to grow worse, and the Communist Party itself split into several groups, which demanded complete liberty of expression inside the Party. Lenin feared a definitive split.

116

He was, therefore, obliged to seek allies. Zinoviev and Kamenev followed him, but Sverdlov, the man who knew most about the Party organizations, was dead, and the insignificant Kalinin was inclined to support Trotzky. The only useful ally to whom Lenin could turn was Stalin, with his numerous connections with all levels of the Party.

In his first article on 'Divergences' Stalin attacked all the other fractions, including Trotzky's 'Tzektrauss,' the working-class opposition of Chliapnikov, Kollontai, Medveviev, and Miasnedov, the 'Centralist Democrats' Sapronov, Drobniss and Smirnov, and the 'buffer group' of Bukharin.

On the following day Lenin published an article in which he referred to the theory which Stalin had been proclaiming so widely. The Tenth Pan-Russian Congress of the Communist Party was due to assemble on the 8 March, 1921, to adopt the principles of the N.E.P.—the New Economic Policy.

But six days before this date the famous Kronstadt revolt broke out. This revolt was a sign of a situation without precedent. The mutineers were not rebelling against the Soviet system—but they demanded Soviets freely elected and the abolition of the dictatorship of the Communist Party.

The threat to the power of the Soviets came no longer from the class enemy, but from the active strata of the population, rendered conscious by recent events. The sailors who in 1917 had been called 'the glory and pride of the Revolution,' and who were its first active agents, had now taken up arms against those who had been their leaders during the days of October 1917. The workers of Petrograd sympathized with the rebels.

The Gulf of Finland was still frozen. Detachments of the Red Army, under the supreme command of Trotzky, succeeded in crossing the ice and seizing the fortress. The Communists did not take things lightly. Nearly 40,000 sailors, captured with arms in their hands, were executed by the command of Trotzky and Dzerjinsky.

In one respect the uprising was to Lenin's advantage. It enabled him to reunite his party. By his prudent tactics he contrived to avoid alarming such leaders of the opposition as Chliapnikov and Lutovinov, who were to some extent involved in the Kronstadt revolt.

Stalin was allotted a new mission. He was entrusted with the elaboration of the famous resolution as to the unity of the Party, which, confirmed by the Congress, was to become an organic law that made it possible to exclude all such members as organized a clandestine revolt within the ranks of the Party. This was a decisive weapon, which enabled him, ten years later, to expel all his enemies from the Party. It was so useful to him at the decisive conjuncture that one is inclined to ask whether, in 1921, he had not foreseen the use which he would be able to make of it at the opportune moment.

The Congress adopted, not only this resolution, but also the N.E.P. It ordered the abolition of confiscations and requisitions of the peasants' wheat. It permitted a certain liberty of private industry and commerce, so that the peasants might be able to procure certain commodities without delay, and be encouraged to sow their fields. The artisans were declared to be self-employed, and their co-operative union was granted the same rights and privileges as the trade unions of the heavy industries.

This was a total reversal of the current policy. The transition was violent. Only yesterday the Tcheka—which with the introduction of the N.E.P. became the G.P.U.—was shooting artisans and tradesmen who had concealed the smallest amount of their goods or products. To effect the reversal an iron grip and a profound knowledge of local personages and of the workings of the Party machinery was indispensable. A Commission, known as 'the N.E.P.,' was established by the Politburo. The Commission needed a president. Lenin's choice for the post was Stalin. He seemed the best man for the job, and he was becoming indispensable as the Party administrator.

Stalin was completely engrossed in his new task as controller and conciliator. Very often he had to travel into distant regions or remote provinces where the authorities were finding it difficult to apply the N.E.P.

There was an extraordinary improvement in the economic condition of the country. For the majority of the Communist leaders the new situation was only provisional, and such differences of opinion as occurred related merely to the tactics to be employed.

Stalin, at Lenin's request, took action to prevent the Party from tumbling into the 'alluring and dangerous' abyss opened up by the N.E.P. What was needed was a 'purge'—the first!

It was during this period that Lenin began to exhibit the first symptoms of the malady which was to prove fatal. Towards the close of 1917 he began to complain of vertigo, of fatigue and insomnia. He was tormented by headaches of increasing frequency. Then, one day, he suddenly felt so giddy that he had to cling to the nearest article of furniture to save himself from falling. As soon as his illness began to cause him serious anxiety, he considered the necessity of creating a post from which all the strings of government could be pulled. But it is obvious that many of the Soviet leaders failed to realize the real importance of this new post.

Zinoviev, on hearing of Lenin's illness, hastened to Petrograd. He was afraid that Lenin would be succeeded by Trotzky. He knew that in that case he would not remain much longer at the head of the Third International, and that Trotzky might examine his dossier too curiously.

He had a plan: An alliance with Kamenev which, to hold its ground, would have to secure the co-operation of a secretary of the Central Committee, who had a firm grip of the Party machine and was inaccessible to the influence of Trotzky. Stalin appeared to be the man.

The Second Pan-Russian Congress elected a new Central Committee, which in its turn appointed the new Politburo, and three secretaries: Stalin, Molotov and Rudzutat. On the 3 April, 1922, the plenary assembly of the Central Committee elected, in accordance with Lenin's proposal, a Secretary-General: Stalin. That post he holds today.

Trotzky, for his part, basking in the glory of his victory in the Civil War, which the masses persisted in attributing to him alone, continued to display the utmost contempt for the Caucasian, who devoted himself to commonplace daily tasks. But Stalin knew that he had only to play his cards, and to wait, in order to become, thanks to the Party machine of which he had now complete control, the master of the U.S.S.R. What he needed, above all, was prudence, and patience. He had more than enough of both.

In his capacity as Secretary-General, Stalin had to edit Lenin's declarations. Lenin's health was rapidly deteriorating. From the spring of 1922 the Politburo held its sessions at Gorki, under his roof. The ailing leader was disquieted by the latest development of the N.E.P., and it exasperated him to see that the 'recession' of Socialism, which he had recommended, was more and more assuming the character of a retreat.

He now suffered his first attack of hemiplegia. He lost the power of speech, and could not move his right arm or leg. For several weeks his condition remained unchanged. Then periods of improvement set in; they lasted from half an hour to a couple of hours, alternating with further crises. It became necessary to reach a decision in respect of Lenin's successor.

Stalin had made a useful 'conquest' through friends of his wife. Iagoda, an official of the G.P.U., who had qualified as a pharmacist, was a protégé of young Sverdlov, who was often a guest of the friends of Mme. Stalin. Before the revolution he had attempted to associate himself with Sverdlov's wealthy family, by marrying one of his cousins. But some jewels disappeared—and their door was henceforth closed to him. After the Revolution Jacob Sverdlov assisted him, appointing him, among other things, Vice-President of the Council for Physical Culture.

The Secretary-General of the Party was not slow to recognize the uses of an Iagoda. The head of the G.P.U., Dzerjinski, an old Polish revolutionist, was a man of absolute integrity, but Iagoda was a 'careerist' of unknown origin. Since his judicial dossier contained a reference to the theft of jewels, he could be entrusted with very special missions. . . .

One thing made him particularly interesting to Stalin: he was keenly interested in toxicology, and the toxicological cabinet of the G.P.U., in the charge of his friend Dr. Kazakov, was a valuable Party asset. Stalin himself was greatly interested in poisons.

Lenin was still struggling against his malady. In October 1922 he felt sufficiently recovered to return to Moscow and resume his usual occupations. The physicians had authorized him to work from 11 a.m. to 2 p.m. and from 6 p.m. to 8 p.m. on condition that he rested completely for two days in the week. But on the 17 December, 1922, he had a further attack of hemiplegia, and the paralysis of the right side became permanent.

On the 30 December the First Congress of the Soviets of 'all the

Russias' made a historic decision: the Union of the Socialist Soviet Republics, the U.S.S.R., was founded. On this occasion Stalin, as Commissary for the Nationalities, officiated as spokesman, making one of his speeches in 'the new style.' It was brief and simple; displaying nothing of the bad taste and false pathos which had so often marked his speeches.

CHAPTER XVIII

LENIN'S TESTAMENT, AND THE CONQUEST OF POWER

L ENIN, in his lucid moments, was considering the means of strengthening the Party and avoiding a baleful conflict between his successors, who were making all preparations for a battle for the supreme power.

Stalin, who had a valuable ally in the person of Molotov, President of the Orgburo, an auxiliary organ of the Politburo, continued methodically to place men on whom he could rely in the Party machine and the Central Commission of Control. 'Technical Secretaries' to the Politburo and Orgburo were appointed. They soon became the real masters of the Party machine, while they still remained the private secretaries of Stalin and Molotov. Stalin also created his own personal secretariat.

A conjuncture of events which he was quick to exploit enabled him to develop this service to a high pitch of perfection. He was to find it of incalculable advantage. A Czech engineer, Oldrich Karlik, came from Moscow to instal the first system of automatic telephones (Viertouchka) for the members of the Politburo and the Central Committee. The first installation included only one hundred telephones. The private secretaries of Stalin—Mekhliss and Gricha Kanner—got into touch with the engineer, and he installed an instrument which allowed Stalin to listen to all conversations.

Inspired by the typically Russian love of theoretical discussions, and also by their curiosity in respect of the new automatic telephone service, the members of the Central Committee derived a great deal of pleasure from the protracted exchange of ideas regarding the Party situation. The question of choosing Lenin's successor, and a new Secretary-General, was very much to the fore.

Stalin often passed the whole night in his office, listening to these conversations. His private secretaries, Kanner, Mekhliss, Bajanov and Toustoukha, were often to witness this curious scene. Kanner, in

1928, made a few allusions to these 'nocturnal vigils.' He also spoke of the disappearance of the engineer Karlik, who had accompanied him to Irkutsk and Novosibirsk in order to instal the same kind of apparatus, and whom no one had seen since then. Having been too talkative, Kanner himself disappeared into the cellars of the G.P.U. Mekhliss and Bajanov succeeded in fleeing the country.

Thus Stalin kept himself informed as to the most private thoughts of the other members of the Central Committee, and when it was necessary to act he knew where the blow should fall.

He paid many a visit to Lenin, who lay sick and helpless in the Kremlin. The physicians had postponed the invalid's removal to Gorki, considering that the journey thither would be too fatiguing.

One day Stalin received an incomprehensible letter; it was in Krupskaia's handwriting, and it bore her signature. He immediately called her on the telephone: 'Nadiejda Constantinovna, don't send me any more of these notes. It isn't Vladimir Ilyitch who is writing them—it is you; I don't require your instructions.'

Krupskaia insisted, and ended by losing her temper.

'Volodia will recover his health one day; you'll be sorry. . . .'

Stalin hung up the receiver, having retorted, angrily: 'I am not going to be taught what to do by a bird-brained woman.'

One may take it that Stalin yielded to the angry impulse because he knew that the circumstances—the state of Lenin's health—made it possible for him to do so. Already there was a change in the balance of power.

Krupskaia complained to Lenin, and Stalin received a note in the tremulous handwriting of the invalid: 'After your coarse and unpardonable behaviour to Nadiejda Constantinovna, there is an end of personal and kindly relations between us. Lenin.'

These lines were written by a dying man, surrounded by women. As a matter of fact, Lenin continued to write to Stalin through the same amanuensis, although the notes which he dictated were becoming more and more irritable.

Early in February 1923 Stalin received from Krupskaia a sealed envelope, bearing an inscription in Lenin's handwriting: 'To be opened after my death.'

It was to be supposed that the envelope contained important instructions from Lenin. Stalin convoked a meeting of the Politburo.

Zinoviev, who had come from Petrograd, declared: 'The envelope ought to be opened immediately.'

Stalin, we know, is extremely prudent; and he has little respect for the conventions when the future of his political career may be in question. It is difficult to believe that he had not found an opportunity of acquainting himself with the contents of the envelope before it was officially opened.

When opened, the notes it contained were brief—and they did not spare the majority of the Soviet leaders.

Zinoviev and Kamenev were described as 'hole and corner politicians.' Bukharin was 'a scholastic'; not a Marxist; weak in dialectic, bookish and lacking in realism, but 'sympathetic.' Piatakov was described as 'a good administrator,' but, like Bukharin, 'not fit for political leadership.' Trotzky was 'not a Bolshevik.' But 'this fact must not be held against him, just as one must not blame Zinoviev and Kamenev for their attitude in October 1917.'

As for Stalin, the 'Old Man' found no political fault in him. But —and this judgement must have been to some extent inspired by his retort to Krupskaia—'he is inordinately coarse and brutal. He is also capable of taking advantage of his power to settle personal disputes.' After admitting that 'rudeness is an admissible trait in the mutual relations between Communists,' Lenin adds: 'Nevertheless, one must consider replacing Stalin by another Secretary-General, who, having the same qualifications, would be pleasanter in his dealings with his subordinates.'

Stalin, having read the notes, had a question to ask: 'Do you think it necessary, comrades, to ask Ilyitch to revise these notes in any way?' The members of the Politburo, having all been criticized by Lenin, were unanimous in supporting Zinoviev, who, feeling himself to be the most injured (for he regarded himself as Lenin's successor) exclaimed: 'The notes have no political value. They must be put in the archives. That's all they're fit for.'

This is the origin of the famous legend of 'Lenin's Testament.'

In March, Lenin suffered another attack of hemiplegia. He found it almost impossible to take any nourishment, and speech was becoming more and more difficult.

The Twelfth Pan-Russian Congress of the Communist Party was held in his absence from the 17 to the 25 April. On this occasion the results of Molotov's activities as organizer were apparent. The secretaries despatched into the provinces were firm supporters of Stalin and his group; and although the Party organizations of Petrograd and Moscow were controlled by Zinoviev and Kamenev, while the Ukraine, and its President, Petrovsky, were inclined to waver, the majority of the Congress was in favour of Stalin.

Zinoviev, who was lacking in character but not in intelligence, saw danger ahead. But on the Central Committee the majority were in his favour, he having to read the report in Lenin's place.

Men like Stalin understand how to take advantage of everything —even of apparent set-backs. It was easy enough to excite a reaction against Zinoviev, who was regarded as a usurper, and guilty of *lèse-majesté*. Trotzky would have suffered the same fate if he had not suspected Stalin's strategy. On the new Central Committee, appointed by the Twelfth Congress, Stalin's group had a majority of twelve votes. His secretariat had gained control of the party machinery.

In May Lenin was removed to Gorki. Towards the end of July his condition had slightly improved. He began to walk again, leaning on a walking-stick, and on the arm of his wife or sister. He began once more to take an interest in political affairs. But he suffered from frequent relapses. Fits of extreme excitement often mask the progress of paralysis. Lenin wept and shouted, just as Stendhal did, who died of the same malady.

Between two attacks Lenin sent for Stalin. During one of his short visits he was alone with the 'Old Man.' On returning to Moscow Stalin convoked the Politburo. 'The "Old Man,"' he said, 'doesn't want to go on suffering. He has asked me for a poison to shorten his sufferings. He would make use of it only if they became intolerable. . . .' A confused discussion followed.

Stalin, in August 1923, wrote a letter to the Executive Committee of the Comintern, which contained a masterly analysis of the situation. He concluded that 'during the present phase' it would be impossible to Sovietize Germany. He proposed an alliance with the Social Democrats, who could be eliminated later. This letter was actually a first exposition of the tactics of the 'Popular Front.'

The time had come to decide on the direction to be followed by the foreign policy of the U.S.S.R.—and by Stalin himself. For the moment, he spoke of the glorious lot of Comrade Trotzky, who would soon be given the task of leading the German proletariat, the vanguard of the industrial proletariat of Europe. And Trotzky already saw himself in Berlin, the leader of the world revolution. He was ready to leave the Communist Party of Russia to 'all these provincials'—to Stalin, Kamenev, and Zinoviev. While waiting for his hour to strike, he was relaxing in the Crimea, with his wife. Other Soviet leaders followed his example, but Stalin and Molotov remained in Moscow, strengthening their position.

Zinoviev was on holiday at Kislovodsk, a watering-place. But Stalin's attitude filled him with anxiety. Though he had not the vigour and eloquence of Trotzky, he had great experience of organization, and as a cynical opportunist he was not hypnotized by the mirage of an immediate world revolution. He was fond of the proverb: 'It's better to hold one's ground than to run.' He understood very clearly that when Stalin and Molotov had completed their task of organization the triumvirate would have served its purpose, and would be replaced by Stalin's personal dictatorship. In order to prevent this he decided to resort to one of those bargains which his master Lenin had so often been able to effect.

But this time he had bitten off more than he could chew. If we study the innumerable intrigues which were woven about the Kremlin, we are struck by the prevailing lack of earnestness by which they were qualified—excepting those conducted by Stalin himself.

Secretly, Zinoviev convoked a meeting at Kislovoksk. Vorochilov, Ordjonikidzé, Lachévitch, Bukharin, Evdokinov (secretary of the Petrograd Committee), Dzerjinsky, Kalinin and Kamenev were present. He also sent a telegram to Stalin, asking him to come and discuss the situation inside the Party.

On the 30 September, 1923, in a cave known as 'the Cave of the Dead Mule,' there was a strange assembly of Bolshevik leaders. It would be known to historians as the 'Conference of the Troglodytes.' In order to avoid curiosity and indiscretion, the leaders went out for a walk, which ended at the cave. There they spent nearly three hours, debating and exchanging opinions. They sat on the damp rocks, and Lachévitch often remarked that he at least had gained something from the conference: namely, a violent attack of sciatica.

Kamenev had not left the Crimea, where he was diligently courting an English journalist, Claire Sheridan, who in 1921 had made a bust of Lenin. Stalin replied by a telegram: 'I have other things to do than to chatter with a lot of loafers.'

Zinoviev did not read the text of this telegram, which Mekhliss, the leader of Stalin's secretariat, had shown to the secretaries of the Politburo and the Orgburo.

No decisions were reached, Vorochilov and Ordjonikidzé having declared that without Stalin they could not express any opinion.

On the 6 October Stalin, in response to the repeated requests of Ordjonikidzé, arrived in Kislovodsk. At the meeting Zinoviev com-. plained that 'the secretariat has organized a veritable dictatorship inside the Politburo.'

After prolonged discussion a compromise was proposed by Stalin: Three members of the Politburo would be delegated to the Orgburo, to direct the activities of Molotov and the secretariat. The three delegates were: Trotzky, Bukharin, Zinoviev.

Stalin knew well enough that this was a 'rotten' compromise.[1] Trotsky considered he was too big a man to concern himself with such petty details as the appointment and control of provincial secretaries. Bukharin, a scholarly person, was known to detest the problems of organization. As for Zinoviev, head of the Red Commune of Petrograd, he could not absent himself for very long, lest Stalin put his own men into the local committee.

In their turn, the military took a hand; they were waiting for Trotzky's return to Moscow. Once he had rested himself he would 'put himself at the head of the opposition.' On the 5 December a resolution was voted *severely condemning the special privileges of the bureaucracy and restoring the right of criticism.* It was an artful move; autocriticism is seldom dangerous.

At the same time, as an external sign of his authority, Zinoviev obtained, through the intermediary of his friend Evdokinov, the decision to rename the city of Elizavetgrad, Zinovievsk. Vorochilov promptly proposed that Tsaritzin should henceforth be Stalingrad. Kamenev gave his name to a small town of no particular importance. Gatchina, near Petrograd, took the name of Trotzky. Tver became Kalinin; Perm, Molotov; Vladikavkoz, Ordjonikidzé; Samara, Kuybichev. Even an individual without real influence, like Rudzutak,

[1]'Rotten' was the expression which Lenin applied to alliances which had no lasting effect. 'Unsound' might be a better translation.

honoured with his name a modest village on the Volga which was known as 'The Fleas.' Tomsky was the only one to refuse this honour.

But the masses were still waiting to hear what Trotzky had to say. There is no doubt that if at this moment the head of the Red Army had openly joined the opposition, the Politburo would have been swept away.

Stalin said little, but he knew that the moment for action had arrived. He left Moscow for the Crimea, where he found Trotzky. This visit was one of those gestures which few have the sense to make at the critical moment. In his *Memoirs* Trotzky certainly mentions the fact that 'although he was ill, he signed the Politburo's decision of the 5 December, 1923'; but he gives no hint as to the circumstances in which Stalin succeeded in obtaining his signature. Yet this was an act of irresponsibility on his part which can only be likened to a political suicide!

Once more, it was Stalin's secretary Kanner, whose indiscretions finally cost him his life, who revealed to his colleagues the details of this journey:

'Comrade Stalin went straight to Comrade Ordjonikidzé's villa, where I joined him an hour and a half later, for I had first to send some telegrams for Comrade Stalin. When I reached the villa I found Comrade Stalin radiant with delight: Trotzky had consented to add his signature at the foot of the Politburo's decision of the 5 December. His interview with Stalin was brief. He had come accompanied by Pavda, and after some five minutes' conversation he announced: "The decision of the 5 December corresponds with my point of view. I am signing it." Pavda tells us that Trotzky was much flattered by the fact that Stalin had made the journey especially in order to see him, and that it was certainly this that induced him to add his signature.'

Stalin knows how to flatter when flattery is needed.

When *Pravda* published on its front page the statement that 'Comrade Trotzky entirely approves of the line of the Politburo and has signed the resolution of the 5 December' the opposition suffered a terrible shock. It felt deserted by its leader at the very moment when it should have struck the decisive blow.

Various persons of minor importance sought to persuade Trotzky to amend his fatal error. Piatakov went to the Crimea and explained to Trotzky the exact position, and the trap into which he had fallen. The head of the Red Army thereupon wrote a further letter which he gave to Piatakov. He declared that the presence of his signature under the resolution of the 5 December did not by any means indicate that he shared the disastrous attitude of the majority of the Politburo.

Piatakov took the letter to Moscow. It was read at the Party meetings. It produced a certain impression, but the favourable moment had passed.

Zinoviev exclaimed that Trotzky should be court-martialled immediately. But Stalin waved his hand disdainfully. 'There are more immediate dangers!'

There were indeed. His listening-post had reported several conversations between Krupskaia and Piatakov, who asked whether Lenin was still capable of signing a protest against the policy followed by Stalin and the Politburo. Piatakov—or so he stated in Paris, when in 1928 he was acting as commercial representative of the U.S.S.R.—wanted to read this declaration at Party meetings, in order to bring about a reversal of the situation created by Trotzky's signature.

Krupskaia had replied that 'she would take it upon herself to get Lenin to understand and sign.' She added that 'she was preparing, in according with Lenin's indications, a new "testament," treating Stalin and company with greater severity than the former document.'

Stalin had no time to lose. Convoked by him, the Politburo adopted a resolution severely blaming Trotzky for his 'direct attempt to discredit the Party apparatus,' and proposed that he should take a holiday in the Caucasus.

On the following day Kanner saw Iagoda enter Stalin's office, accompanied by two of the physicians who were attending Lenin. 'Feodor Alexandrovitch,' said Stalin to one of these physicians, 'you must go at once to Gorki, for an urgent consultation in respect of Vladimir Ilyitch. Guenrikh Grigorievitch will accompany you.'

That same evening—it was the 20 January, 1924—Kanner, who was in and out of the room, overheard a few snatches of a conversation between Stalin and Iagoda: 'There will soon be another attack. The symptoms are there. He has written a few lines (Kanner saw a

ı

few lines in Lenin's distorted handwriting) to thank you for sending
him a means of deliverance. He is terribly distressed by the thought
of a fresh attack. . . .'

On the 21 January, 1924, the fatal attack developed. It was terrible, but it did not last long. Krupskaia left the room for a moment
in order to telephone. When she returned Lenin was dead. On his
bed-table were several small bottles—empty. At a quarter-past seven
the telephone rang in Stalin's office. Iagoda announced that Lenin
was dead.[1]

---

[1]The question of 'Lenin's poison' has often been raised and discussed. We shall
see in the following chapter how it was treated by Trotzky and Stalin's group.
Kanner's account has never before been published; it was given to us by a colleague
on Lenin's secretariat, who had left the U.S.S.R. It seems to us, in any case, that
Lenin's condition was such that any active intervention on his part in the affairs of
the State or the Party, even by correspondence, could not have taken place; which,
however, does not mean that there could not have been some machination of the
kind of which the history of the struggles between the Communist fractions is so
full. On the other hand, the fact of furnishing the means of an eventual euthanasia
by suicide might well appear, in this case, a gesture of pure humanity.

CHAPTER XIX

THE END OF THE TRIUMVIRATE

On the day of Lenin's death Trotzky was on a train making for Sukhum, on the Black Sea, where the Politburo had sent him for a compulsory 'cure.' He heard the news at the Tiflis railway station, from the leaders of the local Committee of the Party. He telegraphed to Stalin, in the ciphered code of the local Committee.

Stalin replied at once: 'The funeral will take place tomorrow. You cannot return in time. The Politburo considers that in view of your state of health you must continue your journey to Sukhum.'

On the verandah of a sanatorium, where he was lying wrapped in blankets, Trotzky learned that Stalin had deceived him; the funeral was later than Stalin had pretended.

Why did Stalin think it necessary to ensure that Trotzky would not attend Lenin's funeral? The first explanation that occurs to one is political in character. If Trotzky had been present at the funeral he would have had to make various speeches. He would have become the centre of attraction of the crowd of some three millions of persons who, in spite of the terrible cold, passed in procession before the coffin. In the eyes of the military detachments, the party delegations, and the citizens of the capital and the provinces he could easily have figured as the successor of Lenin.

Trotzky proposed another explanation. 'Stalin must have been afraid that I might connect the death of Lenin with the conversation in the Politburo on the subject of poisons.'

'I did not resume personal relations with Kamenev and Zinoviev until two years later, after they had broken with Stalin. They ostensibly avoided any discussion of the circumstances of Lenin's death; replying by monosyllables and refusing to meet my eyes. . . .'

One does not quite understand the reason Trotzky gives for his discretion at the time. It was Stalin who read the famous Oath over Lenin's coffin. Thousands of pilgrims, assembled in the Red Mecca, saw his face and heard his voice for the first time. They spread the news over the vast country that they had seen the successor to the first Bolshevik leader. Hitherto Stalin had worked in the background, inside the mechanism of the State and the Party.

By openly presenting himself as a candidate for the heritage of Lenin he was, of course, exposing himself to all sorts of dangers. The group of the Forty-six was unwilling to come to terms with him, and Piatakov had a new scheme of his own. He managed to convince Krupskaia that the question of the 'Testament' must be submitted to the Politburo.

'I told her that the Politburo had decided to conceal the existence of the "Testament," ' he himself declared in Paris, in 1928, before a group of personal friends who met from time to time at 55 Avenue de Suffren, in the apartments of Jean Arrens, Councillor to the Soviet Embassy. 'I told her too that the document was filed in the archives: "You must ask for it to be read on the occasion of the coming Pan-Russian Congress, and if it isn't read you must threaten to read it yourself." '

Krupskaia, as a member of the Central Committee, was automatically a member of Congress, with a consultative vote.

She asked Stalin for an interview. He received her in the presence of the head of his secretariat, Mekhliss, and the head of the organization department, Syrtzov. As he was ignorant of the object of her visit, and was afraid that some sort of 'provocation' might have been devised by Krupskaia and Trotzky, he preferred to have witnesses. The interview took place on the 18 March, 1924, in Stalin's office.

'I had never seen Krupskaia in that condition,' Mekhliss told his colleagues of the secretariat. 'She came in and began immediately, almost shouting: "I gave you an envelope sealed by Ilyitch with instructions to open it after his death. What have you done with this envelope?"

' "The Politburo has no information to give you, Nadiejda Constantinova. . . ."

' "It's a question of the Testament of Vladimir Ilyitch, of his last wishes. The Party must be told of them. I warn you that if you don't read the Testament during a session of the Central Committee, I shall publish it myself—I am the testamentary legatee. I have to fulfil a mission which he entrusted to me on the day of his death. . . ." '

She went on shouting for some time. When she had gone Comrade Stalin exclaimed, in an irritable tone: 'Old witch! Stupid, birdbrained woman! A shrew!'

A few days after Krupskaia's visit to Stalin, Trotzky returned to Moscow. While resting he had completed a pamphlet, 'The Lessons of October,' dealing with the Bolshevik Revolution. In this he attacked Zinoviev and Kamenev, describing their attitude during the period preceding the insurrection of 1917, their 'treason,' their hesitations, their alliance with that *petit bourgeois* Maxim Gorki, and their dubious relations with the Mensheviks, themselves the lackeys of Kerensky. Calling them 'two *petits bourgeois* who have strayed into our party,' he held them entirely responsible for the failure of the German revolution in the autumn of 1923. 'Zinoviev could not act otherwise at the head of the Komintern. One can't ask a lapdog to be a Great Dane,' said Trotzky to a 'youth delegation' which came to welcome him at the railway station on his arrival from the Caucasus.

By speaking thus, he enabled Stalin to evade, without too much difficulty, the problem presented by the testament. Taciturnity is better than imprudent eloquence.

Zinoviev and Kamenev hurried off to Stalin in a state of panic. They decided that Kamenev had to read Lenin's 'testamentary notes' at a secret plenary session of the Central Committee. It was agreed that he would hint that while he admired Lenin as a leader of genius, one should not forget the state of his health when he wrote the 'Testament.' He invoked Lenin's article on the Central Commission, in which he reminded his readers that the essential thing was to remain united after his death, and to continue to lead the labouring masses. In the meantime Stalin sent Syrtzov to Trotzky, in order to warn him that if he entered upon a discussion in the Central Committee concerning the 'Testament' the letter would be read in which he wrote of Lenin, in 1908: 'Lenin, that professional exploiter of the ignorance of the members of his party, who provokes sordid quarrels and incites the revolutionaries to attack one another, calumniating them, dividing and dominating them by his criminal and stupid ambition. The whole edifice of Leninism is based on lying and falsification. . . .'

The letter was dated long before Trotzky's adhesion to Lenin's party, but its publication would undoubtedly have caused a violent upheaval in the country in which the cult of Lenin, and of his mummy in the mausoleum of the Red Square, had recently been inaugurated.

Trotzky was obliged to accept a compromise, and he himself saw to it that there was no discussion.

In May 1924 was held the Thirteenth Pan-Russian Congress, with 748 delegates, and 881 members of the Party. Stalin had to defend himself on another ground: that of ideology. Trotzky, as usual, insisted that the Russian revolution must be regarded as the first chapter of the world revolution. The Comintern needed fresh leadership; the watchword of the Soviets must be 'permanent revolution.' But the majority of the members of Congress were peasants and officials, who were not greatly impressed by the slogan of 'world revolution.' They condemned the programme of the Trotzkyite opposition, describing it—as everything was described that did not agree with the prevalent tendency—as 'a *petite bourgeoise* deviation from Marxism and revision of Leninism,'—a convenient formula.

However, when a new Central Committee had to be elected, Stalin flatly rejected Zinoviev's proposal that Trotzky and his supporters should no longer be elected.

'It is too soon as yet to risk a decisive battle with Trotzky,' he said. 'Our position isn't strong enough yet. We'll wait until the Fourteenth Congress.'

Stalin knew how to wait. He is never impatient, and this apparent lack of enthusiasm is only a deliberate tactical expedient. Together with his taciturnity, it makes him a formidable adversary. He wanted to retain a counterpoise to Zinoviev and Kamenev in the Central Committee and the Politburo; and Trotzky was still at the head of the Red Army. Stalin decided upon a measure of which he alone foresaw the future consequences. The triumvirate must be transformed into a septet, by the addition of Rykov, Bukharin, Tomsky and Molotov.

When the new Politburo had been appointed, Stalin assembled all its members, with the exception of Trotzky, in his apartment.

'We thought it as well to keep Trotzky in the Politburo in order to avoid an open conflict in the country, and in the Party. We must devote ourselves above all to developing the economic measures proposed by Congress. But Congress has described Trotzky's attitude as that of a *petit bourgeois*, a revisionist in respect of Leninism, and we must be united, so that Trotzky cannot profit by our occasional differences.

'*For this reason I propose that we always meet at my place in private committee before each official meeting of the Politburo, in order to agree beforehand as to our decisions.*'

The proposal was accepted. Mekhliss recorded the gist of it in a secret minute which was signed by each of those present. The triumvirate was at an end—but Stalin's power increased enormously.

CHAPTER XX

THE SECRET OF STALIN'S ASCENT TO POWER

THE Septet appeared a somewhat eclectic combination. It was divided into three groups. On the Left were Zinoviev and Kamenev. Stalin and Molotov, controlling the mechanism of the Central Committee, represented the Centre. Rykov, President of the Council after Lenin's death, with Bukharin and Tomsky, formed the Right. For them the N.E.P. was not a mere tactical manœuvre, but a decisive change in the policy of the Government. The supplementary members, Kalinin and Rudzutak, were affiliated to the Right: Dzerjinsky hesitated between the Right and the Centre.

The situation was becoming more and more threatening toward the dictatorship of the Communist Party. The whole of Lenin's system of agrarian reform, based on direct exploitation, without the utilization of hired workers, was threatening to collapse, while the prosperous peasants, the Kulaks,[1] were becoming more and more numerous. In trade, private enterprises were continuing to spring up everywhere. In industry private initiative had created thousands of small workshops and factories which sold their products to the peasants. Labour co-operatives were becoming more frequent.

In the autumn of 1924 it had become evident that the private section of the nation's economy was becoming more important than the socialized section. The Statistical Institute, which prepared secret reports for the Politburo, made an alarming discovery: 72 per cent of the national economy was in the hands of private persons!

When Rykov informed the Politburo of this fact, Stalin wanted a Communist to check the figures. Krumin, a member of the Central Committee and editor of the Government's economic journal, was entrusted with the task. He came to the conclusion that the Institute

---

[1]The Kulaks are prosperous peasants who have succeeded in acquiring a certain amount of property at the expense of the poor and less able peasants.

was mistaken. Private enterprise did not account for 72 per cent of the national economy, but . . . for 73 per cent.

Seven years had now elapsed since the seizure of power, yet the principles of the Bolshevik Government had not been established, while representatives of other parties, such as the Mensheviks, were filling important posts. The Politburo and the Soviet Government were obliged to reckon with them, just as the different fractions of the Communist Party had to reckon with one another.

But Stalin, at least, was able to profit by the chaos. While others were eternally discussing questions of principle, he devoted himself to two enterprises. The first, which we have already noted, was the systematic conquest of the mechanism of the State by the mechanism of the Central Committee and the Politburo, which he already controlled, though he was as yet careful to ensure that his mastery of it was not too obvious. The second was the elaboration of a new theory, destined to replace Lenin's theory, which, according to Stalin, was useful only in navigating the tempests of the initial or post-bellum period.

The measures adopted by Stalin and Molotov during the next few years were so many steps toward supreme power. Unless we study them as a whole we shall not perceive the actual mechanism of their progress.

By means of the pretext that after Lenin's disappearance a strict and permanent control of the mechanism of the Soviet State had become a sheer necessity, Stalin and Molotov created a whole network of commissions in conjunction with the Politburo and the Orgburo. Among these comissions were: The Commission for Agriculture; the Transport Commission; the Industrial Commission; the Financial Commission; the Commission for Foreign Affairs; the Commission of Public Security; and the Military Commission.

Some of these already existed in a rudimentary form. In 1924 each of them was equipped with a large office and a director, who was in each case a member of the Central Committee. To complete this structure, a Special Commission was created. This Commission was to serve Stalin as a springboard. But it had a very modest title: 'The Commission for the Circulars of the Central Committee.'

The Politburo approved of the creation of this 'technical commission,' without attributing any great importance to it. This was
just what Stalin had desired. Stalin's mode of action was to avoid all
show, and to offer explanations only when it was no longer possible
to avoid them—and when the end was achieved.

The Commissions rapidly became actual Ministries. All steps
taken by the People's Commissars had to be ratified by a corresponding Commission. Now, the orders of these Commissions were communicated by means of notes officially known as 'circulars,' which
they drew up in agreement with the Secretary-General of the Party,
and which were centralized in the 'Commission for the Circulars of
the Central Committee.' They were drafted, on principle, in accordance with the decisions of the Politburo or the Central Committee;
but the official references became increasingly vague, and finally the
Secretary-General exercised a very wide personal initiative, which
no one required him to justify in any way.

Stalin found that he needed a group of technicians who were
members of the Party and absolutely trustworthy. He recruited
them from among the young men who frequented the 'Salon of the
Palace of the Red Sailors,' whose central figures, as we know, were
Stalin's second wife and her four friends—Léra Rubtzova Malenkova,
Ida Volodarskaia, Moussia Ignatieva, and Rosa Ulitzkaia.

The secretary of the Commission for the Circulars, the very
driving-wheel of Stalin's whole machine, was a young Party member, Boris Bajanov, the son of a physician of Mohilev-Podolsk, who
was personally recruited by Molotov.[1]

Having perfected his tactical use of the Commission for the
Circulars, Stalin began to plan another conquest. He wanted to gain
the adhesion of Lenin's 'Old Guard'—of the 'Old Bolsheviks' who
continued to exercise authority as Lenin's fellow-conspirators, and
whom the younger members of the Party treated with reverence,
impressed by their spectacular attitude and their oratorical vigour.
He himself, at this time, had no means of attracting the masses, and
as he was fully occupied with the silent conquest of the twofold
mechanism of power, the moment for spectacular publicity had not
yet arrived.

[1]Bajanov afterwards became Secretary to the Politburo and the Orgburo, replacing Nazarietian and Rostoptchin while remaining at the head of the Commission
for the Circulars, etc.

Trotzky gave his own explanation of this phase of Stalin's activity: 'The "Old Bolsheviks," the "old" young revolutionaries of the Tsarist era, were not often, alas! story-book heroes. There were among them many who did not display sufficient courage when it came to arrest, police inquiries, and deportations. . . . Having become Secretary-General of the Party, in 1924 Stalin built up, in his private quarters, a complete file of all the members of the Party. By threatening to reveal their past he reduced them to servile obedience.'

According to the Secretariat of the Politburo, the percentage of such 'Old Bolsheviks' in the two categories was sixty. If we are to be objective, we must recognize that the method of pressure exerted by this means was not Stalin's invention, and that it continues to flourish in many countries other than U.S.S.R.

CHAPTER XXI

THE NEW DOGMA

THE check to the German Revolution, and the disappearance of the hope of the outbreak of a world revolution, called for the elaboration of a new tactical and strategical dogma for the Russian Communist Party and the Comintern. As a realist whose feet were firmly planted on the earth, Stalin was not content with abstractions.

The task which he had set himself, because events had necessitated it, was no easy one. Lenin had proclaimed *urbi et orbi* that the Russian Revolution was only the first phase of the world revolution. The active circles of the Party no longer knew where they should seek the revolutionary truth. In order to attract the young men and to make sure of their reserves, they would have to offer a sufficiently attractive ideal.

Stalin, who was not as yet the 'inspired leader and source of all wisdom,' did not appear to consider himself capable of accomplishing this theoretical transfer without help. In order to do so he appealed to his old Viennese 'guide,' Nicolas Ivanovitch Bukharin. A member of the Politburo and editor-in-chief of *Pravda*, as well as the head of the department of propaganda, this naïve and ardent individual, 'a veritable child of thirty-five,' as they called him in the Politburo, was the darling of the Party youth. Always on the alert for a new theory to explain a situation or elaborate a suitable tactics, he had for some time been absorbed in meditation.

One day Stalin invited him to discuss, between themselves, the situation inside the Party. Mekhliss, permanent witness of the Secretary-General, was present.

'Nicholas Ivanovitch,' said Stalin, 'we are, with you, the "Himalayas" of the Politburo. The others are just rubbish—excepting Trotzky. But Trotzky isn't a Bolshevik. He would like to force on the peasantry the heavy burden of an insensate super-industrialization, at their expense, and the expense of those people of middling position whom Lenin has told us to spare, in order to preserve the alliance between the workers and the peasants.[1] . . . One must elaborate a new dogma, adapted to the new circumstances, in order to show the members of the Party that we are true Leninists and that Trotzky is merely a Menshevik who has lost his way.' And Stalin expounded the theory of 'the building of Socialism in a single country,' without waiting for the triumph of the world revolution. He required the theoretician to transform this idea into a 'basic doctrine.'

Bukharin needed no persuasion. In him was the love of those dialecticians who are fond of adapting theories to realities; the soil was already prepared. The press had been dealing with the subject for months past; reversing the method of the true creators. The theories under discussion may be stated thus:

'. . . It is not necessary to wait for the victory of the world revolution before inaugurating the building of Socialism in Sovietic Russia. Being a vast country, covering a sixth part of the globe, Russia is endowed with economic possibilities which are completely harmonious. She represents in herself *a world economy in miniature*—an economic microcosm (so the scholastic Bukharin explained). The essential thing is to isolate Sovietic Russia from the capitalist sector, from the world economy, by a Socialist autarchy, in order to forestall attempts on the part of the outer world to restore the capitalist economy. . . . One must, therefore, stress Lenin's idea as to the capitalist encirclement of the first Socialist State, and the permanent danger incurred by this State, at the same time pointing out that a peaceful co-existence of the two sectors is possible so long as one sincerely rejects the idea of armed aggression. . . .'

Stalin accepted Bukharin's plan. But in another conversation he proposed to complete the new theory:

'. . . If we adopt the building of Socialism in a single country—in the U.S.S.R.—without waiting for the help of countries more developed industrially,' said Stalin, 'we shall need first-rate factory managers, engineers, and organizers. In the beginning we should have to send for foreign engineers. All these people will have to be well paid, and their material situation cannot be the same as that of a

[1]This was the principal theme of the oath pronounced by Stalin before Lenin's coffin.

simple working-man. Consequently the egalitarian deviation must be rooted out as quickly as possible. . . .'

It is curious to note the regularity with which any theory which did not correspond to the necessities of the moment was described by Stalin as a 'deviation.'

The first hints of the new doctrine began to appear in the press. To begin with, the imagination had to be powerfully impressed. In a pamphlet by Karl Marx, which was republished in 1867, and which was devoted to a criticism of the Gotha programme of German Social-Democracy, Bukharin found the following sentence on p. 33, lines 10 to 12: '. . . it is childish to think that the Socialist régime would immediately see the establishment of a total equality of material conditions in society. . . .' That was all. But it offered the possibility of evoking the supreme authority of Karl Marx to justify the new dogma and the new tactics which were already taking shape in the Politburo. Young people educated in the Marxist cult had to accept this thesis of the Gotha programme.

Now it was possible to begin the actual construction of the so-called Socialist system. And it was based—a fact which had hitherto escaped most of the commentators and observers, hypnotized by labels—*on the practical abandonment of Leninism.* In 1924 some 75 per cent of the national economy was still in the private sector; and when the Socialist sector began to regain the whole of the national economy, it was all done under the slogan of abandoning the preliminary necessity of a world revolution and condemning the theory of equality of pay.

Stalin remained faithful to his tested manœuvre. Before himself, as a screen, he set Bukharin, who had to take the first blows by which the opposition of the Left attempted to regain their lost positions. A veritable tempest discharged itself upon him. 'This is a revision of Lenin and Marx,' Trotzky protested. 'An ignoramus, an illiterate, a poor scholastic, a pope in the Party,[1] attempts to deface the works of Lenin and Marx and to serve an unsavoury hotch-potch to the Party. . . .'

Piatakov and Olminsky paraphrased the story of Roland's mare —a sally of Marx's during an argument with Bakunin: 'She was a wonderful mare, but unhappily she was foundered. Your mare is

[1]Bukharin was descended from a family of priests.

broken-winded, Comrade Bukharin. You have made a mess of your homework in the class of your ignorant professor, Joseph Stalin.'

Karl Radek and Dimitri Manouilsky, who specialized in anecdotes, were full of droll stories of the building of Socialism in a single country:

'Bukharin has introduced a mathematics à *rebours*,' declared Radek. 'He descends from $n + 1$ to n. And these are his results:

'The building of Socialism is possible on the world scale:
'Therefore it is possible in a single country.
'Therefore it is possible in a single city.
'Therefore it is possible in a single street.
'Therefore it is possible in a single house.
'Therefore it is possible in a single w.c.'

Bukharin paid no attention to these attacks. He was protected by his sincerity. In the spring of 1925 he published an article in *Pravda* in which he appealed to the peasants: 'Enrich yourselves!' he exclaimed. This gave the opposition their chance, and they launched a fresh attack upon the majority in the Politburo. 'Stalin has become the leader of Thermidor,' cried Trotzky, in the Party meetings. 'He openly favours the Kulaks. He wants to liquidate the dictatorship of the Communist Party.'

An extraordinary session of the Politburo was convoked. It was obviously impossible for Stalin to defend Bukharin's unfortunate slogan. As we know, nothing matters to him but the distant aim which he has set himself. He does not allow himself to be influenced by personal loyalty or friendship. He dropped Bukharin, and took part in the vote that severely censured him.

But during the same session he took the opportunity of striking Trotzky the blow which he had been meditating for years. It was true that Trotzky, through lack of character, had always given way to opposition, and that his reactions had been mere verbiage.

'The Civil War was over long ago,' said Stalin. 'The U.S.S.R. are no longer threatened by any war. Comrade Trotzky should, therefore, be moved to another post where he would be more useful: that of President of the Goelro (Electrification of the U.S.S.R.). I propose to appoint, as Commissar for War and President of the Revolutionary Council for War, Comrade Michel Frunzé, the conqueror of Wrangel. . . .'

The decision was voted unanimously. Trotzky gave way without a protest. In voting against Trotzky, Zinoviev and Kamenev were pursuing personal ends. They hoped now to take advantage of the Bukharin affair in order to split the Stalinist majority in the Politburo. Following the example of the Secretary-General, they invited the other members of the Politburo, with the exception of Stalin and Bukharin, to a meeting in Kamenev's flat. They attempted to organize an anti-Stalinist pentagon—but they got no further than talking it over.

Then Stalin, taking this action as a pretext, ceased to convoke them to the meetings of the Seven. The new grouping had resulted in eliminating the two members whom Stalin had found most inconvenient.

In order to deprive Trotzky of the command of the Red Army, Stalin ran a great personal risk: by appointing Michel Frunzé to the post. For the first time, and perhaps for the only time, he had before him a man always ready for action, and capable, if need arose, of using the revolver which he never laid aside.

On arriving in Moscow—ere his first appearance at a session of the Politburo, to which he had been co-opted as supplementary delegate, Frunzé declared: 'I propose to manage my Commissariat as I think best. I am responsible to the Party and I shall give reasons for my actions. But I won't put up with being badgered with super-fluous instructions.'

The tone of this declaration displeased Stalin, and when Frunzé began to appoint the commandants of the military district, without previously consulting the Politburo, Stalin convoked his 'pentagon.' 'Comrade Frunzé,' he said, 'will have to be called to order.'

'Impossible,' Rykov and Tomsky replied. 'Trotzky, Zinoviev and Kamenev would take his part. Kalinin and Dzerjinsky are friends of his. If he jibs we shall have to retreat, and the prestige of the Politburo will suffer a serious blow.'

Stalin had to wait in patience, but not for long, for he realized that a Frunzé would not be content, like Trotzky, with mere words.

One day, having come to the Politburo to see Stalin, he was kept waiting for nearly a quarter of an hour by Torstukha, one of Stalin's secretaries. 'I have no time to waste,' said Frunzé. 'Comrade Stalin must see me immediately.'

'You know, Comrade Frunzé,' Torstukha replied, 'it is we who give orders here.'

'What?' cried Frunzé, in sudden fury: '*This* is what gives orders!' And clapping his hand to his Mauser, he opened the door of Stalin's office.

The incident coincided with alarming reports from Iagoda. In October 1925 Frunzé dismissed the commandants of many of the military districts. He appointed men chosen by himself—or by Zinoviev and Kamenev—in Moscow, Leningrad, Kharkov, Minsk, and Orenburg. In Orenburg an ex-officer of Wrangel's army, a certain Karanov, boasted that he would shortly be transferred to Moscow, where a military *coup d'état* against Stalin was in preparation. But a month before the convocation of the Fourteenth Pan-Russian Congress, in view of which Zinoviev and Kamenev were making preparations for a decisive attack upon Stalin and Bukharin, Frunzé, suffering from intestinal ulceration, died under an anaesthetic. He was given a splendid funeral.

On the eve of the convocation of the Fourteenth Party Congress, Stalin had to deal with yet another danger. Kamenev and Zinoviev attempted to repeat their habitual manœuvre: to induce the Party organizations of Moscow and Leningrad to vote in the same sense. With the help of the Ukraine, which was still wavering, it might be possible to unite 350 of the 650 votes against Stalin.

But Stalin had the Party machine under his control. He could force upon the Congress whatever decisions he desired. In his political report he demanded sanction for his new theory of the building of Socialism in a single country.

Stalin manœuvred with extraordinary and unscrupulous cunning. The long hours which he had passed with Molotov during the sessions of the Commission for the Circulars had enabled him to make a thorough study of the mechanism of the State. He was beginning to feel sure of himself. His quiet reserve was in impressive contrast with the emotional manner of other orators, who were given to wild gesticulations, and the repetition of commonplaces or empty phrases. For the first time the delegates of the Congress felt that they

K

were confronted with something more than a mere Secretary-
General and Party administrator.

Once more Trotzky allowed an opportunity for action to pass.
He let his friends, Piatakov, Radek, Radovsky and Préobrajensky
waste their time in lobbying for votes. A great political future could
hardly be built on abstention, or fear.

The Fourteenth Congress approved of the general line followed
by the Politburo and the Party by the crushing majority of 560 votes
against 61, with 29 abstentions. Zinoviev and Kamenev were check-
mated.

The new Politburo, appointed by the new Central Committee,
included neither Trotzky, nor Zinoviev, nor Kamenev. Their places
were filled by Kalinin, Dzerjinsky and Vorochilov. Two new supplementary delegates made their appearance: Kirov and Andréev.

CHAPTER XXII

STALIN AND THE POLITBURO

As soon as the Fourteenth Congress had broken up, after appointing a new Central Committee, Stalin submitted to the latter his resignation from the post of Secretary General of the Party. This, it is true, was merely a matter of principle, since he was certain to be elected with a crushing majority. As a matter of fact, the following vote of confidence gave him a majority of 85 per cent.

This manœuvre had a twofold object. In the first place he spoke of his devotion to Lenin, so that the great operation of socialization was placed under the posthumous authority of Lenin, neutralizing, by this very fact, the oppositions of Right and Left. In the second place, Stalin was seeking to create, in this federal republic, whose framework had hardly been completed, the notion of duration and continuity. Since it was impossible to base authority on the tradition of centuries, or even of decades, the immovable illusion of continuity had to be created in the psychology of the masses by the deification of the memory of the founder of the U.S.S.R. Later on, the development of this notion would make Stalin himself a sort of symbol of the Soviet Union.

The year 1926 confronted Stalin and his Politburo with considerable economic difficulties. The receipts of the tax in kind were small, and would not suffice to feed the industrial regions and the Red Army. Of the five million tons of grain needed half had to be bought at a fixed price. The total production amounted to 7.5 million tons, of which about 2.5 millions entered into the category reserved for the open market.

From this one example it may be seen that everything had to be done in the name of Lenin.

In the summer of 1926 Stalin consulted the President of the Agricultural Commission of the Politburo, Iakovlev-Epstein, in connection with the supply of cereals. A plenary assembly of the Central

Committee was convoked. The debate on agriculture became a debate on the manufacture of goods to satisfy the requirements of the peasants. This debate was so lively that the President of the Council of National Economy, Dzerjinsky, and his senior assistant, Piatakov, nearly came to blows. Dzerjinsky, who had a weak heart, collapsed; that same evening he died. The terrible founder of the Tcheka disappeared—in consequence of a mere dispute as to the percentage of textile fabrics to be produced in the region of Moscow. He was replaced on the Economic Council by Kuibychev.

Stalin, who was obviously uneasy, declared at a meeting of the Politburo: 'It must be admitted that we are approaching the critical point of the existence of the Soviet power. The Central Committee has been unable to offer an immediate solution. But the line of action to be followed is laid down: we must proceed to the rapid industrialization of our country. Otherwise the "peasant Acheron" will swallow us up. . . .'

At the same meeting Stalin submitted the list of new industrial undertakings which had to be established—a list drawn up by the Industrial Commission. The industrialization of the U.S.S.R. was beginning; and this beginning coincided with a great disturbance in the ranks of the Party.

Zinoviev, forgetting the hatred which divided him from Trotzky, and the pamphlet on the 'Lessons of October' in which Trotzky had attacked him, sent emissaries to his enemy. One of them, Michel Ivanov, the leader of the metallurgical trade unions of the Ural, was afterwards the leader of the technical section of the commercial representatives of the U.S.S.R. in Paris. There, one day, he described his first interview with Trotzky in this connection:

'I went to see Comrade Trotzky in his flat in the Kremlin, and I told him, without beating about the bush, why I had come to see him. At first he seemed to be surprised. "What, it is Zinoviev who has sent you? He wants to work with me after dragging me in the mud?" I repeated what Comrade Zinoviev had told me before I started: "The essential point is actually to fight Stalin, to defeat him politically, to prove to the Party that his methods are those of a usurper, and to expose the Thermidorean character of his dictatorship. The rest of us—the true Leninists—can come to a friendly arrangement between ourselves. . . ." '

Trotzky accepted.

In August 1926 the new allies held a secret meeting in Moscow, when they decided to form an illegal fraction within the Party. Krupskaia was present at this meeting. But all these Communists are people afflicted with complexes. They are constantly on the rack between their devotion to certain ideas—old or new—and the principle of fidelity to the Party; and at the same time they are obsessed by their doubts as to the real orientation of the 'Bolshevik truth.' Thus, on the very morrow of the meeting, one of the participants, a certain Lazarev, repented and went to see Stalin, telling him of Krupskaia's intervention, and what Zinoviev and Trotzky had said.

The response was immediate. That very evening Zinoviev's flat was broken into, and the famous letter written by Trotzky in 1908 was abstracted: the letter which was full of insulting references to Lenin. Shortly afterwards a photographic reproduction of the letter appeared in the Leningrad party newspaper, the cradle of the new opposition.

It was preceded by these words: 'This letter, sent by Comrade Trotzky to the social traitor Martov, and found on his premises when he was arrested by the Ogpu, is now in the personal archives of Comrade Zinoviev.'

The Politburo then published, over Stalin's signature, an important decree: 'Discussions are authorized only before the Party Congresses, and not before conferences. The action of the opposition is contrary to the statutes. If it persists the matter will be submitted to the Central Commission of Control with a view to excluding all those who refuse to obey the statutes.'[1]

Zinoviev, Kamenev and Trotzky realized that they had got themselves into difficulties. They sent Stalin a letter intended for the Central Committee: 'We repudiate all activities directed against the statutes of the Party. We undertake to avoid any future violation of the statutes and to act as disciplined members, while reserving our right, guaranteed by these statutes, to apply to the Party Congress to settle our differences with the present leadership.'

But Stalin already had a firm grip of the reins. In November 1926 the Party Conference, on his initiative, deplored the 'amoral and cynical Trotzky-Zinoviev alliance.' And in December a plenary

[1] The decision of the Tenth Congress gave this right to the Central Commission.

meeting of the Executive Committee of the Third International adopted a parallel resolution. Zinoviev was replaced at the head of the Comintern by the Bukharin-Manulsky tandem, seconded by Piatnitzky.

The year 1927 opened under somewhat disquieting auspices. The industrialization of the country was proceeding but slowly. There was talk of sabotage, of embezzlement, of criminal negligence; and sanctions were liberally applied. On the other hand, the attempts to attract the average peasant into the kolkhozes were rarely successful. In March, in view of a report of Iakovlev-Epstein's which declared that collectivization was proceeding 'at a tortoise's pace,' Stalin proposed to appoint a new director of the Agricultural Commission. Andre Andréev, a candidate for election to the Politburo, was nominated.

In May 1927 Leonid Krassin, Commissar for Foreign Trade, a very old friend of Stalin's, was invited by the latter to engage in a private conversation. They met in a villa at Gorki, close to Lenin's old home. Stalin had invited a number of those who were then his intimate friends: Bukharin, Ordjonikidzé, Rykov, Kalinin, Vorochilov, Molotov, Kouibichev, Menjinsky, and Mekhliss. They met in a little park, where they played at *gorodki*—a popular game, requiring both strength and skill, of which Stalin was very fond. The dinner was served in the Caucasian style, and Stalin himself bled the sheep, so that a Caucasian fry could be prepared.[1]

Krassin had a definite theory as to the proper course to be followed: a reconciliation, economic and commercial, with the capitalist world, a consolidation of the Imperial Russian debt, and an offer of investments in the Ural and Siberia to the British; new loans and short-term credits for the purchase of machine tools in England and the United States.

A few days later the 'die-hards' of the British Government organized a raid on the Arcos[2] premises in London. On the 26 May the British Government broke off relations with the U.S.S.R. On the 7 June, in a railway station, a young Russian assassinated the

---

[1]Trotzky mentions this custom in his book, as demonstrating Stalin's 'personal physical sadism.'
[2]Arcos: the Sovietic commercial mission in London.

Soviet Ambassador, Voikov. The international tension increased.

In the Politburo, Stalin declared: 'It is evident, even to a blind man, that the capitalist countries want to take advantage of our political and economic difficulties and our disagreements, in order to bring about a conflict, first of all between the U.S.S.R. and the adjacent countries, and then between the U.S.S.R. and the entire capitalist world. We have not a moment to lose. While increasing our efforts to breach the united front of capitalism, we must accelerate our military preparations. The time is limited. . . .'

In October 1927 Marshal Vorochilov, promoted to this rank with Budienny, Blucher, Iégorov and Tukhatchevsky, presented to the Politburo a report on the measures taken to bring the Red Army up to date. From the technical standpoint its modernization was the work of Tukhatchevsky. The army was being rapidly mechanized. Twelve armoured brigades were being formed, and an air force of 6,000 planes, while professional soldiers were taking the place of the territorial divisions. The Politburo unanimously approved the plan.

Towards the end of the same month a serious fact was brought to light. Of the Old Guard, the true nucleus of the Party, consisting of some 6,000 Bolsheviks of the period before the 1917 Revolution, 80 per cent were anti-Stalin. Zinoviev, Kamenev and Krupskaia had succeeded in enticing them into opposition.

Stalin's secretary, Kanner, relates: 'Nazaretian, and Mekhliss, who was at this time editor-in-chief of *Pravda*, came to see Stalin in the afternoon, to inform him of the results of the voting of the different groups inside the Party. Stalin, after listening to them, observed that the Old Bolsheviks were fossils. 'But one must not underestimate the importance of their vote. If we allow the eighty-three to continue their propaganda inside the Party, the State will be reduced to inactivity. Instead of appreciating the measures proposed in proportion to their real importance, I am often obliged to think of how I can avoid giving the opposition an easy pretext for attacking them. I have made up my mind. They must be faced with an ultimatum: they must submit to the Party, and resume their place in it, or they must continue the conflict outside it—against the Party, against the Sovietic State which is directed by the Party. *Then we shall crush them as we have crushed the other hostile groups. It will not be the Central*

Commission of Control but the Ogpu which will take charge of that operation.'

In the whole history of Stalin's life we do not find any equally precise and positive expression of his notion of the way to deal with the internal conflicts of the Party. In these words we find a complete and precise definition of the tactics which would inevitably lead him to exterminate his principal enemies, who in his opinion were identical with the enemies of the Party and the Soviet State.

But many years were to pass before he had decided to take 'physical' action against them. This is one of the most curious aspects of the mentality of a member of the revolutionary Order who was on the way to becoming a true statesman. He could not as yet make up his mind to employ brutal force against his 'own sort.' But when he at last saw that the employment of force was a practical necessity —and he was never a man to arrive at sudden convictions—the machinery of reprisals began its infernal work.

On the 9 November, 1927, he requested the Politburo to exclude Trotzky and Zinoviev, 'guilty of serious infraction of the statutes,' from the party. On the 14 November an extraordinary assembly of the Central Committee and the Central Commission of Control confirmed the decision. In December it was ratified by the Pan-Russian Congress of the Party, which at the same time decided to apply the same measure to the active leaders of the opposition: Kamenev, Radek, Préobrajensky, Rakovsky, Piatakov, L. Smirnov, Mdivani, Lifchitz, Smilga, Sapronov, Boguslavsky, Sarkiss, Drobniss, and V. Smirnov. The excluded members were dismissed from their posts, and those of them who took part in a demonstration on the 7 November were deported to the regions of the Volga or the Ural.

Adolphe Joffé, one of the most prominent members of the opposition, who had organized its 'clandestine centre,' committed suicide, leaving a letter to Trotzky. In this he besought Trotzky 'to fight the usurper Stalin by all the means habitually employed by revolutionaries to strike down the enemies of the people.' He was the first victim—a voluntary victim—of the struggle between the Communist leaders. But as blood calls for blood, his death inaugurated an era of bloodshed.

As usual, the new Central Committee proceeded to hold elections to the Politburo. Among the supplementary members of the Polit-buro, in addition to Kaganovitch and Mikoyan, an Armenian who was an intimate of Stalin's, and Ouglanov (next secretary of the Moscow Committee, who had already been of great service in the struggle with Kamenev and Zinoviev), were two senior Ukrainian officials: Petrovsky, President of the Ukrainian Republic, and Tchoubar, President of the Council. The titular members of the Politburo were: Stalin, Bukharin (the permanent originator of theses and dogmatic theories), Vorochilov, Kouybichev, Rykov, Tomsky, Kalinin, Molotov, Ordjinokidzé and Kirov (the only man to figure in the whole of Stalin's career as a genuine personal favourite).

On the 19 January, 1928, Stalin summoned to his office the head of the G.P.U., Menjinsky, his senior assistant, Iagoda, and the secretary of the G.P.U., Bielienki. Mekhliss was present during the conversation that followed. All the members excluded by a decision of the Central Committee and the Control Commission had to be interrogated. The head of the G.P.U. did not receive this order with any show of enthusiasm. An old Bolshevik of Polish origin, an admirer of the works of Oscar Wilde, and an admirable pianist,[1] he cherished no particular hatred of the opposition. At the time of the Civil War he had not hesitated to warn Trotzky that Stalin and Vorochilov were intriguing against him.[2] Among the members of the opposition were some of his old friends.

On returning to his office he called up Kamenev on the telephone and asked him to come at once. Kamenev came, accompanied by Zinoviev, Trotzky and Radek. Menjinsky informed them that he would be obliged to arrest them if they resumed any sort of clandestine activity.

'Many of our comrades have been arrested already,' said Trotzky. 'They are militants of no great importance. They have been compelled to sign lying declarations concerning their activity, involving me, with Zinoviev, Kamenev, Radek and Piatakov.'

'Who forced them to sign these declarations?'

---

[1]Condemned prisoners, on their way to the sinister cellar in which they were executed (having to cross Lubianka's inner courtyard), often heard the strains of Chopin being played by the head of the G.P.U., who had installed a grand piano behind a screen in his office.

[2]Trotzky mentions the fact in his memoirs.

'Iagoda.'

On the following day Menjinsky wore a singular expression when he received his visitors. The fact was that Stalin, having been warned by Iagoda, had called on him, accompanied by Mekhliss. They had talked for more than an hour.

'Well, Comrade Menjinsky,' Trotzky remarked, 'have you verified my declaration?'

'Yes. It may be perfectly true. . . .'

'What? May be? Show me the declarations signed by our friends, and I undertake to prove that they are untruthful.'

'That's impossible, Lev Davidovitch. . . .' Kamenev intervened:

'Do you understand, Menjinsky, what these tactics are leading up to? You'll end by shooting the lot of us in your cellar.'

Menjinsky, with a pensive air, went over to the piano without replying. He played the first bars of 'Solvieg's Song' from Grieg's *Peer Gynt*.

'Stop playing! Stop!' cried Kamenev. 'I insist that you shall tell me, as an old revolutionary and a Bolshevik, if you believe that Stalin, after shooting us, could by himself ensure the final victory of our party in its struggle for world power?'

Menjinsky stopped playing, and looking straight into Kamenev's eyes, he exclaimed: 'But why did you ever allow him to obtain the immense power which he is wielding already? Now it's too late. All the Secretaries of the local Committees are on his side. If you begin to struggle against him you will shatter the Party machine. Yes. Break up the whole Party just to get the better of this one man. Do you understand? Do you want to dig the grave of our Party dictatorship and allow the Kulaks and the Nepmen to invade the stage? I am an old Bolshevik; I belong to Lenin's cohort; I shall do everything to hinder the break-up of the Party. But I shall obey the orders of the Politburo, and of Stalin, the Secretary-General elected by the Central Committee. I recommend you to do the same.'

This dramatic conversation soon became generally known. Menjinsky kept a secret diary, while Iagoda wrote a detailed report of it for Stalin's benefit, in which he gave a distorted version of his leader's statement—hoping to inherit his post.[1] This conversation produced a great impression. The leader of the opposition, in a

[1] Trotzky speaks of this too in his *Memoirs*.

declaration read to the Politburo in February 1928, made the promise to submit to the decisions of the Fifteenth Congress and to observe the discipline and the statutes of the Party.

'I don't believe them,' said Stalin. 'But we must make the experiment of readmitting them to the Party. I feel that I am under a personal obligation to do so, in order to prove that I am following the instructions of Ilyitch, and that I am loyal and impartial, even toward my personal enemies.'

This was a skilful manœuvre, for it tended to absolve Stalin from any future responsibility for the fate of members of the opposition. When the Politburo came to consider the question of their fate he would insist that its vote must be unanimous.

It was obviously not the official desire to 'follow the advice of Lenin' which induced Stalin to effect this apparent reconciliation with the Trotzkyites and Zinovievists. He foresaw the approach of another danger, and, like an experienced tactician, he devised a policy so balanced that he could take his stand on either side at will.

His prevision was justified. The necessity of building up, as quickly as might be, a heavy industry which would serve as the basis of the war industry which would make it possible to modernize the army, compelled him to accelerate the tempo of industrialization and of the collectivization of agriculture. The question of the necessary means was discussed with considerable heat.

Carrying in his arms a child of Trotzky's, and attacked by the members of the Right, who had been his chief supporters in his struggle against Trotzky, Stalin had to manœuvre as a member of a fraction. Only the greatest strength and the clearest vision could save him from losing his way in the zigzag course imposed upon him by circumstances, and enable him to avoid the innumerable snares which lay in wait for him.

In order to deal with the members of the Right 'deviation'— Bukharin, Rykov, Tomsky—it was necessary to deprive them as quickly as possible of the support of Kalinin and Petrovsky. This task was confided to Mekhliss. While Petrovsky was absent from Kharkov, the G.P.U. of the Ukraine arrested his brother and transferred him to Moscow. He 'confessed' to being the agent of an organization which Petliura had set up in Poland, and was executed six days after his arrest.

In the summer of 1928 Stalin convoked in the Kremlin a military conference which included all the district commandants with their chiefs of staff, and promised in a long speech to take all possible "measures to ensure that our army shall be a modern army, well equipped, and well provided with armoured cars and aeroplanes." The army agreed to support Stalin in his plan of industrialization at the expense of the peasantry.

CHAPTER XXIII

THE STRUGGLE AGAINST THE RIGHT

H AVING elaborated the tactics of his struggle against the Right of the Politburo, Stalin hesitated for a long while before applying them. As always, he decided to act under the impulse of an eventual pretext. Kanner, his private secretary, tells how it happened:

Towards the end of October 1928 Stalin received a visit from Ordjonikidzé, who seemed greatly disturbed.

Members of the Right were organizing their forces in Moscow, where they were in touch with Uglanov, in order to prepare for a *coup d'état* inside the Party. The Red professors—Slepkov, Stetzki, Maretzky and Eichenwald; the secretaries of the trade unions—Dugadov, Bassov, Verba and Smeliansky; the heads of administrative departments—W. Schmidt, Eismont, Kaburov, Grinko; and lastly, some of the officials of the G.P.U.—Artusov, Katzenelbaum, Mironov, Salski, Epstein—took part in this 'legal' conspiracy. They wished to take advantage of the plenary session of the Central Committee and to ask for the appointment of a new Secretary-General of the Party. Uglanov had been promised the support of the Ural. The Leningrad Committee was still wavering. The Ukrainians were only waiting for a favourable moment for striking a blow at Stalin, who was planning the collectivization so detested by the provincial Committees. At the same time Bukharin was willing to overlook the attacks which Zinoviev and Kamenev had made upon him. He admitted the necessity of concluding a general agreement directed against Stalin—an agreement between all the members of the oppositions, Leftist and Rightist, including Trotzky.

In order to avoid misunderstandings and discussions after the victory over Stalin, and also, perhaps, because the new allies distrusted one another, the substance of the agreement was recorded in a document which Bukharin consigned to his strong-box in the Politburo. All these 'conspirators' produced the impression of people trying to overtake a carriage which was some way ahead of them, and of whose route they were not quite certain.

By the day following the consultation of Kamenev and Bukharin, Stalin had been informed of the nature of the interview. Iagoda was keeping watch over all the leaders of the opposition, wherever they might be. He had learned that in reply to a telegram which Kamenev had sent to a certain Maltchikov, a confidential agent of Trotzky's at Alma-Ata, a message had been sent from this distant city. Addressed to Kamenev, it contained only a single word: 'Agree.' By this message Trotzky associated himself with the 'legal conspiracy.' By the evening of that same day a photostat of the document was in Stalin's hands. The fact is that when Kanner ordered the private safes for the members of the Politburo, the locksmith Kolobov was ordered to provide duplicates of all the keys; and these duplicates were handed over to Stalin.

When he could not avoid it, Stalin abandoned his usual prudence and deliberation. He sent for Vorochilov, and together they decided on important changes in the command of the military districts. By the following day all the commandants who were old members of the Party had been replaced. Politically neutral, the new commandants were not greatly interested in the conflict between the Bolshevik leaders. Among the new men was Tukhatchevsky, who was appointed to Moscow.

Special emissaries of the Secretariat were sent into the provinces, in order to inform the local Committees and their secretaries, who were under Molotov's orders, of the creation of the cynical and unprincipled 'super-bloc' of Stalin's adversaries. They were asked to verify the loyalty of all the Party officials. The power which Stalin had at his disposal, in the name of the Party and the Politburo, was ready for immediate application. Then, and only then, Stalin convoked the Politburo. There was no need for further restraint. He made a frontal attack. He began with Bukharin, speaking as one who was the master of the situation, and accused him of chameleon-like and anti-Leninist policy.

The name of Lenin—like that of Marx—was always a touchstone for the men of all parties, under whatever circumstances. Everything that was undertaken was always done in the name of Lenin, and under cover of the traditional Marxist jargon, even when the matter in question was the abandonment of the basic theories of the two prophets of Communism. This habit has created, and is still creating, a certain confusion in the mind of the general public, among pseudo-qualified observers, and even among the politicians of foreign countries.

'It's a lie!' exclaimed Bukharin. 'You have invented a fable for the use of the *durfatchki* and simpletons.'

'Do you know this, Nicholas Ivanovitch?' Stalin handed him the photostat of his agreement with Kamenev. 'What have you to say?'

It was a dramatic moment. Rykov and Tomsky demanded the suspension of the session. Stalin, supported by the majority, refused the suspension. He cited the mysterious affair of the negotiations in Paris between Sir Robert Horne, ex-chancellor of the British exchequer, and the Soviet *chargé d'affaires* in Paris, Bessedovsky, a member of the opposition of the Right, concerning a political and financial agreement between Britain and the U.S.S.R. The latter had suggested, through the intermediary of a Scottish manufacturer, the granting of a loan of £500,000,000, in exchange for a monopoly in the supply of the machine tools required for the new Soviet industries. The U.S.S.R. would have acknowledged the old Tsarist debts, would undertake to dissolve the Comintern, and would discontinue all propaganda in the British Empire.

The members of the Right, greatly disconcerted, declared that they were anxious only to defend their 'political platform.'

'Well, then,' said Stalin, 'tell us what your platform is. I shall convoke a plenary session of the Central Committee so that you will have an opportunity of defending it.'

At this meeting of the Central Committee the members of the Right found themselves almost without supporters; their provincial friends thought it prudent to refrain from intervention, and to await a more favourable moment. There was, therefore, no real discussion, and after a mere reading the theses of the opposition were rejected by a majority of 75 per cent of votes, with 20 per cent of abstentions.

After the vote had been declared Bukharin, Rykov and Tomsky announced their resignation from the Politburo. Stalin, however, refused to accept their resignation; it was too soon for his purposes. He did not wish to assume the sole responsibility for the physical destruction of his enemies. He preferred to begin by defeating them on ideological grounds, in order to appear, not as a man defending his own cause, but as the 'true representative of supreme justice, mobilized in the defence of the Revolution, its conquests, and its future.' At the same time, he proposed to exile Trotzky, in order to avoid the danger of some sort of provincial *pronunciamento*. It may be that he was also endeavouring to create abroad a centre of fixation for the opposition, which would enable him to keep a closer watch on its sympathizers until he was able finally to annihilate them.

In November 1929 the Central Committee declared that the propagandist ideas of 'the opportunists of the Right' were incompatible with the quality of Party membership. It proposed once more to exclude Bukharin from the Politburo and to address a warning to Tomsky and Rykov.

Once again, Stalin temporized. He did not think the moment had come to exclude his two enemies. First he must purge the administration and place men at its head of whose devotion he could be sure: as he had already purged the Party, in order to avoid the disorganization of the mechanism of the State. From the political standpoint the situation was clear enough: Stalin had conquered the Politburo and the entire Party. Henceforth no opposition of importance could arise within its various departments. He could now devote himself immediately to the solution of the tremendous problems which confronted the U.S.S.R. There was no longer any need to discuss their conformity with the abstract and contradictory ideologies which were merely fractions of the Marxist theory dissociated by contact with the realities of life.

Before the convocation of the Sixteenth Pan-Russian Congress of the Party, which was to open on the 26 June, 1930, the Politburo elaborated its first Five-Year Plan. The international situation called for its early publication. In Germany the party of Adolf Hitler was meeting with considerable success; its victory was more than probable, and the threat of war was becoming more definite.

CHAPTER XXIV

COLLECTIVIZATION : THE FIRST FIVE-YEAR PLAN

HAVING become the undisputed master of the Central Committee of the Party, and of the Politburo, Stalin proceeded to the implementation of decisions relating to the industrialization of the country and the collectivization of its agriculture. His actual power was tremendous. But having made sure that he had plenty of elbow-room, he firmly refused to make a show of it. Although he confronted the country as a dictator, he was a dictator of a very peculiar kind. He did not wish to give orders; he obtained obedience by means of suggestion.

Moreover, since 1924 he had not occupied any official position in the State. He acted simply on and within the Party. The experience which he had acquired during the long period of conflict, and the first twelve years of the existence of the U.S.S.R., had enabled him to perfect his tactics, which as time elapsed became more and more dynamic, more and more logical. They had brought him to his present position, in which he found himself in a certain sense *above the controlling mechanism of the State and the Party.* He was becoming increasingly taciturn, and in his speeches, which were growing more infrequent, the old seminary style was giving way to simplicity of expression.

He convoked the Sixteenth Party Conference in order to make detailed preparations for the Sixteenth Congress, and the political slogans which would have to be introduced there. The struggle against the kulaks was at its height. The local authorities were at no particular pains to explain just what the kulaks were. Thus, a local secretary in the Northern Caucasus—Cheboldaiev, who was afterwards shot in consequence of his excesses, which led to a terrible famine and a peasant revolt in that region—had only this to say:

L

'For me, a kulak is any peasant who does not sell all his grain to the State.'[1]

In a 'directive circular' Stalin declared: 'One must rely entirely on the poor peasants and consolidate the alliance with the moderately prosperous peasants in order to engage in the decisive struggle to annihilate the kulaks as a social class.' Of course, to annihilate them as a social class did not mean the physical extinction of the kulaks. But the local authorities had no time to draw the distinction; moreover, Stalin had issued stringent orders through the Agricultural Commission of the Central Committee. He asked for prompt results; those who failed to produce them would be treated as saboteurs.

Now, in the majority of regions the number of kulaks, according to the official statistics, amounted to 40 per cent of the peasantry. The annihilation of these peasants 'as a class'—by driving them from their holdings, evicting them from their houses, confiscating their sheep and cattle and horses, and deporting their wives and children to Siberia—often ended in physical extinction. It would be supreme hypocrisy to pretend that Stalin and those around him did not know what results would follow from obedience to their circulars. Although various explanations may be offered for the purges and the bloody reprisals against the enemies inside the Party, who would themselves have acted in the same way if they had been victorious, the frightful cruelty of the period of peasant collectivization cannot be excused on the human plane, whatever its results may have been on the economic plane. The dead will not benefit by the better organization of agriculture, and the sum of suffering accumulated during the process of collectivization surpasses human realization.

It came to a regular civil war in slow motion. Against this terrifying background collectivization was effected at an ever-increasing pace. In 1928 the agricultural land in the hands of the *kolkhozes* amounted to 1,400,000 hectares. In 1930 it was 30,000,000 hectares.

Then Stalin felt that the time had come to absolve himself once more from personal responsibility for what was happening. Under

[1]Senator Vandenburg said, in 1946: 'For me everything that is not against the New Deal is Red.'

the title, 'The Vertigo of Success,' he addressed a severe warning to all those who had been 'intoxicated by the success of the collectivization and had forgotten the necessity of sparing the peasants unnecessary suffering.'

The article produced a great impression; but for the peasants, in their distress, the mere fact that Stalin appeared to regard them with compassion was encouraging. It was followed on the 3 April by a 'Reply to the Comrades in the Kolkhozes.' It repeated the theme of the previous article, recognized 'the mistakes and blunders committed,' and promised to repair these errors. It did not, of course, promise to resuscitate the dead; but it established a positive contact with the survivors. It told them that 'Leninism severely condemns the policy of reprisals against peasants of moderate means', and promised that all those would be punished who should violate the principle that peasants should exercise free choice of entry into the kolkhozes.

Stalin thus became to the peasants a sort of 'Little Father,' who listened to their complaints and endeavoured to right their wrongs. The fact that he himself was the immediate origin of their misfortunes was beginning to escape them. An image was taking the place of the reality. It is a paradoxical fact that these terrible years of collectivization saw the origin and increase of Stalin's popularity among the Russian peasants, although more than three millions of them—men, women and children—had paid with their lives for the 'vertigo of success' of the local Soviet authorities who were merely executing the draconian commands contained in Stalin's circulars.

On the 26 June, 1930, at the height of the collectivization and industrialization, the Sixteenth Party Congress assembled. Stalin, in a political statement, described the Congress as 'the Congress of the general offensive of Socialism upon all the fronts.'

As a matter of fact the industrialization of Russia was proceeding at a dizzy pace. The great barrage on the Dnieper was under construction, while at Krematorsk and Gorlovka enormous factories were being built in which tractors would be produced. The locomotive factory at Lugansk-Vorochilovgrad had been rebuilt. In the Ural engineering workshops and chemical factories were being established, and the stupendous Kouznetk-Magnitogorsk Combine was nearing completion. In Nijni and Moscow enormous automobile factories were springing up, and in eleven months a gigantic tractor manufactory had risen from the ground in Stalingrad.

Stalin was at the centre of all this activity. He had familiarized himself with economic and industrial questions, and he did not hesitate to express his intention during his conferences with engineers and commercial directors. It is true that the special conditions which were then obtaining facilitated his judgement. The means at his disposal were the total resources of an immense country, and no considerations of private interests had to be taken into account.

Nevertheless, he had to deal with difficulties of a political order with which he was constantly confronted. For example, there was a movement among the managerial orders which were now described as the 'technocracy.' Stalin published another article—a word of warning.

His speeches and articles were becoming more and more infrequent. Their purpose was merely to expound theses or advance theories, as Lenin, Bukharin and Trotzky were fond of doing. Any utterance of his addressed to the public was an act of government. In order to keep trace of the precise evolution of events it becomes important to discover the intention of such utterances and to place them in their logical order. We shall then perceive the continuity of Stalin's governmental activities; and only then, since Stalin refuses to explain his words or his actions, and since his speeches and articles are always devoted to a decision which has not only been formed, but which has been at least partially realized.

Thus, when Stalin uttered his warning to the engineers he had already decided what means to employ against them, and these took the form of the 'exemplary' trial of Chakhty, the trial of Ramzin,[1] and the summary execution of Paltchinsky. At the same time the first link was forged of the chain that would one day drag Rykov to the cellar of the G.P.U.

In the meantime the progress of industrialization was undeniable. The share of industrial production in the national economy of the U.S.S.R. had increased to 54 per cent and the level of production

[1] A secret agent of the G.P.U. placed among the technocrats.

was 180 per cent as compared with the pre-war figures.[1] Heavy industry was developing at a truly surprising rate.

But the political fever of the country was not abating. The number of members of the opposition to be imprisoned or deported was continually increasing. Secret committees were formed in the Ural, in Siberia, in the Ukraine, in the Caucasus. Gori, the birthplace of Stalin, became the seat of a secret committee formed by the opposition in the heart of the Communist Party of Georgia. Lastly, Trotzky, from his place of exile, contrived to communicate with the leaders of the opposition. He even gave them directions. 'Be calm and tranquil for the moment. Seem to become reconciled with Stalin. War is approaching. When it comes, the true Leninists will save the Socialist fatherland.'

In some cases events were so complicated that one can no longer distinguish between friends and enemies. A prominent member of the G.P.U., Sacha Blumkin, who in 1918 had assassinated the first German Ambassador, Von Mirbach, in Moscow, returned from Constantinople, where he was at the head of the network of Soviet espionage. He brought with him a letter from Trotzky, who wrote to Radek from Prinkipo. Radek, fearing a trap of the G.P.U., and suspecting that Blumkin might be an agent of Iagoda's, asked Stalin for an audience, and handed him the letter as a pledge of the sincerity of his conversion. Nevertheless, this did not prevent him from continuing to work in secret against Stalin in Comintern circles. Blumkin was shot for abusing his authority.

The content of the letter impressed Stalin profoundly. It determined the form taken by the final phase of his struggle against the opposition. Its consequences made it of such importance that it deserves to be reproduced here:

'*You asked me when we last met in Moscow what the tactics of the opposition ought to be. Here they are:*

[1] This refers to the war of 1914-18. It is true that the industrial development of the U.S.S.R. had attained gigantic proportions. But this was not due entirely to the action of the Sovietic governments. In the twentieth century the progress of industry had accelerated throughout the world, and had reached an astonishing pace, and the technical progress realized during the war and the next few years gave this development a fantastic impetus. On the other hand, from the close of the nineteenth century, and up to the Revolution, Imperial Russia had been effecting a 'normal' development, without the stimulus of revolution, which would undoubtedly have produced remarkable results.

'*Stalin is a man without any principles. He believes that his presence at the head of the Party is enough to ensure the victory of Socialism. From this point of view he is psychologically sincere, although the thirst for power, and the pleasure of displaying this power, play an important part in determining the behaviour of that morbid personality, Stalin.*[1]

'*But he is fundamentally the grave-digger of the proletarian revolution in the U.S.S.R. and throughout the entire world. . . . At a certain moment the régime will simply transform itself into a régime openly anti-working-class and anti-Socialist, despite its official ensign of a Socialist country.*

'*All that remains is to wait for the inevitable war, in which Stalin's régime is doomed to founder, to snatch the power from his hands and save the Socialist fatherland. Stalin's policy will lead the country toward the catastrophe; we shall then be justified in reversing it, as Clemenceau, at the time of the* 1914-18 *war, wished to overthrow the incapable government which had preceded it.*[2]

'*Certain comrades, above all the young men, ask whether it would not be more reasonable and easier to eliminate Stalin physically. I do not think so.*[3] . . .'

The letter, which is very long, ends with a glance at the situation of the U.S.S.R., the international situation, and the work of the foreign Communist parties. Blumkin, who was very proud of carrying so important a document, copied it and had a hundred duplicates made. Thus published, the letter was discussed in the opposition groups, and even in the prisons and the distant regions of Siberia, to which so many members of the opposition have been exiled.

Stalin, of course, was well aware of these tendencies. In order to prepare a decisive counter-attack he sent for Menjinsky and Iagoda. This was in May 1931.

---

[1]Mere objectivity compels us to admit that the description which Trotzky gives here would fit all the Communist leaders equally well.

[2]Trotzky's logic is certainly more than contestable. From the moment when the régime of Stalin is doomed to founder, one should forge ahead, instead of considering the vague plans of a Clemenceau who in any case had employed legal constitutional methods.

[3]There we have it ! Why all this verbiage if one is not to 'eliminate Stalin physically'—Stalin who is the source, the personification, and the symbol of all evils?

CHAPTER XXV

THE GREAT PURGE APPROACHES

FOR a long while past, Stalin had been considering a plan. He expounded his ideas in a long conversation with Menjinsky. The latter, ill and spitting blood, made notes of the conversation in the private diary which he kept hidden in his office safe.

'The more we persecute our opponents,' Menjinsky declared, 'the more popular they will be throughout the country. Remember the results of the Tsarist repression!'

Stalin did not agree with him. According to him, the Tsarist régime did not depend on any social class, apart from a few representatives of the nobility and the great landowners. On the contrary, his régime, born of the revolution, had created new and especially favoured strata: the whole of the bureaucracy of which Trotzky speaks, all the 'kolkhozians,' 'ennobled' by labour, with their special rewards, and all the Stakhanovists, with salaries ten times as large as the basic wage. By reinforcing the position of these social strata and decapitating the opposition one would consolidate the State. In a country like Russia, where the people have no tradition of popular government, a few millions of well-disciplined Party members, relying on five to ten millions of privileged citizens, will suffice to make the mechanism of the State proof against all attack.

There were a number of sensational trials, and the prisoners, found guilty, were sentenced to capital punishment. So far the accused were almost exclusively specialists—technicians, engineers, or officials 'without party ties,' who were in touch with the leaders of the opposition.

One by one, all the People's Commissariats were 'sifted.' The technique of obtaining confessions had been perfected by Iagoda. For that matter, it was quite familiar to the leaders of the opposition, who had seen it at work when they were still on the other side of the barricade. It had been known for some years past that Iagoda arrested the families of suspects in order to force the latter to confess. People knew, also, all the details of the 'third degree'—the use of the blinding lamp—a method universally employed—and the 'perpetual movement,' in which the accused were forced to run without resting round the 'anthropodrome' provided by the G.P.U.

In 1925-26, when the G.P.U. began its struggle against the enriched 'Nepmen,' these methods were applied to force the *nouveaux riches* to reveal their hiding-places and their savings. Trotzky, Zinoviev, Kamenev, Bukharin, and other promoters of the anti-bourgeois terror, were well acquainted with these methods, and had never protested to the Politburo—although at that period the least protest would have compelled the police to renounce such practices. But they were employed against 'class enemies,' which justified 'all and any means of conflict.' The men of the opposition, and their leaders, now had the methods applied to themselves which they had regarded as normal when they themselves were in power. The terrible police machine which was set going in order to crush them without pity was neither invented nor perfected by Stalin. It was an integral part of the Soviet State which Lenin and Trotzky had erected after the insurrection of October 1917.

But Stalin the statesman—and he had become a statesman—understood that it would not suffice to crush this opposition. It would be necessary to cement the new summit of the Party, to ensure its permanent cohesion, by an esoteric theory reserved for the exclusive use of the Russian summit of the new Communism.

On the 21 December, 1933, which was his fifty-fourth birthday, Stalin delivered an address before an intimate circle of friends and members of the Politburo, at which some of his private secretaries were present. Thanks to Gricha Kanner, we are able to record the details of this address; which was of capital importance in the ulterior development of the U.S.S.R.

'The doctrine of "Socialism in a single country," ' said Stalin, 'establishing a provisional autarchy in the U.S.S.R. while awaiting the victory of Socialism in other countries, grants us the possibility of defending our economic and social system, for an unlimited period, in a purely economic struggle, co-existing with the non-Sovietized sector of the world economy. But one danger is becoming more and more menacing: the danger of war with Hitlerian Germany. This danger determines the whole policy of the U.S.S.R., its diplomatic tactics, and the lines of its economic development.

'In order to reinforce the social fabric of the U.S.S.R. the Politburo will see to it that the percentage of favoured citizens becomes larger and larger. While in the *kolkhozes* there are 70 per cent of peasants who were of moderate means and are not contented with their present situation, there are 30 per cent of peasants and agricultural labourers who were poor and who have now experienced a veritable social elevation. They represent a sufficient foundation for a stable U.S.S.R. Among the labourers too the ratio of 30 per cent may be maintained. Thus the Sovietic State may be assured of a normal development.

'Within the Soviet State the Communist Party must remain the same "Order of professional Revolutionaries" as it was during the struggle against Tsarism. This is the more necessary inasmuch as the prospect of an inevitable war necessitates the renascence of a guided patriotism and an undercurrent of national pride calculated to strengthen the army. The same national plan necessitates reconciliation with the Church. Thanks to the Order of professional Revolutionaries, there is no danger of concessions of this kind leading to political degeneracy. . . .

'Those members of the Communist Party who occupy the more conspicuous posts will, of course, have a higher living standard than the ordinary workers. But they will enjoy this higher standard only as *organizers*, in order to ameliorate the conditions under which they work, and not as members of the Party. As soon as any one of them is demoted to another post of less importance to the State this apparent privilege *will have to be withdrawn*. . . .

'If we can make sure of a continual supply of young pupils in the school of Socialism, *our State will be able to survive indefinitely without any risk of the social degeneration which might be provoked by the inequality which we shall tolerate provisionally. It must not be forgotten that the realization of the Five-Year Plans and the elevation of the general standard of life will render this inequality less and less perceptible.*'

This address made a deep impression on those who heard it, though they had often been disconcerted by the gravity of the sufferings and sacrifices imposed upon the masses at the beginning of this first Five-Year Plan. Nadiejda Alliloueva embraced Stalin in public, saying: 'Now I understand the real meaning of your "general line." '

In his famous 'Letter to the Komsomolietz Ivanov,' published in *Pravda*, Stalin repeated the same theses in a more moderate form. Mekhliss, the editor-in-chief, gathered a few young friends about him in order to explain Stalin's esoteric dogma. 'But we must not only have a dictator,' he concluded. 'This leader must be the supreme source of the essential directives of the Party, which will itself be the cuirass of the State. We shall pass through a long and difficult period: and during the whole of this period our Secretary-General must be blindly and unfailingly obeyed, as the supreme and infallible authority of the Party. . . .'

It was Mekhliss who undertook the task of glorifying Stalin, who from this moment was embarked on a process of veritable deification. The principle had to be translated into reality without delay. *Pravda* began by filling its pages with references to Stalin by which the dictator was elevated to the level of Lenin and Marx. Mekhliss's description of 'Leninism-Stalinism' became the official designation of Stalin's 'general line.'

Innumerable addresses from kolkhozians and workers—declarations from the remotest corners of the U.S.S.R.—written in more or less flowery language, never ceased henceforth to give support to the veritable personal cult of Stalin, and an official legend endeavoured to date the first manifestations of the 'genius of the Father of the Peoples' from the period before the revolution. The historical truth was, of course, disregarded.

It will be understood that the 'old ones' were not prepared to accept the transformation of the Koba of yesterday into the ruling genius of today. Radek, who in his new post of 'Rector of the University of the Workers of the East' enjoyed a good deal of leisure, took this opportunity of asking the celebrated question: 'Who will be the infallible commentator of Marx after Stalin's death?—Comrade Budienny's mare!'

The quip was repeated everywhere. It was repeated to Stalin, to Radek's misfortune. After the affair of Trotzky's letter Stalin had regarded him with some confidence, but in 1937 his jest landed him in the prison of Iakutsk. Other enemies of Stalin's published pamphlets or leaflets in which they ridiculed the new dogma of personal glorification, describing him, in Trotzky's jargon, as 'the grave-digger,' 'the Thermidorian,' or 'the Bonaparte in power.'

Iagoda soon discovered the authors and printers of these attacks. Most of them were sentenced to ten years' imprisonment and per-petual deportation to Siberia. Some, who 'confessed' to being agents in the service of foreign systems of espionage, were shot. For the moment the victims were persons of secondary importance only. But blood was flowing, and blood calls for blood. Presently it began to flow from higher and higher sources.

Serge Kirov, an extremely influential member of the Politburo, and the friend of Stalin, to whom the latter had dedicated his book: 'To my dear friend and beloved brother,' was the chairman of the Leningrad Committee. He publicly approved of these measures: 'These are the lees of our Party; degenerates, paid agents of foreign powers, scum, lustful vipers.[1] They must all be pitilessly exterminated. . . .'

And as though to go one better than Mekhliss, he assured the local Committee of Leningrad: 'It is the greatest good fortune that our country has a Stalin at its head. He can bring about a Ninth of Thermidor without Barras, an Eighteenth Brumaire without Bona-parte, remaining always what he is: a revolutionary genius, an experienced tactician, a man who is building Socialism, and who will one day build it on the ruins of the old, rotten capitalist system. All our hopes are in Stalin, our well-beloved chieftain and our master, the great master of the world's workers. Those who are yapping at his heels are ignoble rascals who deserve a revolver-bullet in the nape of the neck.'[2]

The head of the Leningrad G.P.U., Medvied, by way of an echo of this discourse, executed nineteen members of the Communist youth who had belonged to the secret committee of the opposition, and who as a matter of geographical convenience were described as 'Finnish spies.'

The third bloody period of the U.S.S.R. was beginning.

---

[1] He was the first to employ this expression, which enjoyed great popularity.
[2] His appreciation would be kept in mind by the executioners of the G.P.U.

CHAPTER XXVI

EXTERMINATION OF THE OPPOSITION: THE FIRST PHASE

STALIN's esoteric doctrine has undoubtedly a certain moral value. Applied to the realities of life, it led to a series of measures of which one cannot speak without shuddering. The most appalling thing about it is that the internal logic of the theory is bound to lead to the practices followed by the Soviet Government, and that *politically speaking it is justified*. But in order to realize an enterprise so ruthless and so cruel, one must possess such obstinacy and natural insensibility as are fortunately not vouchsafed to the great majority of human beings.

In January 1934 the Seventeenth Congress of the Communist Party assembled. Its 1,225 delegates with deliberative votes and its 736 consultative delegates represented 1,900,000 members of the Party and 1,000,000 probationers, or about 3,000,000 Communists grouped under the standard of 'Leninism-Stalinism.' It is they who form the framework of the Sovietic State.

In his political report Stalin described it as a 'Congress of Conquerors': 'Our country has rid itself of its mediaeval and outdated envelope. From an agrarian country it has become an industrial country. From a country of small individual holdings the U.S.S.R. has been transformed into a land of expansive collectivist and mechanized agriculture. . . . Socialist industry represents 99 per cent of the total industry of the country. Socialist agriculture occupies 88 per cent of the whole cultivated area. . . .'

A new Politburo was elected. It comprised: Stalin, Molotov, Kouibychev, Ordjonikidzé, Vorochilov, Kalinin, Kirov, Andréev, Petrosky, Tchoubar, Mikoyan, and Lazar Kaganovitch. The deputy members were: Beria, secretary of the Committee of Transcaucasia and head of the Tiflis G.P.U., Voznossensky, the new President of the planning Commission, Jdanov, second Secretary in Leningrad, Iéjov, the new third Secretary of the Central Committee, and Cherbakov, the new secretary of the Moscow Committee. The young men were thus well represented.

Stalin, in order to keep the power in his own hands, had to hold on to the tiller with all his might. Despite arrests, deportations and executions, the secret committees of the opposition continued their activities. The programme of the younger malcontents was becoming ardently revolutionary. They no longer demanded 'a *coup d'état* inside the Party'; they issued appeals to the peasants and workers and officials, calling upon them to overthrow 'the ignoble régime of oppression installed by Djugachvili.' Trotzky, from his exile in Barbizon, sent more and more definite instructions. His son, Leo Siedov, wrote openly: 'One need not be scrupulous as to the tactics and methods to be employed in the struggle against Djugachvili. A tyrant deserves to be fought as a tyrant.'

This was the appeal to the knife.

The whole fabric of the U.S.S.R threatened to collapse if its rulers betrayed the least weakness. In March a serious discovery was made in the Kremlin. A pharmacist employed in the Kremlin nursing-home—Moïse Rosenfeld, a nephew of Kamenev's—had proposed to poison several members of the Politburo. He had also made plans for a military *coup d'état*, thanks to the complicity of the military commandant of the Kremlin, Peterson, a Lett. They were denounced by a confederate, Pastukhov. The opposition insisted that the entire conspiracy was a provocation engineered by Pastukhov, an agent of Iagoda's. Rosenfeld and the conspirators confessed that they wanted 'to get rid of Stalin and his Politburo and regenerate the leadership of the Party.'

This time there was a fight to the death between the principal Communist leaders. All caution was thrown to the winds, and no one recalled the posthumous advice of Lenin. This was not a conflict between class enemies, but an internecine battle between fractions of the Party whose limits were vague in the extreme.

During this period—a crucial period for him—Stalin, who trusted no one, subjected Rosenfeld and his accomplices to a personal interrogation. His confidence in Iagoda, who after Menjinsky's death had become the head of the G.P.U., with the title of 'Commissary-General for the security of the State' was not complete. Menjinsky's private diary, found by Redenss and submitted to

Stalin, told the latter that he could not place absolute confidence in the heads of the secret police.

Rosenfeld declared that Kamenev and Zinoviev were completely ignorant of the conspiracy, but that its political aim was in correspondence with the slogan, 'Back to the Politburo of Lenin.' A number of executions followed. Kamenev and Zinoviev, who had certainly been on the fence for years past, were tried by a secret tribunal and sentenced to five years' imprisonment for moral complicity. Their long journey to the grave had begun.

In the summer of 1934 Kirov unearthed a conspiracy amidst the garrison of Petrozavodsk, in Soviet Karelia. At its head was the chief of the local government. Fifty-six members of the Party were executed. In August there was fresh trouble in the Ural. A secret centre of opposition had been organized at Sverdlovsk by the secretary of the Ural Committee, Tabakov, and his assistant, Lepa. These two were in touch with centres of the secret opposition in Leningrad, Moscow, Tiflis and Kiev, and had entered into relations with Kamenev and Zinoviev, who were serving their prison sentences in the Ural.

In the secret correspondence which had been discovered Stalin was described as a 'miniature tyrant,' an 'amoral degenerate,' and a 'Genghis Khan.' The writers advocated 'a revolt inside the Party which would throw Stalin and his "tail" of depraved climbers into the refuse-bin.' They also demanded the return of Kamenev and Zinoviev, who would re-establish the true political line of revolutionary Leninism. The head of the G.P.U. in the Ural—Deitsch, a friend of Iagoda—was in touch with the secret Centre. Pamphlets had been produced by the police printing-press at Sverdlovsk.

The 'Stalinites' and their enemies were now caught up in a mesh of circumstances from which neither could escape save by the destruction of the adverse party. To refrain from the crucial engagement would have been equivalent to suicide. One hundred and forty-five members of the Party were shot after confessing that they were spies and saboteurs. Technicians and specialists, charged with similar offences, who had spent two years in the prisons of the Ural, confessed to having received directions from the 'secret centre.' Their confessions were made on the understanding that they would be pardoned; nevertheless, they were shot. The affair of the 'clandestine centre' was marked by the forfeit of 350 lives.

On returning to Moscow, Kirov proposed that the Politburo should deal finally with Kamenev, Zinoviev, and their friends, now in the prisons of the Oufa. Once more Stalin gave proof of his prudence. Despite the difficulties of the moment, he always bore the future in mind. It would obviously have been convenient to get rid of such obstinate enemies; they would continue to cause disturbances and to justify them by describing them as 'Leninism.' But he felt that he should not liquidate the two ex-members of the Politburo and the ten ex-members of the Central Committee so long as they enjoyed a certain prestige in the eyes of many Party members, and so long as they could still function as the standard-bearers of the opposition.

But the ground was shifting under Stalin's feet as he advanced, and fresh dangers were threatening him on every hand. Iagoda complained that Kirov was plotting to supplant him at the head of the service. He described him as an adventurer, and produced a dossier according to which Kirov, while serving in Astrakhan as head of the political section of the army, had married the widow of a White officer—herself a spy of Denikin's—who had disappeared soon after her marriage, taking with her some secret military plans of the greatest importance.

On the following day Iagoda, after listening to the encouraging advice of his colleagues, called on Stalin in order to give him the Kirov dossier. Their interview was private; but Stalin's secretaries, who were at work in the next room, saw that Iagoda was deeply flushed when he took his leave. Stalin, who accompanied him, said· 'I warn you that I hold you entirely responsible for ensuring that the contents of this filthy thing that you call a dossier shall never become known.'

After Iagoda's departure Stalin himself burned the dossier in his office fireplace.

On the 1 December, 1934, something happened that started the great repression which Stalin had for years been meditating, but had hesitated to begin. Kirov was assassinated on the premises of the Party Committee of Leningrad.

For once, Stalin did not restrain his wrath. He ordered a special train so that he could hurry to Leningrad and conduct the inquiry into the affair in person. When Iagoda turned up at the railway station as though to accompany him, he informed him, brutally: 'On this train I have no need of you nor of your services.'

Iagoda himself asked for an engine to take him to Leningrad. The railway officials refused to oblige him. A paradoxical situation: the head of the G.P.U., before whom the whole of the U.S.S.R. trembled, could not even impose his will upon the railway officials. Evidently the latter were protected by an order from Stalin himself. But Iagoda did not admit defeat. He had an old aeroplane at his disposal, a U-2. He flew off, taking four hours to cover the 350 miles from Moscow to Leningrad, arriving before Stalin.

The murderer, Nicolaev, declared that he had killed Kirov out of jealousy. Kirov was his wife's lover. But Nicolaev was an ex-member of the G.P.U. of Leningrad, and had made use of a pass signed by Medvied. He was also a member of an organization in touch with the secret centre of the opposition. Interrogated by Stalin in person, Nicolaev insisted that his only motive had been jealousy.

The affair was followed by a veritable avalanche of reprisals. For once, Stalin seems to have lost his sangfroid and to have done what he had never done before: he openly accepted responsibility for the executions that followed. In addition to the members of the camouflaged opposition of Leningrad, of whom 467 were shot, several thousand members of the same group, who had been arrested or deported during the last three years, were executed in prison or in their place of exile, often in the Arctic regions, where they obviously could not have been involved in the attack upon Kirov.

This was the beginning of the abject career of the bloodiest 'purger' of all times—Nicolas Iéjov. Stalin sent him to Minsk, Kharkov and Kiev in order to 'sift' the heads of the G.P.U. Balitsky was arrested as an accomplice of Skrypnik,[1] who as a monarchist student had belonged, before the Revolution, to a group of the extreme Right. Pilar von Pilschau, head of the Minsk G.P.U., was shot as 'a Baltic baron who had entered the Party by trickery.'[2] It

[1]A member of the Politburo of the Ukraine accused of separatism. He committed suicide.

[2]Pilar von Pilschau was admitted to the Party on the personal recommendation of Lenin, who knew him well. He was responsible for the famous 'capture of Savinkov,' lured into Russia in 1924 by Pilar's secret agents in Warsaw.

was recalled that Balitsky and Pilar had conferred with Iagoda before the latter had submitted to Stalin a dossier incriminating Kirov. It was obvious that Iagoda's own position was anything but secure.

Kamenev and Zinoviev were tried for a second time in Leningrad, whither they were brought from their Siberian prison. After a conversation with Stalin they admitted their moral complicity in the assassination in exchange for the promise that they would not be executed. They were condemned to ten years' imprisonment and sent to the notorious 'insulator prison' of Yakutsk.

The reprisals covered the whole country. Stalin returned to his former principle of disclaiming all responsibility. He was attempting to stand apart from and in a certain sense above the purge; when orders were given they emanated officially from one of the numerous organs of power, but never from him.

It was not enough to dispose of the Old Bolsheviks physically. Confessions had to be extracted from them. Kamenev, Zinoviev and others had to admit their 'moral complicity' in the assassination, and their offences, not against Stalin, but against the Party. The Party emerged from the internal rupture with undiminished prestige, since the heads of the opposition accused themselves merely of having acted as 'bad Bolsheviks,' and admitted that under these conditions the punishment which would be inflicted upon them would be justified. As for Stalin, in the eyes of the masses he had to appear, in a sense, a victim of fatality, powerless to oppose the onward progress of that justice of the Party and the country which functioned with all its collective mechanisms in such wise that he personally could not change its direction. The necessities of Communism are as pitiless as the Fate of the Greek tragedies.

On a journey to Kislovidsk, Stalin went first of all to see his intimate friend, Ordjonikidzé, who for the past year had been seriously ill. In the presence of Mekhliss he endeavoured to convince his friend of the absolute necessity of 'radically liquidating the abscess of the opposition by tearing out its deepest roots.' There was a lengthy discussion.

'I can't accept the execution of these companions of Lenin under a disgraceful accusation,' Ordjonikidzé maintained. 'We shall discredit our Party in the U.S.S.R. and abroad. The Committee could not survive such executions.'

Mekhliss, in his articles, made subsequent reference to the theories and arguments which Stalin developed in order to convince his friend. They were represented as a long dialogue.

'The unity of our Party, its absolute unity, is the only guarantee of victory in the coming war,' said Stalin. 'These fellows conspire even in prison; they are dreaming of the war which is coming and which will enable them to overthrow us. The least set-backs in this war they will utilize against us. It is precisely their reputation as Lenin's old companions that makes them more dangerous than the emigrés abroad. They could destroy the Party itself. And without the framework of the Party the Soviet State could not survive. ... . The fact that they are alive is enough. If there is ever the least possibility of complicity on the part of the G.P.U. and Iagoda, they will deliberately set themselves up as the spiritual leaders of the revolt. . . . Then it will be too late, and we shall only be increasing the most serious risks. Be frank: are you certain that they won't do everything they can to attack us, even if the only possibility of doing so took the form of a military defeat?'

Ordjonikidzé gave an evasive reply. Stalin insisted.

'They will destroy us, and they will throw a dead cat on our tomb and on the tomb of our State.[1] *We must be the first to throw the dead cat.*'[2]

After this discussion Stalin convoked the other members of the Politburo to a conference in Molotov's villa. This figures in the history of the struggle against the opposition as the 'Third Conference of the Kislovodsk Troglodytes.' It was decided unanimously that Zinoviev and Kamenev should be retried. Ordjonikidzé responded by writing a letter in which he broke off all friendly relations with Stalin and the other members of the Politburo. This was his last political gesture; a little later he committed suicide.

On returning to Moscow Stalin himself supervised the preparations for the trial. The new public prosecutor, Vichinsky, an old Baku acquaintance, was entrusted with the inquiry and the interrogatories. A special prison called 'the prison of the Politburo,' was

[1] A Georgian custom: when a man has killed his enemy by vendetta, he throws a dead cat on his grave.

[2] By this Stalin means that who have been executed must be discredited in the eyes of the nation.

prepared at Lefortovo, near Moscow. Iagoda had not the right to enter this prison.

Stalin was often present at the interrogations. Sometimes he had long conversations with the accused. Mekhliss, in exchanging opinions with the members of Stalin's secretariat, said that the Secretary-General of the Party requested the accused to express their contrition in order to prove that they were truly ready to do anything to serve the Party, as they had done when they spoke from the platform during the Seventeenth Congress. There they had pledged themselves, having admitted their 'grave and unpardonable offences, to do everything in future to merit the forgiveness of the Party and to serve it in accordance with the commands of Lenin, without regard for their lives, and by executing all the orders of the Party and its leaders—the Politburo and the Secretary-General.' It was of this pledge that Stalin was reminding them. Since after the last trial he had kept his promise, and since despite their admissions they were sentenced only to ten years' imprisonment, they continued to hope.

While preparations were made for the trial, a ruthless purge was inflicted on the foreign Communist parties, and especially on those of adjacent countries. Ninety per cent of the foreign Communists living in the U.S.S.R. were shot as spies of their governments. It must be recognized that some spies had really slipped in among these foreigners, but it is equally certain that the percentage of such spies was negligible. The more prominent members of the foreign parties were called to Moscow so that they might be arrested and deported to Siberia or executed.

The new president of the Comintern, George Dimitrov, the hero of the Reichstag trial, lent his authority to this implacable 'purge.' It was actually an 'internal' operation on the Communist world. The majority of the victims were the 'real, genuine' Marxists. But the liberal, *bourgeois* world, which had been in the past extremely feeble in its reactions when the Bolsheviks were exterminating the *bourgeois*, whom they described as 'class enemies,' were now perturbed by the massacre, although its victims were responsible for ruthless destruction in the past. By such a paradox as history has often recorded, humanitarianism showed itself utterly inconsistent, extending its sympathies in a selective manner which could be explained by nothing more than total ignorance of the facts.

By a special decision, the Politburo ordered the verification and renewal of the membership cards of the Russian party. Henceforth membership of the Party would be individual; groups would no longer be admitted as a whole.

During this drastic purge the new Constitution of 1936 was published, 'the most democratic in the world,' which, if it were applied in the spirit of its provisions, might well correspond with that definition. Tremendous popular festivals were held throughout the country, and in Moscow, under the presiding genius of Stalin. The new slogan was: 'How good it is to live in the U.S.S.R.!' At the moment when they were preparing to strike the hardest blow at the heart of the Party, Stalin and Mekhliss did their utmost to show the dictator's solicitude for the masses of the people.

In August 1936 the trial took place of Zinoviev and Kamenev, together with Evdokinov, Bakaiev, Pikel, I. Simonov, Mratchkovsky and others. They publicly confessed to crimes which it was materially impossible for them to have committed, and even while confessing to them they protested their indefectible attachment to the Communist Party and their fidelity to the Party and all its commands. They seemed actually to vie with one another in their professions of faith, and in confessing the phases of their moral degeneration. The world, which could make but little of the whole affair, was surprised and disconcerted, and quite a number of literary men seized the opportunity of writing successful 'psychological' novels.

The accused were sentenced to death. The Supreme Council of the U.S.S.R., elected by universal suffrage, and the supreme legislative body, in which Stalin was a simple deputy, rejected their appeal. Kamenev, Zinoviev, Smirnov and Ter-Vaganian asked to see Stalin. He visited Kamenev only and had a long talk with the prisoner in his cell.

CHAPTER XXVII

EXTERMINATION OF THE OPPOSITION: THE SECOND PHASE

THE trial of Zinoviev and Kamenev echoed through the world like a thunderclap. In the U.S.S.R. the impression was literally overwhelming; and within the Party the dismay and exasperation of the members were extreme. Ordjonikidzé was right; the first executions inevitably led to other executions, and to further suicides.

Stalin was mistaken: the measures taken were not enough to render the opposition powerless. The emotional reaction throughout the country was unfavourable to him. During the close of the trial the Tchekists on guard in the court house, with their commander-in-chief, Major Dubovitch, at their head,[1] were seen to weep when Kamenev, aged and bent, in a pathetic peroration asked his family to forgive him for the suffering he had caused them.[2] He recalled the fact that this was the third time he had stood before a Soviet tribunal. In an indirect fashion he explained the political reasons for his 'confessions.'

'The war is approaching. It will expose our country to deadly peril. We must stand united around Stalin in order to avoid defeat and catastrophe. All that diminishes the absolute and supreme authority of Stalin threatens our Soviet land with deadly danger. . . .'

One feels that during his talk with Kamenev in the prison cell Stalin may have expounded his 'esoteric dogma,' as developed by Mekhliss.

Not long after the execution of the prisoners, Iagoda fell into disgrace. In September 1936 the head of the G.P.U., Marshal of the Tchekist forces, was dismissed without explanation and appointed Commissar . . . for Posts and Telegraphs! His place was taken by

---

[1]Under the name of Ianovitch he had been in Paris as the representative of the G.P.U. when General Kutiépoff was kidnapped.

[2]His family had been placed under arrest in order to expedite his 'confessions.'

Nicolas Ivanovitch Iéjov, Secretary to the Central Committee. A cantankerous little man, suffering from tuberculosis, he was of working-class origin, and he detested all the representatives of the revolutionary intelligentsia. He was generally hated. With the instinctive malice of the incurable, he selected for assistant a certain Zakovsky, from Odessa, a sometime quack and a pickpocket, who in 1917 became the leader of a group of 'Anarchist Individualists,' who distinguished themselves by a series of robberies, rapes and murders. His headquarters in Kharkov—at 5 Sadovo-Kulikovskaia Street—soon became a regular storehouse of stolen articles. In 1918 he joined the Bolshevik Party, and in the Tcheka became the head of the 'Section of Combat against Banditry.' He was particularly well known for his direct participation in 'cellar' executions, and for his trick of shooting accused persons in his own office. Appointed to Leningrad after the assassination of Kirov, he introduced practices there beside which those of his predecessor Bakaiev, were extremely anodyne.

Iéjov and Zadovsky got to work. In November 1936 Iéjov submitted a report to the Politburo, in which he demanded plenary powers for the 'great purge.' They were granted unanimously.

While Iéjov was at work inside the Party, and even within the ranks of Iagoda's forces, Stalin continued to accelerate the industrialization of the country, and to develop a definite foreign policy. We know that among the Marxists, whatever the matter actually in question, it was the universal rule to proceed by way of establishing a thesis, antithesis, and synthesis, in accordance with Hegelian theory. Stalin went to work in the same way, but all his Marxist theses were in the last resort adapted to the necessities and requirements of the national continuity of Russia.

The ideological scion imported by Lenin was undergoing a progressive transformation under the influence of the stock into which it was grafted. Communism was no longer an ideal which one sought to realize at any cost. It had adapted itself to the vital needs of a people which was beginning, after and during all its trials, to enter upon a stage of convalescence.

Trotzky's prophecies were being realized. He, from beyond the frontiers, had never ceased to attack Stalin, accusing him of 'liquidating the Revolution,' of dragging the country into the paths of a *bourgeois* nationalism, and of consecrating the final betrayal of the 'revolution in permanence.' He also fulminated against the execution of the Bolshevik leaders of the earliest vintage, forgetting that he had collaborated with them at the time of the anti-bourgeois terror, and that during the Civil War he had been responsible for the execution of tens of thousands of human beings, even if they were Communists.

In the interior, Iéjov was elaborating the plan of a new purge, to be carried out by the G.P.U., which had now become the new Gugobezs, the Department of State Security in the Commissariat of the Interior—the N.K.V.D.[1] In his detailed reports he kept the Politburo informed of his labours.

Lists of suspects had been drawn up which comprised *only members of the Party*. The purge began with the N.K.V.D. itself, 'in order to root out Iagoda's people.' The Commissariat for Foreign Affairs was rapidly purged of 'foreign spies.' The Commissariat for War was subjected to a 'verification.' At the same time, in the Ukraine, the Caucasus, Bielo-Russia and Uzbekistan, 'separatist traitors to the Socialist fatherland' were eliminated.

Petrovsky, Tchoubar, Béria, Kaganovitch, Mikoyan and Kalinin did what they could to check the ardour of the 'great purifier and glorious chief of Soviet counter-espionage,' as the terrified editors of Moscow were already calling Iéjov.

But Stalin supported him, though without committing himself. 'In affairs of this sort,' he said, 'it is better to strike hard rather than leave intact any nests of dangerous enemies. Remember the wars of religion, and the inquisitor who said that God would recognize the innocent later on and separate them from the guilty. Nicolas Ivanovitch is our inquisitor. He will submit his accounts to the Party later on.'

Nicolas Ivanovitch felt that he had been given his head. He arrested, according to his lists, all the ex-members of the opposition who had repented and had been readmitted to the Party: Piatakov, president of the State Bank, Sokolnikov, Bukharin, Krestinsky, Rakovsky, Rykov, Radek, Serebriakov, and many thousand persons of minor importance. Tomsky committed suicide when the agents of the N.K.V.D. came to arrest him.

[1]The N.K.V.D., the Commissariat of the People in the Interior, afterwards became the M.V.D., the Ministry of the Interior.

Even in the N.K.V.D. itself Iéjov and Zakovsky assembled the senior officials, surrounded them with guards drawn from a provincial detachment, and treated them to a discourse which began as follows: 'You people here are all scoundrels, spies, traitors, mercenaries sold to the enemy. . . .'

One evening Redenss entered Iéjov's office, and, in Zakovsky's presence, spat in his face. Iéjov shot him down with his revolver. In the same way he killed Ivan Miejlaouk, an old Bolshevik, ex-Commissar of the Soviet pavilion in the Paris Exposition. That same day he informed the Politburo that Bulanov, sometime Iagoda's secretary, arrested in December 1936, had confessed that Iagoda had told him to 'sprinkle the walls of Iéjov's office with a vaporizer containing a poisonous gas.' Iagoda, being arrested, had already confessed his crime, and also his participation in the murder of Kirov, the poisoning of Menjinsky, Maxim Gorki, and Kulovshev, and finally, his intention to poison Stalin.

The officials of the old G.P.U. were now living in a veritable inferno. They were shot down without trial in the very cellar in which they had executed so many other victims. In Moscow, 187 were so executed; in the provinces, nearly 3,000. One thing is certain —that if by some miracle the 'Whites' could have seized the power in the U.S.S.R., they would never have exterminated as many gold-laced Tchekists as did Nicolas Iéjov. Thus Immanent Justice appeared to manifest itself by striking those who for eighteen years had been the vilest of assassins. But in order to do so it assumed an aspect no less hideous.

More than 4,000 members of the opposition were shot without trial. Then, once more, two spectacular trials were staged. Piatakov, Radek, Rakovsky, Rykov (ex-President of the Council), Bukharin (the scholarly theorist), Préobrajensky, Grinko, Krestinsky, Sokolnikov, were brought to trial. A secret tribunal condemned the diplomatists Karakhan, Zuckermann and others. Ienukidzé was shot about this time, although he had relied on his volume of reminiscences, in which he extolled Stalin.

This execution of Stalin's most intimate friend alarmed the ruling circles. Henceforth no one could feel safe from Iéjov. Stalin, who, when 'the cause' was in question, had no regard for the ties of friendship, was logical even when his own feelings were involved.

His was an inhuman logic, but he obeyed it without flinching.

Ienukidzé's Christian name was Abel. Trotzky took advantage of this when in one of his articles he put the Biblical question to Stalin: 'Cain, what hast thou done with thy brother Abel? Cain Djugachvili shall be thy name in Russian history after this hateful murder.' The retort was immediate. Mekhliss ordered the Sovietic press to give Trotzky the surname of 'Judas.'

The great penance was nearing its culmination in the purging of the army. One could already feel which way the wind was blowing when Radek, in the course of his trial, recalled his relations with Colonel Smutny, aide-de-camp to Marshal Tutkatchevsky. Here was an undeniable clue.

The affair presented no complexities. Feeling that their hour had struck, a number of the military leaders decided to defend themselves. They knew that only one thing could save them—the disappearance of Stalin, who was overturning the established order of things in the Politburo. General Sinilov, the new commander of the Moscow garrison, was regarded by them as capable of organizing an attempt upon Stalin during one of the military reviews in the Red Square.

Two men were at the head of this conspiracy, which never got beyond an embryonic form: Marshal Tutkatchevsky, and an army commander of the first rank, Yakir. They were of different social origin. Tutkatchevsky belonged to the lesser nobility. An officer of the Imperial Army, he entered the Red Army in the hope of becoming a Bonaparte.[1] He was an extremely gifted officer, and the real creator of the modern Red Army. Yakir, a Jew from Kichinev, ex-anarchist, ex-student of Odessa University, was promoted divisional commander in 1919, during the civil war in the Ukraine.

When Tutkatchevsky went to London to attend the funeral of George V he was a guest at a social evening organized for the Soviet generals by the military attaché of the U.S.S.R. in France, Krantz-Vientzov, living at 24 Avenue de Saxe. In the course of a conversation respecting the anti-Stalinian opposition, Yakir, a fervent admirer of Trotzky, expressed the opinion that the army must long for his return. No more was said then, but the G.P.U. was informed,

[1] So he told a French officer, a fellow-prisoner in Germany, who published a volume of reminiscences in Paris.

and all those present were inscribed on Iéjov's famous list of suspects.[1]
When Tutkatchevsky felt that danger was threatening him from
Iéjov he tried to get into contact with Radek, in order to establish a
'political platform' for his agreements with Sinilov, a convinced
member of the Party, who would never have done anything without
obtaining some sort of direct political patronage for his action.

Radek himself was on the point of being arrested. He betrayed
Tutkatchevsky, as he had betrayed Blumkin.[2] This enabled Iéjov to
compromise Tutkatchevsky politically, for it would not have been
possible to execute one of the most popular marshals of the U.S.S.R.
on account of a dispute in the Party ranks. By means of double-faced
agents abroad, he managed to provide the too confiding services of
several foreign countries with false information regarding Tutkatchevsky's intended act of treason in favour of Germany. This information reached that guileless politician, Benès, who immediately
forwarded it to Stalin.

On the 1 May, 1937, Tutkatchevsky was present at yet another
military review in the Red Square. But he was no longer commandant of the military district of Moscow; he had just been appointed to the district of the Volga. His disgrace was obvious; there
was a vacuum about him. When, as usual, he went to mount the
governmental platform and take his place beside Stalin, two officials
of the G.P.U. barred his passage. During the ceremony he remained
on ground level, among the small fry.

Early in June, Vorochilov convoked, in his Moscow office, all
those who had taken part in the banquet at 24 Avenue de Saxe, and
also their friends. They were Tutkatchevsky, Yakir, Putna, Kork,
Eidemann, Ouborévitch, Krantz-Vientzov, and a few others. They
found themselves facing a complete council of war: Budienny,
Blucher, Vorochilov, Iégorov, Timochenko and Chapochnikov.
The army would soon have to play a decisive part in a war which
Stalin regarded as inevitable, so he preferred to preserve appearances.

After the first executions of the 11 June, 1937, others

[1]The story of the banquet at 24 Avenue de Saxe, and the details of the
Tutkatchevsky affair, were told in 1939 by the Soviet General Krivitzky, sometime
chief assistant to Tazvedupr (Second Bureau) and published in the Novy Mir.
Krivitzky himself was assassinated in 1940 by Soviet agents.
[2]Radek succeeded in saving his life. He was not sentenced to be shot, but died
later on in the Yakutsk prison.

followed; but the names of those executed were not made public.[1]

The 'great purge' of the soldiers was the last step before the stabilization of the quasi-theocratic régime which Stalin and his group had perfected on the eve of the second world war. Repression, like all the proceedings of the State, has its internal logic. It could end only with the disappearance of the grand inquisitor Iéjov.

The 'glorious chief of Soviet counter-espionage' had become the second most important man in the U.S.S.R. The extermination of the officials of Iagoda's G.P.U. had earned him the greatest popularity throughout the country, and especially in rural districts, which had suffered so much from their exploits during the period of collectivization.

'Iéjov is our avenger,' said the peasants.

Undoubtedly Iéjov was abnormal. Had he not been so he could never have performed the horrible task which he had undertaken. Once he had begun, he could not stop, and his psychological mechanism revolved upon a single idea, which had become a real obsession; to discover fresh conspiracies.

On the strength of the 'confessions' of several members of the Government of the Ukrainian Republic whom he had executed, he accused two members of the Politburo, Tchoubar and Petrovsky, of being 'secret separatists.' Tchoubar was excluded from the Politburo and deported. Petrovsky, already shaken by the execution of his brother, died of fear and resentment.

The last prominent victim of Iéjov's was Marshal Blucher. Iéjov accused him, after he had defeated the Japanese on the hills of Tchang-Kou-Feng, of being . . . a Japanese spy. Blucher hanged himself after arrest in order to avoid the humiliation of being interrogated.

This was the last drop that made the vessel overflow. Vorochilov proposed to send Mekhliss to Khabarovsk in order to investigate the charges made against Blucher. At the same time a number of members of the Politburo, including Béria, himself a prominent Tchekist, demanded the cessation of the purges, which had lost all political meaning. In response, Iéjov in person presented to Stalin a report on the members of the Politburo who were 'compromised' and in-

[1] The Red Army colonel, C. Kalinov, in his book, *The Sovietic Marshals Address You*, gives the numbers of the victims of the military purge.

cluded in his dossier. Vorochilov, Béria, Koganovitch, Mikoyan, Voznessensky, and even Molotov figured among the suspects! To this report Zakovsky added a note in his own hand concerning the interrogation of those who had denounced the members of the Politburo: 'The confessions were made by the accused without constraint and on their own initiative.'

This may have been true. The accused, having made fantastic confessions in respect of their own crimes, may have felt that it was in their interest to involve the members of the Politburo in their affairs, in the hope of gaining time.

But Stalin seized the opportunity of calling a halt to the 'bloody saraband.' Not having *officially* accepted any personal responsibility at the beginning of the operation, he could not himself take the initiative in bringing it to an end. He might one day be reproached for not stopping it sooner. In giving way to the collective initiative of the Politburo, he remained in the background. He left the entire responsibility for the whole operation to the Politburo. The principle of never giving direct orders, and of keeping himself aloof from the melée, was strictly observed.

The decision to have done with purges was adopted without discussion. It was obvious that the authors of the purges, Zakovsky and Iéjov, would have to disappear. Zakovsky was cashiered, accused of sadism, and shot. It was impossible to deal so expeditiously with Iéjov. He had been too conspicuous and too highly placed. Like Rykov and Iagoda, he became Commissar of Posts and Telegraphs. Then, quite unobtrusively, a gathering of physicians of the N.K.V.D. declared him insane. He was interned in an asylum near Leningrad, and on the day of his arrival he hanged himself from a tree in the park.[1]

Béria succeeded to his post. A number of Commissions of rehabilitation were set up in the interests of the members of the Party, and the officers in exile and in prison. Among those rehabilitated were the future Marshal Rokossovsky and General Rodimtzev. More than 6,000 officers, officials, engineers, professors and journalists were liberated. Stalin would soon have need of them.

---

[1]According to certain military refugees, who wrote of the incident after the second world war, a placard was hung round the neck of the corpse. It bore the words: 'I am carrion.' This was his 'spontaneous confession.'

CHAPTER XXVIII

THE APOTHEOSIS OF STALIN

THE struggle within the Party and the purges were over at last. Stalin decided when they should stop, as he decided when the collectivization should cease. He addressed the nation in order to consecrate the new state of affairs, and emitted the slogan: *Our most precious capital is man. We must appreciate this capital and give it the attention it deserves.*

The framework of the Soviet State was strengthened and consolidated. Agriculture, since the collectivization, was practised on new foundations, and its yield had increased. The industrialization of the country was far advanced and the great masses of the people had gained in security. The 'privileged individuals of the régime,' whom Stalin had reckoned to be 30 per cent of the population, were beginning to feel comfortable. They were no longer afraid of the régime, since they were born in it, and represented its framework. Throughout the country tremendous popular manifestations were organized, the culminating point being the festivals of the nationalities of the U.S.S.R., which were held in the Red Square.

But all Stalin's activities were influenced by anxiety in respect of the international situation, which in the Kremlin's opinion was becoming more and more menacing. Once again Stalin addressed the nation. His intention was plain: it was to give the non-party citizens a renewed faith in themselves and their future: without such faith they could not be asked to agree to the sacrifices which the war already on the horizon would render inevitable. Once more Stalin defined the rôle of the Communist Party in the U.S.S.R.

'One may accept it as a general rule that as long as the Bolsheviks preserve their ties with the great masses of the people they will be unconquerable. But let them lose contact with the masses, let them break their alliance with them, and they will rust and lose their strength and become nullities.[1]

'The mythology of the Greeks numbers among its heroes the celebrated Antaeus, son of Poseidon, the god of the Ocean, and Ceres, the goddess of the Earth. He was regarded as invincible.

'What gave him his strength? It was this: that whenever, in the midst of a fight, he found himself in difficulty he recovered his strength by touching the Earth, the mother who had given him birth and had nourished him. He had one enemy who by taking advantage of this weakness conquered Antaeus. By lifting him up he deprived him of contact with the soil, and so was able to strangle him. This enemy was Hercules.

'The Communists put us in mind of Antaeus. Like him, they are strong only because they are allied with their mother, the masses who gave them birth, fed them, and educated them. So long as they remain attached to the people no one will be able to vanquish them.

'This is the secret of our invincibility.'

Such language may surprise us in a man who built up a State and attained to power over heaps of corpses. But the case of Stalin is full of complexities.

From the beginning of his revolutionary activities, and long before his first contact with Marxism, he had dreamed of the ideal earthly paradise of Tchaadaiev. Later on he had become a convert to revolutionary Marxism, as revealed to him by Lenin. But he had never been an absolute convert to this doctrine. Lenin, Trotzky and Bukharin had always served an abstract Deity, reasoning on an intellectual and almost supra-human plane.

Stalin, on the contrary, had his two feet firmly planted on the earth. He was in the grip of the realities of life, and being always conscious of the psychological tendencies of the masses, he was always aware of any change of orientation. His address is important and significant, not because of the conclusions which it draws, nor because of its sudden affirmation of respect for humanity: the important fact is that he judged it necessary to express it, and that he, a realist, and an intuitive thinker, thought the prevailing tendency in

---

[1]Stalin is addressing the Soviet masses, which explains why in the midst of this discourse he pauses to explain the myth of Antaeus. One sees how carefully he expounds it in order to render his argument comprehensible to the masses.

the Soviet masses so powerful that he had to take it into account and in a sense to appropriate it.

He was then sixty years of age, and the years had changed him. He had tempered the Caucasian violence of his gestures; he walked slowly, always with measured steps and a slightly rolling gait, like that of the brown bear of the mountains. He spoke more deliberately and never raised his voice.

Morally, the years in the seminary, the secret terrorist activities, and above all the apprenticeship to the profession of statesman upon which he had entered in 1918, had marked him profoundly. His taciturnity had become nearly a mania. On the other hand, he reflected and meditated deeply. He had succeeded in passing through one of the most turbulent periods of history without falling into any of the innumerable snares and pitfalls that lay in wait for him, and he foresaw those that the future might hold for him. So far he had always been able to discover a way of attaining his ends, while around him more brilliant, more sensitive, more intelligent and more cultivated men had lost their footing and had finally been exposed as useless and excitable chatterers. They had often drawn the attention of the world to themselves—by their actions at the beginning of the Revolution, and later, by the tragic, sensational and 'incomprehensible' circumstances of their disappearance. However, they have left but few traces, while Stalin has become one of those men who share with a very few others the direct responsibility for the destiny of the contemporary world. One may regret it or rejoice in it, but such is the fact.

Political stability being assured, at a price which few would have had the courage—some say, the criminal courage—to pay, Stalin devoted himself to his task as the supreme guide of the State in which he had retained, and erected into a permanent system, the compulsory labour camp.

The old Red Army had become a national army. The portraits of those ancient glories of the army, Alexander Nevsky, Kutuzov, Suvorov, Nakhimov, Skobelev, and the like, had been replaced, on the walls of the Military Academy, the military schools, and the barracks, by the effigies of Marx and Engels.

Stalin judged it opportune to stop the campaign against the

Orthodox Church. He was actuated not by sympathy but by necessity. Trotzky, in exile, protested indignantly. But Stalin was not
greatly impressed by the dogma of pure Marxism.

In 1939 he introduced a fundamental reform of capital importance; but as he refrained, as his custom was, from explaining his
action, it escaped the notice of foreign observers. The U.S.S.R. had
based the State on the Party cell.

Unwillingly, no doubt, but feeling that he could not do otherwise, he restored the family, the household. In creating the new code
of the family he hit two targets with a single stone. The proposal
was debated for months in the course of a vast referendum-discussion
in which all the basic organizations of the U.S.S.R. took part. Thus,
the masses, whom their rulers had always wanted to persuade that
they were participating in the creation of the Socialist State, had the
illusion that they were playing an active part in the elaboration of
the laws. This impression was all the stronger inasmuch as the laws
in question related to the family, divorce, adultery, and alimony,
which meant infinitely more to the citizens of the U.S.S.R. than
deciding whether a red-haired Chvernik or a brown-haired Mikoyan
should be President of the Supreme Council.

The new code surpassed all the codes of the capitalist countries in
its essentially 'bourgeois' rigidity. The Russian wife, who for a long
while past had been as defenceless as the wives in Latin countries,
now became the veritable mistress of the home. Law suits that
excited general interest ended in the infliction of severe penalties on
husbands who had attempted to bend their wives to their will by
means of force. Delay in the payment of alimentary pensions was
punished by five years' imprisonment. Divorce was rendered extremely difficult.

'Our country's New Woman' is celebrated by Stalin in his
speeches, and he periodically receives mothers of families in the
Kremlin in order to decorate them with the insignia of the 'Heroic
Mother.'

In the meantime the Red Army had given a good account of
itself in a first test. The Japanese had for some time been waging war
—without declaration—against the Russians on the frontiers of
Outer Mongolia. The new commander-in-chief in this region,
Joukov, who was trying out the new armoured divisions, reported

a decisive victory. He had annihilated an entire Japanese army which he had succeeded in encircling.[1]

The Eighteenth Pan-Russian Congress of the Communist Party assembled in the spring of 1939. This was the apotheosis of Stalin. The glorification initiated by Mekhliss had become a veritable deification. It was followed by spectacular demonstrations.

The right to own property was extended, and those who had the means to build new houses could leave these to their heirs.

In the streets the private cars of the generals and factory managers drove past the thousands of clerks and artisans and labourers who crowded the trains of the Underground, whose luxurious stations still failed to produce the illusion of social equality between the workers at the base of society and the new bureaucracy.

Stalin does not attempt to dodge the question. He admits the increasing inequality, and even justifies it. All things considered, this is equivalent to a confession that he was afraid of that *trahison des clercs* which was the ruin of certain countries at war with the 'Third Reich.' Stalin buys his *clercs*—at a very high price. Exceptional 'men of destiny' often act as diviners; they are able to detect the direction of subterranean currents, invisible to the eyes of others, and so they assure their own continuance. In reality the irresistible tendency to *embourgeoisement* was at work in the minds of the privileged citizens.

The Eighteenth Congress appointed a new Central Committee, which in its turn elected a new Politburo. It was composed of out-and-out Stalinists. Beside Stalin himself, it included Molotov, Mikoyan, Béria, Kaganovitch, Andréev, Jdanov, Kalinin, Voro-chilov, Tcherbakov, Khroustchev, Voznessensky, Bulganin, Chver-nik, Malenkov, and Kossiguin. Two-thirds of these were new men, the personal candidates of Stalin, the 'boss.'

Stalin's hands were now free. His authority was unlimited; yet for the last fifteen years he had held no official position in the Government. This facilitated the maintenance of his prestige as supreme arbiter; he soared above the State, giving only directions of a general order.

The Stalinian legend was created. Official biographies remodelled his whole life, effacing everything that could lend any prestige to

[1]He successfully repeated the same manœuvre several times against the Germans.

N

those of his enemies who had disappeared, and the historians re-wrote the history of the U.S.S.R. Artists erased from their paint-ings the features of men who were no longer influential, and even promoted Stalin to the front rank of their groups.

The Georgian Djugachvili had become not only the absolute master of the new Russia, but the symbol of its continuity. This he owed not entirely to his own will, and the will of his group of followers, but also to the fact that this operation was in line with the will of history, and the country's instinct of self-preservation at a time when it was about to suffer a test in which its existence would be at stake. The sixth sense which is so amazingly developed in Stalin enabled him to divine the direction of the psychological urge of the masses on which he has allowed himself to be borne forward. In so doing—whether we like it or not, whether we criticize him or admire him—he appeared as the authentic creator of the new form of social and economic life which had emerged from the vast Russian crucible.

It is true that in order to attain power he waded through a sea of blood. It may be that if he had not had within him the atavisms of an Ossetinized Georgian, of a descendant of the convict populations of the island of Dju, of the terrible warriors of Genghis Khan, and of crafty, vindictive, cunning mountaineer ancestors, he would have stopped half-way to the goal, shrinking from the hecatombs without which he could never have reached the summit of power.

That power he desired; he created and shaped it, asserted it and defended it with all his might, with all his cunning, with all his pitiless cruelty; with all the frightful logic practised by the Order of Professional Revolutionaries. In 1939 he was already completely and consciously responsible for his rise to supreme power.

All that he had lived through since his days in the Tiflis seminary would have been enough to fill the most exceptional of lives. But for him this was only a curtain-raiser. The second world war was about to put the strength of the new Russian State to a terrible test, and to place him in the very centre of international actuality.

CHAPTER XXIX

STALIN AND FOREIGN POLITICS

WHEN Stalin entered upon the crucial period of the Second World War he was handicapped by the manifold results of the peculiarities of his intellectual and political training. This period, which began with Munich, is still with us. His apprenticeship in this domain was long and complicated, and in a certain sense it is still continuing.

With Churchill and Roosevelt, Stalin is one of the very few statesmen who through all the changing vicissitudes of the last few years retained their faculty of influencing and shaping the destinies of their contemporaries, instead of allowing themselves to be carried away by events. But the Georgian is profoundly different in character from the other two.

Churchill, a tireless and tenacious fighter, unshaken in adversity, whose greatness was revealed during the tragic hours of 1940–42, and Roosevelt, a genius at improvisation, owe much to their eloquence, to the attraction of a life lived openly, unshadowed and unstained, in the traditional setting of a well-established order.

Stalin, as we now already see, is a man of a very different stamp. Dull, without brilliance, without eloquence, he seems in the eyes of the world a sort of political abstraction of extra-human reactions; the millions of portraits which reveal his features do not make them more familiar; as a personality he is always in the background; and the history of his conquest of power is not such as to arouse much sympathy.

In order to understand and explain the motives of his attitude and his movements on the international chessboard, one must, of course, go back to the dominant ideas and prevailing conditions of the time when he was passing through his late apprenticeship.

Stalin has seldom been out of Russia, and only for very brief periods. He has never come into real contact with the world and

cannot be said to know it. His famous sixth sense, an infallible guide
to action within the frontiers of the U.S.S.R., a sort of radar which
enables him to detect the orientation of the psychological urges of
his own people, has failed him almost entirely in his relations with
the outer world. The psychological realities of the world beyond the
Soviet frontiers escape him altogether, or his vision of them is distorted. Knowing nothing of their solid foundations, he under-
estimates their importance. For a long while his notion of the outer
world was conventional and schematic.

In this respect he was utterly different from the other Bolshevik
leaders of the internationalist period. The latter had become strongly
Europeanized by years of life abroad. In their speeches, their writings,
their conversation, and even their spontaneous confessions during
the great trials, they seemed always conscious of foreign audiences,
which, for that matter, were always prejudiced in their favour. Even
Trotzky, who could never be consoled for his failure to drown the
West in blood and fire, felt closer to the West, which in its turn
understood him and absolved him—even pitying the tragic fate of
the incendiary !—Stalin took not the slightest interest in the West,
and he did not hesitate, if it suited him, to treat even foreign Communists in the most offhand manner. Over and over again he con-
tradicted or misinterpreted them, but this did not diminish their ill-
rewarded though fervent admiration. One day it will tire them.

Deprived of his trump card, his almost infallible instinct, he
began to look about him for a substitute, something that would give
him confidence in himself, since he never trusted the opinion or
advice of others.

He found the solution in a meticulous and pedantic study of
international problems and of diplomatic history, as well as in keeping the closest watch on his diplomatists. This study yielded results.
The extent of his knowledge in this domain began to surprise the
statesmen who came into contact with him. Roosevelt, Churchill,
Eden, Stettinius, T. V. Soong and Victor Hoo, negotiating with
Moscow in 1945, were astonished by the degree of his erudition and
by his memory. But this cold science, this knowledge acquired by
scholastic methods and hard intellectual labour, did much to poison
the relations between the Allies in the Second World War. It was
constantly leading to deadlocks which resulted in a dangerously

charged atmosphere. Often enough the guide himself lost his way in a kind of labyrinth. For all these reasons, the activities of the Soviet diplomatists were dominated by a veritable documentary fetichism. Treaties, conventions and agreements were for Stalin the only positive basis of his relations with the world, whose psychology remained a mystery to him.

This peculiar intransigence became even more rigid after the end of the war, when the Kremlin's diplomatic portfolio was full to bursting-point. It contributed to an international tension in an atmosphere full of distrust, apprehension and misunderstanding.

The Western diplomatists, seeking the new solutions demanded by the changing conjunctures of life, felt that they were constantly coming up against an impenetrable curtain. The representatives of the United States, always impatient for results—in their famous New World efficiency—were those who suffered the most. The delegates of the West tried by negotiation to create a fresh atmosphere. The representatives of the Kremlin referred to the literal contents of dossiers full of stipulations which Stalin insisted must be strictly observed. They seemed actually to rejoice in the most exasperating juridical chicanerie.

On the whole, Stalin adopts and enforces a mode of procedure which is in diametrical opposition to the suppleness of his internal activities; a mode of procedure which suggests the comparison of a ballet dancer who, lest he should lose his footing on an unfamiliar stage, has put on shoes with leaden soles.

The official Russian attitude toward Germany is unique. Germany has always exercised on Stalin, as on all the Bolsheviks, a veritable fascination, but a fascination full of apprehension. Stalin has never taken his eyes off Germany. His whole view of world politics is conditioned by his relations with Germany—the traditional, immediate and real source of danger to Russia.

In all that relates to international affairs, Stalin's prudence has often been expressed in surprisingly emphatic forms, though the rhythm of his action is often astonishingly slow, even exasperating. Not only does he proceed with velvet tread, but all his actions are slow and gradual. Thus, if Hitler succeeded in taking him completely by surprise on the 23 June, 1941—a fact which cost the Russians dear

—this was not because for once in a way that second-rate statesman Ribbentrop hit on a successful ruse. It was Stalin himself who, according to his own statement to Churchill, 'thought he had six months before him'; in other words, he had been unable to follow Hitler's rhythm of action.

The very organization of the Department for Foreign Affairs was conceived in a manner by no means propitious to rapid accomplishment. Stalin reinforced Lenin's methods of control, and created others. A new special commission was set up for the examination of documents. After the successive dismissals of Zinoviev and Bukharin, the presidency of this organization was confided, on Stalin's initiative, to his confidential assistant, Molotov.[1]

This was not enough for him. He insisted that every question, after it had been discussed by the Commission—whose sessions he systematically refrained from attending—must be submitted to the Politburo. He himself was always the last to vote, on the pretext that he did not wish to influence his colleagues. Very often he required the final sanction of the Central Committee.

This cascade of superimposed precautions appeared to have only one purpose: to avoid all responsibility, even indirect, in activities which were still new to him, and whose mechanism threatened to involve him in its complications. Often he accepted initiatives of which he did not wholly approve, but which were supported by a formal decision of the majority, behind which he escaped observation. These tactics he still applies. . . .

At the same time he proceeded indefatigably with his technical apprenticeship—the study of historical and diplomatic problems.

He insisted on keeping directly in touch with the representatives of the U.S.S.R. in foreign countries. (This he did only in a semi-official manner, since until 1941 he held no post in the Government, and his post as Secretary-General was constitutionally speaking only a private function.) His manner of conducting dialogues of this kind tells us much about the man.

In a long conversation with Raskolnikov, the Soviet Ambassador in Sofia, he surprised the latter by his ideas and his way of attacking

[1]Finical, undecided, but obstinate, Molotov often went farther than his master. Entirely devoid of diplomatic suppleness and ability, even before the rupture with the West at Lancaster House, he is said to have persuaded Hitler, by his intransigent attitude in Berlin in November 1940, to attack the U.S.S.R.

problems. Raskolnikov, an ex-officer of the Imperial Navy, turned diplomatist, discovered with surprise that Stalin, whom he knew only as an official of the Party, knew more than he did of the historical aspects of the thorny question of the Straits.

After some hesitation, Raskolnikov confessed that his recollection of the period in question was at fault. Said Stalin, 'I will tell you: it was in the time of Paul I, in 1798. Breaking with London, Paul signed a treaty of alliance with the Sultan and obtained this right. Pitt's agents organized his assassination and rendered the treaty void.'

Raskolnikov felt like a schoolboy reprimanded by a master whom he feared and disliked. Hoping to revenge himself, he taxed his memory: 'You are forgetting the treaty of 11 September, 1805, signed by Alexander I, which gave our warships the right to pass through the Straits in both directions.'

Stalin smiled again. 'I see that our diplomatists are trying to improve their knowledge. . . . The treaty of which you speak did exist, but it was as stillborn as the Treaty of San Stefano. The Turks refused to let Russian ships pass through the Straits, because Napoleon had promised the Sultan his aid and protection. . . .'

Another Soviet diplomatist, Bessedovsky,[1] appointed First Councillor of the Embassy in Paris, had a long conversation with Stalin. This interview showed that Stalin's ideas were already extremely comprehensive, and that he counted largely on the private contacts which he had contrived to achieve.

In accordance with his usual tactics, Stalin began by disconcerting his visitor. 'I have just been reading a ciphered telegram from the French Ambassador, Jean Herbette, giving the Quai d'Orsay various biographical details relating to yourself. It also mentions some of your failings . . . alcohol, for example. . . . It gives an account of a speech which you made in the Danzig Rathaus, before some of the members of the Senate, after you had had a drop too much. . . .'[2]

After this preliminary admonishment, Stalin analysed the diplomat's activities in Tokyo. Having consulted certain notes, he added:

[1]While exercising the functions of chargé d'affaires in Paris, Bessedovsky, threatened by the Tcheka, leapt over the wall of the Embassy garden one night and demanded the intervention and protection of the French police.

[2]Bessedovsky, who records this conversation in a book published in 1932, says that Herbette's telegram was deciphered by a certain Malakhovsky, in the Commissariat for Foreign Affairs.

'We have already proposed to Paris that the Russian debt should be paid in sixty-six annual instalments of 60,000,000 gold francs. Try to see Briand and Poincaré, and also Monzie and Dalbiez, in order to settle this question. When this has been done Roumania and Poland, allies of France, will be pacified. Peace is an absolute necessity for me at the present time, both in Europe and in the Far East. . . .'

His conceptions of the German problems were likewise determined by all manner of complexes, quite unintelligible to those who have not studied his career, and who do not allow for the Russian continuity, which exerted an increasing influence on the revolutionaries who had now become statesmen. Like almost all the disciples of Lenin, for many years he had great hopes of the Sovietization of Germany, which country, as we have seen, is for the Bolsheviks the most powerful piece on the international chess-board.

Year after year Stalin repeated the sentence pronounced by Lenin in the Second Congress of the Communist International in Moscow: 'The day when Germany becomes Soviet the knell of the capitalist world will sound.' This conviction was deeply rooted in Stalin's mind; so that he spoke of an alliance which would make Germany a new Federative Republic, which would 'overthrow the walls of the capitalist world as the trumpets of Joshua overthrew the walls of Jericho.'

But he saw things refracted through the prism of his customary prudence. He feared to bring discredit upon Bolshevism, and above all upon himself, by concluding an alliance with the Germans. Obviously, if Germany were Sovietized the formula: 'The Germans, having become Soviet, have come over to us,' would suffice to neutralize the popular hostility.

This attitude was to a certain extent defined and developed in a conversation with the Russian chargé d'affaires in Berlin, Bratman-Brodovsky, a Pole, a native of Lodz, who asked for instructions regarding the signing of the Germano-Soviet treaty of friendship and non-aggression.[1] He said, in this conversation: 'I am, of course, in favour of closer and closer relations with Germany. The desire of its rulers to get rid at any cost of the Treaty of Versailles ought to be

---

[1]Bessedovsky, in his memoirs, reports this conversation, of which he was informed by Bratman.

exploited to the utmost by our diplomatists. We could constitute "a pool of malcontents" to prevent the realization of the projected Western *bloc* against us, and to bring into power in Germany the Nationalist elements which favour a revolt against Versailles. A clash between Germany and the Allies could only end in her defeat, and by a Sovietization of the Reich. If such were the result of our policy in Berlin, the verdict of history would be a *pokhvalni list* (satisfecit).

'But we must not be led astray. The German Nationalists are ready to accept our help in order to fight the Peace of Versailles; but as soon as they are in power they will become our most dangerous adversaries. Our friendly relations with Germany can be justified or implemented only by the Sovietization of the country. Otherwise no lasting alliance between them and ourselves is possible.'

Behind the Marxist jargon one hears a *leit-motiv* of the eternal Russia which guides the Bolsheviks in the direction indicated by Slavism, and toward the historical conflict between the Slavs and the Germans, fought out on the great plain of Eastern Europe. In 1945 the Potsdam Agreements attempted to impose a solution: the return of East Prussia, an ancient Slav territory conquered by the Teutons.

By the strange irony of destiny, Stalin, the disciple of Marxist materialism, was in actual practice following the recipe of the most bourgeois sociologist of the century—Gustave Le Bon, one of whose volumes was always on his desk. '. . . One cannot govern a people by attending only to its material needs; one must also, and above all, take its *dreams* into account. . . .'

Thus, it was on regarding the world through a screen coloured by the fear of Germany that Stalin learned the part to be played by a Russian ruler in international politics. He saw the Germans as dangerous enemies, and this for two reasons: one was provided by the ideologists of the Bolshevists, and one by the deep inducement of the historical continuity of Russia, which was fundamentally anti-German.

The policies and attitudes of France, Great Britain, and their neighbours, actually interested him only as regards their repercussions on the enterprises of the Reich, which were engendered by the exceptional dynamism of the Germans. This organic dread, justified and confirmed by the events of 1941 to 1945, was as keen as ever after the conclusion of the Second World War.

Those who would really discover the fundamental reasons of Russia's attitude after the war would find them in the German question. This explains the series of apparently confused attempts, from 1936, to effect a rapprochement with the Hitlerian Reich. It was the German question, again, which enabled Molotov's new theory of 'the third phase in the development of world capitalism' to supersede Litvinov's conceptions, and to bring about the German-Russian Agreement of the 23 August, 1939. But these are not actions undertaken with absolute liberty of thought, and in cold blood. One can accept only with a certain reserve the popular image of a spider, installed in the Kremlin, trying to enclose the rest of the world in a complicated web. As a matter of fact, Stalin himself was struggling in its toils and seeking to escape from them.

When National Socialism became supreme in Germany, Stalin's apprehensions assumed an ever acuter form. He constantly bombarded with questions and pieces of advice the Sovietic organs of information abroad. The *Razvedoupr* and the *Ino* were asked to supply full and precise information and to redouble their vigilance. These two organs, the first directed by General Berzine, a Lett by origin, and the second by Artouzov, an ex-officer of the Austrian Army, who after being taken prisoner had become a convert to Bolshevism, were often in disagreement in their judgements of affairs. Stalin, following his natural tendency, nearly always accepted the views of the pessimists.[1]

When Ribbentrop had become the political heir of Bismarck, and attempted, after signing the naval agreement with Lord Halifax, to revive Wilhelm the Second's old plan for the partition of the world, this attempt to obtain a free hand in the East was profoundly disquieting to Stalin. Berzine declared—and Krivitzky said the same thing in Washington—that he could not sleep for thinking of them.

Yet Churchill had made certain categorical statements; for example, in conversation with the Roumanian diplomatist, Gregor Gafenko, who tells us in his memoirs: '. . . "Of course," Churchill said, "our British Government might come to an agreement with Germany. There's no doubt of that. It would be enough to give

[1]Memoirs of Krivitzky, published in Washington.

carte blanche to Hitler. But what could we share with Germany? The world? The world is not ours to share. If by some aberration we were to surrender to Hitler what does not belong to us, we should soon be unable to defend against him what does belong to us. . . ." '

In so saying, Churchill was not only expressing his personal opinion. The 'young men,' Duff Cooper, Hore-Belisha, and the rest were with him. Further, on the occasion of his visit to Moscow in 1935 Eden took pains to convince Stalin that England was not inclined to listen to the siren songs of Hugenberg and Ribbentrop; besides, the two emissaries of the Third Reich had already departed from London with empty hands.

But men are always ready to believe statements that confirm a preconceived opinion. Stalin was no exception to the rule. He began to listen more and more attentively to the I.N.O., whose director insisted that the British Government was prepared to sign an agreement with Hitler which would give the Third Reich a free hand in the East. It is true that Chamberlain was behaving as though he were seeking to justify many of Moscow's anxieties. Churchill, not in power, devoted himself to landscape painting and bricklaying. The international situation seemed to justify the pessimism of the U.S.S.R., which foresaw an alliance of the entire bourgeois world against the State which Stalin had solemnly proclaimed was 'the first Socialist State in the world.'

CHAPTER XXX

DIPLOMATIC GENERAL POST

FOR Stalin, still hesitating to enter upon the path that was plain before him, the path which the U.S.S.R. seemed destined to follow, the close of the year 1935 was a decisive turning-point in foreign politics.

Although until 1939 the foreign policy of the U.S.S.R. would officially remain a policy of collective security, the first symptoms of the change, which could only lead to the conclusion of the Molotov-Ribbentrop agreement of 23 August, 1939, were beginning to reveal themselves. It was in fact in December 1935 that a conference of the Politburo was held in the Kremlin,[1] at which the military leaders were present, together with the officials who directed the foreign policy of the country.

Speaking of the U.S.S.R., Charles Bohlen, counsellor to the State Department of Washington, an expert in Russian affairs, and one of the initiators of the anti-Soviet American attitude, refers to Stalin's distrust of the outer world as one of the principal reasons for not allowing normal relations with Moscow. He might have gone farther, evoking another complex which plays an even more imperative part. The Kremlin, which, according to tradition—a tradition emphasized by propaganda—inspires the outer world with a sense of dread and misgiving, is itself under the constant influence of the same feelings! It exists in a state of perpetual apprehension of the dangers which it sees accumulating beyond its frontiers. It considers only how it can frustrate the attacks preparing against the U.S.S.R., for which the Third Reich is obviously mainly responsible!

The treaty of January 1934 between Pilsudsky and Hitler increased Stalin's fears. This treaty, as Moscow saw it, was the clearest possible proof of impending trouble: it was like a milestone on the route of an aggression against Russia.

[1] A detailed account of these events, so significant for the future, is given by General Krivitzky.

As the adjutant-in-chief of the Razvedoupr, General Krivitsky knew that the I.N.O. had communicated the content of the 'Gentleman's Agreement' between Pilsudsky and Hitler to Stalin, and also the substance of the conversations between Colonel Beck and Goering, which had taken place in the Bielowierz Forest during the famous hunt in which the aurochs was the quarry. These agreements and conversations, actual or imaginary, or touched up a little in support of German policy, all seemed to promise Hitler the assistance of Poland in the event of war between the U.S.S.R.. and Germany.

General Berzine, at the head of the Razvedoupr, expounded, in a personal audience, the standpoint of his organization, which differed considerably from that of the I.N.O. According to Berzine, Pilsudsky's aim was simply to divert the German armies from Poland, leaving two paths of invasion open to them: the Baltic corridor—Lithuania, Latvia and Esthonia—and the valley of the Danube. The Polish statesman did not intend that Poland should be the battlefield on which the Russian and German armies would meet.

It was obvious that the purely military value of Pilsudsky's plan was to be regarded with caution. The old marshal was only an amateur, in spite of the pride that gave him such confidence in his own talents as a strategist. The Battle of Warsaw, which in 1920 checked the advance of the Soviet invasion, was conceived and realized by General Weygand, against the advice of the Polish leader, who often refused to meet the General, contenting himself with an exchange of notes.

Nevertheless, the information fell upon fertile ground, at precisely the right moment. . . . Stalin was tormented by the dread of a great coalition of the capitalist world against the U.S.S.R. Serious efforts were made to prove the contrary. Louis Barthou, though he could not be described as a pro-Bolshevik, crossed Europe in order to propose to Stalin a North-Eastern pact, which should include the Baltic countries, Poland, and the Great Powers, with France at their head, as a common guarantee against German agression. But at this very moment Colonel Beck justified Stalin's suspicions by clearly disclosing the true and secret aim of the policy which he was pursuing. While she proclaimed herself a partisan of the *status quo* in the Baltic—Poland had treaties with Latvia, Esthonia and Finland—she firmly refused to participate in the 'Treaty of the North-East.'—'This treaty', said Beck, 'might be regarded as an infraction of the Polono-German Treaty.' The Baltic corridor remained open to the Germans.

Nevertheless, the French Government wished to continue its policy. Pierre Laval decided to leave for Moscow in order to sign a treaty of alliance. But Stalin hesitated, and argued the point with Litvinov: 'And what if Laval's journey is nothing but a trick, an attempt to make the Germans regard us as responsible for the encirclement of the Third Reich? Are we to pull other people's chestnuts out of the fire? At the moment Hitler has other fish to fry, somewhere in the Rhineland. Today Laval comes to us, but if tomorrow Hitler should fall on the U.S.S.R. he wouldn't lift a finger. . . . We have reliable information that he and Paganon are building up an anti-Communist front in France, and that he is prepared to ally himself even with pro-Nazi elements.'[1]

Stalin was merely repeating the statements of the I.N.O.

Nevertheless, Litvinov insisted that Laval should be received. The encounter of the Mayor of Aubervilliers and the Georgian was not without its picturesque aspects.

'Can you guarantee,' asked Laval, 'that the French Communist Party will adopt a patriotic attitude in the case of a military conflict with the Third Reich? Our Communists persist in declaring that they recognize only the fatherland—the U.S.S.R.'

'Apply to the Secretary-General of the French Communist Party, Jacques Doriot,' Stalin replied. 'He will answer your question. I am not qualified to speak for him. But I do know that Jacques Doriot is as determined as we are to fight the Nazis wherever they find them.' He certainly did not foresee that in 1942 Jacques Doriot, in the uniform of a first lieutenant of the S.S., would inspect his faithful P.P.F. in the Ukraine.

At last the Franco-Russian treaty of mutual assistance was signed. But when Stalin, who likes to have things in plain writing, wanted to define the practical obligations of the two parties in a military convention, Laval began to jib. There were too many opponents of such a convention. Among them was General Weygand. This was the end of the attempt to resuscitate a Franco-Russian alliance on the pre-war model.

From this one may draw certain conclusions. Stalin did not fail

[1]Details given by Krivitzky.

to do so. Obviously a Franco-Russian military alliance would have made it impossible for Hitler to effect his famous unilateral liquidation of the Versailles Treaty, or even the re-armament of Germany. But the psychological climate did not favour an alliance, and the politicians allowed themselves to be beguiled by the illusion that it could be replaced by vague political combinations, or military conventions with countries of secondary importance.

Stalin, who had barely begun to familiarize himself with the intricacies of the diplomacy of this period, had yet to realize the fact that the statesmen of democratic nations were not their own masters. Not realizing that they had to discuss all problems and convince a parliamentary majority, he only saw duplicity or disquieting reservations in their delays.

It must be admitted, moreover, that the situation was a difficult one. Even the most perspicacious of men, free of all preoccupations as to the course to be taken, and unburdened by the responsibility for actions which would involve his country, would have found it difficult to make his way through the European imbroglio of the moment. Especially if he was looking at the world from Moscow.

Anyhow, things were not developing favourably for the U.S.S.R. Such resolute enemies of Soviet Russia as Sir Samuel Hoare, Neville Chamberlain, Sir John Simon, and Lord Halifax were now in control of the foreign policies of Great Britain. Under these conditions, after the conference of the Politburo of 1935, the U.S.S.R. entered upon a new course. But this course was not plotted by Stalin without a number of deviations; and each of these, like all the modifications of Stalin's policies, left a bloody trace.

One of the results of this conference was the provision of a new pivot which made it possible to change at will the orientation of the axis of Russo-German relations. Now the real game had opened.

In the first place, the Soviet Ambassador in Berlin, Khintchouk, a Jew who had replaced Krestinsky, was dismissed and consigned to the executioners of the N.K.V.D. On the 24 April, 1936, the treaty of friendship and neutrality signed in 1926 reached its term. Born of the Treaty of Rapallo of 1922, it was almost a treaty of alliance, and it called for the close collaboration of the military staffs. After the seizure of power by the Nazis there was still some contact between the military circles of the two countries.

Litvinov, an ardent partisan of the resurrection of the *Entente Cordiale*, proposed to Stalin that the treaty of 1926 should not be renewed. He tried to show that the merest shadow of a new *entente* with the West would be enough to snaffle Hitler, and enable the countries threatened by the Third Reich to complete their new armaments. Stalin appeared to be interested by Litvinov's plan, which gave to the abstract notion of collective security a reality reinforced by a regional pact.[1] Several other members of the Politburo approved of Litvinov's idea. In the opinion of the Soviet Second Bureau, he might very well be sent to urge his proposal upon Paris and London. The majority of the Politburo decided against this. Here, indeed, there was no question of a resolution imposed by Stalin, as it might have been imposed by a Hitler or a Mussolini, whose collaborators respectfully waited upon their will; but none the less Stalin was responsible for it, as the conductor of an orchestra is responsible for the performance of a composition, even if for some reason he folds his arms and allows his orchestra to follow the rhythm imposed by the first violin, or marked by the big drum.

The conception which superseded Litvinov's ideas was a new theory excogitated by Molotov, and entitled 'The Third Phase in the development of World Capitalism.'

Since Bukharin had been expelled from it the real master of the Comintern was Molotov, who was also President of the Council of the U.S.S.R. Always laden with innumerable dossiers, and, to quote a comparison then in vogue, 'distilling boredom throughout the day,' he was determined to assert his prestige. He too had excogitated a 'theory,' as all the leaders of the Bolshevik rank and file had done before him. If one wished to make one's name in this Marxist world one had to be a theoretician. Molotov's theory is not complicated, and its scientific value is at least contestable. Nevertheless, it exerts a considerable influence over world events, for Stalin accepts it and that is enough. History sometimes makes use of a rickety chariot. . . . But if it does make use of it the chariot is worth examining.

[1]Details given by General Krivitsky, who as adjutant-in-chief of the Second Bureau of the Army was directly concerned with the matter.

Molotov asserts that the Fascisms, in general, represent 'the supreme phase of world super-imperialism.' Fascism must infallibly provoke a series of world wars, in the course of which 'universal capitalism will inevitably break down and give way to Socialism.'

At the moment when this theory was enounced it corresponded to a certain state of mind in the Soviet rulers. It seems to us that one can hardly award, without reservation, the title of 'brilliant theoretician' and 'source of all wisdom' to a man who, like Stalin, took this intellectual effort of his assistant seriously. At all events, Stalin would derive 'useful elements' from the application of Molotov's theses. Moreover, as a safeguard Molotov had a special recipe.

He promised Stalin and his disciples the profitable rôle of the *tertius gaudens*, joyful and contented! This political argument was completed by an economic theory which the enemies of the liberal economy would find equally encouraging. The economic crisis of 1930 was declared incurable, for 'the co-ordinates of the cyclical crises of the *bourgeois* régime coincide with those of the general crises of the capitalist world economics.' Henceforth the U.S.S.R. has only to wait in order to witness the collapse of the enemy's economy, already tottering to a fall.

Decidedly, after a certain point the great Marxist theory does not attain a very high intellectual standard. Nevertheless, Molotov's doctrine was accepted and consecrated as 'the practical application of Leninism-Stalinism.' In reality, it provides an apparent Marxist justification when one proceeds in contradiction to the very early principles of Bolshevism.

o

CHAPTER XXXI

TOWARD MUNICH

As the first swallow announcing a timid Spring in the relations between Germany and Russia, Stalin selected the diplomatist Youreniev. His flight, however, was only a brief one.

Before he was Ambassador to Berlin he had been Ambassador in Rome, in Prague and in Tokyo. In accordance with tradition, he had to call on Stalin before leaving for Berlin. The Secretary-General of the Party never failed to counsel prudence; and he did not wish the new Ambassador to go too far. He advised him 'to listen rather than speak.'

He hinted that the new Ambassador's task was to restore the relations of friendship and confidence with the commercial and industrial circles in touch with such Russo-German societies as the Deroutra, the Deroupetrola, the Deroumiekh, and others. . . .

Before presenting his credentials to the Führer, Youreniev visited the Leipzig Fair, which always attracts a number of pro-Russian merchants and manufacturers. Here he made a short but suggestive speech, which at the time, like the majority of really significant political indications, attracted hardly any attention.

However, his delicate mission was frustrated in an unexpected and deadly fashion. A representative of the Razvedoupr in Western Europe, a certain Ignace Reiss, began by suddenly going over to Trotzky's side. He established contact with Trotzky's son, Léon Siedov, who was in charge of the underground activities of the anti-Stalin groups of the Left. Reiss gave Siedov complete details of the Politburo's decision to apply Molotov's theory and to renew friendly relations with the Third Reich. Naturally, the Trotzkyite press of the whole world took this opportunity of beginning a new campaign against Stalin, accusing him, on this occasion, 'of betraying Leninist Communism in general, and in particular the German Communist

Party, which had thousands of its members in the camps of Goering and Himmler.'

Now, the internal situation was still dangerous for Stalin. The great purge was at its height. The commanders of the Red Army and the heads of the N.K.V.D. had not yet been passed through the bloodstained sieve of the purgers. An accusation of collusion with Fascism might be fatal to the lord of the Kremlin, who was not yet entirely his own master.

This was one of the occasions when Stalin displayed his extraordinary and disconcerting cleverness in domestic affairs. As soon as there was any question of taking action at home, like Napoleon, who before Waterloo had found in 1815 the boots of his Italian campaign, Stalin recovered the assurance which enabled him to crush all obstacles and to wade with his customary unconcern through fresh torrents of blood. With unprecedented celerity he turned aside the blow which had been aimed at him. Youreniev was one of those who paid the penalty. Recalled to Moscow, he was accused of secret dealings with the German Fascists. A certain number of high officials of the Commissariat for Foreign Affairs, arrested as long ago as 1936 for Trotzkyism, were 'put into the same basket,' on the pretext of their alleged treason and their attempt to establish a friendly understanding with Hitler.

In reality, Stalin was very adroitly returning the ball to his enemies, who were frustrating his foreign policy and restricting the liberty of movement which he had found so indispensable. The machinery of repression functioned without a break. The sometime Vice-Commissar of Foreign Affairs, Karakhan, the husband of the celebrated dancer Semenova, the departmental Director, Zukermann, Youreniev, and many other diplomatists were all tried at the same time. Now, in 1917 Youreniev and Karakhan had been members of Trotzky's 'inter-departmental' organization in Petrograd, which in August of that year was merged into the Bolshevik Party. Stalin thus 'established' the fact, in public opinion, that 'Trotzkyism had become a faithful agent of German Fascism.' The expression was that of the public prosecutor, Vishinsky.

The trial was held behind closed doors; as was the trial of the Marshals. The prisoners disappeared for ever into the cellars of the N.K.V.D.

Now Stalin endeavoured to free himself of the enemy's control. Reiss, who was regarded as dangerous, was assassinated on his way from Lausanne to Geneva, having been drawn into an ambush by his ex-secretary and mistress Lydia Grosovska.

It was then the turn of Trotzky's son, Léon Siedov, who died mysteriously in a Paris clinic, where he had been operated on for an intestinal occlusion. Trotzky brought an action, openly accusing Stalin of having organized an attempt upon his son's life. The inquiry resulted in no definite conclusion, and one more mysterious affair was added to the many ambiguous episodes of the struggle between Stalin and Trotzky. Thus, General Krivitzky was assassinated in Washington just as he was preparing to lay before President Roosevelt the proofs that the Molotov-Ribbentrop agreement was only the conclusion of a policy inaugurated long before by Stalin, and applied for the first time in accordance with instructions given to Youreniev.

That same year, in August 1940, saw the disappearance of Trotzky. He was assassinated in Mexico by a man of many mysterious identities, who purged his crime in a comfortable cell of the model prison of Mexico City, where he received, every month, a considerable sum of money from an unknown source. The disappearance of Trotzky was a fact of tremendous importance. But at the moment, despite its sensational aspect, and the impression produced on the public, even the specialists in international questions failed to realize the full significance of the event.[1]

[1]Under the title 'The Disappearance of Trotzky and Stalin's Policy,' the author published in the *Journal de Genève* of the 17 September, 1940, an article explaining its precise significance. He wrote: '. . . concerning a number of events of the last few years which have influenced international politics but have attracted no more attention than any series of unrelated incidents. Such were the visit to Paris of the Prince of Wales, before the conclusion of the Franco-British alliance; Marshal Goering's speech in the Nuremberg Congress in September 1938, which described the programme of the foreign politics of the Third Reich, making for the first time a direct attack upon England—in which the majority of observers saw nothing more than a manifestation of the effervescent temperament of the Führer's second-in-command. Such too were the Russo-German negotiations many months before the conclusion of the Pact.

'The same fate seems to have been reserved for the death of Trotzky, the sole official, tenacious and eloquent rival of Stalin for the title which both had coveted with equal ardour, the title of "Head of the World Revolution." Yet this event was destined to exercise a considerable influence on the U.S.S.R., and on international politics. The direct repercussion of this death affected Stalin personally, and the whole of the U.S.S.R.

After the wrecking of Youreniev's plan the foreign policy of the U.S.S.R. found itself in the same predicament as before. The attempt to entice the Third Reich into a profitable collaboration had failed. But the Reich had reached the stage when it would have to decide upon a definite course in order to exploit its military preparations, which were inevitably directed against Central Europe before attacking the West or Russia.

Stalin was perfectly familiar with the theories to this effect elaborated by generations of German economists and soldiers, like Friedrich Naumann, the author of *Mitteleuropa*, written in 1915, a year before his death, and the 'geopolitician' General Karl Haushofer, the teacher of Hess and Hitler, who had converted them to the traditional ideas of the apostles of German expansion.

For Stalin, as he has often asserted, the German orientation toward the south-east comprised two contradictory elements. The first of them was favourable: the prospect of a clash between Germany and Great Britain. The second was plainly to his disadvantage: the annulment, at a certain moment, of the strategical mortgage on the Third Reich of the Czech fortress.

In 1938, on the eve of the Sudeten crisis, Stalin wanted the two antagonists, Litvinov and Molotov, to enter the lists with their hostile conceptions, and he wished the conflict to be fought to a finish with-

---

'Stalin was being constantly disturbed by Trotzky's accusations of having betrayed the spirit of the world revolution. Greatly superior to his rival in scholarship and eloquence and mordant wit, the indefatigable exile never ceased to harry him....

'... Thus, when after the execution of the so-called Germanophile generals, Stalin began to put out feelers in Berlin for a rapprochement, Trotzky did not fail to disclose these negotiations in his articles....

'... Finally, during the last few months, Trotzky had called openly for a revolt against "Cain-Djugachvili." Now Stalin is delivered from all the preoccupations and anxieties which Trotzky was causing him. Henceforth the world-revolution has only one leader; a leader who can engage the U.S.S.R., without the risk of being called to order by the Communist Party, *in all the tactical deviations that may be necessary. He can pursue the most devious courses without dreading the vigilance of Trotzky. He can manœuvre in absolute liberty, knowing that his actions will be neither commented upon nor exposed; he can exploit the antagonisms between the capitalist countries, and the possibilities offered by armed conflicts; he can embark resolutely on a course of recovering all the old Russian territories, making use of the Panslavist ideal in order to profit by the strength of the new nationalism....*

'... Obliged to deal with the tendencies of neo-Nationalism, Stalin himself, accustomed to outstripping evolution when he judges it to be inevitable, may be constrained to preside over the liquidation of the revolution so dreaded by Trotzky ...' (*Journal de Genève*, 17 September, 1940).

out his direct personal participation.[1] Litvinov asked for the immediate signature of an agreement with England and France to resist Hitler's certain attack upon Czechoslovakia. He referred to the Congress of Carlsbad, in the course of which Henlein, the Sudeten leader, formulated the demands which he presented to Benès. He referred to the aerial pact with Bucharest, giving the Soviet Air Force the right to fly across Roumanian territory in order to assist the Czechs. He declared that this would be enough to encourage Prague's determination to resist aggression. According to him, London and Paris would be ready to enter the conflict if it were seen that the U.S.S.R. was definitely taking the part of Benès.

Stalin likes things precisely expressed. He asked Litvinov why he was assured of these things. Litvinov referred to Ambassador Maïsky's conversation with Winston Churchill, who told him that he was preparing to deliver an important speech.[2] Stalin, who was on his guard, appeared to be impressed by the objections of several members of the Politburo, and of Molotov in particular, who suspected a ruse of Churchill's; so obvious that no one with any critical spirit could have failed to detect it.

According to Molotov, the aerial pact, secretly signed between Titulesco and Litvinov, had been annulled by King Carol, who had warned London of it when he announced his coming visit to England.[3]

Berzine declared that according to the information received by his service, Churchill's attitude, as declared to Ambassador Maïsky, was sincere. At the moment England was powerless from the military point of view, but she could not follow a policy of compromise with Hitler. Berzine also insisted that his informants in the Wehrmacht were positive; if it were publicly known that England, France and Russia had firmly decided to support Benès, the German General Staff would use every means of opposing Hitler's attack upon Czechoslovakia.[4] The Third Reich would thus find itself held up on

---

[1]As head of the Razvedoupr, General Berzine was present at this discussion, and he sent his notes and his recollections of the discussion to his adjutant Krivitzky; who reproduced them in his memoirs.

[2]This speech was delivered on the 9 May, 1938.

[3]King Carol visited England in 1938; but on the eve of Munich Roumania had once more agreed to allow Soviet aeroplanes to fly across her territory.

[4]The German archives produced during the Nuremberg Trial proved that the German generals, on the eve of Chamberlain's intervention, were preparing to overthrow H tler.

the frontier of Bohemia. Benès was certainly unfortunate: neither Stalin, nor the British, nor the French decided upon the gesture that would save Prague.

Berzine had noted a few questions of Stalin's which indirectly supported his theory. But the majority of the Politburo, with Molotov at their head, felt that Berzine's advice was in flagrant contradiction to their 'conception of world politics, already approved by the Politburo, according to which the inevitability of the attempts of the Capitalist Powers to reach an agreement with Hitler at the expense of the U.S.S.R. had been established.'

At the close of the discussion it was decided that a new Ambassador, Merekalov, should be sent to Berlin. Astakhov, First Secretary, would assist him. 'Stalin,' Berzine noted, 'did not take part in the voting.'

As always when a serious decision involving future policy had to be taken, Stalin kept out of the way. He preferred to allow the various tendencies to present their theses inside the 'dictatorial shell.' On no account was he willing to assume the responsibility for an Anglo-Germanic agreement directed against the U.S.S.R. He had no great confidence in all the reports of I.N.O., nor in those of Berzine.

It must be recognized that Stalin's hesitations had their counterpart in Great Britain. But it must not be forgotten that Churchill is subject to extremely complicated rules, born of a long tradition of democratic affairs. If the breath of the oncoming tempest seemed to invite statesmen to bow before an inescapable fatality, Stalin himself would find it easier to oppose its approach. For him, public opinion was practically negligible, and he had not to convince a Parliament. If instead of finessing and taking evasive action he had adopted a definite attitude he could justly have laid claim to the title of 'inspired Father of the People.' Then, it may be, the U.S.S.R. would not have had to mourn some 17,000,000 of human lives, cast away between 1941 and 1945.

So Stalin gave way before the majority of the Politburo. But this did not mean that he would not act as he himself thought fitting. He engaged in a manœuvre which was peculiarly characteristic: he encouraged Litvinov's feelers toward the conclusion of a Franco-Anglo-Soviet air pact, which was destined to be grafted on to the other air pacts of Central Europe. Through a personal letter from his chief secretary Tovstoukha, Stalin gave Litvinov to understand that he had no objection to prudent soundings in Paris and London with a view to the conclusion of such a pact.[1] But if a brick were dropped anywhere, Tovstoukha, an absolutely devoted disciple, could be sacrificed and repudiated as having misunderstood or misinterpreted the true significance of the Chief's verbal instructions.

Stalin's stratagem was ingenious in its cynicism. If the British and the French accepted the combination, this would greatly reduce the practical repercussions of Molotov's thesis.

Thus, Stalin made it possible for the chief of the Commissariat for Foreign Affairs to continue its policy despite the decisions of the Politburo. Of course, he could not do so without being very strictly controlled by Stalin, who, fearing to be confronted by an accomplished fact, closely supervised all the actions and utterances of the heads of the diplomatic service. Raskolnikov, Bradovsky-Bradman and Bessedovsky have given in their memoirs a perfect demonstration of Stalin's habit of giving directions, safely camouflaged, but definite, in the course of strictly personal conversations.

The manœuvre upon which he had now embarked was at the bottom of the famous duplicity of the Soviet's foreign policies, which was so often discussed during the years 1938–39, and which observers found so profoundly disconcerting. But if there was duplicity it was not merely a matter of Stalin's bad faith. That would have been too simple.

He had already weighed up the different factors controlling the situation. A constructive revolutionary, he tended to avoid theories based on the collapse of the political, and above all the social and communal scaffolding of other countries. Unlike Molotov, he was already beginning to lose faith in such collapses. He was already sensible of the power of the United States, behind the French and English, and he had no intention of giving direct offence to this mighty combination. A realist, a man of practical solutions, he was beginning to lose faith in the absolute value of purely ideological attitudes. This proved greatly to his advantage in connection with his foreign policies.

The situation was particularly complicated, and the international

[1]Krivitzky's *Memoirs*.

conjuncture was fluid and unstable. By acting in his habitual manner he assures himself of a means of defending himself, if need be, against the accusation that he is a social and national traitor should an agreement with the Nazi Reich, such as Molotov foretold, be concluded.

But his favourite sociologist, Gustave Le Bon, has taught him that 'revolutions cannot destroy the mental structure of a people when this has been built up during a long past. They change only its outward appearances.' Now, the mental structure of the Russian people is fundamentally Germanophobe. In the patriotic cement which Stalin employs to stiffen the psychological attitude of the Red Army, the traditional hatred of the Russian masses for Prussian militarism is one of the principal ingredients. The famous film, *Alexander Nevsky*, showing the Teutonic invasion and its collapse, was produced in response to his personal request, and its production was supervised by his secretariat.

In his opinion, which he has expressed on a number of occasions, the Romanoff dynasty was not discredited by the events of the 9 January, 1905, when the workers proceeded to the Winter Palace in order to present their *cahiers* of grievances to Nicholas II, and were shot down. According to him it was finally discredited by the famous speech delivered in 1916 by the Liberal deputy Miliukov, who, violently attacking not only the Government, but the Empress, complaining of her interference, punctuated every paragraph of his diatribe by the question: 'Was this a case of stupidity or of treachery?'

It must be admitted that Stalin's opinion would seem to be justified. The fusillades of 1905 did not prevent the peasant masses from remaining loyal to the Tsar, as they proved at the beginning of the first world war. It was the rumour of treachery that struck a deadly blow to the Imperial prestige, creating such a void around the throne that a mere riot in the capital developed into a revolution.

We have now come to the eve of Munich. Stalin has completed the bloody purges of the Party and the mechanism of the State. His personal authority has been finally established. It is comparable to the authority of the Tsars. The least imprudence on his part would destroy his prestige and be exploited by his enemies.

The failure of the first attempt to effect a rapprochement with

Germany called for increased prudence on Stalin's part. Molotov and the other Bolshevik leaders did not have to achieve the semblance of infallible deities. But Stalin, having become the personification of a new autocracy, had to act with particular caution. He knew that he could not mobilize or galvanize the masses of the U.S.S.R. for war except by calling upon them to defend the country against the Teutonic menace.[1] The result was that Litvinov's instructions recommended him to require his representatives in Berlin to exercise the utmost prudence in carrying out the directions of the Politburo in respect of the Sovieto-German rapprochement.

Arriving in Berlin, the new Ambassador, Merekalov, presented his credentials on the 5 June, 1938. In the customary speech he spoke of the treaty of friendship and neutrality of 1926 as the effective basis of the mutual relations of the two countries. Once more, this fact of definite historical importance escaped the attention of the chancelleries and the press. Yet this speech had been edited by Stalin himself, in collaboration with Litvinov and Molotov; it deserved greater attention.

Then, in conformity with Litvinov's instructions, Merekalov made himself inconspicuous. He shut himself up in his office at 7 Unter den Linden and avoided any interview with Ribbentrop or his Secretary of State, Baron Weizsäcker.

Meanwhile, in Moscow the balance of forces between the representatives of the two theories remained unchanged.

Stalin, for tactical reasons, began to pay longer and longer visits to Sotchi on the Black Sea. There he spent the time with his children in his new Villa Nadejda, built by a Russian architect of French origin, Auphane. He thus avoided participation in the lively discussions of the Politburo, and even refrained from communicating his opinions by telephone, pleading 'lack of information and distance.'

When it was understood in Moscow that Runciman favoured the Third Reich in respect of the Sudeten problem, Molotov urged more vigorously than ever the necessity of negotiating with Berlin,

[1]François Mauriac, who cannot be suspected of excessive sympathy for the U.S.S.R., does not lose sight of this aspect of the question. In an article published in the *Figaro* he asserts that 'military action, even if desired by the political leaders, could be rendered impossible merely by the opposition, even the silent opposition, of the 190 million inhabitants of the U.S.S.R.'

lest Chamberlain and Hitler should come to a definite agreement behind the back of the U.S.S.R. Nevertheless, Litvinov proved obstructive. Stalin, from Sotchi, supported him, and his position was strengthened by the speech delivered on the 12 July by the French President du Conseil, Edouard Daladier, at the banquet of the *Provençaux de Paris*. Daladier declared, with emphasis, that 'the solemn pledges of France to Czechoslovakia are sacred and ineluctable.'

On his part, Benès appeared determined to resist. He disregarded Chamberlain's advice to demobilize his army, but he could not actually resist without a definite pledge from Moscow. In July he wrote a personal letter to Stalin, asking for written confirmation of the unequivocal attitude of the U.S.S.R. He wanted a reply from Moscow which he could publish.

Stalin received this letter at Sotchi. The majority of the members of the Politburo were on vacation, and their vacations were as sacred as the week-ends of the British politician. A summer secretariat— Andréev, Chtcherbakov, and Malenkov, the new Secretary of the Central Committee, and a protégé of Molotov's—was attending to current affairs. Litvinov was absent on leave. His assistant, Potemkin, was at sea. In the interim the Commissariat of Foreign Affairs was under the direction of a second assistant, Dekanozov.

On receiving Benès' letter Stalin, contrary to his usual custom, interrupted his holiday and returned to Moscow by air. Such a flight was exceptional. The aeroplane, 'The Wings of the Soviet,' which he formerly used on his journeys, had crashed; the giant aeroplane 'Maxim Gorki,' intended for his use, was destroyed by accident or sabotage. It was only by chance that he had not taken his place in it on the day of the catastrophe; his daughter Svetlana had been taken ill. After this, remembering Lenin's advice, he had carefully avoided aeroplanes, 'for leaders must not needlessly risk their lives.'

But this time he set off with Vorochilov in the personal plane of the head of the Red Army, a tri-motor built by Toupolev and baptised 'Lenin.' It was during this flight that he suffered for the first time from asthma. When the plane reached a height of more than 10,000 feet he had a severe attack. His physicians definitely prohibited any further flights. He disobeyed this injunction only on exceptional occasions; for example, in December 1943, on the occasion of the Teheran Conference, but then the aeroplane was provided with a pressure cabin, and two physicians accompanied him. Even with these precautions the pilot was forbidden to climb higher than 1,500 feet, and this involved the choice of a very long itinerary. The plane stopped twice on the way, and Stalin reached Teheran, where Roosevelt and Churchill were awaiting him, nearly two days late.

The extraordinary meeting of the Politburo after the receipt of Benès' letter was entirely devoted to the international situation. The representatives of Razvedoupr and I.N.O. were convoked in order to make their reports.[1] I.N.O. was hardly reassuring. Its informants in Paris, London, Prague, Berlin, Warsaw and Rome believed that Chamberlain was about to enter into an agreement with Hitler. After being received in Downing Street, the Sudeten leader Henlein had a two hours' interview in Prague with Hodja. I.N.O. professed that Lord Halifax had asked Hodja to settle the Sudeten question with all possible speed by ceding the territories in dispute to the Third Reich.

Still more alarming information had been received respecting Lord Halifax's conversations with Captain Wiedemann, a confidential agent of Hitler's, who had come to London. He was reported to have explained that the demand of the Reich was inspired by purely strategical motives; it wished to safeguard the right German flank in the event of a war with the U.S.S.R. Halifax was reported to have replied that the British Government would use its influence in Prague and in Paris to obtain the consent of the Czechs to the demand of the Reich. Further, the reports of I.N.O. referred to the influence of the Anglo-German financial agreement over the Austrian debt (concluded on the 1 July, 1938), and to the hopes of the City that the Sudeten affair would be settled. Finally, there was a long account of the talks in Berlin, in June, between Etienne Flandin and Yaroslavl Priess,[2] the Czech financier and manufacturer.

The Politburo voted against the despatch to Benès of a written reply from Stalin. One can understand why Stalin came to Moscow: if he had not left the decision to the Politburo it would have seemed that he must have taken control one way or the other. In any

[1]Krivitsky.
[2]Preiss played an important part in the campaign to induce Benès to yield to Hitler. He died in 1945, before trial, in Prague.

case, the Soviet Ambassador in Prague was instructed to inform Beneš orally that the U.S.S.R. was ready to execute the obligations imposed upon it by the alliance.

The prudence of the Politburo proved to be justified. Almost at the same moment an event occurred in Warsaw which was decisive for the future of Europe. Colonel Beck, who had for so long been Hitler's factotum in Central Europe, had told the Soviet Ambassador to Poland that Soviet air crossings would constitute a violation of the Polish air-space and that the Polish Air Force and anti-aircraft defences would oppose any such passage. Beck thereby confirmed his attitude; he was delivering the Czechs to Hitler, and facilitating Hitler's occupation of their strategical positions. However, he received his thirty pieces of silver: the region of Teschen.

CHAPTER XXXII

MUNICH

AT this period there occurred a personal crisis in Stalin's life, which was for him an event of the greatest importance. It is evident that he did his utmost to prevent his private affairs from attracting attention. But he could not prevent gossip, and there was a great deal of gossip, not only in the Kremlin, but more or less everywhere in Moscow. Political critics were less vocal, but the tattlers made up for their silence. The gossip related to the preparations for his divorce from Rosa Kaganovitch, sister of Lazare, member of the Politburo.

Stalin might profess the most extreme Socialism, and the dogmas of the Bolshevik Party; he might declare himself to be a materialist and atheist, regarding with contempt all bourgeois prejudices relating to the family and its obligations; but in spite of this he had, throughout his personal life, really remained a convinced *petit bourgeois*.

His enemy Trotzky reproached him to the end of his life with having celebrated the religious obsequies of his first wife. His mental prejudices ended by provoking incessant quarrels with his second wife, Nadiejda Alliloueva, the daughter of the old revolutionary, who at the age of seventeen had become a member of the Party. Twenty years younger than her husband, she had always insisted on preserving the completest independence in all her actions, refusing to concern herself with household duties, or even to look after her children, Vassili and Svetlana, or her brother-in-law Jacob, who was sent to live with his maternal grandmother, or Stalin's adoptive son Boris. She devoted herself to Party affairs, in the co-operatives and the fabric of the State.

Stalin's traditionalistic ideas did not suit the ardent Nadiejda, who wanted to remain a Bolshevik in her private life. The tragic and mysterious death of this young woman weighed heavily on Stalin.

It was to make him forget all this that his friends urged him to contract a third marriage.

Rosa Kaganovitch, on her marriage, retired at Stalin's request from her work in the propagandist department of the Central Committee. Still young, and very handsome, she spent whole days with Nadiejda's two children. Once a week she gave a musical evening and a dance. These evenings gradually became meetings which were known as 'Rosa's salons,' and which spiteful tongues began to discuss with a certain malevolence.

Then, one day, the quiet family life of the Stalin household was disturbed by an event of public significance. Lazare and Rosa had three brothers, Michael, Moïse, and Iouri, all of whom occupied high posts in the Administration. Marshal Vorochilov spoke one day of the 'Kaganovitch dynasty.' The phrase was seized upon by their enemies, and a few weeks later the terrible purger Iéjov accused two of the brothers of a whole series of crimes, including sabotage, malversation and peculation.

Rosa did her utmost to save them. Stalin intervened, but decided to seek a divorce. He could not possibly retain his wife without running the risk of compromising the abstract image of the infallible head of the U.S.S.R., created in accordance with the famous esoteric dogma.

But all these affairs were distressing to him, since they occurred at the very time when he was restoring the solidity of family ties throughout the country, and confirming the authority of the wife in the home.

In 1938 the U.S.S.R. was at the cross-roads. While the main direction and remoter aim of his foreign politics were always present in Stalin's mind, the way in which he ought to negotiate the difficult crossing was not very clearly apparent.

The information which he received was as usual contradictory. In these circumstances Stalin adhered to his basic principle. He tried to obtain as much information as possible while endeavouring to perceive, through his personal informers, the realities which so often escaped them. By endeavouring to maintain an absolute objectivity, he detached himself from all the ideas inspired by his own theories and conceptions. In this he was entirely successful, which unfortunately cannot always be said of the majority of people at work in the international arena. He then got the Politburo to send the Vice-Commissar for Foreign Affairs, Vladimir Potemkin, former Ambassador to France, on a long inquiry.

Potemkin was a personal protégé of Stalin's; a member of a well-to-do middle-class family, who had taught history in a private school. Having joined the Bolshevik Party at the time of the Revolution, he began his diplomatic career in 1919 as President of the Repatriation Commission installed by the U.S.S.R. in Constantinople, whose mission was to secure the return of those who had followed General Wrangel. He was the author of a *Diplomatic History of Europe* which had achieved some success in the U.S.S.R., and also a *Diplomatic Encyclopaedia*.

It is interesting to note that at such an important conjuncture, and for so extensive a voyage of research, Stalin did not select an 'original' Bolshevik, but preferred to apply to a man who had spent the greater part of his life outside the Party. This choice shows that he considers a man of such experience, familiar with the traditions of Russian diplomacy, to be better able than a pupil of the pure Marxist school to interpret European events.

Potemkin visited Western Europe, the Balkans, Turkey, and Greece. Stalin wanted to know where he stood, and when the 'artichoke-leaf conquests' in which Hitler would inevitably engage were going to begin.

At the very moment of Potemkin's departure I.N.O. presented the report of one of its best foreign residents, a certain Maslov, whose network was spread in Switzerland. The conclusions of this report were definite: Hitler would not risk aggression against the U.S.S.R. until he had made sure of his supplies of Roumanian petrol and had conquered the Czechoslovak bastion. This latter, indispensable condition had a twofold aim: to safeguard the route by which his supplies of petroleum reached him, and to liquidate any threat to the German right flank.

Here he was dealing with certainties: the strategic value of the Bohemian and Moravian quadrilateral was a long-established notion which had been defined by dozens of German strategists. It is surprising to find that this axiom was neglected by Chamberlain and the majority of the Western politicians—always excepting Winston Churchill.[1]

Directly he had received this report, Stalin sent for Astakhov. As an exceptional measure, Astakhov was allowed to address the Politburo. This young, brilliant and imaginative diplomatist had already distinguished himself in Japan by his personal initiative in advocating a close understanding with the Japanese Empire. An adventurous spirit, he sometimes went too far. Nevertheless, Stalin employed him as confidential informant and agent.

According to Astakhov, I.N.O.'s report was well founded. The U.S.S.R. could avoid any German aggression for a long while to come if it could manage to convince Hitler, by a courageous diplomatic manœuvre, that it would not be opposed to the creation of a Mitteleuropa under German hegemony, nor to a penetration of the Reich in the direction of the Mediterranean and Asia Minor. In this case there would be no isolated Russo-German war. It would be replaced by an Anglo-German war, almost a world war, in which the United States would intervene.

The battle for the two variants of the future war was raging around Stalin, who so far had not declared himself.

Litvinov believed in the possibility of a British recovery if Germany should attack Czechoslovakia and if the U.S.S.R. were to give the latter military support.

But opinions were still divided. The famous unity of the Kremlin was still an illusion; again there were furious discussions inside the 'dictatorial shell.' And Stalin, the Dictator, sought above all things to avoid issuing orders.

Potemkin, on his return, confirmed the gist of Litvinov's opinions. But he reported certain details which largely neutralized his optimistic opinion, and gave Stalin food for serious thought. Beck would act as Hitler's accomplice, and Stalin deduced from this that one could hardly expect a world war against Germany. France, allied with Poland, could not side with the U.S.S.R. if the latter were to fight the Poles.

In view of all these circumstances Stalin thought it necessary to make London and Paris understand that the U.S.S.R. would not

[1]Churchill's opinion in this respect never varied, and during the second world war it dictated his idea of the best spot for the landing on European soil.

P

take part in a war in Western Europe. Evidently he did so, not in order to apprise them of his intentions, but to make Hitler understand them, and in this way he hoped to avoid drawing upon himself the concentrated thunderbolts of the Third Reich. Further information confirmed Stalin's prognosis without entirely elucidating the situation.

Taciturn and morose, he counselled an increased prudence. He did not dare to clash with the Third Reich and figure as the only adversary. Europe was sliding towards Munich, and Stalin restricted himself to the rôle of observer—uneasy, attentive, but powerless. He could not play an open hand. Against the opinion of the majority of the Politburo, he tried to manœuvre. He struck off at a tangent, giving tacit approval to the efforts of Litvinov. But it is certain that without this tacit approval the son of the Bialystock rabbi, now in control of the foreign policy of the U.S.S.R., would have been promptly liquidated by the agents of Iégov.[1]

Litvinov repeated on several occasions, in a solemn and official manner, that the Red Army would be ready to succour Czecho-slovakia if attacked by Germany, provided Poland would allow the Soviet troops to cross her territory. Beck never missed an opportunity of declaring that he would oppose such action. His Ambassador in Paris, Lukasievitch, made repeated approaches to the Quai d'Orsay and to French politicians, exposing the absurdity of an intervention on the Sudetenland question.

Finally Stalin was obliged to surrender the reins to the Molotov group. He still maintained his principle of leaving each fraction of the Politburo free to assert its own opinion, and to exploit its possibilities and justifications. The final synthesis would depend on events. He postponed his own intervention till the last possible moment. . . . Here we find the basic conception of his course of action, already decided upon, in the international domain. Despite all its divagations it had now assumed a definite form. Henceforth he applied it in all his political and military strategy. Later on he would have occasion to display it over and over again, and even to popularize it in such war films as *The Third Blow*.

This rule consisted in refusing to take the initiative of the attack, or of events which directly led to action. He prefers that the initiative

[1] See Krivitsky.

should always be left to the adversary. He does not react hastily to the first movement of the forces opposing him. He always holds back for a counter-offensive delivered with all the means at his disposal once he understands the deployment of the forces brought into action by the other side.

Continued observation of this system, which sacrifices tactical activity to a 'strategy à outrance,' can but strengthen the impression already mentioned: Stalin works slowly. But this deliberation is not to be explained by surrender to a mere psychological habit. It is rather a system, a plan of action well tested and carefully thought out.

In the month of August 1938, which was to decide the fate of the peace, Stalin returned to Sotchi. Breaking through his usual habit of refusing to deal with matters of State during his vacations, he instructed the Commissariat of Foreign Affairs to keep him constantly informed as to the trend of events. One of the senior officials of the Commissariat, Pavlov, was appointed to maintain the liaison between the Villa Nadejda and the Blacksmiths' Bridge. Copies of all the ambassadors' reports were immediately forwarded to Stalin. Even if he did not wish to give orders, he wanted to know exactly what was happening.

At the end of the month he convoked a meeting of the military leaders. In addition to Vorochilov and Timochenko, the Chief of the General Staff, Marshal Chapochnikov, the great strategical expert, and General Berzine, were present. The Führer had recently made a great show of inspecting the Siegfried Line and crossing the Kehl Bridge. Further, Germany had announced that more than one and a half million men would be recalled to the colours for the autumn manœuvres. It was decided to increase the strength of the Soviet Army to two millions. But spectacular measures would be avoided, and manœuvres would be restricted to military districts.

While treating his old friend Vorochilov with every consideration, Stalin replaced him as Commissar for Defence by Timochenko, with Joukov as Chief of Staff. Chapochnikov became Chief of the General Staff. These three men were old acquaintances. Chapochnikov had for a long while been Stalin's teacher in military affairs, and had worked out all sorts of tactical and strategical problems with him.

In Stalin's home at Perkhouchkovo, near Moscow, there was a study, equipped with maps and a library of military classics. In the past he had, of course, commanded detachments of the Red Army, and even entire fronts. But that was in the days of improvised warfare, fought by armed bands with limited effectives. The coming war was one of a very different character. The U.S.S.R. was about to confront the best army in Europe, commanded by officers who knew their trade and possessing the most learned Great General Staff in the world.

Like all the Bolshevik leaders, Lenin included, Stalin was a great admirer of Clausewitz. The maxim that 'war is the continuation of politics by other means' had long been the corner-stone of Stalin's military structure. But this maxim, after all, was only an outline. Stalin wanted to familiarize himself with technical questions, with the complicated handling of model armies, with infantry, aviation, artillery, armoured cars, and the army service corps.

In Stalin's house Chapochnikov held a small class.[1] The pupils were: Stalin, Mekhliss, head of the political department of the army, Jdanov[2] and Pushrepibichev, the new head of Stalin's secretariat. One day they discussed 'the Battle of Borodino,' which the French call the Battle of the Moskova, and the mistakes committed by the two adversaries. On this occasion Stalin drew his own conclusions, which revealed his fundamental idea—one which would be usefully applied in the years to come. He said: *'The strategical and tactical solution of a battle decisive for the campaign ought necessarily to include the pursuit of the political objects of the war. Battles are not fought exclusively to win the war, but also and above all to win the peace.*

'We ought to go back to the ancient rule that the commanders-in-chief of countries at war should be at the head of the governments of their countries.'

Thus, on the eve of Munich, Stalin, who in practice was in control of all the domestic politics of the U.S.S.R., was already prepared to direct its foreign politics, and even to orientate the coming

[1] The Soviet General Bagratov, who attended these conferences as Chapochnikov's private secretary, gives some descriptions, in the journal *Questions d'Histoire*, of the classes held in Stalin's house.

[2] Secretary for Leningrad.

military operations in the sense of his political conceptions.[1] But just as he had proceeded by gradual steps in the conquest of power, so he waited for the propitious moment for intervening, as ruler of the U.S.S.R., in the international domain and the military field. He would never depart from the prudence which counselled him to show his hand openly only at the moment when the success of the operation for which he was accepting responsibility was, if not already achieved, at least in sight.

Once the Munich affair was over, an incident occurred which was not only very curious, but which presented a certain humorous aspect. It had an important bearing on the future.

I.N.O. forwarded to Stalin some gramophone discs on which were recorded the secret conversations between Hitler and Chamberlain. According to these records, Chamberlain would have left Hitler free to undertake a crusade against the U.S.S.R.

The notion of fabricating such records, of imitating the voices of the alleged speakers, is not a new one. In 1937, at Geneva, Georges Oltramare's supporters had tried to produce the gramophone record of an alleged conversation between Léon Blum and the communist Nicoll.

But things were very different in the case of the spurious Munich records: which shows what mental confusion and emotional instability prevailed at this moment in Moscow, even among the most tortuous of politicians, who were familiar with every description of ruse. The discs were given to I.N.O. by one of its Russo-German agents, a certain Rittmeister von Faltz, a German born in Russia, who vouched for the existence of a score of reproductions, and claimed to have bought his records from Martin Bormann at the price of a million marks. It is possible that this explains the rumour that was current later, to the effect that Bormann was a Soviet agent. . . .

The Politburo sent for Astakhov to come from Berlin. What did he think of the matter? Astakhov, an inveterate advocate of an *entente* with the Reich, and a man who would stick at nothing, thought the records constituted a weighty argument, and eagerly

[1] As a true statesman, with an eye to the historical bearings of events, Churchill understood Stalin very well. Hence his attitude after 1943.

adduced evidence confirming the plausibility of the imitated conversation. He once more insisted on the necessity 'of signing an
agreement with the Third Reich which would forestall Chamberlain's action.'[1]

Inside the dictatorial shell there were what one calls 'various
movements,' but the atmosphere was such that Molotov's supporters
had the best of it. Then the partition of Czechoslovakia, on the
15 March, 1939, between Hitler, Beck, and Horthy, gave the
President of Council the upper hand.

Nevertheless, as matters now stood, while the conflict behind
the scenes in the Politburo and the Eighteenth Pan-Russian Congress
was at its height, it was concerned only with the tactics to be
followed.

The principle matter was settled: everyone, Stalin included,
believed that Chamberlain was urging Hitler to embark on a crusade
against the Russians, and that the Soviet Government would have to
take steps to divert the Germanic flood, and to direct it toward the
valley of the Lower Danube, and then the Balkans and Asia Minor,
where General Liman von Sanders and General von der Goltz had
already spent some time as the representatives of Prussian militarism.
It was believed in Moscow that British interests in these regions were
so important, and that France had invested so much capital there,
that the British Empire and its ally, despite the Halifax-Chamberlain
influence, could not remain mere spectators.

At one moment these previsions were partially realized. On the
13 April, 1939, Great Britain and France gave their joint guarantee
to Roumania and Greece, having already given it to the Poland of
Colonel Beck. Chamberlain, who had been obliged to accept the
seizure by Hitler of the quadrilateral of Bohemia and Moravia, with
its strongly fortified mountains and forests, was now trying to
prevent the collapse of the Little Entente.

Saradjoglou, the Turkish Minister for Foreign Affairs, who considered that he was on very good terms with the U.S.S.R., was sent
to Moscow, in order to obtain the signature to a pact of mutual
assistance, which would lead the U.S.S.R. to take its place in the
'safety girdle.' But he was got rid of without much ceremony.

---

[1]This confirmation, which to say the least of it was imprudent, led to his deportation in 1942 to the Franz-Josef archipelago.

Stalin's reserve was based on several motives. On the one hand, he distrusted Western diplomacy, to which he attributed quite as much Machiavellian cunning as it perceived in his own actions. On the other hand, he could not help feeling sceptical as regards the efficacy of new *ententes*, after the abandonment of the key position of Czechoslovakia.

Lastly, there was an essential fact—a fact, and not words or agreements—which for him represented a decisive test. Litvinov, in his day the advocate of collective security, had declared that England and France would make war to prevent Germany from laying hands on Roumania's petroleum, and that this represented for Russia a real guarantee against German aggression. Now, on the 23 March, 1939, Gregov Gafenco, Minister for Foreign Affairs in Bucharest, *signed, without being prevented by London or Paris, an agreement with the German Ambassador, Fabricius, which guaranteed Roumanian petroleum to the Third Reich.* While others quibbled about a problematical security, this agreement gave Roumanian petroleum to Hitler provided he renounced his plans of invading the Balkans, and confined his aggression to the object indicated in his *Mein Kampf*: namely, the great Russian plain. The chances of an Anglo-German conflict due to the action of the Reich in the Balkans and the Middle East were annulled. History, without a word of warning, accepted its orientation on the 23 March, 1939.

From this time onwards Molotov and Astakhov found it possible to manœuvre the new Politburo. And it was on this occasion that the singular *soi-disant* omnipotence of Stalin became evident. Even while admitting that he could impose his will and his ideas, he never did so. In the interior of the 'dictatorial shell' he acted, during this crucial period, as a controller and co-ordinator rather than a dictator.

The 'supreme Collective,' the Politburo, discussed affairs and acted on its own. Stalin's famous speech, in which he announced that 'the U.S.S.R. refuses to pull the chestnuts out of the fire for others,' can be interpreted in various fashions. He does not pledge himself in any precise sense, except as regards the theoretical interests of the country. But another speech, which is little known, but which constitutes a whole programme, was delivered by Molotov in the Supreme Council. In this speech he openly stigmatized 'plutocratic capitalism,' borrowing the term . . . from Goebbels! By employing the term 'plutocratic' he revealed the fact that Russia's choice had now been made.

Stalin listened, impassive, to the speech of the President of the Council, approved by the Politburo. Just as there was a frantic outburst of applause he left the hall and went to the smoking-room. To the last moment he remained faithful to himself. For him, the supreme skill is to avoid admitting that one is influencing events, but to have the appearance of experiencing them, almost as a resigned and . . . paternal observer.

CHAPTER XXXIII

THE RUSSO-GERMAN TREATIES

THE new Politburo elected by the Eighteenth Pan-Russian Congress of the Party was, as we know, composed of men whose devotion to Stalin was complete. All had accepted his authority, and he could henceforth act as he thought fit, or hold his peace, like an oracle which as often as not is silent. Three young men were now prominent: Malenkov, destined to become First Secretary of the Party; Kossyguin, and Voznessensky; the second being one of the principal organizers of Russian industry, and the last the President of the State Plan. This shows to what extent Stalin emphasizes the industrial questions.

The situation created in Central Europe by the disappearance of Czechoslovakia should have incited all the governments to take up their final positions. The Ambassador in Paris, Suritz, and the Ambassador in London, Maïsky, gave periodical information of conversations relating to different proposals. But Stalin no longer believed in the sincerity of the West. He was convinced that there was a conspiracy against the U.S.S.R. His instincts, and his rather primitive notions of the outer world, put him on his guard against the foreigner; his realism orientated him in accordance with the rules of Marxist historical realism, and what in Western statesmen was really a certain amateurishness, or even an exaggerated nonchalance, appeared to him an eternal and dangerous conspiracy.

When the new Politburo assembled Litvinov presented a report, but the predominant voice in the debate was that of Molotov. For the time being he was justified by events. He still believed in the possibility of launching the Nazi icebreakers against the Western Powers. Stalin, on the other hand, knew that in spite of all his fantastic political notions, Hitler had inherited from Bismarck an aversion to a war on two fronts. His military staff was even more definite. He therefore argued that if the U.S.S.R. should conclude a formal alliance with England and France, the Third Reich would not risk a war.

In short, in his dread of an upheaval in the U.S.S.R., Stalin even cast doubt upon the dogma that a world war launched against the Anglo-Saxons by Hitler would benefit Soviet Russia. But this Ariadne-thread was not enough to guide him through the maze of the international situation; and he did not stick to his idea. More-over, Maïsky's reports from London declared that Great Britain would never sign an alliance with the U.S.S.R. comprising a guaran-tee of the Soviet frontiers in the Far East. Her position in India made such an alliance impossible. Consequently, the danger of a Japanese attack on the U.S.S.R. was increased.

Merekalov departed to his post as Ambassador to Berlin, pro-vided with a written memorandum which he was to present to the Under-Secretary of State, Baron Weizsäcker, after calling on Wiehl, Director of Commercial Relations. The obvious intention of this stratagem of Stalin's was to discover the basic intentions of Germany. Moscow had sent orders for munitions of war to the Skoda works before these had fallen into German hands. He now asked the Germans if they were going to deliver this material. He received a satisfactory reply. Wiehl assured Merekalov that the Skoda contracts would be punctually fulfilled.

Proceeding to the second part of his mission, Merekalov ques-tioned the Under-Secretary directly as to the German reactions in the event of 'serious incidents on the Polono-German frontier.' In view of the hesitating answer received—the Under-Secretary was visibly reluctant to accept the responsibility for a precise reply—Stalin's emissary submitted a memorandum which stated that: 'Ideo-logical differences have never exercised any influence over the Russo-Italian relations. Nor have they in the past constituted a stumbling block for Germany. The U.S.S.R. has never exploited against Ger-many the disagreements between Germany and the other Western States. The U.S.S.R. sees no reason why it should not maintain normal relations with Germany—relations which might be con-tinually improved. . . .'

Whatever Stalin's formal attitude might be, by permitting and even recommending the presentation of this document he fully assumed the responsibility for a definite attitude toward future eventualities.

The Under-Secretary repeated the assurance that the Skoda works would deliver the material in question, and added that the request already presented by Astakhov in respect of maintaining a Soviet commercial representative in Prague had been answered in the affirmative. The results of the probe were conclusive. The Third Reich was ready to engage in negotiations.

At the moment, Stalin did nothing; save for a gesture which is always equivalent, in the U.S.S.R., to the adoption of a definite position. He still took no part in the Government, but he ordered an important change in the directing personnel. On receiving Mere-kalov's report the Politburo decided to entrust the post of 'Chief of Foreign Affairs' to Molotov, instead of the aged Litvinov.[1] To a foreigner, as yet unaware of Molotov's political thesis, Molotov seemed a neutral personality; and his new functions merely indicated that the Kremlin wanted to have its hands free to negotiate with the West as well as with the Third Reich.

Despite this decision, Stalin did not wish to lose the opportunity of once more obtaining information as to British intentions, so that the decision taken on the 30 April was not made public by a ukase of the Supreme Council until the 3 May. Stalin kept it secret for four days because a British delegation then in Moscow was negotiating with Litvinov.

On the 1 May Litvinov was to be seen on the rostrum in the Red Square at Stalin's right. On the 2 May he received the British Ambassador in order to discuss the clauses of the air pact proposed by London and Paris. The delay in making his supercession public was due to the necessity of discovering what the governing classes in England were really thinking. Stalin remained faithful to his usual methods during the new phase of foreign policy. As soon as he had authorized this new zigzag, he 'disappeared' anew. It was Molotov's turn to screen the Georgian Janus, but while he was left free to act as he thought fit, and Stalin maintained his policy of 'not interfering personally in foreign affairs—the apanage of the President of the Council,' he none the less retained an indirect control. This he did through the medium of his intimate friend, Marshal

[1] Molotov was President of the Council of People's Commissars.

Vorochilov, President of the Military Commission of the Politburo.

The task assigned to Vorochilov in this post was given a plausible official explanation. The military questions to be discussed with the Western Powers, who would be obliged to despatch a mission, were important, and in spite of the famous memorandum presented in Berlin by Merekalov, Stalin wished not to commit the U.S.S.R. until a final conclusion was reached. Now, Vorochilov did not share Molotov's opinion; so that Stalin, by keeping in the background, was able to 'play on two tables.' One really has the impression that he wanted once more to remind the Politburo that there were two possible issues in respect of the existing situation . . . moreover, in case of need he would be able to dissociate himself from Molotov. His mastery of intrigue and his system of twofold precautions were now brought to bear in the international domain. This semi-with-drawal was facilitated by the fact that he was fulfilling no official function.

Molotov and Vorochilov could act only as official personages. He himself left Moscow for Sotchi, despite the international tension, which was daily increasing, several weeks earlier than usual, leaving Molotov to make the best he could of the first practical application of his theory. It was a move of the greatest subtlety. He disposed of a power and an influence which officially had no existence, but which were actually so great that he sought as far as possible to conceal them.

Other members of the Politburo now went on leave to their villas in the same neighbourhood as Stalin's.

By a special decision of the Politburo, evidently taken at the indirect instigation of Stalin, Molotov was invited to remain in Moscow until the end of September. He was seconded by Malenkov, whose vertiginous ascent dates from this summer, and who *ad interim* exercised the functions of Secretary-General, and by Jdanov; while he was closely watched by Vorochilov.

Vorochilov believed in the possibility of a politico-economic military alliance with England and France, and he was instructed to make himself agreeable until the last possible moment to French and British military circles. Malenkov was still inexperienced, and might be excused for mistakes committed during his negotiations.

If the negotiations with the Third Reich were successful Stalin would not accept direct responsibility for them. He knew that an agreement with Germany would not be popular with the Russian masses, and that it would certainly upset the Communists all the world over. By leaving the whole apparent responsibility to others he achieved the end he desired—which was to produce the illusion that the affair was arranged and settled without him, that it was due to decisions taken by those who were actually ruling the U.S.S.R., on whom he himself, in conformity with the principles of Soviet democracy, could not impose any line of conduct. *It would never be too late to claim merit for anything whatsoever if it was deserved and if all went well.*

Left to himself, Molotov progressed very slowly, and in a hesitating fashion. He acted so slowly, and with such reserve, that the German Ambassador, Count von Schulenburg, and Ribbentrop, who received the Ambassador's reports, were unable for some time to understand whether Molotov did or did not desire an agreement with the Third Reich.[1]

The vagueness which Stalin evoked by his evasions persisted—and produced results. Weizsäcker found himself obliged to send for Astakhov, now *charge d'affaires* in Berlin, on the 30 May and the 11 June, in order to ask him a direct question. Astakhov told the Under-Secretary that the Government of the U.S.S.R. had firmly decided to 'proceed resolutely toward a political and economic agreement with Germany.' It was Astakhov who referred, *en passant*, to the agreement between Catherine II and Frederick of Prussia, in respect of the partition of Poland. Stalin always preferred to make suggestions through a third party.

According to the notes of the Wilhelmstrasse, Astakhov explained: 'We do not wish to be the instigators of a new partition of Poland, but if circumstances and the disastrous policy of Colonel Beck should lead Poland to become the lackey of British Imperialism and provoke a war with Germany we should never take advantage of this in order to attack the Reich, which would be in a state of legitimate self-defence.' The allusion was plain.

It is permissible to believe that this conversation was immediately reported to Stalin by Astakhov, for he was suddenly summoned to Sotchi, to which he travelled by aeroplane. He spent five days there,

[1]The Wilhelmstrasse Archives.

and returned directly to Berlin, without passing through Moscow. Had Stalin, in departing from his customary behaviour, given personal instructions to Astakhov, or was he content to obtain precise information as to the German reactions?

In the Politburo the final decision had been taken. It could have been modified only in the event of a new conjuncture—the unexpected offer of some exceptional advantage which the Western Powers were evidently unable to make. Astakhov was, therefore, sent back to Berlin, obviously furnished this time with Stalin's personal instructions. He was to go to Dragonov, the Bulgarian Minister in Berlin, and confide to him, in private conversation, the firm decision of the Soviets to conclude an agreement with the Third Reich. This Bulgarian was regarded as so far committed to the German cause that King Boris preferred not to confide in him.

Astakhov fulfilled his mission adroitly. On the 16 June Dragonov called on Woermann, the Director of the Department for the Balkans. He was greatly excited. He had just had a sensational conversation with the Russian *charge d'affaires.* He was trying to make the most of the incident, speaking of the advice he had given to Astakhov, who had spent nearly two hours with him. The Bulgarian insisted on the perturbed condition of the Soviet representative, who had spoken 'with the greatest vivacity, and with a wealth of gestures, and stammering at times.'

Woermann hastened to hand on this news to Under-Secretary Weizsäcker, who evidently realized the importance of Astakhov's initiative, which might modify Russo-German relations, and thus, the whole international situation.

Needless to say, it was Stalin, who did not officially appear in the matter, who directed operations from a distance. All the transactions of that period between the Reich and the U.S.S.R. bore his invisible signature.

It was at Ewest, near Berlin, on the 27 July, that Astakhov, on the express authorization of Stalin, at last revealed the broad outlines of the Russian policy. This does not mean that Stalin already believed without reservation in the possibility of arranging a pact with Hitler; but in case such a pact should be possible, he stated its conditions. And these were his maximum demands; and up to the last moment he doubted whether Berlin could accept them.

They were far beyond the competence of Schnurre, who in his report to his chiefs made no secret of the state of mental confusion to which he was reduced.

In fact, Astakhov made it clear that Stalin had decided to take part in the partition of Poland in the event of a Germano-Polish war. He wished also to regain possession of the ancient Baltic provinces of Latvia, Esthonia and Lithuania; and he confirmed the fact that the U.S.S.R. wished to secure certain strategical interests in the Gulf of Finland; and further, he wished to recover Bessarabia.

Schnurre carefully committed to memory all that Astakhov had said; but, being positively thunderstruck, he contented himself with smiling amiably, and finally invited the Russian to attend the celebrations on the *Tag* of the German Arts in Munich. However, he 'approved most warmly of Molotov's idea' that 'despite appearances, the Anti-Comintern pact was not aimed against the U.S.S.R. but against the City and Wall Street.'

Moscow had chosen to make this singular declaration at the moment when the Mongolian Army commanded by Joukov, supported by four brigades of armoured cars and some 500 aeroplanes, had just inflicted a humiliating defeat on the Japanese. Schnurre had evidently carried out his instructions, in trying to persuade the Russians of the advantages of German mediation in the Far East. In view of the possibility of assuring the neutrality of the U.S.S.R. in Europe in the event of war between Germany and the Franco-British allies, and the inestimable advantage which his Western frontier would afford, Stalin might hope for a *de facto* annulment of the anti-Comintern pact. Yet the great and essential idea of this pact was to get Japan to drive the Russians out of China!

On the following day, Schnurre, who had had time to consult his superiors, telephoned to Astakhov. He told him how greatly interested he and his superiors had been in the conversations of the day before.

When Stalin received Astakhov's notes at Sotchi he appeared to hesitate no longer. Never yet had the Russian State obtained such colossal advantages without costly efforts. Strangely enough, it was the will of history that this should happen at a time when power was in the hands of an internationalist party led by a Georgian. But Stalin, of course, had been absorbed by the national Russian continuum, as had so many before him in the course of the centuries.

Molotov could not quite believe in Hitler's 'Chinese present.' He applied to the Ambassador Schulenburg for confirmation of the facts. Schulenburg confirmed all that Schnurre had said, proving that the promise was to be taken seriously. Henceforth the ground was cleared for the German-Soviet pact.

In his conversations with the British and French generals Vorochilov did his best to bring forward the question of the Baltic countries. It was a small affair compared with Hitler's generosity. But Paris and London could not give guarantees in respect of it.[1] Even had they been willing, the French and British Governments—which, for that matter, did not keep step with each other—could not pledge themselves, and the United States, with its large Baltic population, would certainly be refractory.

[1]On the 10 June, 1939, the author published in the *Petit Journal* an article—'What Stalin Wants'—which was completely confirmed by subsequent events. He wrote:

'. . . As regards the foreign politics of the U.S.S.R., the lessons to be drawn from Litvinov's departure were definite and precise. Stalin wished above all to liberate the diplomatic action of Soviet Russia from anything that might seem like a Genevan mortgage, or from any restraint due to common action with the democratic Western Powers. . . . In this way a warning was given to all, and above all to the Powers on both sides, that henceforth the U.S.S.R. would act . . . entirely as it pleased. Being assured of a free hand, the Kremlin was prepared to exploit its freedom. Unfortunately—and this is a serious fault—the West persists in refusing to see the reality. As against all the facts, against the evidence itself, people persist in trying to persuade us that the Soviets are eager and impatient to adhere to security pacts conceived on the lines laid down by Halifax and Chamberlain.

'At the very moment when Molotov was disclosing one of the chief obstacles to the conclusion of the agreement, the expert journalists were announcing with satisfaction, and without the least accent of irony, that the only cause of delay was the existence of "a few purely formal difficulties." They dare not admit that the differences of standpoint are profound and serious, and that the skilful "hesitations" of Moscow are merely making things easier for Stalin—who is bent on obtaining the maximum. . . . He will not alienate his liberty of action unless he is treated as being on the same footing as the other parties to the negotiations—and above all, Great Britain. . . . There must be automatic intervention in the event of aggression against any of the parties. The more fully Russia becomes conscious of the importance which the West attaches to an alliance with her, the more exigent do her rulers become. It is highly probable that if a guarantee is given in respect of the Baltic countries, Molotov will ask for a guarantee in respect of the Far East. . . .

'. . . Moscow is in no hurry to conclude an agreement with the West. She has not forgotten that after Munich the West wanted to turn the German forces of aggression eastwards. *But she seems to be in possession of data—of assurances?—which free her from all anxiety in this respect.*

'As long as this is the case she will continue her policy—a very skilful one: to delay matters, to yield, if she yields at all, only in return for a very great price.'

(10 June, 1939.)

Accordingly, the Western Powers were not offering Stalin what he needed, whereas the Germans, whom he feared, were ready to grant his demands beyond anything that he could reasonably have hoped. It is true that he had asked a good deal, and that without the presence of the Western military missions in Moscow it is improbable that Hitler would have been so generous. At all events, after a delay of a few weeks the conversations between Astakhov and Schnurre inevitably ended in the agreement of the 23 August, 1939.

At Sotchi, on the 17 August, Stalin received a telegram from Molotov; a long conversation over the telephone followed.

Ribbentrop had just transmitted a first message intended for Stalin in person, defining the clauses of the treaty which Germany was proposing to the U.S.S.R. In all these negotiations the Wilhelmstrasse persisted in addressing Stalin, although he occupied no official post in the Government. Hitler was not deceived by this ruse.

Nevertheless, Stalin continued to finesse. After receiving Molotov's telegram he wanted positively to refuse any consultation by telephone. He did not know how far 'the carrots were cooked,' and he preferred that Molotov, if anyone, should risk indigestion. He therefore restricted himself to advising the President of the Council to submit the message to a private session of the executive trio, Molotov, Vorochilov and Malenkov. Molotov was insistent. The Soviet leaders played their cards carefully: no one was ready as yet to accept responsibility for so grave a decision.

But while Stalin was shilly-shallying with Molotov the German Ambassador requested a fresh, urgent interview. He explained by telephone to Pavlov, Molotov's secretary, that he had received an addition to the message for Stalin, and wished to transmit it. The conversation between Moscow and Sotchi was interrupted in order that the matter could be considered. On the following day, at 6 a.m., the dialogue was resumed.

When Schulenburg had transmitted his addendum, it appeared that the situation called for an immediate decision, and that no adjournment was possible. The Germans, in fact, announced the precise conditions of the future treaty, and demanded, officially, that they should at once be submitted to Stalin. They wanted to force him at all costs to adopt a definite position. They also announced that

Q

Ribbentrop 'intended to come to Moscow to discuss the treaty . . . with Stalin.'

Realizing the gravity of the case, Molotov insisted that the Politburo should assemble under the presidency of Stalin himself. Stalin was obliged to agree. The score was so difficult to interpret that the conductor could no longer remain off stage; moreover, he ought to garner the results of his prudence, patience and cunning. His adroitness was such that he seemed to be consenting to receive the offerings of destiny, which presented him, on this occasion, with all the advantages he had desired. His triumph in this passage of intrigue was complete.

On the morning of the 19 August he took the plane for Moscow. The mechanism of the operation which was to transform the world conjuncture was forging ahead, and Stalin, profoundly impassive, followed whither it led. This was due not merely to a reasoned attitude, but to the special quality of his nerves. At this historic moment Stalin remained faithful to himself, and it was suddenly obvious that his apprenticeship as an international politician was completed. So far he had been dangerous only to his enemies at home; but from August 1939 the outer world was obliged to take him into account; and whatever his official attitude might be henceforth, the instinct that inspires the reactions of the masses understood and accepted the fact that it was he alone who should be regarded as responsible for the international enterprises of the U.S.S.R., regarded as 'disastrous' by some and as 'salutary' by others.

He exploited the German affair to the best advantage. There again the counter-project elaborated in accordance with his indications was rather vague. . . . But he foresaw the signature of a special protocol 'on all the points on which the high contracting parties are interested in the domain of foreign politics.' The agreement would be valid only if the special protocol was initiated simultaneously by Berlin and Moscow. Stalin signified his intention of signing the pact only if the Reich satisfied all the demands of the U.S.S.R.

He risked his whole hand. Either the Germans would not sign the pact at all, or they would ratify Russia's demands by reinforcing in an unlooked-for manner the strategical position of Moscow in respect of the decisive struggle between the Russians and the . . . Germans ! The manœuvre was on the grand scale. Stalin judged that the Germans had already involved themselves too far to retreat. On the other hand, the Allied military missions were still in Moscow.

On the 21 August the German Ambassador sent Molotov a personal message from Hitler to Stalin, which proposed that the Führer should send Ribbentrop to Moscow. On the 21 August, at 5 o'clock in the afternoon, Stalin telegraphed his acceptance of the proposal:

'To the Chancellor of the German Reich Adolf Hitler: I thank you for your letter. I hope the Germano-Soviet pact of non-aggression will mark a favourable and decisive turn in the political relations of the two countries. The peoples of our countries need to entertain peaceful relations with each other. For Germans, the conclusion of a pact of non-aggression lays permanent foundations which make it possible to eliminate political tension and establish peace and collaboration between our countries. The Soviet Government has authorized me to inform you that it agrees that Monsieur Von Ribbentrop shall come to Moscow on the 23 August.'[1]

The negotiations between Molotov and Ribbentrop continued throughout the night of the 23 August. Stalin smiled, now mockingly, now with resignation, as though submitting to things imposed by others, and happening without any desire of his. The agreements signed represented the absolute maximum, beyond which he would not engage himself, even by a harmless phrase. On the other hand, he was always endeavouring to discover the fundamental political ideas of the Third Reich. Obviously, he did not avoid conversations with Ribbentrop. The latter, exuberant and excited, noted that his host was extremely well-informed in respect of international affairs; also, that he spoke his mind freely.

Speaking of Tokio, Ribbentrop declared that the Third Reich considered that it could contribute very effectively to smooth out the differences between the U.S.S.R. and Japan. 'There are limits to our patience,' Stalin replied. 'If Japan wants war she can have it. The U.S.S.R. is not afraid of Japan and is prepared for any eventuality.'

Despite this rebuff, Ribbentrop was still jubilant. He believed that he had achieved stupendous results. Moreover, all the Germans present in Moscow seem to have lost their heads, believing that they had achieved the acme of diplomatic adroitness. They welcomed all Stalin's pronouncements with enthusiasm.

[1]Secret archives of the Wilhelmstrasse.

Speaking of Italy, Stalin observed that Mussolini would certainly not be satisfied with Albania alone—'mountainous and scantily populated and presenting no interest.' Was it possible that he had his eyes on Greece?—he innocently asked Ribbentrop, who preferred to change the subject, and launched into a dithyramb in honour of Mussolini, 'an energetic man who does not allow himself to be intimidated, as he proved during the Ethiopian war.'

'Come, come!' said Stalin, with the same spurious candour. 'For my part, I thought the Ethiopians were armed only with spears and clubs, and that Samuel Hoare and Laval were trying to calm Mussolini rather than intimidate him. . . .'

He continued to speak ironically. Referring to Turkey, Ribbentrop declared that London had spent five millions on anti-German propaganda in Ankara. 'You underestimate the Turkish statesmen,' Stalin replied, coldly. 'According to my information the English spent a very much larger sum on the purchase of Turkish politicians.'

Respecting France, Stalin confined himself to remarking: 'The French Army is worth consideration. . . .'

But the conversation turned back to England: 'England is weak at the present moment in a military sense,' said Stalin, 'but if you attack her she will fight with cunning, obstinacy and courage.' As Ribbentrop only grimaced, he added: 'It is surprising that a few thousand Englishmen should rule India. This is due to a certain illusion on the part of weak peoples as to the strength of the colonizing powers. However, the British Army is weak; so is the British Navy; and the Air Force lacks pilots. All that is true. But in spite of all, Britain is still an Empire which dominates the world. The explanation is to be found in the stupidity of the other countries, which allow themselves to be hoaxed by a spectre that no longer exists. . . . I know the anti-Comintern pact frightened the City and the small traders. . . .'

Ribbentrop, trying to be witty, replied: 'The people of Berlin, who are famous for their shrewdness and their sense of humour, often say that Stalin will end by adhering to the anti-Comintern pact.'

Stalin replied, in a bantering tone: 'When the bankers of the City join the British Communist Party I will willingly subscribe to the anti-Comintern pact, but not before.'

During the celebrated banquet Stalin proposed a toast to the Führer. But this he did in peculiar terms: 'I have been told that the German nation has a great love for its Führer. Consequently I should like to drink his health. . . .'

Proposing four times in succession a toast in honour of the pact of non-aggression, Stalin stressed the fact each time that he was drinking 'to the honour of the German nation which has given the world illustrious scientists and brilliant writers and musicians. . . .' The Germans, in their euphoria, took all this as a great compliment. It was not until later, in 1942, that they spoke of 'the insults which they had to endure from the horrible Stalin.'

At the close of the banquet Stalin declared, this time without irony, by way of wishing *bon voyage* to Ribbentrop: 'Together with the Soviet Government, I take the new pact very seriously. I can guarantee on my honour that we shall never let our partners down.'[1]

The future would confirm the fact that after the elimination of several of the players round a green table the partners of the day before inevitably became adversaries.

On the 25 August the Moscow newspaper *Troud*, in an article signed 'Syndicalist,' stressed the fact that 'the necessities of foreign politics will never prevent us from repudiating the mediaeval and pseudo-scientific theories which are beginning to flourish in Central Europe.' The allusion is plain, and it was said that Stalin's Secretariat had been instructed to request the newspaper to say what it thought of the racial theories of the Germans.

The Germano-Soviet pact was signed. Stalin was pledging himself during a period of international activity of exceptional complexity, in the course of which he would try to maintain as long as possible the Russo-German *mariage de raison*, while yielding nothing in the various disputes which arose during the logical development of the opposition of German and Russian interests.

Whatever might be thought of Stalin, his partners and his foreign adversaries would henceforth have to admit his real worth, and the strength which he had built up; and the additional support which his enterprises derived from his opportune evocation of the national continuity of Greater Russia.

[1] Archives of the Wilhelmstrasse; Schmidt's *Memoirs* and Gafenco's *Questions o History*.

CHAPTER XXXIV

THE WAR AND COMMUNISM

THE extraordinarily rapid issue of the war against Poland surprised Stalin. It was as little expected by him as it was by the Western countries.

On several occasions messages from Berlin, forwarded by the Ambassador Schulenburg, invited the Soviet armies to enter the eastern portion of Poland, which was reserved to them by agreements duly signed. But on two occasions, at Stalin's orders, Molotov evoked technical reasons for postponing the entry of the Red Army upon a neighbouring territory. Then, as a result of these delays, a truly picturesque discussion began between Moscow and Berlin.

The People's Commissar for Foreign Affairs informed Ribbentrop that the moment his troops entered Poland, the U.S.S.R. would issue a declaration of war, by which 'it ordered the Red Army to advance to protect the Poles . . . against the Germans!' It was only after a brisk exchange of messages that Molotov accepted the formula, 'to protect the Polish populations,' without mention of Germany.[1]

Stalin was anxious to avoid affronting the profound anti-German feeling which prevailed among the Russian masses. At any movement undertaken in common with the Germans the real feelings of the people would find utterance, despite the pronouncements of the diplomatists and the praises of the undertaking in question. And when his collaborators were vocal, Stalin was dumb. Whenever they said too much he reacted as usual.

On the 9 September he spoilt the effect of a declaration of Molotov's, who was rejoicing to see his theory justified by events, and indulging in futile demonstrations. Molotov wrote to the German Ambassador: 'Kindly convey my congratulations and greetings to the Government of the German Reich on the occasion of the entry of the German troops into Warsaw.'

[1] Secret archives of the Wilhelmstrasse.

Two days later the newspaper *Troud*, which Stalin had already employed to publish various inspired notes, printed the following: 'We cannot rejoice at the spectacle of the misfortunes of a neighbouring people; if it is true, in the words of the Russian proverb, that every man is the architect of his own good fortune, the peoples in misfortune ought to inspire the same pity as individuals suffering grave afflictions.'

In order to justify the invasion of Poland, and to reserve an eventual possibility of collaborating with the Western Powers against the Third Reich, a specious explanation was invented: 'After the capture of Warsaw by the German troops Poland ceased to exist as an independent State.'

In reality, the efficacy and drive of the Panzers and the Luftwaffe surpassed all expectations, and Stalin had no wish to see them installed on the national frontier. He certainly wished to occupy Eastern Poland, but as he had lost none of his well-known Machiavellism, he repudiated from the outset the accusation that he had committed an aggression against the Polish State.

In signing with Ribbentrop the agreement of the 28 September he had to choose between two attitudes. He ended by declaring that he was opposed to the survival of a Polish State, even in an amputated form, in order to maintain his 'justification' of the occupation of the territories of a State which had disappeared. In exchange for this, Germany renounced her claims on Lithuania, and he thought he had created the impression that Hitler alone had committed the odious offence of occupying regions which were ethnically Polish, while he had occupied only the Ukrainian and Bielorussian regions.

But he was still responsible. In the future he would show himself profoundly attached to the principle of 'buffer-States,' which he would support as independent countries, while transforming them from within, as he did with Czechoslovakia in 1948.

During the winter of 1939-40 it was difficult for Stalin to discover the warlike intentions of the German and Western Staffs. Poland had been crushed in ten days. But the French Army was intact, and the British Navy ruled the seas. Admiral Fraser and Churchill had both declared that 'the conqueror will be the nation that retains the control of the seas and oceans.' This was the 1940 version of the famous proverb, that England loses all her battles except the last. It was not without effect, but the Wehrmacht had revealed an unsuspected strength.

In view of the contradictory information supplied by Razvedoupr and I.N.O., Stalin decided to take personal control of a special information service. He created five networks which were intended to operate in touch with the Chancelleries and the military staffs of belligerent and neutral countries, and so provide him with valuable and reliable information.

One of these networks was installed in Switzerland: it was known as the Red Orchestra (*Rote Kapelle*), and employed some thirty agents. Four other networks were active: Sorge's Red Dragon in Japan, the Koslovsky network in Italy, the Oumansky network in Mexico, and the Pavlov network in Turkey. Thanks to this organization Stalin was able to keep informed as to certain matters of capital importance to him. The heads of some of these networks did a masterly job, and were often summoned to Moscow.[1] Stalin used to ask his informants very concrete questions.

The differences in the mentalities of Stalin and Hitler became evident on this occasion. The Führer believed only in a military solution—in the necessity of crushing his adversaries. Stalin understood that by exploiting the threat of superior strength it was possible to win without risk—and he had a horror of risk—battles more important than those which are fought in the battlefield. This is still one of his essential characteristics, and at the present time it is determining the foreign policy of the U.S.S.R., even more than the dread of the atomic bomb.

Another aspect of Stalin's mentality in 1940 was that he had the sense to limit his demands; he had not experienced the vertigo of success.

After the end of the Second World War, when Jdanov wanted to

---

[1]One of them, Rudolph Rado, a Hungarian, left Switzerland before the Swiss police had discovered the 'Red Orchestra' network. He stayed in Dordogne with a false passport. In a circle of his intimate friends, refugees from Strasbourg, he related picturesque details of the operations of the networks, and the dealings of their heads with Stalin, who was fond of referring to Pitt and his 'personal network.' Rado's accounts have elucidated this part of Stalin's action. On the other hand, the legal proceedings instituted against the Red Orchestra caused a great sensation in Switzerland, and the American General Willoughby made certain revelations in Washington regarding the operations of the Sorge network, one of whose survivors, Peter Tauber, has published sensational revelations in the Paris press.

authorize the Soviet Army to intervene and place the Communists in power in Finland, Stalin sent him these written instructions:

'Finland cannot have the Communists in political power unless this is the wish of its workers and peasants. The Soviet Army has no concern with the internal political conflict in Finland. This people has the right to complete and absolute independence.'

It is to be regretted that Stalin did not display the same attitude toward certain of the countries of Central Europe and the Balkan peninsula. But, one may ask, what would have been the situation if the Roumanians, or Benès, had met the Communist demands with a resistance as firm as that of the Finns? However, there was one very good reason for the special treatment reserved for the latter: Stalin wished to deal tactfully with Swedish neutrality. But it must not be forgotten that in spite of his sympathy for the Finns he did not hesitate, when it was a matter of safeguarding Leningrad, to fall upon this valiant little people, in time of peace, with overwhelming military forces.

From information received through his 'personal network,' Stalin learned in the spring of 1940 that the war was about to enter upon an active phase. The Red Orchestra had been aware, since the winter of 1939-40, of the strategical plans of the Germans for the invasion of Holland and Belgium. We know also that these plans were postponed in consequence of certain misunderstandings in the ranks of the German Staff, and that the decisive blow was to be struck in 1940.

Stalin's dread of seeing the balance of forces turn in Germany's favour was taking an acute form. The provisional associates were in a sort of 'clinch,' each trying to paralyse the other and to prevent him from making preparations for striking a blow.

In London, in proportion as the situation deteriorated, Winston Churchill was exercising an increasing influence in the Government, though Chamberlain was still in Downing Street. In Paris, Daladier was replaced by Paul Reynaud, who was in favour of action.

Stalin knew what was at stake in the new battle in which Hitler had engaged. The stake was the Swedish iron of Koruna, imported into Germany through Norway. It was the famous 'iron route' which had to be cut. Stalin was informed that Germany's immediate *riposte* would take the form of an invasion of Norway, and that an ultimatum to Sweden would demand the right of passage for the German troops and supply columns.

The policy of obstruction was set in movement. A vote was taken in the Politburo. Molotov was instructed to inform the Ambassador of the Reich that the Soviet Government asked that Berlin should not infringe the neutrality of Sweden, and that it would limit its operations to Scandinavia. Molotov jibbed at this. Schnurre, who had gone to Moscow to discuss the increase of economic exchanges, was already complaining that Mikoyan, the Commissar for External Commerce, had on several occasions interrupted supplies on the pretext that the German deliveries were insufficient. He asked for the forecast proportion of twenty-seven to eighteen. When Schnurre appealed to Stalin, the latter refused to intervene in a purely technical question.

But on two occasions, once the invasion had begun—on the 9 and 13 April, 1940—Molotov expounded the Soviet point of view to Schulenburg.'

Stalin's insistence produced some effect in Berlin, and on the 15 April Ribbentrop sent certain explanations. On the eve of the invasion of Belgium, Holland and France, Berlin was beginning to fear a fresh manœuvre by Stalin, under the pretext of preserving Swedish neutrality. Now, according to information received over the personal network, Hitler, in order to terminate the battle in record time, intended to leave only twenty divisions on the frontier of the Soviet zone as covering troops, and of these only six were front-line divisions.

It was at this moment that Stalin took part in a diplomatic action which obviously alarmed the Führer and compelled him to keep a larger number of divisions on his Eastern frontier. This had to be done without risking the rupture of the Russo-German pact: but it was greatly to Stalin's interest to weaken the German forces during the battle of the West, and to set a banana skin, as it were, under Hitler's heels. The operation was, of course, purely egoistical.

The initiative of this venture, which remained almost unknown, was due to Paul Reynaud, who was acting in agreement with Churchill. However, this episode, which was one of considerable political importance, since it elucidated the real character of the

Soviet-German relations, has not been noticed by the historians and politicians who have written memoirs relating to this period. Neither Churchill, nor even Paul Reynaud, has spoken of this attempt *in extremis*; but the evidence of the actors is still extant. Geoffrey Fraser has recently published an account of the matter, and of his negotiations with Ivanov, the Russian *chargé d'affaires* in Paris.

During the German attack Paul Reynaud had decided to initiate negotiations with the U.S.S.R. with a view to concluding a new political, economic and financial agreement, and to send Pierre Cot as Ambassador to Moscow. This undertaking was to be kept officially secret, but its existence had to be confided to Germany, whose armoured cars had already traversed the forest of the Ardennes; so that the spectre of the Russian menace was evoked on the old battle-field of the 1914 war. Stalin and Reynaud knew, of course, that this could only be a vague and remote threat. But they knew also that the German Staff would have to take it into account, and increase the reserves on the Eastern frontier from twenty to fifty or sixty divisions.

For the execution of this manœuvre Reynaud had chosen the British journalist Geoffrey Fraser,[1] who was living in France. In view of the exceptional situation he was appointed attaché to the Cabinet. This appointment of a foreigner as attaché to the Cabinet of the President of the Council was quite without precedent in the history of contemporary France. This detail should have told Stalin that the British Cabinet knew of the affair, and had given it its official blessing. Fraser got into touch with the Soviet *chargé d'affaires* in order to ask him whether Moscow was willing, during the Battle of France, to enter into negotiations for a new Franco-Russian agreement, and to pass the sponge over Daladier's initiative, by promptly appointing a new Ambassador to Paris.

Two days went by. Then Ivanov was authorized to commence negotiations and to continue them in the most open manner. A new ambassador would be appointed by Moscow: Alexander Bogomolov, Councillor of Embassy. Fraser had a number of interviews with Ivanov, who declared that Moscow was favourably disposed toward the conclusion of the new agreement. It should be noted that al-

---

[1] After the attempt was abandoned Fraser had to maintain relations with Ivanov, then at Vichy. Petain's Government then interned him in the camp of Verney, in the Ariége.

though the French press ignored these negotiations at the time, a persistent rumour spread along the routes of the great exodus that the U.S.S.R. was ready to declare war against Germany. The instinct of the crowd, especially acute under such circumstances, had made it curiously sensible of the fact that something was happening between Moscow and Paris during the tragic days of May and June 1940.

But the circumstances were such that Reynaud's initiative, followed by Stalin, did not develop. Two deputies, Fernand Laurent and Ybarnagaray, got wind of the enterprise. They called on Reynaud and threatened to provoke an immediate governmental crisis if the Fraser-Ivanov negotiations were not instantly discontinued. Reynaud had a majority of only two votes in the Chamber. He could not, therefore, persist in this bold initiative. Fraser was formally instructed to discontinue the conversations.

The episode revealed the fact that Stalin was ready to employ any means of obstructing the German operations, since it was in his interest to see the Wehrmacht fight under the most difficult conditions possible. This was not Stalin's only attempt to put a stick between the spokes of Hitler's chariot wheels, which he feared might one day roll upon Russian soil.

Among the Soviet representatives abroad, there was one who could regard herself as the political confidant of Stalin: Alexandra Kollontaï. A survivor, with Stalin, of Lenin's first Politburo, she was a close friend of the master of the U.S.S.R. The daughter of a general, and coming from an aristocratic environment, she had joined Lenin's party from motives of intellectual snobbery. But she was an intelligent and well-educated woman. Stalin had given her a nickname: for him she was 'our Madame de Staël.'

During the great purges Alexandra Kollontaï had lost her husband, the celebrated sailor Dybenko, who had become commandant of the military district of Central Asia. Appointed ambassadress in Stockholm, she soon became 'the personal ambassadress of Stalin,' and took part in many delicate contacts and secret discussions.

It was thus Alexandra Kollontaï who in May 1940 received the mission of doubling the Fraser-Ivanov negotiations. Stalin was afraid, and the episode of Fernand Laurent justified his fear, that the absolute secrecy required in Paris had not been preserved until the date agreed upon. Kollontaï conscientiously proceeded upon her mission. Between the 20 May and the 4 June, when Hitler's armies, having reached the coast of the Channel, were waiting for the Führer to choose between an attack upon Paris or the invasion of England, she informed several members of the diplomatic corps in Stockholm that the U.S.S.R. would not regard the final defeat of France with a benevolent eye. After this psychological preparation, since Stalin was at that time regarded as an accomplice of Hitler, she took a decisive step. She took the initiative of an interview with the Belgian Minister in Sweden. To him she said: 'It is the duty of all the European Powers, the U.S.S.R. included, to oppose German imperialism. The German menace has become much more serious than it was supposed to be. What Hitler wants to realize is a plan of world domination. . . .'[1]

However, the march of history was still too favourable to the Führer. The German intelligence services got wind of Kollontaï's conversations—after a fortnight's delay. In a telegram (No. 1003), Weiszsäcker asked his ambassador in Moscow to protest to Molotov in respect of 'the Germanophobe attitude of Mme. Kollontaï.' But he was ignorant of the real motive of that lady's enterprise.

The defeat of France accomplished, Stalin found himself in the prickly situation he had so dreaded. The U.S.S.R. remained the only Power on the European continent which could venture to match itself with the Wehrmacht; and so far the Wehrmacht was not acting as though for war. On the contrary: the White Book published by Ribbentrop disclosed the secret documents of the French Staff found at La Charité on the Loire, and the plan of General Weygand, who wished to employ his Syrian army in Irak, in Iran, and even in Turkey, in order to approach the petroleum wells of Baku. The anti-Russian arguments and theories developed by the former chief of Marshal Foch's Staff enabled Ribbentrop to pretend that an attack upon the Caucasus was intended.

The Irako-Iranian variant of this theory enabled Ribbentrop to do his best to embroil the Russians with the British and to induce them once and for all to turn their backs on the West. Ribbentrop

[1] Secret archives of the Wilhelmstrasse.

was trying to send Stalin to Iran and the oil wells in the south of that country. Ribbentrop provoked an advance on the part of the Japanese Ambassador in Moscow, who urged the U.S.S.R. to turn away from China and to seize 'the British heritage.' Of course, Ribbentrop did not succeed in launching the Georgian upon these remote and fantastic adventures. Stalin's head was too cool, and his feet were too firmly planted upon the ground. This sort of temptation appeals only to the hazy minds of pseudo-scientific Germans, who, as we know, are given to all sorts of fantastic theories and projects. Stalin, as a realist, knew very well where to draw the line between the possible and the impossible.

Moreover, this undertaking would have involved the abandonment of Red China. Now, as far back as November 1918, in his journal, *The Life of the Nationalities*, Stalin had written a famous article: 'Do Not Forget the East!' In this he declared that the world revolution would never be victorious until the vast masses of the Eastern peoples came to its aid. Since then he had restricted his conception of the Eastern peoples to China. If he embarked upon these unlimited ventures, as Hitler invited him to do, he would leave Hitler's hands free in Europe. Having cleared the board of his adversaries, the Führer would be free to grasp at anything he wanted. Compelled to choose, Stalin played a decisive part in the orientation of Europe in accordance with the historic desires of the Russian State.

Reacting against Ribbentrop's imperious invitation, he inaugurated a system of a kind unexpected in him: a lightning diplomacy. He acted with astonishing certainty. In the middle of June a plenary meeting of the Politburo was followed by a joint session of the Government and the Great General Staff. Both assemblies were presided over by Stalin himself, who thus took it upon himself to determine the general lines of his foreign policy:

The re-annexation of the Baltic provinces lost in 1918, following the Revolution:

The return to the U.S.S.R. of Bessarabia; rectification of the Moldavian frontier; annexation of Bukovina.

Disappearance of the discriminatory régime on the Lower Danube and suppression of the European Commission.

A treaty of alliance with Bulgaria, to which the Dobrudja would be restored, together with part of Thrace, with access to the Aegean.

Annulment of the Convention of Montreux respecting the Straits.

This was more than the maximum programme accepted on signing the Soviet-German pact!

The annexation of Bukovina, in particular, was an infraction of the agreement respecting frontiers.

The realization of this programme would naturally clash with German interests in the Balkans. But before it could lead to an open conflict Germany would have to begin her southward penetration in the Balkan peninsula. Stalin had no illusions. He did not share the enthusiasm of Molotov, who thought that the 'Fascist ice-breaker' might for some considerable time go on working for the new 'King of Prussia'—the Georgian Stalin, installed in the Kremlin.

CHAPTER XXXV

UNCONVERTED DIPLOMACY

So long as Stalin allowed himself to be guided mainly by considerations of a revolutionary and ideological order, there was hardly any danger of an immediate conflict with Hitlerian Germany. In the past the most violent verbal attacks had produced no consequences. But when behind this screen of ideological verbiage the two countries began to muse upon their fundamental historical aspirations the situation was completely changed.

As far as words went, the two disloyal partners were full of precaution: but this did not prevent them from acting, without hesitation or relaxation, in a hostile manner. Molotov and Ribbentrop, the two Foreign Secretaries, shook hands in a spectacular fashion. They continued in their posts, but it became increasingly evident that each was merely trying to paralyse the movements of the other. The hand that was no longer offered to the 'opposite number' now clutched a heavy cudgel, and each of the players waited patiently for the moment to strike the other a deadly blow.

Stalin, engaged in directing this perilous game, knew very well that he was balancing on a tightrope. But his innate deliberation, which he inevitably projected upon others, led him to believe that the German attack upon the U.S.S.R. was still a very long way off.

At all events, in the summer of 1940, Stalin was rapidly advancing toward the realization of his practical aims along the Western frontiers and in the Balkans, without troubling his head over the ideological aspects of the situation. His activities in Russia have been compared with those of Peter the Great. As for the international domain, his attitude in 1940–41 is amazingly like that of Alexander I before the threat of Napoleonic aggression.

The historical parallel is worth remarking. On the 1 August, 1811, the Austrian Minister in St. Petersburg wrote a report on the situation after the Battle of Tilsit. He insisted that the Tsar Alexander was more distrustful than ever regarding the future intentions of

Napoleon, and that he felt that an attempt was being made to hood-wink him until the moment of a sudden explosion. However, the Tsar remained calm. He thought the attack was 'put off until next year.' He would accept the Duchy of Warsaw as a historical fact. He declared that 'the temporary respite had restored his peace of mind, and nothing would induce him to become the aggressor.'

Put Stalin in the place of Alexander, and the views expressed in 1811 might well have been expressed in 1940. Engrossed in the cares and responsibilities of a Russian ruler, Stalin was bound to experience the apprehensions of an Alexander Romanov.

During these crucial months he accelerated the rhythm of his activities, but this was from considerations of a general order.

He knew that war with Germany was inevitable, and he realized the enormous risk of such a conflict, while he did not hesitate to accept it. The regions which he wished to annex would have to serve as a territorial bastion before the frontiers of the U.S.S.R., or at least as an armoured belt. He endeavoured to establish an advanced Russian barrage on the historical pattern of the 'Cossack regions' installed on the southern steppes.

During this month of July 1940 an event occurred of considerable importance, concerning which the historians of the second world war, including Churchill, might have written at some length, but have been silent. Here was one of those prodigious gestures which history reserves for men of exceptional destiny. The most curious thing about it was that on this occasion two men of exceptional character, mutually hostile, different in absolutely every respect, and without previous agreement, were associated in a common undertaking.

One of those men was Stalin; the other, Winston Churchill. In character they had nothing in common; their ways of thought, their lives, and their sentiments were entirely different. Yet at the time when the most insignificant action might have decided the fate of the world, at the very moment when the incomprehension of their entourage was most complete, they achieved something whose significance and results were, and are still, very largely inaccessible to those who profess to be in control of international policies.

Even while he was preparing the defence of Britain, while he was

R

encouraging and inspiring its spirit of resistance by speeches of a truly classical greatness and audacity, Churchill achieved a masterpiece of diplomacy, which adds yet another leaf to his laurel wreath.

On the 9 July, 1940, Sir Stafford Cripps, at Churchill's orders, called on Stalin. Their conversation, which followed closely upon a peace proposal made by Hitler to Britain, lasted more than three hours, and served as the basis of this diplomatic masterpiece.

Sir Stafford Cripps proposed to Stalin what was nothing more or less than 'the unification under the U.S.S.R. of the Balkan countries.' He added that 'the British Government is well aware that the Soviet Union is not satisfied with the régime of the Straits and the Black Sea,' and that 'the interests of the Soviet Union in the Straits ought to be safeguarded.' The Englishman listened without contradiction to Stalin's opinion that 'the Soviet Union is opposed to the exclusive control over the Straits by Turkey.'

Thus, before the menace of the Wehrmacht, now facing the cliffs of Dover, Churchill seemed to be offering Stalin the Balkans, the Bosphorus, and the Dardanelles! In reality the scope of this manœuvre was infinitely more subtle and complicated, and its results more remote, than the offer itself, which had no actual significance. Britain could never consent to the installation or control of Russia in these regions, and as a matter of fact Churchill's whole policy during the war was directed toward preventing such an eventuality.

But Churchill knew that Germany also had her eye on these regions, and that Stalin's favourable attitude toward the German-Russian pact was largely due to the fact that the Western countries were not opposed to the German advance in this direction. He chose this part of the world as the scene of a conflict between the Germans and the Russians, so that at the moment when Hitler was preparing a full-scale attack upon England, the U.S.S.R., by rushing into the temporary Balkanic vacuum, would compel Germany to defend her positions there without delay. It was simple, ingenious, and absolutely classic. But the supreme significance of the affair became clear when Churchill's venture was reinforced by Stalin's. The Georgian was now the master of a considerable sector of international intrigue, and he acted with an adroitness which, like Churchill's, was that of a great statesman.

If he had confined himself to taking the British proposals literally, and acting upon them, he would have exposed himself immediately to a German attack, and would no longer have been able to manœuvre or gain time in any way. These considerations, as well as his habitual suspicion that someone might be playing a double game, decided him to attempt the final operation which gave this diplomatic combination the extraordinary historic form which assured him of this unconcerted collaboration with Churchill.

Stalin ordered Molotov to communicate to Count Schulenburg, the Ambassador of the Third Reich, the substance of his conversation with Sir Stafford Cripps. Schulenburg told this to Ribbentrop.[1]

Stalin delayed three days over the operation. While safeguarding himself in making this communication against the too violent reactions of Hitler, he simultaneously warned Berlin that within certain limits he 'would give the closest attention to the British suggestions.'

At this moment Churchill's interests and Stalin's were parallel. Churchill had to gain time, time to complete the defences of the British Isles; Stalin had everything to lose by a rapid German victory.

Hitler, of course, was unequal to dealing with these two great statesmen. He foresaw probable complications in the East, and did not dare to engage all the forces necessary for a campaign against the British. He did not dare to leave Central Europe and the Balkan area without defence against a lightning thrust from Stalin, who had purposely exaggerated his claims.

Berlin had been aware of the Russian 'menace' for some time. In the telegram No. 2. 3. 132/40, Count Schulenburg tells his superiors that Molotov has very amiably promised to look with a favourable eye on the economic interests of the Reich in Roumania. Now, the 'amiable' disciple of Stalin had just swallowed Bessarabia at a single gulp; and as well as signing agreements with Berlin he had absorbed Northern Bukovina and a piece of Moldavia, under the pretext of securing a direct connection by rail with Lvov.

Molotov's promise of eventual deliveries of Roumanian petroleum meant, according to precedents in German-Soviet relations, that Stalin already saw the whole of Roumania entering the Soviet zone.

Now, the coming fight between England and Germany would almost exhaust the Reich's reserves and supplies of liquid fuel. Under

[1]Secret archives of the Wilhelmstrasse. Teleg. No. 1364, 13.vii.40.

these circumstances, which Hitler had by no means foreseen, he hesitated. These 'hesitations' of August 1940 were felt by a number of German generals, some of whom had received from the Führer explanations as to his attitude: above all, he was afraid of seeing the U.S.S.R. take advantage of the fighting by seizing the Balkans, thus depriving the Third Reich of Roumanian petroleum.

A few days later the organs of the Communist Party of Russia, which were always the first to learn of the intentions of the Secretary-General, Stalin, began a secret propaganda against 'the Fascist imperialism.' Ribbentrop then approached the Soviet Ambassador Chwartzev in connection with 'an article which was definitely provocative with regard to Germany, containing attacks against the Reich, which are consistent with neither the letter nor the spirit of the agreements with Moscow.'[1] The tone of this protest was very much more drastic than the generality of diplomatic protests. In 1945, in this connection, Marshal Goering told the American generals before he was sent to the Nuremberg prison, that Hitler had decided to make war upon Russia in August 1940. This 'decision' was certainly no more than a vague intention. But after a comparatively short lapse of time it ended in the 'Barbarossa Plan.'

Like Alexander I, Stalin was thinking—as he always thinks—of gaining time.

---

[1]Secret archives of the Wilhelmstrasse No. R.M. 21/40.

CHAPTER XXXVI

THE RUSSO-GERMAN STRUGGLE FOR THE BALKANS

As early as 1940 the conflict between the two associate-enemies was becoming more acute. Hitler showed signs of real prudence; he avoided putting his adversary on his guard by suggesting that he would deal with him when the propitious moment arrived. Stalin, who was prepared for anything short of war, pushed his pawns across the board, one by one, in accordance with the system which Marshal Foch had employed in his offensives, and which he had called 'the parrot system.'

Official declarations as to the spirit of the Ribbentrop-Molotov pact continued, but the conflict was becoming one of unprecedented bitterness.

Stalin could afford to give a pawn to Hitler as he advanced toward the Carpathians. It was now for Hitler to trace a frontier beyond which the Soviet forces must not be allowed to penetrate. The first bolt was shot in Roumania; it was intended to stop Stalin before he reached the Danube delta, just where, after the Crimean War, and the treaties of Paris and Berlin, the Bismarck-Disraeli tandem had stopped the Russians. Under the form of the arbitration award given by Germany and Italy in the Hungarian and Roumanian claims upon Transylvania, Stalin saw his plans opposed by the formal guarantee of all the Roumanian frontiers.

There is every reason to believe that Ribbentrop, in his pretentious stupidity, had not even realized the full meaning of his chief's action. He very naturally instructed Count Schulenburg to inform Molotov of the Viennese award, and to explain the reasons for the guarantee given to Roumania. These, as a matter of fact, were purely economic.[1] Schulenburg called on Molotov at dawn, on the 31 August—Molotov, like Stalin, being accustomed to working and receiving callers until the small hours of the morning. Stalin had

[1] Telegram No. 1565, sent by Ribbentrop on the 30 August, 1940.

already been informed of the arbitration, since he had given precise instructions to Molotov. The Ambassador of the Reich found Molo-, tov 'extremely reserved, contrary to his usual manner,' and understood him to say that 'while he thanked him for the information, he believed that the Soviet Government had already been informed by the press and the radio concerning the Vienna conversations. Stalin considered that Germany had violated Article 3 of the Soviet-German Pact by confronting the U.S.S.R. with a *fait accompli* as regarded Roumania, where the U.S.S.R. had important economic interests.'[1]

Confronted by Stalin's dissatisfaction, Ribbentrop instructed his Ambassador, on the 9 September, to call on Molotov's new chief assistant, Andrei Vishinsky, and to hand him a memorandum which was intended to appease the master of the Kremlin. Schulenburg really believed in the possibility of good Russo-German relations. This suited Hitler perfectly, for, as we know, he never kept anyone informed of his real intentions.

Stalin, who was trying to discover these intentions, began another series of probes. On his instructions, Molotov suggested to the representative of the Third Reich that the Vienna arbitration might be balanced by the cession of Southern Bukovina. Berlin, being consulted, replied that the guarantee given to Roumania was definite, and that no further cession of Roumanian territory could be tolerated. By way of reaction to this refusal, Stalin instructed the Sovietic troops to occupy a few small islands on the Kilia, the northern branch of the Danube. Moscow knew that Hitler would not begin a campaign for a few sandy islets, and Vishinsky, as a quibbling jurist, saw in this incident a juridical precedent tending to show that the Reich's guarantee is not always efficacious.

The U.S.S.R. then demanded the liquidation of the Danubian Commission. A discussion followed. Finally, going further still, Molotov proposed to discuss with the German Ambassador the suppression of the important Article 3 of the Pact, which called for a preliminary consultation in questions interesting the two countries. In this duel fought over the heads of their Foreign Ministers, neither Stalin nor Hitler would give way. Stalin made it clear that he too could very well create *faits accomplis* to the detriment of the Third

---

[1]Telegram No. 1815 of the 31 August sent by the German Ambassador to Moscow.

Reich. Hitler replied that Germany had no intention of surrendering Article 3. The 'probes' had therefore yielded a definite result: the Roumanian bar shutting off the Balkans would not be lifted.

Stalin had still to gain time, so that the new People's Commissar for War, Marshal Timoshenko, assisted by Joukov, by working uninterruptedly, could put the Red Army in a condition to stand up to the Wehrmacht. According to the plans of the Great General Staff, the end of the year 1941 was regarded as the earliest date by which Timoshenko's activities could have produced the desired results.[1]

In the meantime, Stalin sought to realize a temporizing policy. Molotov once again sent for Ambassador Schulenburg and gave him a memorandum expounding once more all the litigious questions affecting the Balkans.

In Stalin's name, Molotov asked his visitor to do his utmost to dissipate the 'regrettable misunderstandings' and restore mutual confidence. In this situation of increasing tension Stalin was indirectly addressing Hitler. The effect of this move was to impress and flatter the Führer, by making the discussion a negotiation between 'the great men.' Schulenburg decided to proceed to Berlin forthwith, 'the better to defend the cause of Russo-German amity';[2] which shows that the diplomatic agents engaged in a political operation often devote themselves to their task with a sincerity which may exclude a clear perception of the facts.

Stalin received a prompt response to his overtures. It was more like a blow than a friendly gesture. In fact, a few days later the Tripartite Pact between Germany, Italy and Japan was signed, automatically annulling, to a great extent, the significance of the Russo-German Treaty of 1939.

The *chargé d'affaires* of the Reich, Councillor von Tippelskirch, brought the news to Molotov on the 25 September.[3] He offered the explanation that the Tripartite Pact had nothing to do with the friendly relations between Germany and the U.S.S.R., and was merely an alliance directed exclusively against the American warmongers.

[1]This date was confirmed by Stalin himself in his conversations with Allied statesmen.

[2]His report is in the secret archives of the Wilhelmstrasse.

[3]Telegram No. 1746/33/40—secret archives of the Wilhelmstrasse, published in the U.S.A.

According to instructions received from 'Ram' (as Ribbentrop was disrespectfully called, according to Schmidt, Hitler's interpreter), Molotov's memorandum was carefully examined. A personal letter was sent in reply . . . to Stalin.

'My personal letter to M. Stalin,' said Ribbentrop, 'will contain an invitation to M. Molotov to visit Berlin. We expect this visit, which he owes us after my two journeys to Moscow, and one would like to discuss with him some important questions relating to the fixing of common political objectives for the future. . . .'

On the 9 October fresh instructions reached the *chargé d'affaires* in Moscow.[1] Molotov was to be told that 'the real motive of the despatch of important effectives to Roumania was due to a Roumanian request to organize a German military mission there.' Stalin is not a naïve person: it was clearly evident that Hitler had decided to make Roumania a strong military base. What he was now trying to make plain was that in the event of any intimidation, any resumption of the famous '*Drang nach Osten*,' or an effective threat against the U.S.S.R., Hitler thought he would succeed in forcing Moscow to give way, or agree to submit to the influence of Berlin, and to suffer operations which would enable Hitler to realize his plans of world conquest.

Stalin had not much time to spare. On the 15 October a personal letter from Ribbentrop reached him through Molotov. Dated the 13th, it began: 'My dear Mister Stalin,' and it was very long, though not particularly lucid. After an interminable diatribe against England, the history of the Norwegian and French campaigns, and an abusive description of instances of British perfidy, Ribbentrop declared: 'We Germans have learned one lesson, namely, that the English are not only unscrupulous politicians, but also bad soldiers. Our troops have routed them wherever they met. . . . We know today that this was due entirely to the almost incredible dilettantism and the surprising lack of agreement which prevailed among the political leaders and military heads of England and France. . . . The German military mission which was despatched some days ago at the request of the Roumanians with instruction units of the German armed forces[2]

---

[1]Telegram No. 1832 in the same archives.
[2]These units of instruction consisted at this moment of three divisions. They would soon be increased to twenty, and in February 1941 to fifty.

furnishes our enemies with a fresh opportunity of indulging in empty speculations. . . . Our units might have been destined to safeguard German interests, for the German economy and local interests are closely interdependent. . . .'

After attempting to cajole Stalin in this fashion, Ribbentrop expounded at great length the reasons for the tripartite pact, and repeated the invitation to Molotov: '. . . This visit will give the Führer the opportunity of explaining to M. Molotov personally his ideas as to the form which relations between the two countries will assume in future. On his return, M. Molotov will be able to explain in detail the objectives and intentions of the Führer. . . .'

Stalin did not immediately respond. He convoked the Politburo, so that he might officially indicate the line of conduct to be followed. The Politburo decided to send Molotov to Berlin. On the 22 October Molotov gave Schulenburg Stalin's reply. It was sealed, but was accompanied by a copy.

The form and style of this letter gave the Ambassador reason to believe that it had been dictated or written by Stalin himself.[1] This is the text:

'My dear Mister von Ribbentrop:[2]

'I have received your letter. I thank you sincerely for your confidence and for the interesting analysis of recent events contained in your letter.

'I agree with you that a fresh improvement of the relations between our countries is perfectly possible on the permanent basis of a full delimitation of our mutual interests.

'M. Molotov realizes that he ought to go to Berlin in order to return your visit and he hereby accepts your invitation.

'We have still to agree as to the date of his arrival in Berlin. The period from the 10 to the 12 November is that which suits M. Molotov the best. If this date also suits the German Government the question may be regarded as settled.

'I welcome with pleasure the desire which you express to come to Moscow again in order to resume the exchange of views begun last year as regards questions of interest to both our countries and I

[1] Telegram No. 2236.
[2] Knowing Ribbentrop's weakness for employing the 'von' to which he had no right, Stalin evidently wanted to please him.

hope this desire will be realized after M. Molotov's journey to Berlin.

'As regards a common consideration of certain questions in which the Japanese and Italians would take part, I think, without being opposed to this idea on principle, that it should be subjected to a previous examination.

Very respectfully,

Your Joseph Vissarionovitch Stalin.'

The final date for Stalin's discussion of affairs with Hitler was decided upon. But Stalin did not yet know that this would be the last discussion before the storm. He certainly thought that he would be able to drag it out. And this was assuredly one of his greatest mistakes, to be explained by reactions due to his well-known mentality: it seemed to him that the most important discussion could be prolonged to infinity. While Hitler was afraid that he would not have time to realize his plans before his death, Stalin was in no hurry; he behaved as though he had all time at his disposal. Perhaps he was influenced subconsciously by the fact of Georgian longevity.

At Teheran, in his conversations with Churchill and Roosevelt, he was to say, one day: 'Already, before Molotov went to Berlin, I understood clearly that the war was approaching the frontiers of the U.S.S.R. with giant strides. But I still had illusions as to the date when it might break out.' Subsequent events were to show that Stalin's error of calculation was very nearly fatal to the U.S.S.R.

CHAPTER XXXVII

MOLOTOV IN BERLIN

O N the 9 November Molotov's departure for Berlin, announced for the following day, had the effect of a bomb explosion. Public opinion, the world press, and the diplomatists accredited to Moscow all believed that this was the final consecration of the Russo-German collaboration. 'It seemed,' wrote Gafenko, the Roumanian Ambassador in Moscow, 'that Russia had re-entered the concert of the dynamic Powers. The illusion was general.'[1]

The authorization granted to Molotov to journey beyond the frontiers of the U.S.S.R. was without precedent. For the first time one of the heads of the Soviet Government was to go abroad in order to discuss matters with the head of another government, and even with the head of a State. Owing to the dogma of capitalist encirclement established by Lenin, this journey caused a considerable sensation, and his departure was a solemn occasion. A fanfare gave the signal for the start at the Bieloroussky-Baltisky railway station. All the members of the Politburo and the Government were present —excepting Stalin. He had left for Sotchi, although on the 7 November he was present in the Red Square, at the military review, vigorously applauding a fiery speech by Marshal Timoshenko, declaring

[1]The whole world persisted in deceiving itself. Nevertheless, during the whole of this period the author maintained his own interpretation of the increasingly profound divergences between Moscow and Berlin. At the moment of Molotov's departure a fortunate concatenation of circumstances enabled him, then in Marseilles, to obtain a source of occasional and supplementary information, which proved to be exceptionally reliable, as to the causes of friction between Russia and Germany, and the inevitably negative results of Molotov's interview with Hitler. The author, as usual, sent a clear and explicit article on the subject to the *Journal de Genève*. But the general delusion was so firmly rooted, so general, and defended with such energy, that René Payot, who has a well-earned reputation as an expert in international affairs, refused to publish any articles on this journey, returning the first of them with the inscription: 'Publication inopportune.' He may have been acting in accordance with a certain pressure exercised on his journal, in view of the delicate situation of a neutral country. On the other hand, Berlin organized a monster propaganda in support of the story of a complete agreement with the U.S.S.R. (The original is not to be found in the archives of the Wilhelmstrasse.)

that 'whosoever should dare to cross the Soviet frontier and defy the invincible strength of the Red Army would be annihilated by this army.' This was an allusion to the Japanese defeat of June 1939—and a reminder addressed to Russia's German partner.

However, it was said in the capital that Stalin was still in Moscow, and that he had summoned to his villa at Gorinka, for a special conference, the heads of the army, and Béria, Commissar-General for Security, promoted Marshal of the 'troops of internal security.' As a matter of fact, the conference was to examine a report of Béria's upon the final results of the labours of the Commission of Rehabilitation over which he had presided, and whose aim was to replace in the cadres of the army the thousands of officers deported or interned by the 'purger' Iéjov.

Timoshenko, who enjoyed the unlimited confidence of Stalin, for he had belonged to the Tsaritzin group, had already declared, in Stalin's presence, at certain conferences of the 'Club of the Army and the Red Navy,' that it was time 'to check the Fascist imperialism of Hitler by armed force before it was too late.' Admiral Oktiabrsky in his turn made a speech in which he asserted that the U.S.S.R. could not allow Germany to occupy the Balkans and establish herself on the Straits. There is no doubt that this current of opinion among the soldiers had its effect on Stalin.

It goes without saying that the Georgian and Asiatic revolutionary could not at heart be a veritable *Russian* patriot. But the interests of the State imposed this line of conduct upon him. He could not alter it now; and it served to defend the cause of applied Socialism.

Three carriages of Molotov's special train were reserved for the N.K.V.D. Twelve German officers, assembled for the sake of the cause by the German Ambassador, stood at attention on the platform to the strains of the *Internationale*, which their Führer had promised to 'cast into the dustbin of History as soon as the National Socialists have installed themselves in power.'

On Molotov's arrival at the Anhalt Station in Berlin no band played the official Soviet hymn. Instead of the *Internationale*, the general salute was sounded.[1] A deputy of Molotov's, the Armenian

[1]Details divulged among others by the interpreter Schmidt, commissioned by Hitler to take notes of the conversations during Molotov's stay in Berlin.

Dekanozov, accompanied him. A personal friend of Stalin, once head of the G.P.U. at Tiflis, the head of the central I.N.O., he was regarded as a cunning fellow. He was to replace the insignificant Chwartzev at the head of the Berlin Embassy.

As soon as he arrived in Berlin, on the 12 November, Molotov, whom the journey had not tired, asked for an interview with Ribbentrop. It took place on the spot, at 11.45. Ribbentrop resumed his interminable elucubrations: 'He turns the handle of a hurdy-gurdy,' was what Molotov told his *entourage*. Even in their manner of regarding negotiations the two men were absolutely different. In a style which was inflated even for a German, Ribbentrop held forth interminably upon the great world problems: the defeat of England: the peace, for which the latter country would have to beg upon her knees: 'England is ruled by a military and political amateur called Churchill, who throughout his career has completely failed at all decisive moments, and will fail again this time.' He spoke uninterruptedly for more than two hours.

Molotov was not there to make speeches; he wanted to talk of serious matters; and he suggested that 'Britain's Enemy No. 1,' as Ribbentrop called himself, should 'leave the soil of England, which he regards as already conquered, and pass on to other questions.'

So Ribbentrop changed the disc, and listened to himself delivering a speech of equal length on the Tripartite Pact. 'It is now more than seven years,' he said, with emphasis, 'since I began to work for the strengthening of Germano-Japanese ties.'

The amiable Molotov immediately asked him a rather unkind question. 'Had this seven years' work begun with negotiations with the Japanese?' Ribbentrop, who had been supplying champagne to the Imperial Court of Japan in 1932, did not accept the challenge. He spoke of the Reich's desire to act as mediator between Marshal Chang-Kai-Shek and Japan, in order finally to stabilize 'the great area of Eastern Asia.'

Molotov, who allowed nothing to escape him, suggested that the notion of the 'great area' of Eastern Asia was extremely vague; he would like an exact definition. Whereupon Ribbentrop, tripped up in the midst of his oratorical caperings, made this extremely comical reply: 'This notion of the Great Area of Eastern Asia is new to me also, and as yet I have been given no precise definition of the term.'[1]

Ribbentrop, making the tour of the horizon, spoke of Turkey, which had quickly liquidated the alliance with Great Britain, and had returned to strict neutrality.

Without allowing himself to be outflanked by these gratuitous manifestations, Molotov, who had to carry out Stalin's precise instructions, and who wanted a definite reply from Hitler, whom he was to meet that evening, made a pertinent declaration: 'It becomes necessary to give quite particular attention to the delimitation of the spheres of influence between Germany and Russia. In 1939 the question was only partly settled, and recent facts and events have deprived this settlement of any meaning, except as regards the Finnish part of the problem. What is needed is a permanent ruling.'

At this moment the conversations were interrupted, in order to give the Russian delegates time to enjoy an informal lunch before beginning their interview with the Führer.[2] The Germans present awaited this interview with great apprehension, since they feared an explosion on Hitler's part 'if Molotov spoke to him as he had spoken to Ribbentrop.'

The first encounter between Hitler and Molotov began, of course, with a long harangue from Hitler, who did not waste this opportunity of indulging in one of his oratorical performances, which went on for hours, and usually ended by rendering his auditors 'groggy'. He began by referring to a rule of political realism which he himself had established. Then, doubtless in order to reassure the U.S.S.R., displeased by the action of the Reich in Finland, which was within the sphere of Soviet influence, he announced: 'Probably neither of our peoples has completely realized its desires. But it is admitted that in political life the realization of only 20 to 25 per cent of one's demands constitutes an appreciable result. . . .'

Molotov grew uneasy. The U.S.S.R. had already obtained more than 25 per cent of the results prefigured in the secret protocol; so as soon as he could get a word in, he informed Hitler: 'On my departure from Moscow Stalin gave me precise instructions, and all that I am going to say corresponds exactly with his views.'

[1]Secret archives of the Wilhelmstrasse, No. 41/40 of the 12 November, and *Memoirs* of the interpreter Schmidt.
[2]Secret archives of the Wilhelmstrasse, Führ. 32/40 G. RS.

He thus indicated that if Hitler was dissatisfied with these declarations it would be superfluous to appeal to the 'supreme authority' whose opinions he was presenting.

Reassured by having thus defined his preliminary position, he listened patiently, though with a slight stare of amazement, to the interminable and on the whole rather vague expositions of Hitler, concerning the general lines of the political evolution of the world, the bankruptcy of the British Empire, and the 'pool of successors' who would have to deal with the designs of the United States, who wanted to lay hands on what had been the property of the British.

After a few disarming interventions from Molotov the conversation was definitely interrupted by an alert; an air attack was threatening. It was resumed on the following day. This time Molotov came to the point at once, explaining what Moscow wanted. 'The agreement of 1939,' he said, 'corresponded with a situation which was terminated by the war with Poland. The second phase was ended by the defeat of France, and we have now entered upon a third phase.'

Having clearly explained that the U.S.S.R. considered that the concessions of 1939 were outdated by events, and by the acquisitions of the Reich after its victories in Europe, Molotov tried to ascertain whether the Third Reich still accepted a balance of forces between the U.S.S.R. and Germany. But as Germany had become too powerful after her victory in France, the balance was no longer even.

Molotov then attempted a final elucidation of the situation: if Hitler consented to restore the balance between himself and Stalin— by granting fresh advantages to the U.S.S.R.—this would be a proof that he had abandoned, at least for some time to come, any notion of attacking the U.S.S.R.

Hitler's reply to Molotov was as definite as Stalin would have wished. He refused categorically to enlarge the Sovietic zone, or even to reconsider the question of the presence of German troops in Finland, and mentioned two 'superfluous' acquisitions of the U.S.S.R.: Lithuania and Northern Bukovina, which had not been mentioned in the protocols of 1939.

Returning once more to the attack, Molotov, while emphatically repeating that he was speaking in Stalin's name, frigidly asked Hitler for the 'belt of the Lithuanian coast'—that is, Memel, annexed by Germany in 1939—and for Southern Bukovina—a claim to which had already been advanced, in compensation for the guarantee of the Roumanian frontiers given by the Reich.

'Russia, in the beginning, limited her demands to Northern Bukovina,' said Molotov. 'In the present situation, however, Germany ought to understand that Russia has interests in Southern Bukovina also. However, she has as yet received no reply to this question. . . .'

Here Hitler became almost menacing.

'It would be an enormous concession on the part of Germany if even a portion of Bukovina were to be left to the U.S.S.R. In conformity with a verbal agreement,[1] all ex-Austrian territories should fall into the German sphere of influence. Moreover, the territories which were to make part of the Russian zone are mentioned by name: Bessarabia for example. There is not a word about Bukovina. . . .'

The Germans present expected to see the storm burst. Imperturbable, Molotov returned to the attack. . . . 'According to Stalin's point of view it would be possible and desirable to strengthen the relations between the U.S.S.R. and Germany. But in order to give them a permanent basis certain problems which cloud the air ought to be elucidated. . . . One such is the problem of Finland. If Germany and Russia were really in agreement *this could very well be solved without war*.[2] But there must be no German troops in Finland, and no political manifestations hostile to the Soviet Government. . . .'

Hitler, whose self-control on this occasion amazed his *entourage*,[3] replied: 'It is easy to organize manifestations, but it is difficult afterwards to discover the real instigator.'

The dialogue was becoming embittered. Molotov replied that by 'manifestations' he meant, among other things, the despatch to Germany of Finnish delegations, and the reception in Germany of prominent Finns.[4]

The indefatigable Molotov then touched on the eternal problem

[1]No trace has been found of this verbal agreement.

[2]A fresh war between the U.S.S.R. and Finland.

[3]In his *Memoirs* the interpreter Schmidt stresses more than once his astonishment at Hitler's unaccustomed calm, which he attributed to a major decision which had just ripened in the Führer's mind. It was at this moment that Hitler realized that he would have to attack the U.S.S.R.

[4]Hitler had received Marshal Mannerheim, the hero of Finnish independence, in Berlin.

of the Straits, asking Hitler what Germany would say if Russia were to give Bulgaria a guarantee under precisely the same conditions as that which Germany had given to Roumania.

Hitler replied evasively that 'the revision of the Montreux convention had been envisaged.' Molotov had to repeat his question as to Bulgaria three times before he obtained a reply. According to Hitler 'the problem would present itself if Bulgaria herself were to ask for a guarantee.'

Molotov then referred once more to the U.S.S.R.'s desire 'to obtain a guarantee against an attack in the Black Sea through the Straits, not merely on paper but in fact.' He believed 'that if Germany evinced no interest in the question Turkey might make an agreement with the U.S.S.R.'

Hitler persisted in saying that before replying to this suggestion it would be necessary for him to consult Mussolini. Thus, this second and last conversation with Hitler yielded only negative results. It became perfectly evident that Hitler had definitely decided to stop the U.S.S.R. on the banks of the Pruth, until he thought himself technically strong enough to strike it a decisive blow.

The divorce was consummated in principle, but it was not to the interest of either Hitler or Stalin to announce it openly. The Berlin propaganda still endeavoured to persuade the world that the union, though practically dissolved, was in fact stronger than ever.

Moreover, even in the domain of propaganda Molotov, adopting a ruse suggested by Stalin, had very adroitly 'torpedoed' Ribbentrop's plan. Before the banquet, Ribbentrop had sent Molotov the text of a great speech which was to announce *urbi et orbi* the complete agreement of views between Berlin and Moscow, and their intention of continuing their fruitful collaboration. On arriving at the banquet Stalin's envoy apologized for not having had time to make himself acquainted with the text, being engrossed in preparations in view of conversations with Hitler. He would, therefore, reply in an impromptu speech. A few moments before Ribbentrop rose to deliver the harangue which was to be communicated to the press, Molotov, insisting that his own speech would contain only 'a few improvised phrases,' asked that the address should not be communicated to the press. The Reich's Minister for Foreign Affairs had to renounce its publication, and the effect of the showy propaganda

s

which he had hoped to derive from the visit of the President of the Soviet Council was thus neatly stifled. Nevertheless, the boosting of the incident at the initiative of Berlin continued for some weeks.[1]

[1]The summary of the Berlin interviews constitutes a synthesis of what has been published by various official sources and of notes which have been found in the secret archives of the Wilhelmstrasse, and in the memoirs of Hitler's interpreter, Schmidt. In the reminiscences of his embassy to Moscow, Gregor Gafenko, ex-Minister for Foreign Affairs in Roumania, likewise mentions, but without realizing its significance, the incident of Ribbentrop's and Molotov's speeches, and writes at some length of the effect produced by the interview, thanks to the false appreciation of its real significance.

CHAPTER XXXVIII

TOWARD A RUSSO-GERMAN WAR

ON Molotov's return to Moscow the public boosting of the negotiations was continued. It was all to the interest of Berlin to present the negotiations as a great success, endeavouring to disconcert and even alarm its enemies. Stalin, for his part, had no reason to conceal the truth. If Molotov had returned empty-handed as regards new and positive agreements, he had none the less brought the news that the conflict was inevitable.

Hitler and Stalin both knew what to expect. But each of them thought that he would be able to trick the other, and conceal the moment when he would be ready to attack his adversary. As for the rest of the world, it had fallen into the trap, and continued to believe that the U.S.S.R. and the Third Reich had reinforced their ties. In Moscow the Russophilia of Schulenburg succeeded in putting the diplomatic corps on the wrong scent, and even diplomatists experienced in the affairs of Eastern Europe were completely at fault. Among them was Gafenko.[1]

In the meantime the protagonists of the drama were giving themselves but little respite. On the 20 November Hitler caused Hungary to join the Tripartite Pact; on the 26th it was Roumania's turn. The adhesion of Slovakia and Bulgaria seemed imminent. The U.S.S.R. was in danger of losing its precious bulwark in the Balkans: Sofia. Stalin, in desperation, tried by every means to retard the German aggression. The Soviet Government, the Politburo, the Great General Staff, held many sessions during the second half of November, and the Central Committee of the Party was convoked.

---

[1] The author continued to send to Switzerland articles insisting on the actual results of the Berlin interview, which he called 'the consecration of the Russo-German divorce.' With the same persistence the newspapers refused to publish his articles, which clashed with the current intellectual conformism and incomprehension of passing events.

The problem now was to find some means of impeding Hitler's preparations, and above all to prevent him from occupying bases from which he could launch an attack. The tactics envisaged were directed merely at obtaining results, and all means were regarded as licit. The master of the U.S.S.R. had an adequate experience of affairs, and was totally devoid of 'humanitarian weaknesses.'

There were two solutions to be considered. They were discussed in all the organs of the supreme power. The first was to pretend to adhere to the Tripartite Pact, and to wait until Hitler got entangled somewhere in Asia Minor, or in the basin of the Eastern Mediterranean, into which he was preparing to penetrate. The second was, to continue the policy of neutrality in the face of the Anglo-German duel, without ceasing to reinforce the Soviet Army, and while making sure of Bulgaria.

The first combination was not without its attractions. But the adhesion of the U.S.S.R. to the Tripartite Pact would seem an enormous diplomatic success for the Germans, and might help to eliminate Great Britain from the number of combatants. Hitler would have his hands free, and the manœuvre of multiple betrayals would yield no return. Stalin, consequently, preferred the second alternative: but in his tortuous mind he embarked on a fresh manœuvre.

He was accustomed to profit by the advantages to be drawn from any confused situation. He was to find in the classic arsenal of the diplomacy which he had studied with such application a very ancient formula: It consisted in replying to the offer of a partner by an affirmative, accompanied by absolutely unacceptable conditions.

So Moscow would respond by agreeing to adhere to the Tripartite Pact, but would propose conditions of a kind to which Berlin could not subscribe. At the same time, the bait would be offered to the Reich of fresh concessions in respect of the delivery of raw materials.

The comedy was not easily staged and produced; for during Molotov's visit to Berlin, Sir Stafford Cripps had hinted to Vishinsky at a possible modification of the British attitude toward Moscow, which produced no immediate results. For, behind the white cliffs of Kent and Sussex was the shadow of the United States, with the amazing Franklin Delano Roosevelt. And, as he had several times insisted, Stalin believed that the world war would be won by the Power which had the United States on its side.[1] In short, Molotov's theory of the 'third period' was officially bankrupt.

On the 25 November, at 6.30 p.m., Molotov handed to Schulenburg the reply of the U.S.S.R. Schulenburg immediately forwarded it to Ribbentrop, who by 8.30 a.m. on the 26 November had the Russian text before him.[2]

The unacceptable conditions, easily formulated, were as follows: German troops must be immediately withdrawn from Finland; within a few weeks the security of the U.S.S.R. in the Straits would have to be assured by a pact of mutual assistance between the U.S.S.R. and Bulgaria, included in Russia's southern zone of security, and by the establishment of a base, ceded on a long lease, for the land and sea forces of the U.S.S.R. within reach of the Bosphorus and the Dardanelles; the zone to the south of Baku and Batoum, in the general direction of the Persian Gulf, would have to be recognized as a centre of permanent interest for the U.S.S.R.; Japan must renounce her rights to the coal and oil concessions in North Saghalie; further, should Turkey refuse to agree to a long lease, the necessary diplomatic and military measures would be taken to compel her to comply. Thus Stalin was asking Hitler to become his ally in an eventual war against Turkey!

Hitler replied by setting the German machine at work in Bulgaria.

But London was quick—even quicker than Hitler—to appreciate the situation. The British services reacted wherever this was possible. Taking little notice of the press, which continued to represent Stalin as Hitler's accomplice, the British Government gave active support to the pro-Russian movement in Sofia. The bombs which von Papen's agents placed in the luggage of Sir Hugh Knatchbull-Hugessen, British Ambassador to Ankara, bore witness to Berlin's fears. Turkey, however, frustrated the British efforts, vigorously opposing the signature of a Bulgar-Soviet alliance, which she re-

[1]Stalin was very insistent on this point. In my articles in the Swiss press I had drawn special attention to an article in the *Bolchevick*. It was unsigned, but was attributed to Stalin himself. It showed that the possibility of a world war was not excluded, and that it would be won by the side on which the United States was fighting. I said, moreover, that in 1941 the Reich ought to try to put Stalin against the wall before 'some new fact urges Roosevelt to undertake some fresh, decisive action.' (*Tribune de Genève*, 16 February, 1941.)

[2]Secret archives of the Wilhelmstrasse: Schulenburg's despatch No. 2362.

garded as a hostile action against which she would take adequate measures.

Under these conditions nothing could prevent the glissade of Bulgaria toward the Third Reich. To complete the bewilderment of world opinion, the U.S.S.R. and the Third Reich, while continuing this struggle for the most favourable positions in the event of war, continued to increase their economic exchanges in the vain hope of putting their adversary on the wrong scent.

Henceforth there was nothing vague about the relations between Moscow and Berlin. From December onwards the position was becoming crystallized—a process which must end in an armed conflict. But among the Germans the preparations were pushed ahead much more rapidly, since the Germans knew precisely what they wanted, and would neglect no means of obtaining it.

There were deep-seated reasons for Stalin's deliberation. We have seen already that his character—so different from Hitler's—led him to postpone major decisions, and that this tendency modified his reasoning and his appreciation of the situation; if he had to wait for an anticipated event it always seemed to him that he had still enough time. Moreover, the casuistical spirit reminiscent of his seminary days had become, in the ex-revolutionary, a habit of thought which imposed 'juridical' methods. There have been many illustrious examples of this peculiar mentality among men of Asiatic origin. Attila, before he opened his attack on the Exarchate of Ravenna, had begun with a dispute of a juridical nature, and Genghis Khan introduced arguments of the same kind in his discussion of family affairs.

In this connection, it has been observed that in the winter of 1939 Stalin did not hesitate to fall upon little Finland; but that the previous negotiations—which had failed—had continued for more than two months. He never discarded the notion that it is a convenience, in respect of opinion, and a necessity for men of action, to terminate a pact of non-aggression before attacking another country. He did this in 1945 before the war with Japan.[1] Further, he still had the illusion that Hitler would observe the rules of the political game. For that matter, the Führer had created a precedent by denouncing the treaty of non-aggression with Poland, in the spring of 1939,

[1] Official archives.

several months before the first act of general hostility. Stalin had, therefore, come to regard this attitude as the proof that Hitler would act in the same manner toward the U.S.S.R. In the meantime he reinforced the economic bonds with the Third Reich, meaning to weave a protective net, the meshes of which Berlin would be seen to cut on the approach of the fateful date.

When in January 1941 he received, through his personal network, the first items of information respecting 'the suspect study in the offices of the O.K.W. of military plans with reference to an armed conflict with the U.S.S.R.' he ordered Mikoyan to sign, as quickly as possible, a fresh economic agreement with Schnurre, arranging for larger deliveries of raw materials and petrol.

Knowing nothing of Hitler's real intentions, Schnurre assured Soviet guests at the banquet celebrating the successful conclusion of the negotiations that 'the Führer considers that his friendship with the U.S.S.R. is a necessary element of the decisive victory of the Third Reich over world plutocracy.'[1] The German delegate had been obliged to swallow twenty-two glasses of vodka, which had rendered him incapable of dissimulation; the truth, or what he himself took to be the truth, emerged from vodka as readily as from wine. Those who have participated in Muscovite banquets know something about the matter.

In fact, while in Prague General Nikitin, chief of the divisions on a war footing in foreign countries, assured the directors of the Skoda works of his thanks for a rapid delivery of armoured cars and other material. Hitler appended his signature to 'Instruction No. 21,' his 'Green Plan,' known also as 'Operation Barbarossa.'

Molotov, at Stalin's personal request, asked the German Ambassador to explain the concentrations of German troops in Hungary, where it was said no fewer than sixty divisions were assembled. The Ambassador had heard of these concentrations: Ribbentrop had informed him of them by telegram.[2] 'This movement of troops corresponds,' he said, 'with the necessity of driving the English out of Greece.' After he had replied to Molotov in conformity with the

[1]Official archives.
[2]Secret archives of the Wilhelmstrasse, No. Pol. 1. 1650 Grs.—These instructions were sent to the Moscow Embassy by telegram No. 36; to Von Papen in Ankara No. 12), to Belgrade (No. 11) and to Athens (No. 91).

content of the telegram, Schulenburg received fresh instructions, which gave him greater liberty in respect of his explanations.[1]

Stalin, in the meantime, learned that the invasion of Bulgaria was imminent. On the 15 January Molotov, making no attempt to conceal the gravity of the situation, informed the representative of the Reich, in the most vigorous terms, that 'the Soviet Government and M. Stalin had on repeated occasions drawn the attention of the German Government to the fact that they regarded Bulgarian territory and the Straits as a Soviet zone of security, and that they could not remain indifferent to any threat against it.'

The stiffness of tone of this statement is comprehensible. Stalin had not much to lose. Bulgaria was a turntable from which Germany could take Greece in the rear and quickly reach the Mediterranean and the Aegean. If he could make Hitler abandon the invasion of the country he would be frustrating in the most effective manner the entire offensive of the Third Reich.

At this critical moment an unfavourable factor affected the sequence of events. Despite the visit to Ankara of Anthony Eden and General Dill, chief of the British Staff, in February 1941, Ismet Inonu, who had just received a personal letter from Hitler, informed the British that Turkey took no further interest in the Balkan countries, and intended to devote herself entirely to the defence of her own territories. Sir Stafford Cripps hurried to the rescue, flying to Ankara in a plane placed at his disposal by Stalin.

The Turkish President dismissed all suggestions with a polite but categorical refusal. According to him the obligations of the Balkanic alliance were superseded by the events which had occurred since September 1939. It was impossible to be more explicit: Bulgaria would be left to face the Third Reich alone, without any sort of protection in the rear. Berlin obtained the desired result. Russia's last position in the Balkans was lost. All that remained to her now was Yugoslavia, which, cut off from the rest of the world, could not constitute a serious obstacle to the Nazis.

The Red Orchestra continued to keep Stalin informed; but the date which it assigned to the opening of the German attack was in Stalin's opinion too early. During the last days of February the tension felt in the U.S.S.R. increased. Stalin, always conscious of what

[1]Secret archives of the Wilhelmstrasse, No. 57.

was happening in the masses, even when the famous *vox populi* did not express itself openly, witnessed a demonstration without precedent in the U.S.S.R.

On the 23 February, after a speech from Marshal Timoshenko, devoted to the celebration of the anniversary of the Red Army and the development of the Marshal's favourite theme—namely, that the Soviet armies were strong enough to resist any aggressor—there was a gala performance in the Grand Theatre. Many generals and other officers were present. Stalin was in a box with his daughter Svetlana. While a ballerina, whose liaison with Molotov was semi-official, was executing one of the principal variations of *Giselle*, hisses were suddenly heard. This active nonconformism in the presence of Stalin was a sensational incident. It was a new species of *fronde*, a criticism of Molotov, responsible for the official foreign policy and for the German-Soviet treaty. This very abnormal incident revealed a noticeable degree of tension among the 'clercs' on whom Stalin's régime depended. He felt that he ought to show himself in person in that part of the world for which the Russians feel a sentimental affection: the Slav Balkans.

He waited for the first opportunity. That was provided by Hitler no later than the following day. In a speech, the Führer announced the arrival of the beneficent spring, and spoke of 'the return of the swallows, announcing the liberation of the forces of Nature,' and presaging other events also, of a less bucolic character: the armed forces of the Reich would be able to cross the Danube, now free of its icy bonds, and 'to traverse the mountains, now clear of snow, and covered with flowers and verdant meadows,' in order to fight farther afield and extend 'the installation of the New Order in the world.'

On the first day of March Molotov, on receiving the German Ambassador, told him that he was greatly preoccupied with Hitler's intention of crossing Bulgaria to begin operations against Greece. He seemed much disturbed by the fact that Germany had taken decisions which were contrary to the conceptions of the Soviet Government and Stalin as to the security of the U.S.S.R. He himself had jotted down the text of a memorandum which, after being copied, was forwarded at once to the German diplomatist. The document said, more especially: 'It is to be regretted that in spite of the precautions taken by the Sovietic Government in the course of its *démarche* of the 25 November, 1940, the Government of the German Reich should have felt it possible to act in a manner which inflicts an irreparable wrong on the interests of the security of the U.S.S.R., and that it should have proceeded to effect the military occupation of Bulgaria.'[1]

It is evident that Stalin already realized that the storm had nearly reached his frontiers. His passivity might produce a dangerous result.

Having accepted, though under protest, the *fait accompli* of the Bulgarian occupation, he permitted himself a gesture which was clearly intended to defy Hitler.[2] Yugoslavia alone might serve as the pretext of a demonstration, while creating internal complications affecting the plan of the German aggression. The Belgrade Government was dominated by Tzvertkovitch and Markovitch, two Serbs, more honest than Stoyadinovitch, but inclined to surrender everything to the Third Reich.

This time Stalin himself took the operation in hand. He established personal contact with the Yugoslav Ambassador to Moscow, Milan Gavrilovitch, the leader of the Serb Agrarian Party, of which there were three representatives in the Government. Stalin invited him privately to his villa at Gorinka, near Moscow, where he had a long and cordial conversation with him. He proposed to his guest a Soviet-Yugoslav pact which would enable Belgrade 'to pursue a completely independent policy toward Germany.' In March 1941 this meant, in plain language, a policy of resistance to Hitler.

British diplomacy was following a parallel course; but the Prince Regent, Paul, despite his notorious Anglophilia, and his declared hostility to the entry of Yugoslavia into the Tripartite Pact, did not dare to hold out against his Government.[3]

[1] This *démarche* was prescribed by Schulenburg as early as the 27 February, by 'Instruction No. 403.' On the 1 March the Ambassador, in 'Telegram No. 453,' informed Ribbentrop of the reactions of the Kremlin. (Secret archives of the Wilhelmstrasse.)

[2] Gafenko notes in his book *Les Préliminaires de la Guerre à l'Est*, that Sir Stafford Cripps returned from Ankara to Moscow in February 1941 with the absolute conviction that the Russo-German war was close at hand. Gafenko, who is the proprietor of an important Roumanian newspaper, was well able to distinguish reliable items of information. He made it clear that he was in agreement with Sir Stafford's appreciation of the situation. Now, Sir Stafford had obtained very precise information from the Turkish information service, which had been very ably organized in the U.S.S.R., and had been informed of the conjuncture by General Dill.

[3] As soon as the *coup d'état* had been accomplished Prince Paul was banished from Yugoslavia.

Stalin himself then traced the broad outlines of a possible manœuvre. The departure of the three Agrarian ministers from the Serb Government should produce a political crisis in Belgrade which Prince Paul would find practically insoluble, so that those who were in favour of resistance to Germany would be able to bring off a veritable *coup d'état*. Stalin, of course, was not interested in protecting the national interests of Yugoslavia; but a war in the Balkans might delay the outbreak of the Russo-German War and enable him to gain a little more time. Incidentally, by seeming to support Yugoslavia he gratified Soviet opinion and the traditional pan-Slavic sentiment of the Russians, which he was obliged to take into account. Gavrilovitch became *persona grata* in Moscow. He was privately invited by Marshal Timoshenko to attend a performance in the theatre of the Red Army, where he received a tumultuous ovation from the officers present.

A few days later the Belgrade Government signed its adhesion to the Tripartite Pact. Gavrilovitch immediately resigned and called upon his comrades in the Government to follow suit. The open crisis was followed by a *coup d'état* by which the party in favour of resisting the Third Reich came into power. So far all had happened as Moscow had foreseen.

There was great enthusiasm in the Russian capital. The Yugoslav military attaché was cheered in the streets. At Stalin's order, the 'History of the Russian volunteers of General Tcherniaev during the Serb insurrection against the Turks in 1875-76' was hastily republished. Once more Stalin proposed to Gavrilovitch the conclusion of a treaty of friendship which he himself had elaborated, and which had been rejected by the previous government in Belgrade.

On signing the treaty, Gavrilovitch said to Stalin: 'Are you not afraid that Hitler may attack you?'

'Let him come,' replied Stalin, smiling: 'I'm not afraid of him.'[1]

There was a toning down of claims; all important or spectacular movements of troops were prohibited, save under plausible pretexts, such as the First of May Parade in Moscow and the usual manœuvres in the military districts. Stalin was personally preoccupied with the elaboration of a pact with Japan, intended to secure his frontiers in the Far East.

[1]This conversation is recorded also in Gafenko's book.

CHAPTER XXXIX

INDUSTRIAL PREPARATION: THE PACT WITH JAPAN

SINCE Russia was industrially passing through the Stakhanovite fever of her five-year plans, there was already a certain tradition in respect of production. This consisted in completing a five-year plan in four or four and a half years. Stalin issued another call for·emulation. Already, in 1940, when he judged that the U.S.S.R. could not remain indefinitely aloof from a general conflagration, he had issued the order: 'Complete the present plan in three years!'

On the 27 February, 1941, in the eighth session of the Supreme Council, he intervened in the discussion of the budget, in which he did not normally take part. In the plenary session of the Central Committee of the Communist Party he expressed himself still more explicitly: '. . . The President of the State Plan, Comrade Voznessensky, has given us an impressive picture of our success in industry in general, and in the transport services, the result of the realization of our Five-Year Plans. He tells us also that the rationalization of labour and the distribution of our factories throughout the regions of the U.S.S.R. are already yielding magnificent results. Thanks to the new industrial regions we have created in Siberia, in Central Asia, in the Caucasus, and the Urals, 42.5 per cent of the production of our heavy industry is already concentrated in zones situated beyond the radius within which attacks are possible. But this is not enough. The year 1941 ought to be the decisive year. In 1942 at least 65 per cent of our production ought to come from regions to the east of the Volga. . . .' It would be impossible to speak more plainly. The massive plan of the evacuation of Ukrainian industry was already prepared. It was intended for execution in 1941–42. If Stalin stated this publicly, it was because the machinery was already in place and the operation had begun.

As for the budget for the year 1941, for which the 'approbation of the comrades' was requested, it was purely and simply a typical war budget. Of 215.4 milliards of roubles 71 milliards, or just a third, went on armaments. Moreover, in the departmental budgets 55.7 milliards of roubles were reserved for the construction of strategical highways, workshops for war industries, machine tools for these workshops, and transport, including river transport. This totalled 126.6 milliards of roubles, or about 60 per cent of the total. Nothing less than the intervention of the master of the Kremlin in person was necessary to ensure the acceptance of this budget, astronomical in its proportions for a country at peace.

In this same month of February 1941, Stalin put under contribution all the Party and State organizations which had to co-operate in this domain. This dealt in detail with the measures adopted for transferring to the State the war industries which figured in Stalin's address. Despite the official silence observed in this connection, the Germans were aware of these preparations.[1]

The Pan-Russian Party Conference convoked in the spring of 1941 should normally have paved the way for the Nineteenth Pan-Russian Congress, which, however, had not hitherto been convoked. This time it did not, as was usual, deal with directives of a general order for the realization of State plans. It devoted itself to decisions of a practical order, and the local secretaries of the Party found that they were expected to study the means calculated to accelerate industrial production.

Stalin was the first to propound the problem of secret weapons in all its technical and psychological bearings. He had no wish to have a finger in everything, but as he stood at the centre of power, all initiatives converged upon him, and it was his business to encourage them. On the other hand, as matters stood in Russia, it would not have been advisable for persons responsible for ideas and proposals to attempt to apply or develop them without the official blessing, and the trade mark: 'Inspired by Stalin.'

In the matter of secret weapons, Stalin once again revealed his complete understanding of the Russian mentality. The fetishism of technique which he had helped to create in a people to whom many technical achievements were new and unfamiliar now plays a great

---

[1]Despite their secrecy, Hitler was informed of these decisions as early as February 1941, before his attack upon Greece.

part in daily life. While ready to fight with the bayonet, the soldier of the Red Army experiences for the word *tekhnika* a feeling of veneration greater than that of the Englishman or the American, who is so accustomed to technical achievements that he hardly perceives their excellence. Now, in Russia the Germans have always enjoyed a reputation as excellent technicians. In order to suppress the handicap of an inferiority complex in the Sovietic Army it was necessary to show that the Russian technicians had no reason to envy the Germans.[1]

Stalin was, therefore, anxious to impress the imagination of his soldiers by introducing the employment of weapons which the Germans did not possess. Hence the creation of a special section attached to the secretariat of the Central Committee—the 'Section of Invention.' Obviously, Stalin was proclaimed the direct inspirer of the labours of this section, and from 1939 onwards a number of 'Stalin prizes' were awarded to inventors.[2]

By February 1941 Stalin had decided that it was time to obtain a pact of neutrality from Tokio. The information received from the Ambassador, Jacob Malik, encouraged him to propose conditions. He wanted the Japanese to surrender their concessions in the coal mines and oil wells of Northern Saghalien.

It was Stalin's habit always to negotiate with a weapon in his hands. For him the treaty with Japan had become of capital importance; yet he allowed the negotiations to drag on, clinging to details of the third order of importance—to quote the Japanese Minister for Foreign Affairs, Matsuoka. He held that every treaty should involve a positive acquisition, however slight, for the U.S.S.R. The Marxist revolutionary, the old Bolshevik, had retained, curiously enough, the instincts of a landowner seeking by every means to increase his patrimony. This was also one of his habitual ruses, intended to per-

[1]These considerations were valid for the period of the cold war. This is why Western readers learned almost daily that this or that invention which they had attributed to an inventor or scientist well known to them had been outstripped by a Russian inventor. Recently a film which professed to constitute a serious history of aviation showed an aeroplane of Russian construction driven by a steam-engine.

[2]Amongst others, to the invention of the celebrated 'Katioushka.' Its existence, and its efficacious and spectacular performance, did much to support the morale of the Red Army, despite the defeats of the first part of the war. On the other hand, the U.S.S.R. produced great numbers of armoured cars which were regarded as the best in the world.

suade his adversary that he was in no great hurry to conclude the bargain.

But Stalin was looking for a more immediate result; he hoped that the signing of the treaty with Tokio at this juncture would have a psychological effect on Berlin. Hitler might be impressed if his diplomacy suffered a check, and the imminent assault upon the U.S.S.R. would once again be postponed. It must not be forgotten that this was the obvious motive of everything that Stalin did during this period. Otherwise he would have signed with Japan a pact of non-aggression in 1940. But at that moment he was not yet threatened by the German invasion, and one does not see what interest he would have had at that time in a Japanese-American war.[1]

In dealing with Asiatic problems Stalin found a psychological atmosphere which corresponded with his own. The Japanese, like him, prefer to be silent as to their intentions.

Matsuoka left for Europe without divulging the real object of his journey. He told the journalists that he meant to visit Berlin and Rome. If he spent some time in Moscow it would only be for the usual negotiations: as always in the spring, Japan and the U.S.S.R. renewed their convention in respect of the fisheries off the coast of Kamchatka. It is true that these negotiations were usually effected by less important officials.

Matsuoka spent five days in Moscow, during which he had conversations with Stalin and Molotov. He proposed a pact of non-aggression, to which Molotov, encouraged by Stalin, responded by proposing a treaty of neutrality. Matsuoka then employed one of Stalin's tactical weapons: he went over to the offensive, and demanded the total cession of the northern portion of Saghalien.

Nothing transpired relating to the negotiations between these Asiatics, who preferred a policy of absolute secrecy. Matsuoka continued his journey to Berlin. There he told Ribbentrop as much as he chose of what had been happening in Moscow, and informed the German Minister that as the author of the first proposal to Stalin he would have to make his position clear. He even went so far as to refer 'incidentally' to his claims in respect of Saghalien.

[1]In a nocturnal conversation with Roosevelt in the Soviet Embassy in Teheran, Stalin explained to the President, who accepted his explanation, why he had refused a pact with Japan in 1940, and why he had accepted it in 1941.

Ribbentrop gave his advice to Matsuoka, who listened patiently. 'If the Russians were to adopt a stupid policy and compel Germany to attack them,' said Ribbentrop, 'I think it would be well if the Japanese Army did not intervene against the U.S.S.R.[1] Japan would serve the common cause better by allowing nothing to divert her from the attack on Singapore.'[2]

On the 6 April, the very day when Stalin signed the Soviet-Yugoslav treaty of friendship, the day when the German Luftwaffe attacked Belgrade, and when Schulenburg transmitted Ribbentrop's order to the effect that the Third Reich found itself compelled to begin military operations against Greece, Stalin resumed conversations with Matsuoka. He was actually pressed for time. On the 12 April the agreement was concluded, and the treaty was to be signed on the 13th. The pact of neutrality and non-aggression with Japan would henceforth be the last card in the attempt to delay the German attack upon the U.S.S.R. All the other cards had been trumped.

At the last moment Stalin had withdrawn his demand that the Japanese concession should be annulled, exclaiming to Matsuoka, with an appropriate gesture: 'You are strangling me!' With this gesture the conversations ended, and Matsuoka went to inform the German Ambassador of what had happened and to comment upon the ups and downs of political life.[3]

Despite his final phrase, Stalin was so delighted that for once he broke through his usual habit of taciturnity and reserve. But he did not forget to endeavour to mollify Hitler.[4]

---

[1]Hitler and, consequently, Ribbentrop, were so certain that they would rapidly conquer the U.S.S.R. that they did not consider that they had any need of Japanese help.

[2]The heads of the Third Reich thought the fall of Singapore would provoke that of Churchill's Government, and bring about a compromise peace disadvantageous to England.

[3]Secret archives, telegram No. 883 from the German Ambassador to Moscow.

[4]This explains the sensational appearance of Stalin in the railway station at the moment of Matsuoka's departure. He greeted Matsuoka with a warmth which surprised everyone, as did the very friendly remarks exchanged with the German military attaché Krebs, whose hand he grasped for some time after the departure of the Japanese Minister, assuring him, evidently in order that his words might be repeated to Berlin, that the Russo–German friendship would never end.

CHAPTER XL

STALIN IS TAKEN BY SURPRISE

S TALIN, as a matter of rational calculation, was modest in his triumph. In the meantime the Third Reich had made fresh demands for the delivery of raw materials, and had repeated its protests against the delays in the execution of the agreements already concluded. It went as far as to ask for the admission of its experts to the Soviet railways, whose deficiencies were often invoked by Mikoyan as excuses for the failure to furnish the promised supplies. A representative of the Commissariat for Foreign Trade, Kroutikov, subscribed on the last day of April to the fresh demands of the Reich. Then, in order to avoid giving Hitler cause for dissatisfaction, the diplomats from the countries occupied by Germany were asked to leave Moscow.

But the Balkan campaign had been concluded just as rapidly as Hitler's previous victorious operations, and the Russian intelligence services were already emphasizing the importance of the uninterrupted concentrations of German troops on the Germano-Russian line of demarcation in Poland, as well as their movements in Roumania and Bulgaria.

Insisting that frontier incidents must be avoided, Stalin even forbade the Russians to fly over territory occupied by the German Army. Such prohibitions, however, were not always observed. In a report of the 23 April General Jodl states that 'every day fresh violations of the frontiers, committed by Soviet planes, confirm the opinion of the High Command of the armed forces already communicated to the Ministry of Foreign Affairs by the letter of the 1 March, that this represents a voluntary provocation on the part of Soviet Russia.'

Stalin repeated his prohibition.

At the beginning of May the ruler's 'personal network' fixed a date for the German attack upon the U.S.S.R. It would take place at the end of the month. Stalin then took a step of undeniable signifi-

289

T

cance.[1] Emerging from the privacy and anonymity of the Politburo, on the 9 May he had himself appointed, by the Supreme Council, President of the Council of People's Commissars of the U.S.S.R., thus becoming the supreme executive. This gesture had a twofold significance. While it told the country that the situation was becoming so dangerous as to necessitate, in view of the importance of instant action, the union in the same official hands of the activities of the Party and the activities of the State, Stalin also showed Hitler once again that there was a possibility of negotiation *in extremis* with the U.S.S.R., since he, Stalin, was henceforth at the head of the Government in person, and could give direct, rapid and efficacious replies to such questions as the Third Reich might propound.

But he was grievously mistaken. Each preferred to put faith in what corresponded with his own ideas and his own mentality; on this occasion the individual element took priority over objective reasoning. Moreover, Germany manœuvred with unusual skill. Schulenburg left for Berlin, announcing that he would do his very utmost to dissipate the threats looming over the Russo-German relations. In Berlin he called on Dekanozov, who proved to be hopelessly unequal to his task, and told him that he had obtained Weizsäcker's definite promise that Ribbentrop would ask the Führer to resume his policy of friendship with the U.S.S.R. and to concentrate all his efforts against England.

The Under-Secretary kept his promise. In a report to Ribbentrop he wrote: '. . . I can sum up in a single phrase my opinion as to a Germano-Russian conflict. If each Russian town reduced to ashes had for us the same importance as a British warship sunk, I should advise that the Germano-Russian war should be fought this summer. But I believe that we shall be victorious in Russia only in the military sense, and that in the economic sense we should be the losers. One might perhaps judge that the prospect of striking a mortal blow at the Communist system is sufficient . . . but the only decisive factor is to know whether this would hasten the fall of England. . . . We might, in fact, prolong the war by acting thus, instead of shortening it.'[2]

[1] On the 11 May, in commenting upon this gesture, the author wrote in the *Journal de Genève* that the meaning of the action was clear: Stalin was gathering all power into his hands, since he saw the moment approaching when the U.S.S.R. would have to fight for its existence.

[2] Secret archives of the Wilhelmstrasse. Report No. 998.

Nevertheless, Schulenburg returned to Moscow the bearer of disquieting news. Ribbentrop had declared that the Führer no longer believed in the possibility of the peaceful co-existence of Germany and the U.S.S.R. The Ambassador added, however, that the opposition 'to the Sovieto-German drama' was still powerful.

In this dramatic situation Stalin once more resolved on prudence. At the beginning of June he even refused to receive Sir Stafford Cripps. The situation was no longer the same as in July 1940, when the Wehrmacht was concentrated on the French front. Now he was afraid, and did not want Hitler to believe that he was discussing 'anti-German plans'; the more so inasmuch as by the 4 May the end of the Balkan campaign had been solemnly proclaimed by Hitler in the Reichstag.

It was at this moment that he fell into the trap prepared, for once, by the hand of the master of Berlin. The Reich asked for fresh deliveries of raw materials, and Stalin accepted as current coin Ribbentrop's promise that he himself would come early in July to assist at the final session of the Russo-German Economic Conference!

This was the moment when the 'Red Orchestra' gave Stalin information which finally spoilt his game, just as the Germans had misunderstood the unfortunate beginnings—unfortunate for the Red Army—of the Finnish campaign. For the 'Red Orchestra' stated that the Germans were not prepared for a winter campaign. Their operations, consequently, would have to be completed before the severe frosts, and they would therefore have to begin between the 1 June ánd—at latest—the 15th.

Now, nothing at all happened before the fateful date of the 15 June. On the 17th a goods train brought into the U.S.S.R. some Skoda armoured cars and optical instruments for the Soviet submarines. At the same time the Germans requested Mikoyan to increase the number of goods waggons intended for the transport of the German deliveries. The deception was perfect. Stalin was completely deceived, and on the 18 June he left for Sotchi, where he proposed to spend his vacation. In Moscow there remained only a Vice-President's Council consisting of Molotov, Vorochilov, Malenkov, Kaganovitch and Voznessensky.

It seemed as though things were quieting down. The strictest orders were issued to the army to avoid all incidents on the frontier.

This error of judgement was the most serious which Stalin ever committed; he was still waiting for an ultimatum from Hitler to elucidate the situation, and he refused to believe in an attack without previous declaration. The Russian Staff was still reflecting, held back by the Politburo and by Stalin, when on the morning of the 22 June nearly 3,000 Russian front-line planes were destroyed on the ground, where they were grounded without any camouflage.

The Russian campaign was thus begun under the most unfavourable conditions for the U.S.S.R. The country, and Stalin, were to pass through a terrible ordeal.

War ! . . . Despite the skill, the cynicism, the apparent versatility of Stalin, the outbreak of hostilities, so long deferred, struck a serious blow at the authority of the Lord of the Kremlin. There was a danger that it might have menacing repercussions throughout the country. The danger to the U.S.S.R. and to the Soviet system did not come solely from the armoured divisions, the air force, and the innumerable battalions of infantry brought against them by the Third Reich. The country had barely finished its revolution, and its population had suffered enormously during the Civil War, the terror, and the purges. The number of people who might be tempted to profit by the war in order to settle their account with those who had killed their kinsfolk and their neighbours was truly formidable. On the other hand, whole regions, like the Crimea, the Northern Caucasus, and part of the Ukraine, were riddled with nationalist and anti-Communist movements.

Abroad, it was said that the people would seize this opportunity of turning their weapons against their master. Such, on the whole, was the social and political situation while the strongest army in the world, reinforced by the troops of its Central European and Balkanic satellites, was preparing to attack the U.S.S.R.

A man with less solid nerves would have flinched; a Hitler or a Mussolini would have surrendered to manifestations of rage and gestures inspired by hysteria; a man of the ancient world would have veiled his face. Stalin contented himself with ten days of comparative isolation.

He was confronted with a number of unknown quantities, which he pondered, probably, not without anxiety. It is true that for the principal representatives of the régime the only thing to do, from the egotistical point of view, was to group themselves about their leader. It was probable that the 'clercs' of the régime, whom Stalin had bought at a high price, by giving them a privileged situation, would stand firm.

But in any case the surprise of the German attack resulted, inevitably, in discrediting, to some extent, Stalin's very ability to direct the foreign policy of the country. He found himself obliged to explain, before the most varied audiences, 'why he had ever put any trust in the word of such people as Hitler.' He had somehow or other to explain his error of psychological calculation, which had cost the U.S.S.R. a good part of its air force, and had enabled the Wehrmacht to advance so rapidly into Poland, France, and Yugoslavia, moving towards the centre of Russia.

Stalin remained at Sotchi until the end of the month. The direct line which connected his villa with the Kremlin was in constant use. It was very often Molotov at the other end. Without excessive mental agility, he was calm, imperturbable, obstinate; he had nerves of steel. The two men once again formed a tandem, as in 1912, when Molotov was secretary in the editorial offices of *Pravda*. This time, however, he was not editing a revolutionary journal with a small circulation for the few members of an extremist party. This time he had to save Russia, whose very existence was in danger.

Molotov's first speech, delivered at noon on the 22 June, some hours after the German aggression, in a calm, unemphatic tone, bears in its expressions traces of the style of Stalin's proclamations in the days before the Revolution, when he used to sign himself 'Koba.' The terms employed were crude, but there was eloquence in the concluding passages. 'The Fascist brigands, covered with blood . . . the Nazi assassins. . . . Our cause is just ! . . . victory will be ours !'

As for the country, it was plunged into a veritable stupor. To use a trivial expression, 'it couldn't get over it.' For nearly two years the newspapers had lavished their praises, magnifying 'the great and brilliant Stalin, thanks to whose intelligence our country has not known the horrors of war.' Now, of a sudden, his intelligent policy was shown to be erroneous: Hitler had attacked the U.S.S.R. in time of peace, 'without previous declaration of war, without having made any demands,' as Molotov affirmed in a speech recalling the days of Napoleon. These phrases contain a barely concealed admission of Stalin's tragic mistake. He had been so sure that Hitler would announce his intentions before firing the first shots and dropping the first bombs!

But it is in adversity that strength of character and the true temper of exceptional destinies are confirmed.

While watching over 'the judgement of the people,' Stalin wasted no time; but before reappearing officially he had to wait until the psychology of the masses had undergone a settling process. He meditated, without in any way changing his habits. He entertained relatives, and even some of the comrades of his youth. One of these[1] has given us a few details relating to Stalin's 'ten days of rest and meditation.'

'. . . I reached Sosso's house,' he says, 'late on the afternoon of the 23 June. There was nothing about the villa to remind one of the war. The head of the protection service, the commandant of the troops of the N.K.V.D., Lomakin, had taken no extraordinary measures. Stalin was sitting at his desk, near a great map of the U.S.S.R., which had not been there three days earlier. He had the drawn features of a man who has slept but little. As a matter of fact, he spent the night in conversation with Molotov and Timochenko, and he sent for Béria, who was on vacation at Soukhoum. He said the essential thing was to know what the attitude of the people would be toward German aggression. He expected the German propaganda to exploit the motives of anti-Semitism, and to attempt to obtain support among the older kulaks by waging a campaign against the *kolkhozes*. Béria, who had just been telephoning again, was rather an optimist as regards the general state of mind. . . . Stalin thinks the Red Army inferior in nothing to the Wehrmacht, provided the troops fight; he is convinced that they will hurl the Germans across the frontiers. . . .'

A few days were enough to enable Stalin to realize that in spite of the prevailing confusion, the Russian people as a whole had made up its mind to fight the hereditary enemy which it had faced so often

---

[1] An officer who at the end of the war became Chief of Staff in Budapest, and who passed through 'the Iron Curtain' in 1947, before giving several sensational interviews to a well-known evening newspaper in Paris. So far he has refused to publish his complete memoirs.

since the eleventh century. There was no sign of revolt, and the
active elements of the population recognized Stalin as a leader from
whom they expected action. He must give them victory, for that
alone could make them forget the hecatombs of the past and justify
him historically. Otherwise he would go down to history as a tyrant
who ended his days in defeat and humiliation.

The machinery of State power showed no signs of creaking. The
measures taken to enable the country to resist the Germans were
beginning to make themselves felt.

On the 2 July Stalin returned to Moscow. The powerful, stocky
individual who gesticulated and spoke with such characteristic
deliberation was about to become the pivot of the nation's resistance.

At the front, despite the surprise, the confusion, the rumours of
the first few days, the war had not assumed the aspect of a lightning
attack, such as one had come to expect since 1939. There was no
continuous front. The covering line had been pierced, but large
formations, outflanked or encircled, were continuing to fight. The
Germans were not simply forging straight ahead. An immense order
of battle had somehow crystallized over a depth of some hundreds of
miles, and it was slowly moving eastwards. The German Army was
encountering conditions and methods of fighting of which it had no
previous experience. Despite its lack of air cover, for a great part of
its air force had been destroyed by the first raid of the Luftwaffe, the
Russian Army was fighting tooth and nail. True, there were some
defections; but these were mostly of Ukrainian divisions, Kalmuck
regiments, and Caucasian mountaineers. The numbers of the prisoners
were increased by the presence of uniformed labour battalions.

Stalin had meditated long enough. Morally, the country was
standing firm. On the 3 July the President of the Council broke his
silence. He was counting on the psychological effect of his words,
and when he lifted up his voice for the first time since the outbreak
of the war he was in Moscow. His voice had a new, or rather a
renewed strength. It was warmer in tone, more human.

It was half-past six in the evening when he spoke.

'Comrades, citizens, brothers and sisters, soldiers and sailors, it is
to you, my friends, to all of you, that I am speaking.'

He showed that he did not believe it possible to win this war
unless it were a 'patriotic war,' as was the war of 1812. The peoples

had given their judgement. Victory could be achieved if they were gathered about him, united. He spoke as fitted the occasion. He did not conceal the truth, the whole truth, concerning the military situation. Like a Churchill, who disdains all such specious expressions as 'filling the gap,' 'stopping the draught,' 'offering an elastic defence,' he described the facts as they were: 'The German troops have occupied Lithuania, a great part of Latvia, the western portion of White Russia, and of the Ukraine. Our troops have been obliged to fight a retreating action. Our country is threatened with a great danger.'

He quickly recovered his assurance. He knew what had to be done. His sixth sense once again came to his assistance; and he felt that the people of the U.S.S.R. 'could take it.' He explained that the Germans had obtained an advantage in taking them by surprise, and that their forces were better prepared for war. Incidentally he justified his own policy, saying that the treaty of non-aggression concluded with Hitler had enabled the U.S.S.R. to gain eight months and to expedite its preparations.

He announced that the Superior Council of Defence, over which he presided, had assumed full powers, and he called upon the peoples of the U.S.S.R. to rally round the party of Lenin and Stalin, round the Soviet fatherland. It was not by chance that in these critical circumstances the customary epithet of 'Socialist' was omitted.

The Superior Council of Defence consisted, in the beginning, of all the members of the Politburo, Marshal Timochenko, and Marshal Chapochnikov, Stalin's adviser and military mentor. In this phase of the war, when the military machine was in movement, Stalin thought it useless to appoint a commander-in-chief. The Superior Council was, after all, a war cabinet, and four Marshals—Meretzkov, Vorochilov, Timochenko and Budienny—were in command, after mid-July, from the White Sea to the Black Sea.

Like Hitler, Stalin exaggerated the initial military possibilities, Hitler thought it possible to push a 'lightning attack' as far as the Volga, while Stalin thought he would be able to hold the Germans on the Riga-Dvinsk-Vitebsk-Mohilev-Jitomir-Ouman-Odessa line.[1] Since the victory over the Japanese divisions in

[1]At the Victory Banquet given in the Kremlin in May 1945 to the marshals and generals of the Red Army, he admitted this error of calculation. He also stated that Chapochnikov, who died during the war, without seeing the victory of which he was the first technical artisan, had warned him of the terrible strength of the German army.

Manchuria, he and his generals had indulged in an exaggerated self-confidence.

Stalin was not yet placing himself in the front rank. In accordance with his usual tactics, he avoided accepting the responsibility for the first inevitable checks, before the elements of a 'general strategical counter-offensive' could be assembled.[1] In his novel functions as President of the Council he proceeded with extreme reserve, as though this official post embarrassed him . . . owing to his lack of experience. Thus, although he negotiated with Sir Stafford Cripps in respect of the clauses of the alliance with England, it was Molotov who signed the latter on the 12 July.

During the preliminary negotiations he insisted particularly on two points: Mutual aid, by concentrated operations no less than by the despatch of aeroplanes, armoured cars, lorries, ammunition, and other supplies for the U.S.S.R.; and the acceptance of the principle 'no separate peace to be signed.'

The thesis concerning the 'concentrated operations' assumed in his eyes, as events developed, an increasing importance. He never omitted to refer to it. While recognizing that in the anti-Hitler coalition, 'the Red Army possesses for the moment a force superior to that of the British Army and should be responsible for the principal effort of the war,' he insisted on the fact that the British forces ought to profit by the current operations in the U.S.S.R. by immediately commencing other operations against the Reich in appropriate sectors.

The principle of concentrated operations was propounded once more four days before the signature of the agreement. It was here that the seeds were sown of the mutual incomprehension in respect of the famous second front; it became more serious in proportion as the war continued.

While expressing general ideas, he avoided engaging in purely technical military conversations; he reserved these for Chapochnikov, who negotiated with Lieutenant-General Mason Macfarlane, Admiral Mins and Air Vice-Marshal A. C. Collier. On the other hand, he himself intervened in the economic negotiations carried on between Mikoyan and Lazare Kaganovitch and Sir Laurence Cadbury, representing the Bank of England. He asked for the despatch

[1]See the preceding chapters.

of part of the aeroplanes furnished by America, and added, a little mockingly, despite the seriousness of the situation: 'If it were necessary to pay for these deliveries we should pay for them; we are poorer, perhaps, than the Bank of England, but we too have gold.' This did not prevent him, later, from accepting American lend-lease, which has not yet been repaid.

Seeking to establish useful relations with the Anglo-Saxons under the best psychological conditions, Stalin lured the elderly Litvinov, the world-famous champion of collective security, from his retirement. Litvinov had numerous connections in Great Britain and in the United States; he therefore made him his adviser in matters of foreign politics. On the 8 July Litvinov, resuming his activities as though nothing had happened, made a speech in which he declared: 'We must not leave Hitler any hope of obtaining a species of truce in the West. Our task must be to strike together, simultaneously, without respite or relaxation.'

Since the U.S.S.R. had been enduring the blows of the Wehrmacht, Stalin had endeavoured to establish ties of solidarity with that same West which, from the ideological point of view, had always been his worst enemy.

Stalin, without hesitation, began by propounding a few principles as to the conduct of the war and the internal politics of the U.S.S.R. In his first speech he had spoken of the patriotic Russian war. A Georgian and an internationalist at heart, understanding that the war could not be won unless it were a 'Russian war' against Germanism, he turned his back on the class struggle and its consequences, transferring both politics and the war to the national arena. Whether he wished for this change or suffered it, it was forced upon him by circumstances. He accepted it. He then dictated certain draconian—and ultra-national—measures for the internal security of the Union. All the inhabitants of German origin—who were numerous in the Ukraine and Bessarabia—were pitilessly deported to Siberia—even those who were Communists. Two principal towns, Karl-Marx and Engels, were completely liquidated; the local party secretaries of German origin were likewise deported. On the other hand the doors of the Administration were hospitably open to 'non-party' applicants.

In 1945, in his speech at the Kremlin banquet, at the close of hostilities, Stalin said:

'We ought all to thank the Russian people for its behaviour during the war, which gave us the victory. This people has shown itself capable, at this tragic moment of history, of giving examples such as the world has never seen. We, the Party, and the Soviet Government, had promised this people to endow the country with a powerful army capable of hurling back the enemy on the frontiers. We asked it for enormous sacrifices in the production of arms and munitions. And we were not able to keep our promise, for the enemy has trampled the soil of the country even as far as its capital! *Any other people than the Russian people would have driven us out and replaced us, would have chastised us.* But the Russian people has in spite of all had sufficient confidence in us to enable us *to redress our fault and atone for our mistake.* It has allowed us to organize the defence and to win the victory. Glory to the *Russian People*! Let us offer it our first toast!'

These words—which were hardly understood abroad—meant that the balance of forces in the U.S.S.R. had been modified. If Stalin confessed his error it was not in order to act like a Dostoievsky hero. He could not at that time possibly attribute this national victory to the Party, so he found a way of associating the Party with the victory and of maintaining it in its function of 'guide.'

It was on the same 3 of July, 1941, that the 'scorched earth' order was issued, which concluded with the famous appeal: 'Death to the invader! Let every man fight without thought of retreat, telling himself: I will not die without leaving a German corpse beside me!' He preached implacable hatred for all those who defiled the Russian soil with their tread. His words were a paraphrase, spoken with the same energy, of the words uttered in 1941 by Churchill, when England was threatened with invasion.[1]

Stalin decreed yet other measures. His experience at the theological college enabled him to accommodate himself to one of these better than could his colleagues! He became officially reconciled with the Orthodox Church, which had been the cradle of Russian unity,

---

[1]Since then it has become usual to invite the combatants, not 'to defeat the enemy,' but 'to kill him.'

and which for centuries had stimulated the powers of the country in its struggles against the Mahometans, and against Catholic Poland. This reconciliation was sealed, without demonstrations and without too many references in the press, by the reception in the Kremlin of the Metropolitan of Moscow and seven archbishops. The ex-pupil of the seminary, who threw his cassock over the wall even before he had worn it in order to become a revolutionary terrorist, now, having become the head of the Government of All the Russias, received with great pomp the high dignitaries of the Orthodox Church.

CHAPTER XLI

STALIN ORGANIZES HIS TASK IN TIME OF WAR

D URING the month of July 1941 the course of contemporary history was to be decided. Under the staggering blows of the Wehrmacht, already drawing upon the human and economic potential of the whole of Europe, the Red Army constantly retreated. The whole structure of the Soviet edifice was shaken by the terrible blows. A few fissures were showing in the western part of the country, where defections were taking place. However, despite the defeats, the heavy losses, and the withdrawal from thousands of miles of the front—despite the overwhelming effect on the country's economy, as a whole the young State—and it was not thirty years old—was standing firm. Like certain metals, whose molecular structure becomes closer, and whose coefficient of resistance increases under the vibrations of a violent hammering, Soviet Russia was forging itself. There was no weakening of the military command or the government of the country; the industrial reorganization continued. Contrary to the enemy's expectation, instead of sinking into anarchy the peoples of the U.S.S.R. remained united under a central authority. They persevered in the organized effort which enabled the U.S.S.R. to sustain a modern, technical war, and without interruption to increase its military potential.

From the psychological point of view Stalin's policy had succeeded in resuscitating and reinvigorating the national spirit; in the masses the attraction exercised by the official ideology had given way to other and more actual considerations. In order that equilibrium should be established, in order that it should continue, in order that the technical measures to be taken over the vast stretch of Russian territory should be executed without discussion at every stage, it was essential—since Russia and the U.S.S.R. had never been a democratic country—that the supreme authority should be uncontested, and that it should exercise its power not anonymously, but 'personally.' All the propaganda which had been carried on for years to spread the esoteric dogma,[1] and to make Stalin a symbol of national and historical continuity, had not been in vain. Henceforth, to the end of the war, he would play the part of the catalyser of all the energies of the country, whether military, political, or industrial; a fierce activity inspired all classes, and this miraculous awakening of the patriotic conscience would save the U.S.S.R. . . . and its system of government.

At last the resistance to the enemy had stiffened itself sufficiently. Towards the middle of July a communiqué announced victorious counter-attacks by Timochenko's troops in the region of Smolensk, and enumerated a large number of German divisions which had been annihilated or had suffered severely. The Wehrmacht would need nearly a month to reorganize itself and resume, on the central front, its advance in the direction of Moscow. Even if this were only a temporary check, the maleficent spell was broken; the proof had been given that Hitler's invincible army could be defeated. It had announced that Smolensk would be captured on the 18 July; but it did not enter the city until the 7 August.

The Red Army and its command were still undergoing their apprenticeship before an enemy who had the advantage of the most learned staff in the world, and which had plenty of experience of modern warfare and the complicated handling of armoured units and motorized infantry. All this time Stalin, while still remaining more or less off-stage, was undergoing his further apprenticeship. He was anxious to realize his theory that the head of the Government ought also to be the commander-in-chief of the armies in time of war, so as to make sure that the military operations were in correspondence with the aims of the future peace. He spent four days at the Hotel International in Viazma during the Battle of Smolensk, with Briga-dier-General Basil Sokolovsky, head of Timochenko's staff, and a future marshal.

With the same obstinacy as he had displayed in his studies of diplomatic history, Stalin completed his practical apprenticeship in military matters, familiarizing himself with the requirements of real armies. His experience of civil war had given him only psychological notions in this connection. To handle millions of men on an enor-

[1]See previous chapters.

mous expanse of territory was quite another matter, for which he was as yet unwilling to accept responsibility.

Nevertheless, he resolved to assume the supreme command. Some consider that his delay in doing so was due to his desire to avoid accepting the responsibility for failures; according to others, he was only anxious to perfect his military education.[1]

The whole of his work was reorganized. Before the war most of his time was given to the Central Committee of the Party, where Malenkov was his principal adjutant in respect of home affairs, while Jdanov was helpful as regards his relations with the 'Party brethren,' as the Comintern was commonly called in the U.S.S.R. His intervention in foreign politics and in the military domain were of later date. Now everything was altered.

All this did not prevent him from paying particular attention to questions of foreign politics.

Kossyguin became 'unifier' of war production; Mikoyan was to be director of exchange and commerce for the countries of Central Asia and the Near and Middle East. Lazare Kaganovitch was appointed director of the heavy and chemical industries, and was then entrusted with the Northern Caucasus. Other members of the Politburo were given exceptional powers which enabled them to act like the governor-generals of the Tsarist period, but with veritably dictatorial functions. Béria was appointed to Georgia, where there was a danger of revolt, for the German propaganda had found echoes there. Vorochilov was put in command of the defences of Leningrad; then he was sent to take charge of Western Siberia, which became the principal grain-producing area. Chvernik was responsible for Central Asia.

Malenkov remained at Stalin's side, in order to relieve him of the direction of the Party machine. Molotov saw to the despatch of current affairs, and became the private negotiator who was afterwards nicknamed 'Stalin's Harry Hopkins.'

On the 30 July Stalin had his first meeting with Roosevelt's representative, Harry Hopkins, who had come to Moscow in order to judge of the possibilities of Russian resistance and to negotiate on the subject of Lend-Lease. Despite Hopkins' physical weakness—he

[1]The theory of General Goulichirli.

was ill, and exhausted by his journey—the conversation lasted for three hours and three-quarters. This contact was full of promise. Stalin made a great impression on Hopkins. He gave evidence of a really profound knowledge, even of the smallest details. This was not only because his memory was prodigious;[1] it was above all because he prepared himself meticulously for each interview, and required his collaborators to provide him with a sort of agenda for each question to be discussed. He was very exacting, and fond of surprising his interlocutors by mentioning points that testified to a profound knowledge of the matter under discussion. This was a real quality, but it was also a trick which never failed to impress his auditors.[2]

However, he liked to act a comedy from time to time, playing an impromptu part. The comedian who had first learned his business in Siberia, in amateur performances with the beautiful Vera Delev-ska, was perhaps reminiscent of the barnstormer of Tiflis, or the jester of the Caucasian cabaret, or even the vendor of Oriental carpets. But on the background of his habitual sobriety of speech and gesture these deliberate performances never failed of their effect. When he seized his own throat to show Matsuoka that the Japanese was choking him by his obstinacy, he was obviously indulging in low comedy. But sometimes he rose to a higher level of histrionics, as when he told Roosevelt, with tears in his eyes: 'You are going to discredit me utterly before the Russian people by giving me a Russo-Polish frontier worse than Lord Curzon's? I beg you not to do that. . . .'

Here was comedy of a superior class, which recalls the comedy which Napoleon enacted before the Pope at Fontainebleau. The southern mountaineers are all alike, and a Georgian is no whit inferior to a Corsican.

A true Asiatic, as a negotiator Stalin always likes to be informed as to the personal character and the tastes or failings of any future colleague. Maïsky, who was regarded as having a thorough acquaintance with the leading British statesmen, was asked to prepare for

---

[1]Goering had an equally astonishing memory. During the Nuremberg Trial, for three days he replied to hundreds of questions put by the Allied prosecutors without the least hesitation and without any effort, furnishing precise and ample details of events covering a period of fifteen years.

[2]As it impressed Eden, Harriman and Victor Hoo.

Stalin a memorandum on Churchill, including even his painting, and on the Preminer's ancestor, the Duke of Marlborough.

He likes to stage an environment recalling the conversations or dialogues of antiquity or the Middle Ages. He showers attentions upon his guests, giving them lavish banquets, when the most appetizing dishes and the finest wines are served. Those who participate in the banquets of the Kremlin are impressed by the richness of the menus, composed of dishes of the Russo-Parisian cuisine which the Russian gourmets of the *ancien régime* had caused to be naturalized. Stalin often takes a hand in the composition of these menus, behaving, on such occasions, rather like a *nouveau riche*. By the correct handling of knives and forks the Russian tries to make us forget the famous image of 'the man with the knife between his teeth.' It is the same complex that insists on the strict supervision of the protocol of official receptions and banquets. When in August 1942 Churchill, who had come to Moscow, presented himself at the dinner-table in battle-dress, with no tie, and a zip-fastener, the impression produced on those educated in Soviet etiquette was deplorable![1]

In his first negotiations with Hopkins Stalin thanked the American delegate warmly for Roosevelt's admiring references to the Red Army; after which he quickly passed on to discuss current affairs. The question which he had at heart was the Second Front. He wanted the United States to intervene with the English in order that the latter should 'begin an operation of an amplitude destined to draw some fifteen to twenty-five German divisions.'

Hopkins, who understood the British situation, nevertheless promised to repeat this request to Churchill, and a general agreement

[1]At this banquet, which was fertile in incidents, owing in part to the usual heat of the Kremlin dining-room, Churchill's costume provoked various different reactions. General Wavell was asked 'if this was not the uniform which would be worn by the British troops when they opened the Second Front?' Toward the end of the banquet Stalin proposed a toast to the Intelligence Service, 'so that he would not be mistaken as to his estimate of the enemy forces, as he was during the attack on the Dardanelles, when he induced the First Lord of the Admiralty of that period to stop the attack at the moment when the Turks had exhausted their last munitions.' Churchill was inclined to be highly offended by this allusion, and only the intervention of an American officer, Duncan, cleared the atmosphere. The American declared that if the information services were deceived it was because people like Stalin did not give them enough information. To which Stalin replied, with a hearty laugh, that Duncan had only to ask for information, which would be furnished gratis.

was signed. Stalin made the question of the Second Front his 'bedside sword.' On the 28 September he spoke of it again to Harriman and Lord Beaverbrook. They replied by insisting on a definition of the final aim of the war. Stalin consented to subscribe to part of the terms of the Atlantic Charter, but in spite of Harriman's urging he rejected the paragraph on 'liberty of thought and religion.' The great divergence between the two worlds was emphasized once again in 1941. 'First of all,' said Stalin, 'one must establish a common definition of the word "liberty." '

He was greatly interested in the labours of the six commissions of the Conference. He listened attentively to Harriman, who declared: 'Our aim is the same as that of your British allies: that is to say, it is to give you all possible assistance to struggle against the attacks of Hitler and his cohorts. The American nation attaches a supreme importance to your success.'

But directly after this he spoke again of an immediate Second Front. He wanted a great deal and did not hesitate to ask for it. On reading the protocol of the figures relating to the supply of war material signed by Molotov he observed, ironically: 'That is no more than the production of the one city of Stalingrad.' It spoke of 3,000 planes, 4,000 cars, 30,000 lorries and waggons, 40,000 tons of petrol, 305,000 tons of lubricating oil; total tonnage, 850,000.[1]

This tonnage is impressive, if one considers all the difficulties encountered by the British convoys in the Arctic Ocean, all the human sacrifices, and all the losses in ships and materials. But for the Russians, who at this time were suffering the full weight of the German forces, these supplies seemed very much less than what they ought to have received. The two estimates were irreconcilable. . . .

What Stalin feared above all was that a definite weakening of the U.S.S.R., in the face of a more or less intact British force, would allow Great Britain to instal herself in those regions of Central Europe on whose account Soviet Russia was contending with Germany: the Balkans and the valley of the Danube.

While confident of a final victory over the Wehrmacht, he knew already, after the checks of the frontier battles, the defeats at Minsk, Ouman, and Kiev, and in the Baltic countries, that the war would be long and exhausting. He saw that when once the British forces were

[1]Figures confirmed by Anglo-American sources.

fighting shoulder to shoulder with the Americans, Churchill would try to push toward the Balkans. He was afraid he might see a revival of the Budapest-Salonika-Sofia-Bucharest axis of the first world war, when the Balkans and Central Europe would enter into a British zone of influence, while he, Stalin, would waste the power of the U.S.S.R. in the plains of Poland, the forests of Lithuania, and the marshes of East Prussia.

But there is reason to believe that even if London had shown itself less opposed to his plans, Stalin would none the less have displayed the relentlessness which transformed a whole series of Balkan and Central European countries into satellites, on which, apart from a political alliance, an internal social transformation in the direction of Communism was imposed.

CHAPTER XLII

THE BATTLES OF MOSCOW: CONTACTS WITH THE ALLIES

ON the 2 October, 1941, the Germans launched their first offensive against Moscow. The capital represented their main objective. They were not counting merely on the moral and political effect which its fall would produce. Moscow was a railroad centre of enormous importance, since the principal railway lines, connected by transverse branches, all converged there.

Stalin remained on the spot throughout the battle, attending all the meetings of the Committees for the Defence of the City, the chairman of which was the Moscow secretary of the Party, Alexander Chtcherbakov. In the meanwhile there was a fresh transformation of the supreme command. Timochenko commanded the front from the Black Sea to the south of Moscow, while the capital itself and the front between this and the Baltic were confided to Joukov.

The personal information service, and in particular the 'Red Orchestra,' stated that the date for the taking of Moscow had been fixed by Hitler on the 16–17 October, and that the battle for the capital 'should not last longer than a fortnight.'

The German plan envisaged an attack in the direction of Kalinin, in order to outflank Moscow on the north, and another attack in the direction of Toula, in order to outflank it in the south, and a frontal attack through Viazma, to take the city by assault.

From his shelter, Stalin addressed the population, and gave his promise that Kalinin and Toula should never be captured by the Wehrmacht. The Red Army kept this promise. The Germans appeared before Kalinin on the 14 October, but they were counterattacked by reserves emerging from the forests along the upper course of the Volga, and held up in the city itself. In the centre the Wehrmacht had achieved an important success, seizing Viazma on the 11 October. On the other hand, it was unable to capture Toula.

The offensive was checked. Marshal Bock did not dare to make a frontal attack on Moscow, since the wings of his armies had failed to attain their objectives. Hitler deprived him of his command and ordered a fresh offensive.

Despite the nearness of the enemy, on the 6 November, on the spacious site of the Maiakovsky Station on the Metropolitan Railway, which on this occasion replaced the Grand Opera, Stalin, the Government and the Politburo commemorated the anniversary of the Revolution. Standing on a bench, as in the days when he had addressed the Caucasian revolutionary mob, Stalin spoke:

'Comrades, twenty-four years have elapsed since the establishment of the Soviet system in our country. We have now reached a new phase of the Soviet era. The bloodthirsty brigands of Hitler have attacked us treacherously without any declaration of war, without warning, despite the treaties of non-aggression.[1] We are going to show them that aggression doesn't pay; we are going to exterminate them, and we shall continue to exterminate them until the day when not a single German fascist is left on the soil of our fatherland!'

He announced the German and Russian losses. Both sets of figures were obviously incorrect. The German losses were exaggerated: the Russian losses were diminished—in the interests of the cause.

On the 7 November, at eight o'clock in the morning, he was present at the traditional military parade in the Red Square. The Wehrmacht was at the gates of Moscow, on the eve of its decisive attack; the city had already been attacked from the air, and at any moment the sirens might begin to howl. Nevertheless, the master of the U.S.S.R., with all the members of the Politburo and the Government, appeared on the Governmental platform. Stalin appeared for the last time in his legendary long grey hooded coat, without any decorations or insignia of military rank. A small red star, with a golden sickle and hammer, adorned his cap.

'Comrades,' said he, 'today we are celebrating the twenty-fourth anniversary of the October Revolution under painful circumstances. The treacherous attack of the German brigands, and the war which they have forced upon us, are endangering our country. We have suffered the loss of a certain number of provinces, and the enemy has

[1]He evidently found it impossible to stomach the illegal ('non-juridical') nature of Hitler's attack, by which the Führer had contrived to dupe him.

appeared at the gates of Leningrad and Moscow. There are people who are distracted by the danger and who shriek from the roofs to announce the deadly peril which we were unable to avoid.[1] They are forgetting the much greater difficulties of the year 1918. . . . Today our situation is far more reassuring. Our country is exploiting its enormous wealth; we have an ally,[2] and we have a strong army to defend us. Let us tell everyone: the enemy is less powerful than a few scared little intellectuals imagined. The devil is less terrible than the image one conceives of him. A few months longer, at most a year, and Hitler's Germany will founder under the weight of her crimes.'[3]

It is very doubtful whether in November 1941 Stalin can have believed in the possibility of victory within a year, for on the 16th of that month the Wehrmacht resumed its offensive. On the very day of the attack the frosts of winter set in, and snow fell. Hitler introduced something new in the way of tactics. While maintaining the frontal pressure, he attempted a limited encirclement. Both operations were vigorously conducted.

The Russian riposte took the form of a double encirclement. The enemy centre was opposed only by experienced troops who had already been fighting for months, and were echeloned in depth. They were reinforced by working-class militia, installed in trenches dug more or less at random by the civil population. The fresh reserves were concealed and concentrated on the flanks, but outside the line of encirclement, with a view to a decisive counter-offensive. The second Battle of Moscow had begun, and it developed under the direct participation of Stalin, who took over the command, even to the execution of its details.

Once again Hitler had given his generals a fortnight to take the city, which was almost in sight. Once again the terrible blows of the German Army shook the Red Army. In the centre the Russian lines were pierced in the sector of Narofominsk, and the enemy vanguard

---

[1]This really amounts to a confession.

[2]Obviously Great Britain. At a moment when all the moral forces of the country were put to the test the mere possibility of mentioning an ally was a factor of great importance.

[3]Stalin, of course, was far from being sincere when he said this. He knew very well that the effort of overthrowing Germany by military force would be immense; on the other hand, if countries and governments were to succumb simply under the burden of their own crimes, one doesn't know exactly where we should have been in 1941.

was only eighteen miles from the capital. During the early part of December the offensive reached its most advanced points of penetration. In the north the Germans occupied Khimki, a small port on the Moscow-Volga Canal, some four miles from the city and connected with the latter by trolley-bus.

The danger was extreme. The detachments of the rearguard, exhausted by months of fighting, had at all costs to hold out for a few days longer in order to enable the mass of troops manœuvring for position to complete their concentration. The beginning of the counter-offensive was almost a matter of hours. Several times a day the alarm-bell sounded in the headquarters of the different generals.

'Hullo. . . . Here is Stalin. . . . Make your report.'

'Hold on !' he said, after listening to the report. 'We shall be coming to your assistance in three or four hours' time; you will have reinforcements. . . .'

Of course, his telephone message had often only a psychological value. But the generals were unanimous in declaring that the voice of their chief, calm and deliberate, calling to them often in the dead of night, and speaking words of encouragement, gave them the feeling that they were being powerfully supported from the rear by the country as a whole.

On the 6 December the counter-offensive was opened. The first commander to receive Stalin's congratulations by telephone was General Vlassov, a divisional commander. This was the Vlassov who, being taken prisoner by the Germans, was placed by them at the head of an army consisting of prisoners of war and Russian deserters, and was hanged in Moscow after the end of the war. On the 14th Stalin telephoned his congratulations to General Lielioushenko, who had refused to surrender at Kline. On the 15th he rang up Koniev, who had driven the enemy from Kalinin. On the 16 December a communiqué recording a victory was published over the joint signatures of Timochenko and Joukov. It announced the crushing defeat—probably decisive in respect of the whole campaign—of the Wehrmacht before Moscow.

In this communiqué there is no mention of Stalin, nor of a central command. It was issued directly by the two victors. The following messages were always addressed to the commanders who had won victories, but they emanated, like the decrees of Providence, from the supreme command, which was nothing more than a new mask of the Master's. Everything had to tend toward his glorification, and thereby to strengthen the régime, which was drawing a veil of oblivion over the victims who had paid part of the cost of its establishment. But this veil would be woven of the fresh sacrifices of the Russian populations, who hitherto had never failed in their duty of defending their country, ready to forget the labels which the Marxist ideologists had attached to it.

The victory in the Battle of Moscow brought about a fundamental change in Stalin's position. Externally, however, his attitude was the same as ever. During the past months he had maintained, before the representatives of Great Britain and the United States, an attitude of calm assurance, despite the tragic uncertainty of the situation. Another man would have found it extremely difficult to play the part of the unperturbed ruler; but for Stalin it was no effort to control his nerves, and to meet his visitors with an untroubled countenance. He is kneaded of a special clay, which never ceases to radiate a certain impression of strength and confidence. But he knew that the greatest trials were still to come, and wanted to prove that in any situation there were for him no ups and downs, but only a reasoned and obstinate steadfastness.

Nevertheless, as far as words went he showed a tendency to treat his foreign visitors with rather more confidence after the victory of Moscow. This was, of course, a matter of tactics.

An explanation with London had become indispensable. Eden had decided to go to Moscow for a candid exchange of views with Stalin. There was every chance that the atmosphere would be favourable, since Moscow had pleasant recollections of Eden's visit before the war.[1]

In their interviews Stalin did not beat about the bush. He began, as always, to discuss the question of the Second Front, which the Englishman evidently found displeasing. After trying to obtain certain details of a military nature, which Eden could not give because he was not acquainted with them, Stalin passed on to other questions. Eden listened with open mouth. The Germans were still not far from Moscow, and Stalin was already speaking of the frontiers of the U.S.S.R. after the war. By the territory of the U.S.S.R. he meant

[1]Eden had pleased Stalin greatly. 'This young man will go far,' he said.

the territory held by the Russians on the 22 June, 1941, the day of the German aggression.

Stalin, then, was asking that the Allies should recognize his seizure of the Baltic countries, Bessarabia, Northern Bukovina, Western Poland, the city of Viborg, and part of Karelia. When the war was ended he wanted to sign treaties of mutual assistance with Bulgaria, Roumania and Yugoslavia. In short, he wanted now to ratify all the acquisitions and all the advantages which he had derived from his pact with the Third Reich.

It was impossible for Eden to encourage such demands. Relying on Stalin's liking for Eden, and the esteem which Eden had manifested on many occasions, if not for Stalin's character or his policies, at least for his technical qualities as a statesman, and his intelligence—Molotov declared that he was 'satisfied with the personal attitude of the British Minister,' and asked that 'the understanding effected should be recorded in a protocol.' He was going ahead a little quickly. Eden, of course, did not fall into the trap.

He was able, without affecting it, to escape the influence of the atmosphere of cordiality which prevailed during the preliminary conversations. His decisive argument was that the United States could never give their consent to the final annexation of the Baltic countries by the U.S.S.R. Stalin expressed himself as being gratified by the Russo-Britannic collaboration in Iran, which began on the 25 August, 1941, with the joint occupation of the country, and which took the form of the maintenance of Russian garrisons in the northern provinces, and of British garrisons at certain strategic and economic points in the south, including the shores of the Persian Gulf and the delta of the Shat el Arab, in order to protect the oil refineries of Abadan.

Stalin remembered that Iran ought to have been evacuated at the end of the war if the Anglo-Russian convention of August 1907 had been strictly observed. However, he expressed the usual objection; he added that the U.S.S.R. intended, once peace was restored, to ask for concessions in the oil measures of the five northern provinces.[1] He declared that he had studied, with the greatest interest, Sir

---

[1]References to the substance of these conversations are found in many articles devoted to the subject of Iranian petroleum and published in the monthly review *Questions d'Histoire*.

Edward Grey's conversations with the Russian Ambassador in London, Count Benkendorff, preceding the signature of the 1907 convention. 'England had promised at this epoch that she would offer no objections if Russia obtained, in the five northern provinces of Persia, a concession of the same kind as the Anglo-Persian, which was in process of organization. I believe that on the basis of such an agreement we could establish complete collaboration in Iran.'

These claims were important, but limited. After the ground which had been covered, he was no longer a revolutionary or a political apprentice whose horizons have no limit. The Russian people, on whom he had to rely, was not haunted, like the German, by the idea that it was being held 'cloistered' within too restricted frontiers, or that the real wealth of the world was what had to be taken by force from other peoples. It is just the sense of reality, of 'the degree to which aspirations can be realized,' which makes it an adversary infinitely more dangerous in the long run.

Stalin wanted also to get rid of the new Polish Army formed on the territory of the U.S.S.R., and known as Anders' Legion. 'We have no objection to raise if the Polish legion is sent to fight elsewhere. General Anders is our enemy and would be more useful to you outside our frontiers.'[1]

Before leaving Moscow, Eden's *entourage* told the foreign journalists accredited to the Soviet capital that the British minister was completely satisfied with his conversations with Stalin, and that the latter had asked 'neither for the Straits nor for Persian territories.' During the war it was evidently impossible to make fuller statements. It was easier, less compromising, and more diplomatic to mention 'what Stalin did not ask for' rather than what he did demand.

Whatever the circumstances, he did not 'lose the north.' Nor did he lose, in the west and the south-east, his tenacious and practical view of Soviet interests, which were often but not always those of Russian continuity.

---

[1]Anders, an ex-officer of the Tsarist Army, was a product of the cavalry school, which was suspected by the N.K.V.D. of having been in touch with the organizations of emigré Russian officers in Paris. Taken prisoner by the Red Army in 1939, and confined in the Lubianka prison of the N.K.V.D., he was liberated after the signing of the alliance between Moscow and the Polish Government in exile. He detested the Russians and belonged to the category of Poles concerning whom Stalin, in reply to the statement that the Poles did not like the Russians, retorted: 'Why should they?'

CHAPTER XLIII

THE NEW COMMAND

THE plan of the winter campaign which was to follow the Battle of Moscow was drawn up by Marshal Chapochnikov with Stalin's participation. Stalin no longer concealed the active part which he was taking in the planning of military operations.

However, it may be supposed that the Politburo, while accepting Stalin's initiative, was not unanimous. The theory of the 'brilliant strategist,' though officially accepted, does not appear to have convinced the directing organism of the Party. It seemed, above all, to doubt the military gifts of the Leader; his new appointments were not made public until the end of April 1942, when, on the 1 May, he signed the order of the day in his quality of Commissar for War. He did not forget to ensure that the newspapers should announce the fact that his appointment dated from January 1942.

The motive which induced Stalin to assume the supreme responsibility for the direction of the war was twofold. On the one hand, he could not and would not permit that military leaders like Timochenko, Joukov, and others, who in their turn were soon to become immensely popular, should overshadow his own reputation. On the other hand, the war had become a vast patriotic enterprise which was absorbing all the energies of the country, and in order to avoid being swept aside by the wave of traditional patriotism which has nothing to do with social theories, the Secretary-General of the Communist Party had to see to it that he was borne onwards and upwards by this wave, and even that he seemed to be the motive force behind it. The millennial reactions of the Russian people would thus be travestied as the result of twenty-four years of Communist government!

In the winter campaign the Germans suffered in their 'hedgehogs,' but the trials which the Russian soldiers had to undergo must have seemed almost insurmountable. Moreover, the Red Army was still lacking in heavy artillery. The little it did possess could move only with difficulty through the deep snow. Nevertheless, on the 1 January the Russians recaptured Staritza and opened a wide breach in the enemy lines between Kalinin and Rjev. On the 9 January they achieved a signal success to the south of Lake Ilmen. On the 23rd they occupied the Vieliki-Louki-Bologvic-Mojaïsk triangle. But the Rjev hedgehog, in the centre of the diagonal of this triangle, remained in German hands. A few days later the 16th German Army, under von Busch, was encircled. This offensive was carried out according to a special strategy, incontestably initiated by Stalin himself: an attack by partisans on the rear and communications, simultaneously with a frontal attack by regular troops.

The principle of this strategy was published in a special military periodical, *Questions of Strategy*, issued by the Staff Academy in 1937. An article in this journal analysed the simultaneous operations of partisans and regulars in the wars of the twentieth century. It expounded the ideas of Frunzé, who had died in 1925. It was signed 'Komandarm.' This writer regarded the partisans as a special category of the armed forces of the country, and gave some chapter headings from a manual of 'the Complete Partisan.' The framework of the partisan units was to be provided by the local troops of the N.K.V.D., with all their armaments, which would form, simultaneously, units of shock (assault) troops and a police force inside the groups, in order to prevent the introduction of enemy agents.

We know that the article expounding the action of partisan forces was in reality written by Stalin, who signed it with a pseudonym.

Von Busch was able to hold out until the spring, thanks to the superiority of the Luftwaffe, which revictualled the hedgehogs with the help of Junkers. Nevertheless, along the whole of the front the Red Army realized appreciable gains. But despite these successes, the illusions born of the victory of Moscow were soon discarded by Stalin. He understood that the Red Army alone could not conquer the Wehrmacht, if only because of the weakness of the Red Air Force. He persistently continued his negotiations with Great Britain and the United States. He tried to obtain from the former a new treaty of alliance, to complete the treaty of the 12 June, 1941, which was only provisional. He wanted at all costs a precise and unconditional promise that the British would create a Second Front in Europe. His Ambassador in London, Maïsky, repeated this to Eden and Churchill, always employing the same argument: the risk of weakening the alliance. The allusion was easily understood: if the Second Front were not 'guaranteed' circumstances might compel the U.S.S.R. to refrain from guaranteeing the efficacy of the obligations which it had contracted in respect of the non-signature of a separate peace.

At the same time the diplomatic offensive for the Second Front was being pushed in the United States by Litvinov, now Ambassador. In order to convince Roosevelt of his friendship, and to emphasize his sincerity in the Oriental fashion, Stalin sent his daughter Svetlana to Washington, where she lived under Litvinov's roof. In this connection Stalin often declared: 'I sent Svetlana to the United States as hostage of my friendship for President Roosevelt.' At this moment Stalin's Asiatic memories were in full charge. He combined two terms which for a Westerner were incompatible; the word 'friendship' was preceded by 'hostage.' But in both respects he was doing his best. . . .

Litvinov, who was constantly receiving emphatic requests that he would proceed to action, delivered a great speech in Philadelphia, devoted entirely to the Second Front, which served as a sort of preliminary to sending Molotov to London and Washington. The old champion of collective security sought to play on a familiar string. Then, furnished by Stalin with precise instructions, a fact which was always published and emphasized if need arose, Molotov left in May 1942 for London and Washington on board a Russian bomber which was flying to Murmansk.

Between Stalin's emissary and the head of His Majesty's Government the incomprehension was total.[1] All Molotov's efforts to secure a mention of the Second Front in Europe in 1942 in the final com-

[1]Churchill, in his memoirs, speaks in some detail of Molotov's stay in London, of his mania for sleeping with a revolver under his pillow, and his profound distrust of the British Secret Service and its ability to protect him. Perhaps this is only the picturesque reverse of the antipathy already obvious in *The Unknown War*, published in 1930, when he painted the Bolshevik leaders black! Since then, of course, a good deal of water has flowed under the bridges on the Thames and the Moscova; but despite the alliance imposed by circumstances, the incomprehension persists.

muniqué were in vain. The twenty-year treaty of alliance was signed
by Eden and Molotov on the 26 May.

Having failed in London, Stalin redoubled his efforts in the
United States. Roosevelt, who judged that the chief burden in
Europe was weighing upon the U.S.S.R., showed that he was aware
of the dangerous situation. To the communiqué from London which
spoke of 'a complete understanding,' the communiqué from Washington, to which Roosevelt gave the last touches after consulting
Stalin by radio, added in less lapidary terms: 'A complete *entente* has
been realized between the United States and the U.S.S.R. as
regards the urgent necessity of creating a second front in Europe
in 1942.'

Stalin had all the more need of this diplomatic victory in Washington as imperative reasons had been imposed by military events.
Timochenko's offensive toward Kharkov suffered a humiliating
check, although he had at his disposal an imposing number of new
armoured units, equipped with heavy K.V. cars of forty-five tons,
motorized artillery, and numerous aeroplanes, all hurled against the
panzers of General Paulus and the experienced armies of von Bock.
In the outskirts of Kharkov the new German anti-tank guns, the
terrible 88's, made a hecatomb of the Russian cars. The losses were
heavy, in men and materials, and many prisoners were taken. Timochenko, a personal friend of Stalin's, had put into execution a plan of
offensive entirely approved by the Defence Committee, over which
Stalin presided.

This is why his defeat was afterwards represented as a deliberate
sacrifice designed to delay the opening of the great summer offensive
of the Germans. This explanation was evidently fabricated after the
defeat; but at the time of its production, part of the command and
part of the Politburo, and a great proportion of the population, were
alarmed by a fresh tactical German victory, despite the employment
of newly formed and well-armed divisions. It was felt that the country was disappointed, shaken, and almost disheartened. It was necessary to find a psychological stimulant. This was Stalin's peculiar
province.

In June 1942 he convoked a meeting of the Central Committee
and a session of the Supreme Council of the U.S.S.R., in order to
effect the solemn ratification of the Sovieto-British treaty of 26 May,

1942. It was absolutely necessary to revive the courage of the people by promising that the Second Front would soon be opened.

The measures of supervision which were taken to ensure the safety of Stalin and the Government were symptomatic of the situation. They were decreed by Stalin himself, and they denote the fear of a dangerous repercussion of popular feeling resulting from the serious check suffered by the Red Army. In front of the Metropole Hotel, which was assigned to them as residential quarters, the delegates, forming in ranks of six in the Place Sverdlov, were escorted to the Kremlin under the protection of a large body of armed police, led by Merkoulov, the general in command of the security troops of the N.K.V.D. On reaching the Borovitzki Gate of the Kremlin they were subjected to four successive verifications of their identities, undertaken by special police and officials of the Central Committee and the Supreme Council, who were personally acquainted with the members of the Council and the delegates.

Then all passed through a special room in which they had to surrender their weapons, while on leaving it they were subjected to a fifth inspection which made certain that they had done so. Stalin entered by a little door concealed behind the governmental tribune. As usual, he was greeted by an 'interminable' ovation. There was no time to be lost; and the Master himself had personally taken measures to ensure that all should be done quickly, very quickly. . . . After the lapse of three minutes Béria, at a sign from Stalin, pressed the button of an electric bell. The applause stopped; Molotov mounted the speaker's tribune; he was dressed in a blue suit bought in the United States, and he held in his hand the text of the speech prepared by Stalin. The treaty of the 26 May was ratified unanimously by a show of hands.

During his speech Molotov made special mention of the communiqué from Washington: 'Comrades,' he said, 'this declaration is of the greatest importance to the people of the Soviet Union, for the establishment of the second front in Europe will create insurmountable difficulties for the Hitlerian armies on our front. . . .'

Despite the gravity of the moment, Stalin could not entirely conceal the good humour which emphasized his *sangfroid* and his nervous imperturbability. He was seen to break into a hearty laugh, leaning over toward Kalinin, when in the diplomatic box a Japanese attaché, who represented the absent Ambassador, and had fallen asleep, suddenly woke with a start at the sound of applause, and himself began to applaud loudly the alliance of the U.S.S.R. with Great Britain, which was at war with Japan. . . .

The southern jester, Sosso Djugachvili, still lives on in the brilliant Father of the Peoples, the great comrade Stalin. . . .

CHAPTER XLIV

STALINGRAD

O N the 28 June, 1942, six days after the first anniversary of the German aggression, the Red Army was subjected to another severe test. Against a front of 130 miles, between Kursk and Izioum, Marshal von Bock hurled a breaching force of motorized infantry, armoured divisions, and more than 3,000 aeroplanes. This time the O.K.W. inaugurated the 'Motpulk system,' the autonomous mailed fist, the moving fortress. The formations of assault cars, which also protected the flanks, escorted into the interior of the formation all the necessary weapons; artillery and motorized infantry, anti-tank guns, groups of pursuit cars, the bomber and fighter planes, the D.C.A., the munitions, the supplies, and the repair lorries or mobile workshops. Behind von Bock's 'Motpulks' 195 German, Roumanian and Italian divisions were advancing, ready to fight a gigantic and decisive battle.

The 'Red Orchestra' had informed Stalin of the plan of the O.K.W.: it was to cross the Don, to advance as far as the Volga, to move northwards in order to cut off Moscow and the Soviet armies of the Centre from the Urals, and to enclose them in a vast net. Simultaneously a powerful and independent group would descend toward the Caucasus and seize the petroleum wells of Baku.

Stalin, as soon as he had studied this information, convoked a great military assembly in Moscow. Marshal Chapochnikov, who was dying, was replaced by the new Chief of Staff, Vassilevsky. After prolonged debates Stalin himself summed up the results of the discussions and the decisions arrived at. The strategy adopted was as follows: 'To sell space in order to buy time.' That is, when all is said and done, the eternal Russian tactics. However, they would counter attack whenever the bulk of the forces was more or less protected. The fortified points, the railroad centres, the fords and bridge-heads on the rivers, were to be defended with the utmost vigour, but care would be taken to avoid encirclement, even at the price of extremely

V

rapid retirement, which sometimes—as practice would demonstrate —would assume the appearance of a rout.

From the strategical point of view it was decided to shut off the north so completely that the German offensive would have to turn in a south-easterly direction, so that it could be engaged, at a distance from the north, in the immense plain lying between the loops of the Volga and the Don and the northern spurs of the Caucasus.

The key positions of Voroneje and Kletskaia held firm; but on the rest of the front the Red Army suffered a series of humiliating defeats. General von Mannstein, once Levinsky, passed the Straits of Kerch, seized Rostov on the Don, and thrust onwards to the Central Caucasus, crossing the almost impassable peninsula of Taman, where he was subjected to sudden attacks, while the partisans harassed his troops. On the 9 August the Wehrmacht occupied Krasnodar and the whole of the Kuban, and on the 16th the petroleum fields and refineries of Maikov. It now threatened the Red Fleet's base at Novorossisk.

One disturbing fact revealed a new and terrible danger and threw a fresh light on the state of mind prevailing in the south: on the 10 August Mannstein's advanced guard of armoured cars was wel-comed with enthusiastic cheers from a portion of the inhabitants of Vorochilovsk, whose recollections of collectivization were only too painful. It was the same at Ordjonikidzé. This made it possible for the Germans to begin to form regiments from the Cossacks of the Terek and the natives, who enlisted in their thousands. This was the prodrome of a separatist rot, although for the present it was local. In vain did Stalin send into the Caucasus plenipotentiaries whose duty it was to inquire into the situation.

The whole Soviet system of defence appeared to be breaking down on the southern part of the front. Official communiqués admitted as much, and appealed to the sense of duty of those 'who have shown weakness and can now redeem themselves.'

Stalin was genuinely anxious. The orders which he gave to his ambassadors in London and Washington reflect his anxiety. They were to the effect that his demand for the immediate opening of a Second Front was to be presented in the most urgent terms. His tone became more and more violent. Litvinov admitted to Roosevelt that his master was exasperated, and that his telegrams betrayed his extreme irritation. Molotov was instructed to declare officially that the U.S.S.R.'s powers of resistance were not unlimited and that the Allies would be making a great mistake if they overestimated them. There was an open reference, for the first time, to the possibility of irrevocable disaster.

Roosevelt, whose judgement of affairs was objective, and who was not unfavourably prejudiced against the Soviet leader, nor against the Russians as a whole, recognized the reasonable nature of Stalin's demands. But he replied that the British operations against Rommel in Africa already constituted, in a certain measure, a second front, and they were holding up the crack German formations. Stalin did not accept this explanation, which seemed to him a mere excuse or evasion. Rommel's African Corps consisted of two armoured divisions and one division of light infantry. Such a front was not a centre of fixation; it was merely a slight diversion. On the other hand, he believed that the American forces assembled in Britain already amounted to eight divisions, and that they, with the British and Canadian divisions, supported by an air force superior to that of the Reich, might very well attempt a landing in France with a view to creating a 'veritable' point of fixation. But Churchill maintained his own point of view.

To escape from this impasse, the great 'F.D.R.' advised the two protagonists, Stalin and Churchill, to meet. On the 12 August Churchill arrived in Moscow in an American bomber, together with Averell Harriman. It was the least fruitful encounter—except in incidents. In Moscow everyone—including the foreign press—felt that Churchill was at the time the very last negotiator capable of coming to an understanding with Stalin, of persuading the latter to be patient and to yield to the logic of the British arguments. The two great statesmen were too dissimilar, too completely opposed.

The difference of character, the resurgent hatred of the past, the British Premier's profound antipathy for the 'people of the Kremlin,' his Mediterranean theory of victory over the Reich—all this was bound to inspire, from the very outset, a nervousness and irritability in the mind of the elderly gentleman whose very appearance irritated the Russians. For years past Churchill had been for the U.S.S.R. the personification of 'bourgeos Imperialism'; his profile, cigar in mouth, had figured in thousands of caricatures, with which the masses were perfectly familiar.

There had already been a misunderstanding during the drive from the aerodrome to the British Embassy. According to his habit, Churchill made the V-sign with two fingers. In Russia the word for victory begins with a P and people interpreted Churchill's sign as announcing the opening of the Second Front. This misunderstanding was explained to Churchill. He himself was so nervous that he did not attend the press conferences which he had convoked. The famous banquet in the Kremlin, with its forty-three places, served in the 'Catherine Hall,' was fertile in incidents.

Stalin insisted on the necessity of relieving the strain on the Red Army, and was unwilling to admit that the Molotov-Eden communiqué, and the Washington communiqué, were the expression of a desire, and not the pledge of an immediate and unconditional action. He demanded the redemption of the 'solemn promise' given to Molotov. He laid emphasis on a fact which according to him should have been regarded as of capital importance. He asserted that the Atlantic coast of France was not yet seriously fortified, and that a landing of troops would present no insoluble difficulties. In evidence, he cited his landings in the Crimea, in order to show that the success of such operations depended only on the determination of the command.

Churchill remained uncompromising, but informed Stalin of the preparations for operations in Africa which would serve to draw a number of German divisions toward the Mediterranean. Stalin continued to insist on his own point of view, declaring that all the other solutions were most unpromising.

At last, in the course of a final, nocturnal conversation in Stalin's little house in the Kremlin, Stalin once more explained to Churchill his plans relating to Poland, Central Europe and the Balkans after the war. The interview between these two men of destiny ended in complete disagreement. It is very probable that they already realized that their ideas as to the future status of defeated Germany would be totally dissimilar.

After the departure of the British Premier, on the 19 August, an allied commando force made a raid on Dieppe. Its failure must have proved to Stalin that for reasons of a material order it was not yet possible to open a front on the Atlantic coast of France—especially as the Western Powers would not risk the possibility of very great losses in human lives. Human life is differently valued in Western Europe and in Stalin's monarchy.

On the way to victory the two parties, becoming conscious of the divergences which awaited them, displayed a certain hesitation. Fortunately a third man of destiny, Franklin Roosevelt, intervened; or these divergences, at a time when any maladroit gesture was likely to cause serious trouble, might have proved disastrous to the nations at war against the Third Reich.

It was natural that the British and the Americans should seek to create a situation in which Moscow could not fail to carry out the mission assigned to her. But a certain wavering in Stalin's attitude was becoming perceptible. Stalin, yielding to his characteristic suspicions, thought he detected a duality in the Anglo-American attitude.

Early in August 1942 the ex-Ambassador in Washington of the U.S.S.R.—Oumansky—being in Moscow, slipped into his private conversations with the Allied representatives allusions to the possibility that the U.S.S.R. might envisage an arrangement with Germany. Now, Oumansky was a 'man of straw' whom Stalin employed for confidential bargaining, and Roosevelt, who knew this, took the matter seriously.

The President chose this time to send as his representative Wendell Wilkie, his Republican partner in the two-party administrative system.[1]

Wilkie began by a visit to Kuibychev, where he did his best to convince the Russians that he was a good fellow, who had no desire to complicate matters, and that he was in favour of the immediate opening of a second front in Europe—which had the greatest significance for Stalin.

After a few spectacular and calculated gestures—as when the American climbed over the rail of his box and jumped on to the stage in order to present a bouquet to the *danseuse* Tikhomirova—which amused Stalin greatly—Wilkie set to work in Moscow.

Wilkie was accompanied to Moscow by General Follet Bradley and a number of military experts—soldiers, sailors and airmen—

[1]See Dulles' *On the Road to Teheran*, published in the U.S.A. in 1943.

among whom was Commander Paul Phil, a specialist in the organization of convoys. Wilkie did what was expected of him. He spent
a couple of days in exploring Moscow, giving the impression that he
believed everything that he was told by the people he met, and that
he was duly edified by the N.K.V.D. He then visited the front, spoke
to all the foreign journalists accredited to Moscow, discussed affairs
for hours at a time with Ockanozov and Oumansky, and met
Molotov. On the 22 September he spend two and a half hours with
Stalin, without the United States Ambassador. He gave Stalin a
written message from Roosevelt, and received, then and there, a
reply from Stalin.

The conversations were devoted exclusively to the Second Front
and the American deliveries. Stalin, who in any case would have to
continue fighting, declared that the Red Army would fight to the
last man at Stalingrad, but that it needed victuals and munitions.
Above all he wanted lorries, and accused the British of diverting
some of the armaments intended for the U.S.S.R. by sending them
to the Near and Middle East. He revealed the urgent need of a
declaration concerning a Second Front in order to revive the morale
of the nation.

Convinced, Wilkie declared, before leaving Moscow: 'The best
way of helping Russia consists in opening a Second Front with the
help of Great Britain as soon as the military leaders think it possible.
I believe some of them need to be spurred on by public opinion.
Next summer it will be too late.'

These, of course, were the words of a man who was not a military
expert, nor was he directly responsible for the policy of his country,
but his declaration meant that in the dispute between Churchill and
Stalin, Roosevelt was frankly supporting Stalin. This was the beginning of a singular friendship at a distance. Stalin said, in this connection: 'There is on the other side of the Atlantic a man whose origin
is very different from mine. But he offers you his hand and wins your
heart.'

In the Kremlin, which had become the seat of a veritable command headquarters, Stalin had surrounded himself with a group of
strategists, theoreticians and co-ordinators. Among those constantly
at his side were Timochenko, Vorochilov, whose prestige was purely
sentimental—he was known as 'the saviour of Leningrad'—and

Vassilevsky, who had replaced Chapochnikov. But the pivot of his staff was Joukov, the hero of the victory of Moscow, who had revealed himself as the most brilliant military leader in the U.S.S.R. It was to him that Stalin had confided the task of elaborating a new system of command in the army; the 'war without strategy'[1] which the fifty-seven Soviet armies had formerly fought was now superseded.

According to the official version, Stalin, and Stalin alone, was the author of all these measures. This was only part of the truth. I have already hinted that he acted above all as a catalysing agent, giving impulse and authority to the technical decisions of the talented men of whom Russia possessed so many. This was the proper rôle of a supreme civil and military head; he was like the conductor of the orchestra, who guides and controls the performers. In this art Stalin has achieved the greatest mastery.

Among the solutions proposed, he chose Joukov's.[2] This recommended the constitution of twelve fronts, commanded each by a general who had given proof of his ability. In order that all the fronts should be in close contact, representatives of the supreme commanders would assist each of the generals in command of the twelve fronts. They represented Stalin, and thus the system of personal telephone messages which Stalin had applied during the Battle of Moscow was repeated on a larger scale.

At the most dramatic moment of the Battle of Stalingrad, Stalin sent thither, as his personal representative, Joukov, whose reputation was firmly established, and who enjoyed a tremendous prestige among the troops. He himself made only a single journey to the Stalingrad front, spending a few hours at the north-eastern extremity. But by a subterfuge which would seem a little childish, except for the fact that it produces results, he created his own legend. The slogan 'Stalin is with us!' which was passed round among the combatants, was taken for gospel truth. Not for nothing did the soldiers' songs composed during the Battle of Stalingrad speak of 'Stalin, appearing in the trenches, in the streets of the besieged city, in the valleys, on the hills.' This at all events is true: that 'doubles' of Stalin

[1]A few weeks before this the author had published in the *Journal de Genève* an article on this subject, in which he spoke of the 'War without strategy being fought by Moscow.'

[2]Cf. *Questions d'Histoire*, a monthly Sovietic review.

appeared from time to time at the front.[1] The real Stalin was in the Kremlin.

In October, the crucial month for Stalingrad, he quarrelled with Churchill. The subject of dispute was, of course, the Second Front. As a pretext for his attack on the Englishman he spoke of the case of Rudolf Hess. Stalin demanded that Hess, who at the moment was a mere prisoner of war, who had entered an enemy country in uniform, should be tried immediately as a war criminal.

On this occasion *Pravda* published an article inspired by Stalin as Secretary-General of the Party, of which this journal is the official organ: '. . . Should one regard Rudolf Hess as a war criminal or as a special ambassador of Hitler's to the Court of St. James? Is England going to be turned into a den of gangsters?' Stalin behaved as though he believed that in refusing to try Hess, Churchill was granting him diplomatic immunity, and proving his intention 'to use him for secret and inadmissible negotiations.' Behind this phrase one divines a veiled threat that Stalin himself might take the initiative in such negotiations.

This was assuredly a ruse. It is hardly probable that at this time Stalin could have been thinking of opening negotiations with the Third Reich. But in any case, this fictitious threat of a separate peace was meant to help him to obtain the opening of the Second Front in Europe. All that he said and did pointed in the same direction.

On this occasion the two great men were at odds again. Churchill, after considering the situation, refused to be blackmailed. The British military attaché replied to Vishinsky's reproaches: 'And where would the *first* front be if there were a *second* front?' The allusion was plainly to the relations between the U.S.S.R. and the Reich in 1939 and 1940.

Stalin met with a counter-offensive from Churchill. At this moment occurred one of the most characteristic incidents in the relations between the master of the Kremlin and the man who was freely accepted, during the war, as the master of the British Empire. While violently reacting to the constant contradictions of the Russian, Churchill made a gesture which revealed his absolute confidence in him! One of the most jealously guarded secrets of the war was imparted to Stalin.

[1] Cf. General Goulithlivi and General Tulpanov.

On the 5 November the British Ambassador, Sir Archibald Kerr, called on Stalin at the personal request of Churchill. Their conversation continued for more than two hours. In extremely plain terms, Kerr insisted on the painful impression produced in England by the article in *Pravda*, and two other articles in the provincial press, which accused the English of treachery.[1] On the same occasion, the landing in North Africa, which would take place in two days' time, was announced.

Churchill thoroughly understood the mentality of his 'opposite number,' and he had allowed for the sensitiveness of the Oriental. The landing in Africa was not the second front in Europe for which Stalin had clamoured, but the fact of announcing it represented so friendly and considerate a gesture that the latter was obliged to accept, officially and publicly, despite his profound disappointment, the *ersatz* second front which was offered to him.

Accordingly, on the following day—the 6 November—Stalin delivered a speech in the hall of the Kremlin in which he referred to Churchill's communications, though, of course, without divulging the secret. But in order to raise the morale of the public he explained that any undertaking of this nature was definitely useful: 'Favoured by the absence of a second front in Europe,' he said, 'the Germans and their allies have massed all their available reserves on our front and are hurling them against our south-eastern sector; they have succeeded in achieving a substantial tactical success . . . the absence of a second front in Europe has enabled them to effect this operation without the least risk. . . .'

After this painful admission he sounded an optimistic note: '. . . Nevertheless, sooner or later, we shall have this second front. Not only because we need it, but above all because our Allies themselves feel a need of it as great as our own. . . . Are the Allies actually incapable of organizing a winter campaign on a large scale? Of course not! Their capacity is not to be questioned. . . . Do the opposite ideologies, the different social systems, form an obstacle to co-operation between us and our allies? No, no, and again no!

Stalin ended his address with the words: 'The Anglo-Sovieto-

[1] The article made an attack on the Court, complaining that King George VI was the only head of a nation at war with Germany who had failed to address his felicitations to Kalinin on the 7 November, 1942, the twenty-fifth anniversary of the Revolution.

American coalition has every prospect of conquering the Italo-German coalition.'[1]

On the following day Gregor Alexandrov, head of the section for propaganda of the Central Committee of the Party, published an article which was conciliatory in tone. He said, among other things: 'The absence of the second front is a grave violation by our allies of their obligations toward the U.S.S.R. But we shall be prepared to forget the past as soon as the lack is made good.'[2]

On the 8 November *Pravda* published a Reuter telegram announcing the landing in North Africa. But it made no comment on the incident. Stalin said not a word. Churchill, as obstinate as Stalin, wanted to force the latter to speak. On the 11 November he explained to the House of Commons that Stalin had known of the projected landing—which was true—and that he had approved of it —which was only partially true. He wanted to compel Stalin to make a public declaration.

It is curious to note that from time to time he felt—quite possibly under the influence of the peculiar Russian environment—the necessity, as a matter of propaganda, of 'recognizing his mistakes.' Thus, in the Kremlin, in August 1942, he asked Stalin in the warmest of tones 'to forget the past,' and received the curious response:

'God will forgive you, Mr. Churchill.'

Something of the same kind inspired him during his speech of the 11 November. But Stalin persisted in his official silence. He chose an indirect means of speech, which consisted in granting an interview to the journalist Cassidy, who had addressed to him a questionnaire under three headings.

'. . . In comparison,' he said, 'with the assistance which the Soviet Union is giving the Allies by holding up the bulk of the Germano-Fascist armies, the assistance given by the Allies to the Soviet Union is not very efficacious. In order to increase and improve this assistance one thing only is necessary; that the Allies should promptly and com-

---

[1] He says nothing about Japan, then at war with the Anglo-Americans, and the difficulties of the Allies in the Pacific. But he himself had a treaty of non-aggression with Japan, which was very useful to him.

[2] This contains an optimistic affirmation intended for the peoples of the U.S.S.R., so that the announcement of a landing in Africa might seem to them to afford some relief. But since the end of the war the Soviet press has never ceased to repeat that the lack of a second front in Europe until 1944 was a deliberate intrigue against the U.S.S.R. The suffering and resentment of 1942 and 1943 have not been forgotten.

pletely fulfil their obligations. . . . I think the Soviet ability to resist the Germanic brigands is no less—even if it is not greater—than the ability of Fascist Germany, or any other aggressor nation, to achieve domination over the world. . . .'

But the mention of 'any other aggressor nation which might seek to achieve domination over the world' was singularly reminiscent of the recent conversations with Ribbentrop on the subject of Great Britain and her 'world imperialism.' Here Stalin, without intending it, was speaking the same language as the ultra-reactionary Russians of the nineteenth century, the famous Anglophobes Kathov, Tiout-chev, and Pobiedonostzev, the pillars of the official Pan-Slavism of the days of Alexander II and Alexander III. . . . This, of course, would not escape Churchill, nor would he forget it.

In the meantime, the situation at Stalingrad was changing to the advantage of the Russians. The manœuvre of the double encircle-ment conceived by Joukov, and already applied during the Battle of Moscow, was repeated here on the 12 and the 19 November. The operation was conceived in accordance with a general directive given by Stalin, which went far beyond the local objective. Stalin has cited the words of his master Clausewitz:[1] 'a strategical plan always tends to be imposing, and to aim at remote and important objectives. As a matter of fact, while an operation can always be reduced when cir-cumstances and the resistance of the enemy compel the high com-mand to reduce it, it is, on the contrary, almost impossible to develop a small operation, for the means and the ways of executing it are lacking at the last critical moment and cannot be improvised.'

However, the destruction of the Sixth Army of von Paulus was due very largely to Hitler's obstinacy, and to his constant under-estimation of the forces of the enemy. His orders nailed Paulus to the spot, waiting for the arrival of General Mannstein, who, at the head of an enormous concentration of armoured cars, had been instructed to break through the Russian encirclement. But he did not succeed in doing this, for the output of the Soviet war industries, augmented by consignments from the Allies, was sufficient to outclass the Ger-mans. The motorized Russian artillery developed by Voronov and Chapochnikov, thanks to Stalin's support, and the fighter planes, employing rocket projectiles, destroyed the Panzers. Finally, the

[1] In *Questions d'Histoire*, a Moscow monthly review.

thermite or thermal bomb made its first and last appearance. This produced a temperature rising to 1,800 degrees.[1]

On the 25 January, 1943, Stalin signed his first order to the armies in his new quality of Commander-in-Chief.

After the surrender of von Paulus, which took place on the 2 February, 1943, Stalin's personal reputation was greatly enhanced by this victory, which had a certain symbolic importance. The Supreme Council granted him the title of Marshal of the U.S.S.R., and proclaimed him 'the greatest strategist of all times and all peoples.' These honours were valued by him only because they constituted a means of action. He knew very well, and was constantly declaring, that the final victory was still a long way off, and that among the dangers which had to be faced was one which seemed to him particularly serious: namely, the defection of a section of the population.

This danger was revealed in all its amplitude in the Northern Caucasus. Despite the capture of Rostov on the Don, Mannstein, cut off from the bulk of the Wehrmacht, was still holding the Northern Caucasus. His army was revictualled by way of the Straits of Kertch; and he was able to form more and more numerous detachments of Cossacks from Terek and Kuban, of Tatars from the Crimea, of native Caucasians and of volunteers. When these troops withdrew they were followed by a great proportion of the population.

The U.S.S.R. was in grave peril. Now, for the first time, Stalin was seriously afraid of possible internal repercussions. It was at this moment that he wrote his famous article in *Pravda*: 'Keep Cool!' This put the country on its guard against the tendency to exaggerate successes, and to believe that the enemy could easily be conquered. Examination of the text shows that he was occupied with a new idea, which was born of his apprehensions.

'It must not be thought,' he wrote, 'that the victory of Stalingrad means the final defeat of the Germans. The beast is still in its lair, although we have seriously wounded it. It would take several more Stalingrads to defeat the Germans for good and all. We shall have to work hard, to go on and on producing cars, aeroplanes, lorries, and

[1]The thermal bomb was invented by Stanislas Loika, a mining engineer. The bombs were made at Stalin's command. They were very difficult to make, and their number was so limited that the whole stock of these bombs was exhausted during the battle against Mannstein.

munitions, to conquer the *terrible enemy* who is defiling the soil of our fatherland.'

This was a surprising article. Stalin, who in 1941 had promised to clear the Germans out of the U.S.S.R. in a few months, at a time when the Red Army was definitely weaker than the Wehrmacht, and was suffering a series of defeats, now described the enemy as 'terrible,' as though there had been no danger of exacerbating an inferiority complex of which the Russians had hardly rid themselves. The truth is that behind this phrase another idea was concealed—and this time a political idea: the idea of the possibility of a separate peace, justified by the fact that the *terrible enemy* was still on his feet.

CHAPTER XLV

TENTATIVES IN DIRECTION OF A SEPARATE PEACE

D URING the relative calm which reigned on the Eastern front between the end of the Battle of Stalingrad and the beginning of the last great German offensive against Kursk—that is, between mid-February and the beginning of July 1943—Stalin's method of work was more or less stabilized. While he was devoting several hours of the day to the study of military questions, he was at the same time carrying out a complicated diplomatic offensive. This was the same complicated undertaking as that which he had already pursued during his negotiations with the Third Reich, and he was often to hesitate as to the best course to follow.

For the time being he had to be content with the landing in North Africa. But his acceptance of 'Operation Torch' was purely external. In self-defence he felt it necessary to smile in the face of adversity, since American aid to the West was assuming enormous proportions, and he did not wish to diminish the Russian share.[1] He was greatly preoccupied by the international situation, and the reports furnished by his personal intelligence service in Europe were causing him constant anxiety.

From Switzerland he had received communications from one of his best agents, Colonel Maslov, relating to Franco's attempts to figure as mediator between Great Britain and the Third Reich. The departure of Serrano Suner, the notorious Anglophobe of the Foreign Office, and his replacement by Count Jordana, who was known for his Anglophile sympathies, might have been effected with a view to preparing the ground for secret negotiations between

[1]Between October 1941 and the 1 January, 1944, the United States had delivered to the U.S.S.R.: 7,800 planes, of which 3,000 were flown across; 4,700 armoured cars and anti-tank guns; 170,000 lorries; 740,000 tons of aviation petrol; 177,000 tons of explosives; 1,350,000 tons of steel and 2,750,000 tons of provisions.

the emissaries of Hitler and the British Government in Madrid.

Maslov had informed him of one material fact of capital importance: Franco had evidently—quite by chance—become perfectly aware of the details of 'Operation Torch,' and he had not communicated this intelligence to Hitler, which was proof of his connivance with Churchill.

This is how Franco had learned of the operation: A few days before the landing in Africa an officer of the British Navy, who had upon his person a copy of the plans of the operation, which he was to give to the Governor of Gibraltar from General Clark, had been killed in the course of an air engagement, and his body had been recovered near Cadiz. The Spanish Secretary for the Navy, to whom the document sewn in the dead man's uniform was given, sent it immediately to Franco. The latter gave instructions to the effect that the officer's body should be given to the British military attachés in Madrid, after the secret document has been sealed again and sewn up in the dead man's clothing, as though the Spanish Government had never discovered it.[1]

London, being warned of the incident, did not in any way change the plans of the landing, which gave Stalin the 'assurance' that Churchill was counting on the discretion of Franco. He concluded—suspicious as usual—that this could only be explained by the existence of a secret understanding between Franco and Sir Samuel Hoare, who was regarded as one of the most obstinate enemies of the U.S.S.R. Franco might act as mediator once the landing had been effected, when the English would hold a fresh trump for negotiating with the Reich.

There were other circumstances which gave support to this theory. The aerodrome at Gibraltar was practically undefended, and was divided from Spanish territory by a mere fence,[2] which could have been destroyed in a few minutes by the guns at Taifa. Now, Franco had given orders that special protection should be afforded

---

[1]These details were given in Périgueux in 1943 by Rado, who has already been mentioned in a previous footnote. He was a member of the Soviet network in Switzerland, who at the moment had taken refuge in France. He told the story of the drowned man at the time, but it had seemed the creation of a romantic imagination. However, it was completely confirmed by Sir Samuel Hoare in his book *Ambassador on Special Mission*, and by a letter addressed to Churchill by Franco in 1944.

[2]Confirmed by Sir Samuel Hoare.

around the aerodrome on which the allied planes were assembling in view of 'Operation Torch.'

Stalin's apprehensions seemed to find confirmation in a report, published on the 16 April, 1943, that Jordana had been exploring the possibilities of a separate peace between the Third Reich and 'the Christian Powers.'

While the chimes of the 'Spanish hour' were still ringing in his ears, Stalin found himself engaged in a rather violent controversy with Cordell Hull, Roosevelt's representative, who at the first conference of the allied ministers in Moscow refused to accept the reannexation by Russia of the Baltic countries. Stalin did not give way. He undertook 'to feel the pulse of the Third Reich' in order to clarify the situation.[1]

He was aware of Churchill's desire to achieve at any cost a landing in the Balkans which would have excluded him from those countries. Nevertheless, it was for the sake of these regions that he accepted the risks of war with the Third Reich, and logically he could not give them up.

In May Alexandra Kollontaï was summoned to Moscow. Two days later she returned to Stockholm, accompanied by Alexandrov, the head of the Propagandist Section of the Central Committee, and by Mikoyan, who among other functions exercised those of Vice-President of the Foreign Commission of the Politburo and of Chief of Foreign Trade.

According to the instructions given, the affair should have been conducted with the greatest discretion. To begin with, preliminary contacts with an inconspicuous member of the German Embassy, in order to notify the fact that the U.S.S.R. would be glad of a private exchange of views. Then, a meeting between Alexandrov and a counsellor of the Embassy, and finally, a conversation between Mikoyan and the Ambassador of the Reich, or some other important personage. This was, on the whole, a repetition of the 'Operation Asthakov' of 1939, which experience had made it possible to improve at certain points.

The affair got under way fairly quickly, thanks to a Swedish banker of German origin[2] who was in contact with an attaché of the

[1] Details furnished by Rado in 1943.
[2] Still serving as intermediary in certain negotiations..

Embassy who was entrusted with the work of propaganda in Swedish financial circles.[1] The banker announced the arrival of Alexandrov and 'another gentleman who is the personal representative of Stalin,' who had come to open negotiations, and asked that Alexandrov should be received at the Embassy. He explained that Stalin's representative, who was passing under a borrowed name, could not remain very long in the Swedish capital. Ribbentrop, who was immediately informed of what was afoot, feared to be drawn into a trap, and consulted Hitler. Thereupon Hitler insisted upon an inquiry, in order to discover whether the banker who was acting as intermediary was not perhaps . . . a Jew. He was a Jew. Thereupon Hitler ordered the Germans 'to abandon this intrigue of international Jewry which was trying to hinder the attempt of Madrid to arrive at a truce with the Anglo-Saxons.'

Mikoyan spent only three days in Stockholm, waiting for the return of the attaché. In the meantime the attaché had been severely admonished by Ribbentrop, and Hitler had threatened him that if he did not abandon his suspicious contacts. . . . Stalin now knew where he stood. He knew that Hitler would cling indefinitely to the idea of a peace of compromise with the Anglo-Americans.[2]

---

[1] In 1930 he published his recollections. Part of his book appeared in the *Figaro Littéraire*.

[2] Doenitz, Himmler and others tried to negotiate such a peace during the final collapse.

w

CHAPTER XLVI

STALIN & ROOSEVELT: TEHERAN

ONLY one course remained for Stalin: to bind himself to the Allies until the end of the war. Roosevelt's attitude in respect of the Third Reich was absolutely precise; and he might prevent what Moscow called Churchill's Balkanic frolics. The U.S.S.R., with its 300 divisions engaged, as against fifteen Anglo-American divisions, not counting the divisions which Great Britain and the United States had sent to the Pacific, was the main force. He must profit by the situation in order to settle the problems of the post-bellum period in the sense most in conformity with Russian interests.

Accordingly, Stalin assumed an increasingly friendly attitude toward the United States, and toward Roosevelt himself. As a matter of fact, the relations between the two men were assuming a development and a significance which could not have been foreseen. What Stalin had begun as an ordinary diplomatic game was taking hold of him with a completeness which can be compared only with the impression which Lenin had produced upon him at the beginning of his career as a professional revolutionary. But the orientation of this influence and the direction in which it led him were the very reverse of Lenin's.

In a private letter, written by his own hand, Stalin thanked Roosevelt for the welcome which the White House had extended to his daughter Svetlana. He loved this daughter tenderly,[1] and his personal gratitude was perfectly sincere.

On the 22 May, 1943, he made a political gesture which was intended to show Roosevelt that the peaceful co-existence of the U.S.S.R. and the United States had become a reality. The Comintern was dissolved.

[1] As Churchill had observed, during the improvised supper in Stalin's house on the 14 August, 1942.

We know now, thanks to the revelations of the Spanish Communists, that the liquidation of the Comintern was never completed, and that a secret office, known as 'Institute No. 611,' continued the work of the Comintern at a more deliberate rate, until in 1947 its successor, the Cominform, was created.

Nevertheless, one should not under-estimate the political importance of this official decision.

The non-interference in the internal affairs of other countries on which Roosevelt had insisted as a real guarantee of a peaceful co-existence, became apparently a fact. In the exchange of diplomatic courtesies between the U.S.S.R. and the Allies, Stalin paid his first courtesy to Roosevelt.

These courtesies began to appear in other branches of political life. In a communiqué, Stalin officially recognized the efficacy of American aid, and published the figures relating to the quantities of materials already delivered. The Soviet radio broadcast the communiqué immediately. In order to emphasize his friendly attitude, Stalin instructed Litvinov to publish a statement in Washington.

The renewal of the law of Lend-Lease put an end to the controversy. Stalin kept to his chosen path. Henceforth he would play Roosevelt's card. For the first time in his life he would allow himself to be guided by a sentiment.

At this period he had to concentrate once more on the military operations. He had ended by acquiring an extreme skill, if not in the direct handling of armies, at least in the handling of the officers who exercised the actual command. He intervened in their exploits, introducing those considerations of common sense which in military science are described, on the whole, as 'strategy.' He gave the preparations for the summer campaign of 1943 the aspect of an industrial company's plan of production.

In June, between the 11th and the 23rd, he presided over a series of meetings at which the principal directors of the war industries were present, together with the most prominent soldiers, those who would soon be placed in command on the fronts, and lastly, Timochenko, Joukov and Vassilevsky.

On the very first day of these meetings he himself put the essential questions: 'How many tanks do you want, how many planes, how many motorized guns? At what do you estimate the inevitable losses of material? Can the present rate of production of our industry possibly make up for these losses?"[1]

The Russian artillery had already been organized by Voronov, in accordance with a system of massive concentration elaborated by Chapchnikov and successfully applied before Stalingrad. As for the tanks, it was calculated that the losses might amount to from 65 per cent to 75 per cent of the effectives engaged. The abundance of means was such that these percentages were regarded as acceptable. In order to judge of the scale of this effort it will suffice to recall that for the Dnieper offensive it was calculated that 5,500 tanks would be needed; so that the percentage of losses estimated represented 4,000 tanks. Here the industrialization which had cost the U.S.S.R. so many sacrifices and victims shows the importance of the results which it had achieved.

But in spite of this the task of the Red Army was not an easy one. Stalin realized this, and admitted, in the course of debates, 'that the adversary is still very powerful, is endowed with material of superior quality, and has at his disposal soldiers of great valour and experienced leaders.' At the same time, a new tank, the 'Tiger,' weighing fifty-six tons, equipped with 88mm. guns and heavy armour, was employed as the backbone of the Wehrmacht in the battle of the summer of 1943, assisted by 'Panthers' and 'Ferdinand' anti-tank guns.

The commanders-in-chief of the armies had already sufficient prestige, and had already sufficiently proved their worth, to apply, of their own initiative, the tactics appropriate to the execution of Stalin's strategy.

Stalin this time achieved a decisive psychological victory. By the intentional and very largely feigned dilatoriness of his preparations he made Hitler believe—as Goebbels declared in his journal, *Das Reich*—that the Russians, incapable of defeating the Wehrmacht under normal atmospheric conditions, dared not attack. Persuaded that he must win in the summer in order to give way in the winter, Hitler took the initiative. This was just what Stalin wanted, especially as he knew the spot at which the German Army intended to strike.

He waited patiently until Hitler, becoming nervous, ended by ordering his generals to begin their offensive, which would lead, as

[1]*Questions d'Histoire.*

Stalin calculated, to a disequilibrium of forces in favour of the Red Army.

On the 5 July the Wehrmacht moved to the attack on a front of 180 miles, with masses of 'Tigers' which swept down upon the salient of Kursk. Hitler, recalling the Napoleonic wars, called it an attack of the 'Leipzig' type. The greatest battle of the second world war had begun. It was also to be one of the least known. The Wehrmacht threw in its tanks in massive formations. These consisted of twenty-five to thirty-five 'Tigers,' in pointed groups, followed by seventy to eighty tank destroyers, and numbers of motorized cannon, detachments of medium tanks, and finally, the motorized infantry. The preparatory fire was intense, but of brief duration.

In the first twenty-four hours of the battle Von Klugge lost 650 tanks—more than Rommel had lost during the whole of his campaign! However, in spite of von Klugge's alarming reports, Hitler gave orders that the battle was to continue. During the following days the Germans attacked from the north, while doing their utmost to make progress in the south. Between the 6 and 12 July they threw into the line 6,000 tanks, which were used to reinforce the 7th Panzer division, brought from France.

The German offensive definitely came to a standstill on the 13th. The Wehrmacht had lost 3,000 tanks and 1,200 planes—a fourth of the German planes on the Russian front. The Red Army had lost 1,750 tanks and 600 planes. The superiority of the reserves, which had been made clear during the conferences of the 11 to the 23 July, enabled Stalin to order an immediate general offensive. The moment of which Stalin had been dreaming on the 6 November, 1941, when he made his speech in the underground railway station, had arrived.

Before starting these fresh operations Stalin had constituted an 'operative quartet,' which was to undertake the direction of all battles, leaving to Stalin only the task of remote supervision. This quartet, which was appointed on the 5 June, consisted of: Vassilevsky, Chief of Staff; Joukov, quartermaster; Voronov, in charge of the artillery; Timochenko, co-ordinator.

The brilliant successes of the Soviet Army brought the Russians to the Dnieper; at the beginning of November they were in Kiev. Thenceforth Stalin's armies regularly outclassed the Germans. Only von Mannstein-Levinsky still ventured on counter-offensives, and succeeded in escaping from the encirclements and the traps prepared by Stalin's generals. He fought in the mud and snow, and he made use of the partisans—the anti-Bolshevik Russians—and it was he who in 1943 saved the Wehrmacht from a final disaster.

Stalin did not make Hitler's mistakes; he never interfered in the tactical dispositions of the generals. It was for them to execute the variations on the given theme. Also, he never undervalued the courage of his enemies. Speaking of Mannstein, he said: 'If he had not been one of Hitler's generals I would have made him the senior professor of our Military Academy.'

While the Russian forces were advancing towards the west, Stalin gave constant thought to the political future. On the 19 July he received General von Seidlitz and a group of officers who had been taken prisoner with him at Stalingrad. Under the direction of Wilhelm Pick, he founded the 'National Committee of Free Germany,' whose official aim was to overthrow Hitler and conclude peace. He knew that many German generals were dreaming of overthrowing Hitler and offering an immediate peace to London and Washington. Haunted by the fear of seeing the balance swing too far on the side of the Anglo-Americans, he wanted to make his own arrangements.

Other changes were effected in the country at war. As Commander-in-Chief, Stalin ordered the Supreme Council to create decorations bearing the names of ancient victories. The cadets' colleges were re-established, to enable the orphans of officers killed at the front to follow the career of their fathers. In this way a military caste was created in the U.S.S.R. This exposed the 'Marxist and revolutionary' régime to considerable risks. But even while accepting them, with truly diabolical skill he managed to make these risks redound to his advantage. If in favouring the creation of a military caste in the U.S.S.R. he created 'a mathematical point for the application of Russian Bonapartism,' he himself became a Bonaparte by allowing himself to be proclaimed as 'the organizer and father of the future victory, the greatest military genius of all times.'

One of the principal reasons for this action became evident as October approached. The time had come to engage in final conversations with the Allies. He took the initiative in arranging a meeting à trois with Churchill and Roosevelt. Now, *at this meeting he did not intend to figure as the leader of a party, or as the representative of a militant Marxism.* He did not wish to irritate or repel his allies; he wished to come before them simply as the personification of a vast country, having at his back a people with all its historical traditions and aspirations. As he could not leave Russia, he wanted Roosevelt to come to Moscow. He promised that after the victory, when peace was restored, he would hasten to visit the United States. But if only for reasons of prestige, it was impossible for Roosevelt to go to the U.S.S.R.

On the 20 October he intervened as mediator between Molotov and the British and American Ministers for Foreign Affairs, then in Moscow. Molotov demanded the immediate abolition of the monarchy in Italy, since it was guilty of favouring Fascism. As the refusal of the British and American Ministers became more and more obstinate and peremptory, he terminated the interview. Stalin did not want any serious trouble to occur before he had met Roosevelt. He persuaded Molotov to accept the Allies' point of view.

At the same conference the rejection of the *Anschluss* was voted, and the establishment of a list of war criminals. Stalin insisted most particularly on this point, for he saw in it a definite obstacle to any attempt to make a separate peace with Hitler or his lieutenants. He also proposed the principle of the unconditional surrender of the Third Reich; which Cordell Hull accepted after consulting Roosevelt by radio. Roosevelt, on the other hand, demanded that the 'three Great Powers' should pledge themselves not to employ 'armed force in the interior of the territory of other States without previous and mutual consultation.' Stalin hastened to accept the proposal; as an ex-seminary pupil he knew the value of mental reservations.

These preliminary stages being accomplished, it remained for Stalin to approach the major problem—to discuss with Roosevelt and Churchill how the world should be organized after the war. He knew what Churchill thought; he knew what differences divided them. But Roosevelt, even at a distance, exercised on him a strange attraction, and he was counting on his co-operation.

At the Teheran Conference Stalin had reached the culminating point of his career. It marked the end of his ascent, for there were no more steps to climb. Now, with Churchill and Roosevelt, he constituted the supreme Areopagus which would endeavour to shape the destiny of the world and to trace new frontiers on the map. Neither the revolutionary apprentice, Sosso, nor the terrorist agitator, Koba, nor the Secretary-General of the Communist Party, Stalin, now head of the Russian Government and Marshal of the Russian Armies, had dreamed of one day climbing to these heights of power, which afforded such a limitless perspective of the future. His master Lenin had thought to conquer the world by sowing the seeds of revolution. Stalin was now taking his place in the restricted circle of the representatives of traditionalist governments, who proposed by negotiation to shape a statute for the post-bellum world.

Stalin was at last to meet, not only Churchill, but also Roosevelt, the President of those United States which had always represented, in the eyes of the Russian Communists, an ideal of technical accomplishment. One of the favourite slogans designed to stimulate the rivalry of the engineers and artisans of the U.S.S.R. had been: 'We shall catch up with America!'

He prepared for the meeting with his usual meticulous calm. But those about him noticed a certain meditative reserve, a certain solemnity, an attitude resembling that of a believer on the eve of a great religious festival, or an actor about to enter upon the stage to play the great rôle of his career,[1] a rôle which was not easy to play.

As usual, Stalin had made a careful study of the new personage whom he was about to meet. The liberality of Roosevelt's ideas, his improvisations, which were often touched with genius—such as the exchange of destroyers against bases—and Lend-Lease—his nonconformism, and his outlook upon the future—were all sources of encouragement to Stalin, who had made up his mind to derive the greatest possible advantage from the friendship. As in Pirandello's play, a number of truths were matched against one another, and each of the three men wanted to make the other two respect a large proportion of his own truths; but Churchill, a politician of the old school, subtle but uncompromising, remained on his guard.

Before his departure for Iran, Stalin had prepared a reply to two questions which had already been put to him. One concerned the

[1]Impressions described in the course of private conversations with journalists by Vishinsky, during the Nuremberg Trial, a period when the Russians had not yet become distrustful of contacts with Westerners.

future international organization which was to guarantee peace, and which had already evoked, in Moscow, the conference of the three foreign secretaries. The second question related to Japan.

Stalin attached a greater importance to the question of international organization, since he was anxious to have it 'surmounted' by the organization of the 'Three Great Powers,' of which Teheran, according to him, was to be regarded as a first manifestation. It was feared in Moscow that in an international organization of this kind, a sort of regenerated Holy Alliance, the capitalist States would be in the majority and the U.S.S.R. would be like 'a Socialist island surrounded by a capitalist ocean.'[1]

The famous dogma of encirclement was still present in Stalin's mind, as was the notion that the capitalists, by the very fact of their social position, must be thinking of ways to destroy the first Socialist State.[2] He would, therefore, have to manœuvre in such a manner as to avoid a 'diplomatic encirclement.' Hence his obstinate intention to remain as long as possible 'among the three great Powers.' In a council reduced to this simple expression he would evidently be one against two. But he foresaw that after the war the United States would concentrate on the Western Hemisphere and the Pacific, and that he would remain, in Europe and in the Near and Middle East, almost tête-à-tête with a Great Britain enfeebled by the sacrifices which she had taken upon herself in order to continue her war effort. This would 'safeguard his equilibrium,' which for him had become an *idée fixe*, which he endeavoured, through all his complicated negotiations, to maintain, in order that he might be protected against a 'fresh capitalist aggression.'[3] This was one of the reasons why, despite the efforts of Churchill and Eden, he opposed the entrance of France into the Council of the Three, when he had been one of the first to welcome the French Committee of National Liberation as the provisional government of France—before the United States and before Churchill and without the reservations decided upon by the Conference of Quebec on the 24 August, 1943.

The second question was of more immediate practical importance.

[1]An expression employed by Alexandrov, chief propagandist of the Central Committee of the Party in October 1943, at the meeting of the local secretaries.
[2]A résumé of the essential content of a number of essays on this subject published in various Soviet periodicals.
[3]Article in the journal *Bolchevik* on the preparatory period in Teheran.

At this Conference of Quebec, Roosevelt had declared that the war with Japan should be regarded as on the same plane as the war against Germany. Cordell Hull had already demanded of Stalin, on the 25 October, that the U.S.S.R. should annul its treaty of friendship and non-aggression with Tokyo, and had stated that Roosevelt would discuss the matter without circumlocution. On his side, Litvinov had reported from Washington that the President had asked him on several occasions:

'When are we going to be real hundred-per-cent allies in this war against totalitarianism?[1] Does Stalin really believe that this can be destroyed throughout the world if Japan is left intact? Then he would not have gone to war with the Third Reich save in self-defence, and would allow totalitarianism to flourish in the Far East? I shall ask him this question as soon as we meet, and ask for a clear and definite reply.'[2]

Stalin would not accept this suggestion. He was fighting against the greater part of the Wehrmacht, and could not at the same time fight the Japanese. However, his agents informed him that Roosevelt was subjected to constant pressure by Generals Marshall and Mac-Arthur, who were anxious to secure Russian participation in the struggle against the Japanese.[3]

At his very first contact with Roosevelt, Stalin was surprised and almost disconcerted by an atmosphere such as he had never known. Instead of hostility, or at best, a chilly reserve, he encountered the celebrated Roosevelt geniality, an optimism in human relations, a frank gaiety, and an infectious laugh, which represented the principal ingredients of the famous charm of the Great American, who sought to convince his interlocutors by sympathy rather than by attack.

Stalin felt himself to be in the presence of a friend whom he had known for decades, so friendly and intimate was the atmosphere, as he repeated several times after his return to Moscow.[4] He almost

[1]During the common war against Germany it was a tacit convention to apply the term 'totalitarianism' only to the Powers of the Tripartite Pact.

[2]After the victory, on the 7 November, 1946, at a public meeting at Krassnaia-Presalia, Litvinov described in detail his conversations during his mission to the U.S.A.

[3]At Teheran he agreed to fight against Japan six months after the end of the war in Europe and asked for half of Sakhalin and the Kurile Islands .

[4]In so speaking Stalin was somewhat lacking in the sense of humour. Naturally, the friends he had known for decades were no longer there; they had disappeared in the struggle for power, and the purges.

purred like a cat that basks in the sunlight and voluptuously stretches its limbs. He was beginning to believe that a pleasant manner leads to good relations, and that there was really no need for him to use his claws and pounce. He was discovering a world that was new to him, a world in which there prevailed such an atmosphere as he had never known in the course of his pitiless existence; in which, even when the struggle was at its tensest, one kept one's temper. He did not forget—as his conduct during negotiations was to prove—that he was defending very precisely defined interests, and that a smile, even when it was sincere, was for him merely a weapon—but one as effective as his famous taciturnity. This being accepted, he was more profoundly moved than has been generally believed.

The private or semi-official relations between the two men to which Roosevelt attached such value were facilitated by the President's installation in the Soviet Embassy, on the pretext that there might be a danger of attacks by German agents. He himself took the initiative in his nocturnal conversations, going to see 'Uncle Joe' in the presence of a single Russian interpreter.[1] He behaved like a man who has faith in his own personal dynamism, and who is trying to tame and convert a man who is reputed to be dangerous, but of whose co-operation he stands in urgent need. While he was exploiting this human contact as a tactical weapon, he was also, in a sense, enjoying the game. . . . However, he had great plans for the future: personal considerations and ideological conflicts had no terrors for the architect of the New Deal, above all when there was hope of attaining a better future—a future to be won by tears and blood and sweat, in Churchill's immortal phrase.

Roosevelt's intellectual fireworks, and his constant search for new horizons and new means of reaching them, dazzled Stalin. He discovered, moreover, that the President of the United States had more liberty of action than the master of the Kremlin, who had always to deal with his Politburo. Carried away by this new atmosphere, he overstepped the limits assigned by the officially established theses of the supreme organ of the Russian Communist Party. . . .[2]

The principle of the peaceful co-existence of different social sys-

---

[1] Details were recorded by Colonel James Roosevelt, who accompanied his father to Teheran.

[2] As Vishinsky said in private conversation.

tems was readily admitted; the more so as in time of war the questions of liberalism or constraint in countries which were fighting on the same side were relegated to the background. This enabled Stalin to realize and establish, one by one, the practical deductions deriving from this theory.

Roosevelt often indulged, almost in a conversational tone, in flights of ingenious improvisation which disregarded the mundane spirit of his official *entourage*. The content of these confidential talks was not always confided to the representatives of the Department of State. Stalin, who, as we know, is susceptible to the fetishism of the 'settled thing'—above all, in respect of the promises given by others —kept a watch on himself, and took everything very seriously. It was from these private conversations that so many misunderstandings arose after the war, which contributed to enlarge the gulf between East and West which was once more fully revealed on the death of Roosevelt.

The atmosphere to which he was now subjected was so unusual that something unprecedented happened to Stalin. It did not embarrass him to behave in some respects as a poor relation, dazzled by the wealth of his benevolent colleague. He explained—introducing the subject naturally enough—that the revolutionary expansion and the dynamism of the Russian people were due to its poverty. This poverty was aggravated tenfold by the destruction and devastation of the war. Speaking as a man who was used to dealing with large figures, he estimated the loss and wastage of the war at ten thousand million gold dollars.[1] Finally, he insisted that Germany ought to pay this amount, so that the economic development of the U.S.S.R. might make rapid advances, 'with the benevolent support of the capitalist world.' It was essential to place the U.S.S.R. on an equal footing with other States in the economic competition of the future; in that case their peaceful co-existence would have a solid and lasting foundation. The U.S.S.R. needed only machine tools, chemical installations, petroleum refineries, rolling stock, and articles of current consumption. All these things ought to be supplied by a defeated Germany. Stalin wanted priority in respect of German reparations, with the transference of industrial establishments, and a levy on the

---

[1]Maïsky, who at Yalta had to enlarge on this subject behind the scenes of the Conference, referred repeatedly to this conversation in Teheran.

production of as much of the German economy as was continuing to operate.

Roosevelt, who knew how important the Russian war effort was to the Allies, who was thinking of the economic and political difficulties which would inevitably follow the war, and the possible means of avoiding them, saw that Stalin's proposals had their attractive side. He was above the private interests of the financiers and industrialists, and he wanted to bring Stalin and the U.S.S.R. back into the international sphere of economics. But as he doubted whether Germany, devastated by the war, which he believed it would be necessary to prolong into 1947 or 1948, could satisfy Stalin's demands, he accepted, as the basic compensation to be paid to the U.S.S.R., the sum of ten thousand million paper dollars, of which a long-term loan of three thousand millions would be granted by the United States.

In all these private conversations with Roosevelt, Stalin spoke with emphasis of the sufferings of the Russian people—the sacrifices and efforts of the peasants and artisans, and the combatant forces of the U.S.S.R. These were obviously arguments whose cogency could not be denied. But he resorted to them because he wanted to obtain something. He spoke of the additional dangers that threatened the Red Army. Referring to the participation in the war of Turkish officers 'on leave,' who were training the Musulman units levied by the Nazis in the Caucasus and the Crimea, he sought to obtain Roosevelt's consent to common action against the Straits. In order to convince Roosevelt, who maintained that according to British reports Ankara was fulfilling its obligations to the Allies by forming a protective screen before the Middle East, he produced the text of a conversation between von Papen and Ismet Inonu, in which it was suggested that after the Germans had entered Baku the Turks would take possession of Trans-Caucasia, including Batoum. Roosevelt, however, recalled the promise given by the U.S.S.R., as a future member of the international organization, that it would not seek to settle its quarrels with its neighbours by force of arms. But he accepted the principle of a revision of the Montreux Convention. He atoned for his refusal by a truly surprising promise, from which one sees that in spite of the scope of his outlook upon the future, he was not familiar with certain geographical and historical facts relating to the Old World. He suggested, for example, that a base might be given to the U.S.S.R. in the eastern basin of the Mediterranean, chosen from among the ports of Cyrenaica, or in the archipelago of the Dodecanese, unless indeed both bases could be granted simultaneously !

Roosevelt, of course, did not make this suggestion in Churchill's presence. Roosevelt's advisers were no better informed than Stalin's. When Molotov raised this question in 1947, at Lancaster House, Bevin and Burns gasped for breath—with good reason !

In the conversations *à trois* Stalin's attitude was more prudent. He was at odds with Churchill, who certainly did not like the way things were going, although he did not really know quite what was happening, and he did not share the impetuous optimism of Roosevelt, that dilettante of genius. Nevertheless, Stalin did not hesitate to ask two questions which for him were of essential importance. These related to the future frontiers of the U.S.S.R., and the Second Front. He was evidently trying to get the two questions decided then and there, and to ensure that the Big Three should create a precedent by acting as supreme arbiters. His argument tended toward depriving the small nations which had not had to endure the same sacrifices during the war, not only of their votes, but also of the possibility of airing future grievances.[1]

As regards the frontiers, he was categorical. What he had already told the British in Moscow he now repeated to Roosevelt. He wanted the frontiers of 1941, and also a guarantee against German aggression starting from East Prussia. His ideas as to the future of the Reich were as vague as those of the other two statesmen. In any case he wanted to deprive the future Germany of Prussia, the traditional lair of the Junkers, and to create an independent Bavaria, Rhenania, and Westphalia.

Roosevelt, at this time, was a supporter of Morgenthau, who wanted to dis-industrialize Germany by expelling twenty million of her inhabitants and transforming her into an agricultural country. Stalin did not support this idea: 'One must choose between Morgenthau and Richelieu—and one must choose Richelieu. The Reich,

---

[1] As Stalin foresaw the conditions of the distant future, it may be that he was taking precautions which would be to his advantage when the war was ended, when he would extend his rule to countries in the Soviet zone of influence.

amputated and divided, might either form a customs union or integrate itself economically with its neighbours on the west—with France and Belgium.'

Despite the objections of Sumner Welles and Cordell Hull, Roosevelt adhered to his point of view. He was supported by Churchill, who at this warlike period never lost an opportunity of stigmatizing the German people, and describing it as a beast of prey whose terrible fangs must be drawn once and for all. Having seen a 'war without hatred' under Daladier and Chamberlain transformed into a 'phony war,' he understood that Stalin was right to face the hatred in the hearts of his soldiers. But he did not lose sight of the limits of the possible imposed by the long political history of this ancient Europe, which for a Morgenthau carried away by the indignation aroused by the 'racism' of the Germans, was, as it was for the majority of the Americans, a *terra incognita*.

The militant arguments in favour of the immediate constitution of a second front were presented by Stalin in quite a novel form. After the victories of Stalingrad, Kursk, Orel, and the Dnieper it was a proven fact that at the present time the Red Army could defeat a fatigued Wehrmacht. But in order to dispose of the enemy finally one would have to crush him in his lair. A terrible danger was threatening—and it concerned Great Britain as well as Russia. Stalin's personal intelligence service had warned him of the preparation by Germany of secret weapons which the Third Reich was perfecting with surprising rapidity, in order to give the Wehrmacht a crushing superiority of quite a novel character.[1] In order to convince Roosevelt and Churchill he 'emptied his bag.' He was informed in September of the construction of new types of jet planes, the Messerschmidt 162 and the Arado 234, which could attain a speed of 530 miles an hour, and whose delivery, in series, would begin in the second half of 1944. Despite the Allied bombardments and the lack of raw materials, the output of planes built in underground work-

[1] The documents produced at the time of the Nuremberg Trial included an account of an exceptional assembly at the O.K.W., presided over by General Jodl, in the presence of the Gauleiters. This completed the 'reconditioning' of the Wehrmacht—that is, its reorganization, with the employment of new methods of combat, due to novel weapons, protected by numerous inventors, whose mass production was to begin in April, May and June, 1945.

shops was to amount to several thousands per month.[1] New types of tanks and armoured motorized cannon were put into construction.[2] Finally, new pilotless planes of very long range, which were intended to bring Great Britain to her knees in 1945, by destroying her cities, her industries, and her ports, were under construction.[3] The 'Red Orchestra' had also succeeded in obtaining from an informant in Berlin, who was a member of Hitler's *entourage*, an account of a conversation between Hitler and Goebbels on the subject of an atomic bomb.[4]

It appeared from this conversation that Hitler was certain of not losing the war if he could hold out until the end of 1945, when he would have at his disposal the atomic weapon, as well as heavy bombers which would enable him to destroy Western Europe in three months and strike a violent blow at the United States.[5]

This information, which the American O.S.S. had not received, obtained at a time when the U.S.A. were themselves trying to perfect a weapon of disintegration, impressed Roosevelt, especially as its truth was confirmed by the Intelligence Service, which had contrived to place one of its agents in the 'Red Orchestra.' The British bombers had destroyed the atomic installations of Penemunde, but those on the island of Bornholm were still intact. Information had been received from other sources that the production of Uranium 235 was being undertaken in the subterranean workshops of Thuringia.[6]

Stalin presumed that Hitler was a maniac who was capable of ordering the massive destruction of all the inhabitants of Europe. This weapon must be wrested from him at any cost, and this meant rapid action in Europe. It was on this occasion that Roosevelt informed Stalin of the existence of the 'Manhattan Plan,' whose practical results would be obtained about 1947. Despite Stalin's questions, Roosevelt gave him no detailed information, merely indicating that

[1] In January 1945 the Reich produced 3,125 planes, of which 2,450 were pursuit planes, and until March the output of war material had constantly increased.

[2] The future Royal Tigers and Elephants.

[3] These were the V1 and the V2, which the Allied landing in France compelled the Germans to send into action before they had an adequate stock of them.

[4] Information on this subject was at the bottom of Laval's belief in a revival of Germany, followed by a final victory.

[5] In 1945 the Allies captured on Norwegian airfields a number of heavy bombers intended for the bombardment of the United States in May 1945.

[6] Goebbels broadcast the description of the results of a new weapon producing the effects, on a small scale, of an atomic explosion.

the theoretical problem had been solved by scientists from all countries, and that as the difficulties of the plan were only of an industrial and technical character, the United States would undoubtedly overcome them.

During these same days Stalin returned to the question of the petroleum concession in the north of Iran. Churchill and Eden did not think fit to oppose him at this juncture. It was Roosevelt who proved to be intractable. For him the time for colonial concessions was past; the time had come for technical aid to backward peoples, so that they could themselves exploit the riches of their soil. The end of this war, he thought, would doubtless see the end of the colonial régimes. He declared, moreover, that the President of the Iranian Council, Ghavan-es-Saltane, was opposed to the granting of new concessions, as was the Persian Parliament.

Stalin replied that being himself an Asiatic he would be able to convince another Asiatic, and that he would obtain this concession while pledging himself never to employ force.[1] But he was not unduly insistent. It was in his interest to keep Roosevelt in a good humour; he was capable of moderating his demands in order to leave the American under the illusion that he could always succeed in converting his partners to the most humanitarian conceptions.

In Teheran, all the questions which gave rise to the post-bellum tension had already been evoked; but it is certain also that Stalin had allowed himself to be influenced by Roosevelt's 'human touch,' the more so inasmuch as all efforts were directed toward and through the war, and that ideological questions were relegated to the background. The organic interests of the U.S.S.R. at war submerged the Marxist farrago. If in his enthusiasm as an improvisator Roosevelt went a long way toward granting Stalin's requests, hoping that he was making for a new dawn in the life of the post-war world, Stalin also was attracted by the same cheering prospect. For once, he forgot his chronic suspicion. But he was the prisoner of his past, and of the Politburo; Roosevelt's disappearance would shut him into his cage again.

[1]He was mistaken. To convince an Asiatic one and a half Asiatics are needed. Ghavan, President of the Council in 1947, got the better of Stalin by agreeing to give him petroleum concessions, and by contriving to get them annulled by Parliament, with Mossadeq in command, and with the help of the Anglo-Iranian Company, against which Mossadeq was to turn in 1951.

x

CHAPTER XLVII

BETWEEN TEHERAN AND YALTA

AFTER the first meeting of the Big Three, Stalin felt that he was firmly installed among the world's rulers. Roosevelt had treated him as his equal; so had Churchill, though not without some flashes of temper; victory seemed in sight. As his reserved nature made any demonstration of emotion impossible, and as his tactics called for modesty in moments of triumph, the consciousness of his strength took the form of an increase of physical and moral potential. He felt that he was truly 'the master.' The certainty of his decisions in his common-sensical strategy, the lapidary form of his remarks, often assumed the shape of aphorisms, making him a sort of oracle on whose judgements his military collaborators, the generals and marshals of the Red Army, had come to rely. They said as much in their contacts with Westerners during the euphoria of victory in 1945 and 1946.

On the other hand, a certain coolness became apparent in the attitude of those members of the Politburo who were grouped about Molotov.

As soon as he returned to Moscow, Stalin had to devote himself above all to the preparations for the new Russian offensive in the spring of 1944—Joukov's famous 'mud offensive'—and to the Polish question, which was more acute than it had ever been.

The treaty of mutual assistance between the U.S.S.R. and the government of General Sikorsky had been annulled after the tragic discovery of the charnel-house of Katyn, despite the affirmations of Moscow that the Gestapo had faked the tragic fraud. Churchill's and Roosevelt's attempts to intervene did not prevent the rupture of diplomatic relations between the U.S.S.R. and Poland's representatives in London. Sentimentally and humanly speaking the Polish action was comprehensible, if the official German version is accepted, which holds the Soviet Government collectively responsible for the frightful mass murder. But in the midst of a war against the Third

Reich the decision to demand an international inquiry under the threat of a diplomatic rupture, though dictated by indignation and grief, resulted in consequences of exceptional gravity regarding Poland's future—if only because it furnished Moscow with a pretext for this rupture.

Military necessities compelled Stalin to adopt measures which were essentially favourable to his secret political aims in respect of the future, so that he was killing two birds with one stone.

A conference opened in Moscow on the 6 January, 1944. Stalin requested the delegates—Poles present in the U.S.S.R.—to guarantee the tranquillity of the Polish territory by forming a Provisional National Committee, the nucleus of the future government. The Poles—most of them Communists—agreed, and appointed then and there the future 'Government' of the liberated territories. This could not have been done had the Polish leaders in London shown greater political sagacity. As things were, Stalin played his hand without difficulty.

Meanwhile, he had not lost sight of the question of the Second Front, and was careful to make it impossible for Churchill to proceed to effect a landing in the Balkans. He made repeated applications to Roosevelt, begging him not to allow 'Operation Overlord' to be abandoned in favour of a landing in the south-east of Europe.[1] One of those paradoxes in which history is so fertile came to his assistance. It is doubtful whether Churchill, who was holding fast to his strategic plan, would have agreed to abandon it, if the Germans had not transformed the local situation. Churchill was relying on the support of Turkey. But the Germans, by a lightning operation, had occupied the Italian islands in the Mediterranean, thereby impressing Turkey, which showed itself greatly influenced by this demonstration of German strength, which was capable of acting with such celerity.

Hitler's success against Badoglio's Italian troops in the islands of the Mediterranean had the effect of strengthening the collaboration between the Allies and bringing about the landing in Normandy.

The landing of the 7 June was greeted by Stalin in telegrams of congratulation to Churchill and Roosevelt. On the 10 June it was the turn of the Red Army to move. But it moved in an unexpected

[1]The history of the hesitations and discussions on this subject is sufficiently well known.

direction. Its operations began with an offensive on a secondary front: the Mannerheim Line, between the Gulf of Finland and Lake Ladoga. By attacking here Stalin was pursuing two different aims. He wanted to enter Norway, and thus establish himself in Scandinavia before the victory of the Allies in the west; and he wanted to attract the bulk of the Wehrmacht reserves toward the north-east, in order to facilitate the frontal offensive of Joukov, who was to thrust across Poland.

But if Stalin had over-estimated the possibilities of a rapid allied victory in France, he had underestimated Hitler's powers. On the 28 June Ribbentrop was at Helsinki. The German fleet dropped anchor in the port of Sveaborg. Despite Roosevelt's letter to the Finnish President, the Finns broke their bargain with Stockholm, which led to the rupture of diplomatic relations between Finland and the United States on the 30 June. Marshal Mannerheim continued the struggle with his fifteen divisions, and the seven divisions of General Dietl, two of which were armoured.

At this moment there occurred a curious episode, which gave evidence of Stalin's certainty of judgement, his coolness, and his powers of calculation. He wrote a personal letter to Mannerheim, in which, while he reproached the old champion of Finnish independence for continuing a hopeless war, he assured him of his unshaken esteem for the people of Finland, and their indomitable courage. In Mannerheim himself he recognized 'an honest soldier.'

On the 2 July, 1944, an event of great importance occurred. It did not arouse all the comment which it deserved, although it was at this moment that Stalin took up his personal position with regard to the main questions of doctrinal developments and the actions of the U.S.S.R. He went to Leningrad on the occasion of the manifestations in honour of the martyred city, which for two years had been besieged, bombarded, and starved. There Jdanov made a speech, reproduced by a number of newspapers, which was essentially an expression of the expansionist tendency of the Politburo, carried away by the intoxication of victory, and foreseeing a new 'Marxist apotheosis.'

Jdanov declared: 'The destruction of Fascism, that advance-guard of world imperialism, confronts us with the final phase of *Socialist construction on the world scale*. Our people and our army have been fighting for their country, and they are winning the fight, but their country is also that of all the world's workers. Our victory is an ardent appeal: the hour of Socialism has struck.'

Had Stalin no part in the victory? He declared that he had. For the first time the split between him and the majority of the Politburo was openly manifested.

His reaction to the speech was unmistakable. His words left no one in doubt: the war was still on, and a struggle for influence had begun in the Kremlin. Stalin, who had learned a great deal about the outer world in his contacts with the 'Big Two' of the Western world, was beginning to realize the extent of the dangers which the coming victory would reveal. He distrusted the vertigo of success. As a clear-headed, rational thinker, he knew that the Russian people had been fighting a patriotic war for their country. He was under no illusion—he saw the menace which would arise from the attempt to transform this 'sacred war' into a struggle directed by the Communist Party toward the narrow aims of revolutionary Marxism. He knew this, and he said as much in the plainest terms in his reply to Jdanov:

'The liberation of our fatherland is the work of its people, led by a Soviet Government; our merit has been, to understand how to organize the victory, thanks to our sensible policy of the building of Socialism in a country as backward as was our Fatherland. *Let the other peoples follow the example of the U.S.S.R.! But we must never force them: it is not for us to take the initiative!*'[1]

This conflict of tendencies is still in progress.

The twelve fronts of the Soviet Army were advancing irresistibly towards the west, applying to the Wehrmacht its own tactics of the lightning war, while the O.K.W. was imitating the tactics of the Russian High Command of 1941 and 1942, 'selling space in exchange for time,' on the principle of the 'elastic defence.'

Meanwhile the diplomatic activity between the Allies was re-doubled in intensity. What arrangements would be in force after the war? Stalin was in no hurry to lay his cards on the table. He agreed to accept China as a fourth Great Power. But his representatives at

[1]It is curious to note analogies between these two speeches, and therefore between two policies, in 1951. After the aggressive speech of Molotov in Warsaw on the anniversary of its liberation, Malik, in a speech made on the 25 July, 1951, recalled that Stalin had said: 'Revolutions cannot be exported, and the U.S.S.R. is not trying to intervene and force them on other countries.'

the conference of Dumbarton Oaks accepted the statute of the future
U.N.O. and its Security Council only on principle, while agreeing
to the co-opting of France after the end of the war. They also agreed
to the constitution of an International Court of Justice, a permanent
secretariat, and an international air force intended to fight against any
eventual aggressor. But this acceptance was only on principle, and a
definitive agreement would be necessary later. This was a repercussion of the wrangling in the Kremlin, where the Politburo found
it difficult to pass from the theory of the constant hostility of the
capitalist régime and the dogma of encirclement to the principle of
collaboration.

The autumn of 1944 saw a solution—but a very provisional one—
of a particularly dangerous problem arising from relations between
the Allies. The Red Army was entering the Balkans, and before it
could come into contact with the British, Great Britain and the
U.S.S.R. would have to define the bases of such relations in this part
of the world, where their interests had always clashed with those of
Germany, whose elimination would leave them in a dangerous
confrontation.

Germany was counting eagerly on an inevitable clash between
the Russians and the British, as Goebbels wrote in *Das Reich*; he
believed that the winter of 1944–45 'would see the end of the un-
natural Russo-British alliance.' Germany was not yet crushed as a
military power, and it was in order to avoid this fatal clash, on which
Hitler and Goebbels were basing their hopes, that Churchill decided,
after consulting Roosevelt, that he would himself go to Moscow.
Roosevelt would have liked to discuss matters personally with
Stalin, but Stalin refused to leave the U.S.S.R., and Roosevelt had
to face the Presidential Elections on the 7 November.

Accordingly, Churchill went to Moscow, accompanied by Eden.
This was a sacrifice which was to cost him dear; it oppressed him to
return to the Kremlin, which he had left on the 14 August, 1942,
'terrified' by Stalin's claims. But the sacrifice was a measure of his
greatness.

The moment was doubly dramatic. The Russian troops, on
arriving in Bulgaria, expelled the British *chargé d'affaires*, Gibson,
who had been appointed after the conclusion of the Anglo-Bulgarian
armistice in Cairo. In Yugoslavia Tito openly threatened to hang

King Peter if he returned to the country without his authorization. In Roumania the military exigencies of the Sovietic armies were endangering the régime. Lastly, in Greece the Communist partisans of E.L.A. were preparing to seize power. The British positions in the Balkans were threatened, and the U.S.S.R. was ready to debouch on the Mediterranean and the historic highways of the Empire.

Eden, for whom Stalin had a personal liking, had a curious conversation with the latter during this visit. Stalin said:

'Hitler is undoubtedly a clever man, but he has one capital fault : he doesn't know when to stop.'

Eden's smile was significant. It did not escape Stalin, who added, in an ironical tone: 'You are thinking that I too don't know when to stop. You are profoundly mistaken, Mr. Eden. I know very well when to stop, as you will see !'

The sense of time, and the estimate of the point at which one should stop were, of course, very differently evaluated by the two parties. In every case, considerations of the future have perhaps persuaded Stalin not to exploit to the very utmost the advantages offered by the immediate military situation. On the Graeco-Bulgarian frontier the Red Army had twenty divisions, while in Greece the British General Scobie had only 10,000 troops, and had to deal with the threat of the thousands of Communist partisans dispersed throughout the country. Stalin came to a standstill. In a 'gentleman's agreement' Churchill and he agreed that Greece should remain a British zone of influence, in exchange for which the British were obliged to recognize the rest of the Balkans, and the valley of the Danube as far as Bratislava, as a Soviet zone of influence.

This agreement was undoubtedly the most important diplomatic act of the second period of the second world war. At the crucial moment of the war, when Hitler was trying to gain time in order to start the new technical war, he was finally deprived of the hope of seeing the Allies quarrelling in the Balkans. Churchill's political wisdom had taken the Nazi's trump card.

But had Stalin really stopped 'in time'? Opinions on this point may well differ. On the other hand, the agreement itself was differently interpreted at Yalta by the contracting parties.

The necessities of warfare, the seizure by the enemy of enormous territories, and an important part of the industrial and agricultural regions of the U.S.S.R., had compelled Stalin to appeal more and more urgently to the goodwill of the populations which had agreed to take part in the war and to share in the sacrifices imposed by it.

Once the attitude of the country was determined Stalin acted immediately in the only possible way. The general tendency of the measures taken was perfectly clear: it was a relaxation of the principles of pure Socialism. The liberal States were obliged, in time of war, to resort to a sort of autocracy; the U.S.S.R. was obliged to relax its authoritarianism. Lest the rope should break under the strain, Stalin allowed it to slip. Non-party men began to occupy an increasing percentage of posts in the administration. In order to obtain the maximum effort from the peasants the very principles of collectivism were modified. The promises given to the non-party citizens and the *kolkhozes* gave them reason to hope for a 'liberal' future.

In July 1943 Stalin placed himself at the head of an extraordinary Council of Three, which was to deal with rural, economic, and political affairs. He took an active part in its deliberations, despite his preoccupations as Commander-in-Chief and his control of international politics. He was assisted by two members of the Politburo, Andreiev and Voznessensky.[1]

The trio ratified a change in the very structure of the economic organization, a change which was essential if they were to retain the goodwill of the masses. In order to stimulate the production of wheat, the producers were offered a sort of decollectivization. This was put forward in the form of the promise of a new statute relating to the *kolkhozes*.

In the *Bolchevik* for November 1943 an article by Andreiev, which made constant references to Comrade Stalin, contained an outline of the future statute. By this statute the *kolkhoz* is defined as 'a peasant co-operative,' which applies to the State for the supply of tractors on hire; it also pays a tax in kind. The desire of the *kolkhozians* to enlarge their personal holding is satisfied, even to the length of doubling or trebling the individual patch of soil, and allowing the peasant to acquire as many cows as he pleases.

---

[1] It is highly significant that after the war Andreiev was seriously threatened with expulsion from the Politburo, and Voznessensky was deprived of all his important functions and exiled, in disgrace, to the Ural. Before the war the authorities were more severe with persons 'responsible for all sorts of deviations,' who were chosen as scapegoats, after the condemnation of their zigzag politics.

This statute had never been officially promulgated, but its appearance in the official Party journal, with reference to Stalin, led, on the verge of legality, to a veritable revolution in the *kolkhozes*. As a matter of fact, the direct share of the State, in payment for requisites and the hire of tractors, amounted to 28 per cent. The indirect share —that is, the retention of the minus-value of salaries for the loans furnished during labour—amounted to 14 per cent. Thus, the personal share of the *kolkhozian* amounted to 58 per cent, which means that he had become to a great extent 'emancipated.'[1]

This increase of wealth among the agriculturalists, compared with what was happening in other countries, compelled Stalin, abandoning the ideological theses of Marxism, to do what was possible to limit inflation and to guard against the soaring of prices in the free market. By a series of articles and replies to correspondents published in *Pravda* and *Isvestia*—which constituted Stalin's usual means of establishing direct contact with the citizens of the U.S.S.R.—he inaugurated a campaign of sacrifices 'freely granted' by the *kolkhozians*. He began with a letter to an agriculturalist of the Saratov district, who had offered, as a gift to the State, his wartime savings, which amounted to 120,000 roubles.

'I assure you of my fraternal gratitude. We have not always been very nice to the *kolkhozians*, but this was the fault of the local authorities. I see now that we can rely on our *kolkhozians*, on their love for the Sovietic fatherland, on their will to defend the fatherland to the last.'[2] This is a long way from the Marxist jargon.

A powerful movement in favour of gifts to the State was manifesting itself. It will suffice to say that in the year 1944 this campaign brought in nine thousand million roubles, which proves, above all, the amplitude of the resources at the disposal of the private rural holding. This drain upon peasant savings enabled Stalin to curb the rise of prices in the free rural market.

In order to avoid serious alimentary difficulties, the Socialist State was obliged to appeal to the goodwill of the peasant; and in order to arouse and stimulate this it renounced the principles and the practice of the totalitarian economy. This was a lesson which Stalin had finally understood, and he never forgot it.

[1] Official figures for the 1 January, 1946.
[2] *Isvestia* of Saratov, No. 3,298.

In the Army also he had to satisfy many requirements which were contrary to the Communist régime. The political commissaries were suppressed, and a sort of relative liberalism was re-established. The N.K.V.D. no longer had the right to arrest a soldier without the authorization of the military procurators—of whom, it is true, 70 per cent were ex-members of the N.K.V.D. By an official decree, Stalin promised priority to combatant soldiers, after the war, in obtaining situations in the industries and the ministries, and bursaries for those who wished to continue their education.

After each fresh victory, which he caused to be greeted by salvoes of artillery, in accordance with a tradition borrowed from Peter the Great, he received numbers of soldiers and officers, to whom he delivered some variant of the following address: 'After we have driven out the Fascist aggressors and pirates, we shall continue to build up our State. Thanks to you, we shall repair the ruins and devastations: after you have conquered the Fascists you will preside over the great task of the economic renaissance. The foremost in the battle will also be the foremost in the triumphant activity of Soviet Socialism.'[1]

It was a draft of the future that Stalin was signing—a draft with many duplicates.

He did not overlook the people's love of the Orthodox Church. The Commission of the Orthodox Church co-operating with the Supreme Council received a considerable subvention. Karpov, the president of this Commission, elaborated the draft of a statute for communicants and for the parishes. This statute was officially adopted in November 1944. At the same time the Politburo published in No. 9 of the *Bolchevik* for 1944 a decision which must have sent a shudder through the ghosts of the militant Marxists:

'Those who are not members of the Party we leave absolutely free to go to church. They must not be hindered in their practice of religion and no discrimination should result therefrom. They can occupy the most important posts in the civil and military administrations of the State, and it is strictly prohibited to make any objections to them on account of their religious practices.

'As for those who are members of the Party, militants of rank and members of the youth organizations may be Christians. But the

[1] *Isvestia*, 11 October, 1944.

local committees are obliged to deal vigorously with them, explaining to them that their religious practices are in contradiction to the dogma of dialectical materialism . . . it would, however, be strictly forbidden to exclude them from the Party on account of religious practices. . . .'

That was not all. These decisions were personally announced by Stalin to the Patriarch, who visited the Kremlin before his departure on a journey through the countries of the Near East, and above all through Syria and the Lebanon, to which he sailed on a warship. A report on the juridical situation of the Holy Places, drawn up by the agents of the Patriarch, and tending to show that the Orthodox Church had rights of priority over the majority of the Holy Places, was submitted to Stalin, and approved by him! Finally, in January 1945, Stalin paid a private visit to the office of the Patriarch in the Convent of Novodievitchi.

In March 1944 he had visited the grave of his mother, buried in the cemetery of the Convent of King David. The reconciliation with the Georgian Church was symbolized by his private visit to the Exarch. It is true that in return the Orthodox Church became once more a docile instrument of the new State.[1]

In respect of another question of equal historical importance, Stalin boldly took the initiative. In 1943 he received a delegation from the office of the organization of the World Pan-Slav Union. The leader of the delegation was General Govorov; Marshal Tolboukhin was one day to become its honorary president, and the ex-attaché of the Tsar in Paris, General Count Ignatiev, became a member of the executive bureau.

Stalin did not fail to make a speech on this occasion: '. . . I promise you that the Soviet Union, the majority of whose population is Slav, will support your movement throughout the world with all its might. Slav unity and Slav solidarity have always been the aim of our people. We are entering upon a new era. Germanism has been defeated by the Red Army, which is realizing the dream of Panslav-

---

[1]By restoring the liberty of religious practices, even to young Communists, Stalin was allowing for the traditional attachment of the Russians to the Orthodox Church. This was only increased by the struggle against Catholicism, since for centuries Rome and Moscow, Roman Catholicism and Orthodoxy, had fought each other with the utmost energy. Imperial Russia had no Concordat with the Vatican, a Papal Nuncio was not received, and staff officers could not be Catholics.

ism. But the enemy is not yet finally crushed, and Slav solidarity would make it easier to strangle him if he were to make another attack upon our country. . . .'

Thus, when it was necessary to demand an immense effort from the country as a whole, an effort which could not be extracted by force or by the application of Marxist ideas, Stalin was obliged to open the sluices to sentiments which for centuries had been deeply rooted in the minds of his subjects—sentiments on which some had attempted to graft the imported ideology of Marxism. Moreover, in appealing to the sentiments of the Slavs he was counting on the influence of the citizens of Slav origin in the United States to counterbalance the influence of the Americans of Germanic origin.

But this calculation, with many others, was invalidated by political developments after the war.

CHAPTER XLVIII

YALTA

BEFORE the Conference of Yalta had assembled, Stalin applied himself to organizing his task of controlling and supervising the civil and military activities of the U.S.S.R. so that they might proceed without interruption. At Minsk he convoked an assembly of the commanders of the various fronts. It met in the general field headquarters. He himself attended the meeting, accompanied by his chief of staff, Wassilevsky, and Joukov, his quartermaster. General Antonov acted as chief of staff of the organization.

The principles of the '*coup de grâce* offensive,' as he called it in his order of the day to the Red Army, were perfected.

Contrary to general belief, Stalin, while he liked to be regarded as an 'inspired strategist,' never intervened in the course of operations. But he did his utmost to ensure that in the final stage of the war there should be no hitch at the last moment. He explained this to his generals, often reminding them that the lesson of the war with Poland in 1920 had revealed the dangers of the psychological shock to the morale of the armies in the case of a great victory won by an enemy already half conquered.[1] He did not want the Red Army to suffer even a temporary reverse in this last fight to the death before entering upon the great Polish plain.

Always on the alert to note the psychological tendencies of the masses, he had already realized that the Red Army, no longer being on its own territory, and having stretched its lines of communication to an inordinate extent, was no longer inspired by the ardent desire to liberate the soil of the fatherland at any cost, and that its combative spirit was touched with a certain hesitation. It had been necessary to resort to all sorts of measures in order to revive the warlike ardour of the Soviet troops, which had plainly diminished since the end of 1944.

[1]There is a fuller exposition of this point in the periodical, *Questions of Strategy*.

At the Conference of Minsk he defined the strategical principles, which are really no more than the precepts of common sense, which could be read from the map. The plan which he proposed was one of extreme prudence. The Germans were dug in along a line running from the Baltic to the Carpathians. Their flanks were firmly established. A lightning offensive in the centre, such as Joukov recommended, involved a certain danger. The front would assume the shape of the cusp of a parabola, whose axis pointed toward Berlin, and whose sides might be cut.

However, he had received information to the effect that the Germans were organizing a group of armies which would attack from the south, moving northwards, while another group would thrust southwards from East Prussia, passing to the west of Warsaw. This was the repetition of the manœuvre of the German staff in 1914. Stalin therefore proposed what was known in Russia as 'the strategy of the hyperbola,' whose principal axis was aimed at Berlin, while the wings constantly advanced on the flanks.

Despite the success achieved by the Allies on all fronts, Stalin regarded this as one of the most dangerous moments of the whole war. He thought it so, he declared that it was so, and he acted accordingly.

Goebbels, in each number of *Das Reich*, spoke of the signs that pointed to the inevitable quarrel between the Allies. After the Balkans, the pretext would be found in Poland.

The Governments of Lublin and London had declared war—a pitiless war. Now, Stalin had already insisted that the future government of Poland, which would be subject to the Soviet Government, should accept as the eastern frontier the Curzon line, leaving the territories which were ethnically Ukrainian and White Russian to the U.S.S.R. The Poles installed in London would not agree to this, and finally created a situation which threatened the normal relations between Stalin, Roosevelt and Churchill. The question of Danzig had provoked the second world war. There seemed to be the seed of a third world war in the discussions as to the eastern frontier of Poland.[1]

[1]At Yalta Roosevelt, although he was inclined to compromise, warned Stalin that this question might prevent the organization of a peace after the second world war. This declaration is recorded by Stettinius.

Before a further meeting with the President of the U.S.A. Stalin accordingly tried to enlarge the future Government of Lublin by accepting representatives of the London Government and of the Polish resistance groups, on condition that all should solemnly recognize the Curzon line. In exchange, he promised Poland the territories to the west which she had lost during the centuries of German pressure. This compensation was economically greater than the value of the territories lost in the east. He was evidently seeking to make the new Poland, by gifts bestowed at the expense of the Reich, a friendly country. At the same time, he wished to create a bastion which would bar the Corridor between the Duna and the Dnieper.[1] The London Poles proclaimed that those who accepted the Curzon line were 'traitors to their country.' For the British the situation was complicated by the presence in their army in Italy of 150,000 Polish soldiers.

Among the factors which still further aggravated the situation was the famous check of the Red Army before Warsaw at the moment of the Polish insurrection, led by General Bor Komorovsky, an authentic hero but a rash politician. It is true that Rokossovsky's army suffered a severe defeat in the suburbs to the east of the Polish capital, where it lost two armoured divisions, while powerful German forces inflicted a severe defeat on the Russians before Siedletz, east of Warsaw. Nevertheless, from the purely moral standpoint, this check will be recorded in history as the abandonment of heroic insurgents to their fate. . . .

All the British attempts at mediation were in vain. Stalin was in a difficult position. He was to say, however, at Yalta that he would have preferred to dispense with the Polish Communists if among the other parties he could have found partisans of collaboration with the U.S.S.R. But the interpretation of the word 'collaboration' differs according to the conceptions of the two collaborators: the one who enforces collaboration and the one who has to accept it.

If the Teheran conversations had seemed to owe their existence to the individual action of Stalin, it was quite otherwise at Yalta.

Stalin found himself constantly in difficulties with his colleagues

---

[1] 'I wanted to padlock this corridor and I could not show myself less Russian than Curzon and Churchill, who had granted these territories to us,' said Stalin at Yalta.

of the Politburo. For them the only thing that counted was the immediate advantage which could be derived from the coming victory. The prospect of success had turned their heads, while Stalin, without as yet having any precise views as to the future, felt, with his usual instinctive prudence, that the future as it presented itself to the eyes of Molotov and Jdanov was not the sort of future which one ought to desire.

But he did not know what to do. The course which he ought to follow was not apparent. He was obliged to take the lead in the discussion, being placed, in a certain sense, between two fires. The discussions with Roosevelt and Churchill were becoming more and more prickly, and Stalin felt that certain of the Allies' demands were justified. . . . This, moreover, was the period during which he ought to put forth the greatest efforts. He often received much less consideration from his own people than from those who were facing him at the conference table. Roosevelt in particular, anxious to keep Stalin in a receptive mood, manœuvred with his usual skill, and with a surprising intuitive understanding of the Russian temperament.

Oumansky, the Russian Ambassador in Washington, had often told him of the innate suspiciousness of the Russians, who for centuries had lived on a vast, limitless plain where enemy hordes might appear at any moment.[1] Roosevelt never forgot what he had been told. Thus, at Teheran, when Churchill asked him to dine with him privately, on the eve of the official conversations with Stalin, Roosevelt declined the invitation. Stalin, who was evidently informed of the fact immediately, appeared to be really touched by this refusal; he himself, who had arrived in power after a series of 'personal blocs' in the Politburo, was very sensible of Roosevelt's consideration. At Yalta, Roosevelt continued to observe the same precautions. He did not lunch privately with Churchill until five days had elapsed since the first meeting.[2] At the same time, he formally requested Stettinius to avoid any private conference with Eden, and he missed no opportunity of making Stalin aware of his differences with Churchill, especially in respect of colonial questions.[3]

On the eve of the Conference the Politburo appointed a Per-

[1] In an article published in the Soviet journal *Troud*, Oumansky describes his conversations with Roosevelt on this subject.
[2] Stettinius, in his book on Yalta.
[3] See the first part of this volume.

manent Committee to follow the negotiations on the spot. The president of this committee was Molotov; it included Béria, Malenkov, Bulganin, Vorochilov, and Mikoyan. Stalin's authority was, of course, very great, but for once his traditional tactics of taking refuge behind the decisions of the Politburo turned against him. Carried away by Roosevelt's example, he wanted to form decisions which had not been previously considered by the committee. He even did so. But the Politburo was accustomed to being the supreme official authority; it jibbed at this, and sought to impose its actual authority.

The committee, therefore, sat every day, discussing the questions which would be considered on the following day, and classifying everything that had happened during the day. Very often its discussions were continued late into the night. At midnight precisely Stalin was obliged to dissolve the sessions in order to examine the situation at the front. He had beside him Antonov, Chief of Staff of the armies in the field, the Air Marshal Khoudiskov, and Admiral Kouznetzov. A direct telephone service connected the ancient palace of Prince Youssupov with the headquarters of the Marshals Joukov, Koniev, and Rokossovsky. Reports on the situation were examined, and any divergencies—which, by the way, were frequent—between the reports of the three marshals and their two controllers, Timochenko and Wassilevsky, were scrutinized and corrected. Very often, after fulfilling his functions as Commander-in-Chief, Stalin had to return to the Permanent Committee, where General Poskriebychev and his son Basil Stalin were acting as secretaries.

The result was that Stalin, contrary to the general belief, was less free in his decisions than Churchill and Roosevelt. The men in actual control were to be found, not in the conference chamber, but off-stage, where they discussed matters without camouflage and often without amenity.

The Conference of Yalta began on the 3 February. At the opening of the conference Stalin appeared anxious. On the previous day the intelligence service of the Red Army had arrested in Poland a Colonel Vincency Krassevsky, from London, who had been ordered to organize a revolt in the forest region between Kaunas and Vilna, where the Red Army had already been attacked in June and July by detachments of partisans.

z

Now, Stalin knew that Roosevelt was bound to support the
Poles, and Gromyko had told him of the conversations which Eden
had had with Stettinius, according to which, if the Russians did not
agree to discuss the Polish problem, Great Britain would be obliged
to announce publicly that a deadlock had occurred.[1] The Polish
fissure might open a profound breach in the alliance. But Stalin was
not free to manœuvre as he wished. The Permanent Committee was
keeping a watch on him.

He had another immediate anxiety. The 'gentleman's agreement'
concluded with Churchill and Eden in October 1944 in Moscow was
interpreted by the British otherwise than by the Russians. Lord
Halifax, British Ambassador in Washington, told Stettinius, who in
turn informed Gromyko, that Britain had concluded her verbal
agreement as to the partition of the zones of influence in the south-
east only in order to secure a provisional delay of a few months, with
a view to purely military considerations. According to this arrangement the British would have kept 'a 20 per cent influence' in Roumania, Hungary and Bulgaria. In Yugoslavia and Albania the British
and Russian influences were to be equally divided, while Greece was
to remain entirely in the British zone.

This information had exasperated Molotov, who pretended that
'Stalin had allowed himself to be diddled by the gratuitous gracious-
ness of Roosevelt, who was after all nothing but a representative of
American ultra-imperialism, and whose personal amiability, more
dangerous than Churchill's frank obstinacy, was preparing the way
for the latter.'

The first day was devoted to generalities. In the course of conversation, Stalin gave his opinion of De Gaulle, whom he had
received in Moscow in December. 'He is not a very complicated
character,' he said, 'and he's obstinate into the bargain; he's the most
obstinate man I have ever met in my life!' However, he did not yet
know that De Gaulle had warned Harriman, before leaving Moscow,
that the western countries would in the immediate future find themselves in very great difficulties in respect of their relations with the
U.S.S.R. Stalin, moreover, did not seem very well disposed toward
France.

De Gaulle, he said, 'was not conscious of the realities, for he in-

[1]This declaration is mentioned in Stettinius' book on Yalta.

sisted that France should have the same rights as the Big Three, although France had not done much fighting.' He was deliberately overlooking the fact that without the participation of the French in the war of 1939 a war against Hitler and the defeat of the Third Reich would hardly have been possible, for he, Stalin, at that moment had a treaty of non-aggression with Hitler. He also debated the matter at some length before consenting that France should be allowed a zone of occupation in Germany.

Expressing his displeasure with the different interpretations of certain agreements concluded in Teheran and Moscow, he decided to play his trump card, which ought to make the greatest impression on the Allies, by revealing the actual proportions of the enormous military effort of the U.S.S.R. and the amplitude of its forces. He proposed to listen to a report on the situation at the front from General Antonov.

'I am bringing forward the question of this report on my own initiative. At Teheran I did not agree to allow anybody to intervene in the conduct of the operations of the Red Army.[1] . . . It is simply that I am proud of the success of this army, and it is for this reason that I have asked General Antonov to read us his report.'

Churchill evidently understood the allusion, but nothing could prevent him from saying what he had to say. So, after Antonov's report had been heard, and also the report of General Marshall—who surprised Stalin by the accuracy and the vigour of his improvised speech—the British Prime Minister said coldly: 'I am very glad to hear that the Russian front is approaching Danzig; it is one of the most important submarine bases.'

Stalin took no notice of the remark, but spoke again of the number of Allied divisions in the west: 'About the first of March Eisenhower will have eighty-nine divisions at his disposal; a third of the effectives will consist of armoured divisions. He will have nearly 10,000 tanks and 4,000 heavy bombers,' he was told.

'That does not seem enough,' said Stalin, who was anxious to emphasize the amplitude of the Soviet effort. 'On the Polish front alone we have 180 divisions, against 80 German divisions.'

The skirmish with Churchill continued: 'Our armies have never

[1] An allusion to the intervention of the Allied military attachés in the plans of the Russian General Staff at Mohilev, in 1916 and 1917.

enjoyed numerical superiority,' said the Prime Minister. 'Their superiority depends on our air power and our armaments.'

Stalin was doubtful. The Royal Tigers, the Panthers, had shown themselves to be greatly superior to the British and American tanks. After Churchill had explained the plans of campaign for the spring and summer of 1945, he said, pessimistically: 'I am not certain the war can be ended in 1945.'

The first meeting ended on this note; but a comical incident helped to clear the atmosphere. As a matter of courtesy, during the conversations in the Tsar's Summer Palace, where the Americans were quartered, Stalin forbade his two personal guards, officers of the N.K.V.D., to enter the conference hall. Now, at a certain moment Stalin left the hall by another door in order to go to the lavatories. This was at the end of the session. The bodyguards, no longer seeing him, were literally bewildered, to the great amusement of Roosevelt, who knew the secret of Stalin's disappearance. Stalin returned just as his guards were informing Béria of his disappearance. Roosevelt and Stalin were much amused. Here was a case of kid-napping in Roosevelt's palace, in the style of an American gangster film!

That evening, at the dinner given by the President, all were in the best of spirits. But not for long. When Roosevelt offered a second round of Russian champagne to his guests, Stalin cried: 'Drink up! Drink up! I am ready to supply more champagne to President Roosevelt on credit: thirty years' credit without interest!'

But they soon turned to more serious matters. Roosevelt took this opportunity of persuading Stalin that a president of the U.S.A. had to pay some attention to the opinion of the Poles.

Stalin replied, cynically: 'An enormous proportion of your seven million Poles never vote. I've gone into the matter thoroughly.'

'We'll speak of this again,' Roosevelt replied.

The conversation continued by fits and starts; each speaker taking up his position and testing the attitude of his interlocutors. The talk was now cheerful, now serious. These three men, on whose shoulders such heavy responsibilities were resting, were fond of a jest, but each had a different sense of humour.

At one moment Churchill, carried away by the after-dinner atmosphere, engaged in a fresh bout of arms with the master of the

Kremlin. He rose to his feet, announcing: 'To please Marshal Stalin, I drink to the proletarian masses of the world, of the U.S.S.R., and of England, and I beg to remark that I am the only head of a government here who could be dismissed at any moment by the vote of my people—that is to say, the masses of whom I speak. . . .'

'Then you are afraid of the next elections?' asked Stalin.

'No. And I am proud to know that the British people can change its government whenever it thinks fit.' Vishinsky, who wanted to have his say, intervened: 'I am sure of one thing: the American and British peoples ought to learn to obey their leaders as we obey Stalin.' 'Come and repeat that remark in America, and see the reactions of the people,' was the frigid response of an official of the Department of State.

Towards the end of dinner the conversation reverted to the Polish question, and the veto of the Council of Security of the future U.N.O. Opinions were divided. The ensuing discussion of the Big Three made little progress. It seemed as though they were approaching a deadlock. Then Roosevelt adopted a direct method, as he was fond of doing. He arranged for a tête-à-tête conversation with Stalin, in the presence of the Russian interpreter Pavlov. This conversation was dramatic.[1]

Roosevelt insisted that if no positive result were obtained in respect of the Polish question it would be a lamentable failure on the part of the Conference. It would involve a rupture between the U.S.S.R. on the one side and the United States and Great Britain on the other, just as their victorious troops were about to meet on German territory.

Stalin argued that he had to consider many contingencies. 'I am not omnipotent,' he said. He had to act in accordance with the secular interests of Russia. He could not return to Moscow to tell his fellow-citizens that he had shown himself to be less Russian than Curzon and Clemenceau.

'The frontier has been awarded to you,' said Roosevelt, finally, 'but the matter under discussion is the Polish Government.'

[1]There is no complete and official record of it. Stalin, between the Allies and the Politburo, confided in Roosevelt, who repeated certain of his confidences to Stettinius, who recorded them in his book on Yalta. On the other hand, Pavlov spoke of the meeting to Goulichvili, and by cross-checking these various partial accounts it has been possible to obtain a fairly accurate notion of the conversation.

It was then that Stalin made a series of confidences to Roosevelt, which Stettinius and Pavlov remembered: 'You are mistaken in believing that I am a dictator like Hitler,' said Stalin. 'I am not. Of course, I exercise indisputable authority, and I could impose concessions which I am ready to make, but which my colleagues would not wish to allow. But in this case I have to show them the immediate or future advantages which I should expect from such concessions. Otherwise I should be diminishing my own authority.'

In connection with the question of the Polish frontiers, he was closely watched by the Government of the Ukraine. The Ukrainian question was extremely difficult of solution, owing to the chauvinistic separatism of the Ukrainians. He had to make it clear to the people of Kiev that it was thanks to him that the Greater Ukraine was created.[1]

'Give me the contrary arguments,' he insisted, 'and I undertake to bring Molotov to reason, for it is Molotov who receives the directives of the Soviet Government.'[2]

He agreed to the rectification of the Curzon Line to the advantage of the Poles, but without the region of Lvov, for which Churchill had asked. In exchange he agreed to a compromise: the entrance into the Polish Government which actually ruled the country of representatives of the political and democratic groups in Poland and abroad. He was therefore agreeing to a fusion of all the Polish parties.[3]

Roosevelt agreed, and it was by the private understanding between the President of the U.S.A. and the ruler of the U.S.S.R. that the Conference of Yalta was saved from failure. With this, the certainty of conquering Germany, and the certainty that the war against the Reich would not be transformed then and there into a war between allies, was definitely assured.

The conversation then turned on the question of the veto of the

[1]After the war Stalin asked Beneš, in a friendly spirit, to cede to the Ukraine the Subcarpathian Ukraine, the only region which was still excluded from the Greater Ukraine, and which had set itself up as an independent country in 1939. The dream of the Ukrainian chauvinists was realized by the same Stalin who materialized so many of the dreams of the Russian nationalists.

[2]Even when he seemed to be giving way, Stalin remained on his guard. He did not speak of the Permanent Committee and the Politburo, thus giving the impression that it was the Government of the State, and not the Party, which spoke the decisive word.

[3]We shall see later under what conditions this promise was withdrawn.

future U.N.O. Stalin admitted that Roosevelt was right in calling Molotov's obstinacy nonsensical. Molotov, it will be remembered, asked for the right of veto on the inclusion in the order of the day of any question whatsoever.[1]

Stalin also wanted Roosevelt to confirm the total amount of the reparations to be claimed from Germany—the twenty milliards of dollars, of which ten milliards were to come to the U.S.S.R. 'As agreed between us at Teheran, but Churchill would not agree. . . .'

'Agreed,' replied Roosevelt.

This was the end of the historic conversation between the two men which made it possible to arrive at the Yalta agreements, whose scope and propriety were to be so much debated. However, the general agreement was reached only after a close and often tense and dramatic discussion during the plenary sessions of the Conference.

Churchill still protested against the amount of the reparations: 'They are,' he said, 'too high, and we should have to feed the Germans during the occupation.' Stalin for once lost his temper—a thing that rarely occurred. Contrary to his usual custom, he left his seat and walked to and fro in the hall, speaking with vehemence and gesticulating. One could see what importance he attributed to the question of reparations, which would define the economic conditions prevailing immediately after the war. 'I cannot tell the Russian people that the devastation and destruction which they have suffered will not be repaired by those who behaved like veritable savages. I cannot accept this refusal of just reparations to my people. I cannot go back to Moscow and tell them this: Our allies will not admit our most sacred right to compensation. I will not do it, for I know that my people would be roused to indignation by such treatment on the part of those who are their allies in this terrible war, in the course of which they have fought with unexampled courage and an unprecedented spirit of sacrifice. . . .'

We know that Stalin, like so many great men, does not disdain a theatrical gesture on occasion. But in the opinion of the delegates who were present the emotion which he expressed was perfectly sincere. Its significance is no whit diminished if we recall the fundamental reason of his apprehensions: The peoples of Russia would

[1]Stalin forced Molotov, despite his opposition, to accept Roosevelt's point of view, as he had promised during this tête-à-tête.

demand—and were already most insistently demanding—an improvement of their standard of life, and they would demand an accounting of their rulers. The time was past when any sort of conditions could be imposed upon them.[1]

At the close of his speech, although no agreement had as yet been reached, Stalin went up to Roosevelt and gave him a prolonged handclasp; a quite unexpected gesture. It was as though he wanted to thank him, in front of Churchill, for his understanding of Russian needs, which he had already understood at Teheran. It was probably this incident that afterwards gave Roosevelt the notion of the demonstrative handshake of the Big Three, which was recorded by a widely circulated photograph.

During the debate on the veto, Stalin, doubtless to prove to Roosevelt that he kept his private engagements, made another gesture which was quite contrary to all the traditions. He turned to Molotov, and told him, pointing to Roosevelt and Churchill: 'They are right! You must not make yourself ridiculous by your objections. We cannot continue to insist on the veto of the order of the day. . . .'

Molotov, obliged to give way, did not even attempt to conceal his irritation. He never forgave Stalin, and reverted to the question under discussion. Roosevelt took advantage of the situation by introducing a secondary question, but here again Molotov proved equally intractable. Roosevelt had asked that the U.S.S.R. Air Force should be authorized to use the Hungarian aerodromes, and that a group of American experts should be allowed to examine the effects of the bombardment of the petroleum installations at Ploesti.

'Agreed,' said Stalin immediately. Then, seeing that Molotov wished to intervene, he made a sign of impatience. 'Useless to discuss the matter further; the request is completely justified. As Commander-in-Chief I shall give the necessary orders.' It is to be noted, in this connection, that the Permanent Committee had no right to interfere in the command of the Red Army.

The Yalta Conference came to an end, and the occasion was

[1]Stalin's apprehensions were to be justified; as a man who was always watching the reactions of the masses, he could not be mistaken. At the end of the war the peoples of the U.S.S.R. demanded an improvement of their living conditions and refused to put up with the scarcity of foodstuffs. Millions of soldiers had come into contact with the life of foreign peoples, and it was impossible to conceal the reality from them. The aged Kalinin was, therefore, sent on a propagandist mission to calm their impatience.

marked by a dinner in Churchill's quarters, in what had been Vorontsov's villa at Aloupka.

Stalin arrived between Molotov and Pavlov. He was in a sullen mood, visibly fatigued and irritated. Molotov kept on addressing him confidentially. He too seemed in an irritable mood, as though obliged to take part in a ceremony which he found displeasing.[1] Finally, Stalin came to the point. He told Churchill flatly that the final communiqué of the Conference ought to mention the question of reparations due to the U.S.S.R. Roosevelt supported him. It was decided that the text should declare that the U.S.S.R. had a right to ten milliards of dollars in reparation. Stalin, suddenly relaxing, looked at Molotov with a smile, and pressed Roosevelt's and Churchill's hands. Henceforth he was in the best of tempers, and even spoke in praise of his eternal enemy Churchill:

'I know of no precedent to such courage,' he said. 'Churchill was alone, tête-à-tête with the Third Reich, but his nerves did not give way. He refused to accept the compromise which Hitler proposed in 1940! This will be his great glory in history, for such tenacity is found only in men of unique quality!'

And as though to show that he kept his engagements, he mentioned the recent events in Greece, asking 'simply for information, without wishing to criticize the British.'

At this moment Roosevelt intervened, saying that for his part he did criticize them. When Churchill replied that he hoped that peace would quickly be restored in Greece, but that it would be difficult to form a government representing all the political parties, Stalin agreed: 'You are right; the Greeks are not yet accustomed to political discussions; they prefer to cut one another's throats.'

In the chief instigator of compulsory collectivization and the purges, these words might seem, to say the least of it, surprising; but the fact that he could utter them was an indication of the path which he had followed, and the influence of the war upon his formation as a statesman: this was a spontaneous reply, an incidental comment.

[1]The day before, at a meeting of the Permanent Committee, Molotov complained at some length that Stalin was allowing himself to be beguiled by Roosevelt and Churchill. He refused to believe that these two had any differences; they were acting an Anglo-Saxon comedy, while they were really acting together, and he claimed that the Yalta Conference practically annulled the decision at Teheran respecting the ten milliards of dollars.

As the Balkans always appeared an inexhaustible subject, Churchill asked Stalin to pacify Tito with a view to forming a national government.

'You don't know Tito yet,' was Stalin's reply. 'Nor the extent of his pride. Having become the ruler of a country, he would think himself insulted if I gave him any advice.'[1]

'You cannot hesitate to advise him because you might run the risk of offending him!'

'I certainly do! But I am not afraid of him, and when it's necessary I shall tell him just what I may think it useful to say.'

In conversations on subjects of a general nature Stalin, in a relaxed mood, pointed to the gist of the conceptions which he had formed.

'I am sure,' he said, 'that as long as we three are alive there can be no serious quarrel between the U.S.A., Great Britain, and the U.S.S.R. But what will happen when we have disappeared? We ought to take advantage of our mutual understanding to build a solid house for the United Nations. This is why I want to see the statute of the future organization complete in every particular, to prevent our successors from making a mess of affairs. I assure you that nowadays this is my principal task.'

Stalin showed by this that he had retained much of the mentality of the litigant who attaches a special importance to the written and accepted document. With the end of the war a result had been obtained which he wanted to consolidate and fix once and for all in rigid rules of conduct. It took him a long time to understand that in a world which is constantly undergoing transformation the search for this kind of stability is comparable to the quest for time gone by.[2]

He had still to complete his apprenticeship to the outer world. This he was to do during the arduous years between 1945 and 1950.

---

[1]We know how Tito did react later on to advice from Moscow.

[2]*La recherche de temps perdus.* He has arrived at this notion, surprising in a Bolshevik, because through the historical changes to which he has largely contributed he has acquired a fundamentally conservative mentality.

CHAPTER XLIX

BETWEEN YALTA AND POTSDAM

THE members of the Permanent Committee bowed before the official decisions of Stalin. They could not do otherwise, but they were not resigned. Molotov's ill-temper had increased; he felt that he had been slighted in his capacity of Minister for Foreign Affairs, a minister from whom Stalin had publicly exacted concessions. It was not only that he had been forced to abandon the position which he had adopted; his attitude was the corollary of the tendency of any governing bureaucracy to defend its department against any interference. We see this in every country. But in the U.S.S.R. the absence of any free and responsible public opinion gives a specially acute edge to this bureaucratic particularism. At the 'summit' of the Soviet State it replaces the differences of public opinion in the liberal countries.

Thus, while it bowed before the *fait accompli*, the majority of the Politburo never missed an opportunity of evoking and analysing certain facts which prove that Stalin had been guilty of a political and psychological error when he agreed, however prudently, to make certain concessions.

At the same time, a new theory was beginning to replace the theories of Molotov, which were now out of date. A new theorist had come forward as doctrinal guide. This was Marshal Bulganin, ex-President of the State Bank, who had acquired his high military rank without ever having been in command of armed forces.

Bulganin's theory was one of excessive simplicity, and its actual value was not great. In its presentation it served as an example of the statements which the anti-Soviet politicians elaborated subsequently in order to explain the foundations of the policy which they recommended. If we consider all the mischief that Marxism has done in all parts of the world, we shall see that its influence in this last connection was not the least. Westerners adopted its primitive mode of thought, expounded in rigid and changeless forms. The intelligence gained nothing thereby, and the return to 'synthetic' thought had serious repercussions in the practical domain. 'Experts' made their appearance in the chancelleries, and their petrified science, based on that of the Marxists, was suddenly and quite unreasonably endowed with an aura of infallibility.[1]

The thesis of the Soviet pseudo-savant, which expresses ideas corresponding to the policy which the majority of the Politburo wished to impose, was developed at some length. It asserted, among other things:

'The Anglo-Saxon Powers have admitted the U.S.S.R. to their society only in self-defence. . . . As soon as the war is ended the U.S.S.R. will be subjected to encirclement; the countries in its zone of influence will be torn from it one by one, thanks to the economic and financial superiority of the U.S.A. and the impoverishment of the U.S.S.R., and its zone of influence will be transformed into a new *cordon sanitaire*. . . . It is inevitable that the Anglo-Saxon Powers should attempt to assure their economic, financial and political domination over the future Germany. This would then become a docile instrument in their hands, and a danger to the U.S.S.R. . . . In Asia, China, dominated by Anglo-Saxon influences, will turn against the U.S.S.R. after a period of rapid economic development facilitated by the United States. . . . Thus, despite its dazzling victory, the U.S.S.R. may very soon find itself in a very menacing position. . . . A common front, which could not be formed at the time of the conflict with the Third Reich, could be constituted now, and the future international organization would help to mobilize the public opinion of the world against the U.S.S.R. The Vatican, in view of the number of Catholics in the countries included in the future Soviet zone, would be another factor making for the mobilization of world opinion against Moscow.

'In the face of these dangers, and in order to prevent the creation of a world bloc against the U.S.S.R., the following policy should be adopted: To prevent the formation of a unified Germany. To establish in all the countries of the Soviet zone governments controlled by the local Communist parties. . . . France and Italy are of quite particular interest in this connection.

[1] An example of this pseudo-science was the famous 'X plan,' whose paternity was most seriously disputed by a number of persons.

'Not to allow China to reconstitute her unity and to stimulate the Communist Government of Yenan to continue its struggle against the Chunking Government. . . .

'To favour everywhere the increase of the influence of the Orthodox Church, liquidating the Unriat centres in the Ukraine and Poland, and overcoming the preponderance of the local Catholic episcopates.'

Bulganin's theses were discussed and adopted by the Politburo only a few days after the conclusion of the Yalta Conference. They were accepted by an overwhelming majority. Only Voznessensky, Andréiev, and Kalinin abstained from voting. Stalin was not present at this session; he was at his headquarters in Minsk, where he was drawing up the plans for the final offensive against Germany.[1] His absence, which seemed to have such a plausible motive, was due to a number of complicated reasons. We know already that in Stalin's case it is his silences and abstentions which have the greatest significance. If Stalin had been in Moscow he could not have abstained from voting, and from voting for the new theses, which were really nothing more than the directives of his famous Leninism-Stalinism, applied to the international situation of 1945. Bulganin was, on the whole, his pupil; yet his theses struck a deadly blow at the policy of collaboration inaugurated at Yalta. Here was a dramatic contradiction. Stalin may, however, have had other things on his mind.

Bulganin, it is true, did not speak of attacking the capitalist world. But he revived the dogma that the U.S.S.R. was itself under attack, and all his conclusions are contradictions of the notion of the peaceful co-existence of the two social systems. On the whole, he was expressing the tendencies of Molotov and Jdanov against which Stalin had already protested in his famous Leningrad speech, and resuscitating the classic theories of the Marxists.

All these circumstances made it impossible for Stalin to oppose the theses at that moment by attacking their theoretical basis. To do this, he must have begun by destroying the classic theses and dogmas

---

[1]These theses were not officially published in toto. They were given to the public, one at a time, often in the form of commentaries, in the Revue Bolchevique, and in articles signed by Leontiev, Alexandrov and Koudriavtzev.

of the Leninism-Stalinism of which he had been one of the principal creators.[1]

In practice, once Bulganin's theory was adopted, Stalin left to Molotov the responsibility not only for domestic, but also for foreign politics, devoting himself more and more to the direction of military operations. This modification of the situation, which was not officially announced, had immediate consequences as regards the attitude of the U.S.S.R., in spite of a few last attempts of Stalin's to maintain the spirit of Yalta, due to the fact that he was unwilling to allow anything to change the character of his relations with Roosevelt.

The attitude of the U.S.S.R. toward international problems was clearly changed. If sometimes the change was made in contradiction to Stalin's advice, his formal responsibility as conductor of the orchestra was not lessened thereby. But, as we know, he disliked giving orders.

The first result of the stiffening of Moscow's attitude was the non-observance of the 'Declaration as to Liberated Europe' elaborated at Yalta on the 9 February, which provided for free elections in the countries comprised in the Soviet zone, with the constitution of governments formed by all the democratic parties.

At Bucharest, on the 27th of the same month, Vishinsky, giving free vent to his violent temperament, forced the young King Michael to dissolve Radescu's Government, appointing in Radescu's place the crypto-Communist Grozea, assisted by Bodnareanu, an ex-officer of the Roumanian Army, who had deserted in 1937 and had worked in the U.S.S.R. for the N.K.V.D. The attorney-general, in the High Court of Moscow, so far forgot the forms of diplomacy and the rules of simple decency as to call the King a 'greenhorn', and violently bang the door of his office.

As for Poland, Molotov refused to agree to the advent of the leaders of the democratic parties, a list of whom had been drawn up at Yalta by Stalin and Roosevelt. He informed Harriman that the Lublin Government was the only veritable Polish Government, and

[1]This he undertook to do, but he needed some time to modify his theoretical bases. He progressed step by step, and it was not until August 1930, in a letter dealing with a linguistic problem, published in the review *Questions of History*, that he announced—as always, incidentally—*the non-existence of all the Marxist theses or dogmas* and the necessity of regarding all the theories of Marx, Engels, and Lenin as superseded by events. He treated Marxism as a confectioner treats an egg, filling the shell with his own confections.

that new members could be added to it only if he accepted them.

Then, when Roosevelt, attacked in Congress for his 'concessions without equivalent consideration to Stalin,' sent Stalin a long telegram, in which he declared without circumlocution that 'the Polish question must be settled in accordance with the decisions taken at Yalta, and in order to ensure the favourable development of our programme of international collaboration,' Stalin did not reply until a week had elapsed. It is possible that no one will ever know whether he had allowed himself to be convinced by the arguments of Molotov's group, or whether he was really no longer in a position to impose his own point of view. Or again, as so often happened when he had to come to some conclusion with regard to a matter of foreign politics, it may be that he was afraid of making a mistake. He knew, of course, what he wanted to obtain, but the finer manifestations of the Anglo-American psychological climate still continued to escape him; handicapped by his post, he did not quite know what he ought to expect. At all events, the legend of his dictatorial power in his relations with the Politburo had never been more definitely refuted. This fact becomes plainly apparent if we compare certain comments of Stettinius' with the text of the telegram of reply to Roosevelt:

'We saw Stalin at Yalta,' Stettinius wrote, 'reveal himself as a realistic statesman, despite the difficulties he experienced in making certain concessions which run counter to his basic dogma and also to the interests of the Russian State, which he governs in its Soviet form. . . . I was glad to be able to say that President Roosevelt had found in Stalin a high degree of co-operation. When President Varga asked me if it was difficult to work with Stalin, I replied that he was, in truth, very rough, but also very realistic. . . .'

And here is the text of the telegram sent to the President of the United States—a telegram officially signed by Stalin: 'I recognize that the Polish question is in an impasse. The fault is mainly that of the British and American Ambassadors to Moscow, who insist on completely liquidating the Lublin Government and forming an entirely new government, which is contrary to our agreement. I can accept among the leaders of the Polish party only those who recognize the new eastern frontier of Poland with the U.S.S.R., as well as the other agreements concluded at Yalta in respect of Poland, which do really endeavour to establish friendly relations between Poland and the Soviet Union.'

Even the tone was new. One can understand why a week had gone by. Even the style did not seem to be Stalin's.

The Permanent Committee, in return, opened a true counter-offensive. In London the Soviet representative on the European Consultative Commission declared, on Molotov's instructions, that the Russians refused to enter the Control Commission in Germany, although this declaration was contrary to those made previously, when the fact of co-operation was regarded as established.

Then a telegram from Stalin, accepting, in the main, the famous theory that he had been 'deceived' by his friend at Yalta, was sent to Roosevelt. It contained a protest in respect of the negotiations at Berne between British, American and German officers concerning the surrender of the German army in Italy. Roosevelt had given Stalin warning of the German demand, and had promised to advise him when the negotiations commenced. Now, the telegram claimed that the negotiations were already in progress, and that Roosevelt had been 'deceived by his own subordinates, among whom was Eisenhower.'

Roosevelt replied, very drily:

'I am filled with indignation at the false reports which your informers have sent you. These reports give rise to the impression that it is the job of some of your informers to destroy the friendly relations between the U.S.S.R. and the United States. . . . General Eisenhower would not have undertaken negotiations without informing me. In any event you will be kept constantly informed as was decided at Yalta. . . .'

Stalin was forced to apologize—for others: '. . . I did not doubt your good faith,' he telegraphed. There can be no doubt that Roosevelt, surprised by the sudden aggressiveness of Stalin's attitude, realized, with his usual psychological acuteness, that something queer was happening in Moscow. His telegram attributed the responsibility to the people surrounding Stalin. It is evident that he had not given up hope of influencing the Soviet Government through Stalin, whom he knew pretty intimately. Of this he gave a startling proof on the eve of his death.

On the 11 April he was in the little house at Warm Springs, in

Georgia. His physical strength was failing, but his mind was perfectly lucid. He drafted a message to Churchill, who had asked his advice as to the way in which he should deal with the Polish affair in the House of Commons. He wrote:

'I should minimize as far as possible the Sovietic problem in general, for this problem, in one form or another, seems to present itself daily, and more often than not it ends by subsiding, thanks to Stalin, as in the case of Berne. Still, we must be very firm; so far our conduct has been correct.'

On the 12 April Roosevelt died. His death was a decisive turning-point in the relations between the U.S.S.R. and the West.

Stalin could no longer remind the members of the Politburo that he had a powerful supporter. His position was weakened by the disappearance of a man in whom he had absolute confidence, and who he knew would persevere, against all opposition, in the strict application of the measures decided upon at Teheran and Yalta. Here the personal element had played an enormous part. To 'a friend' of Roosevelt's stature he could make concessions which he would never have made to another. He had proved this at Yalta, and it is certain that despite the necessity of yielding to the tendency represented by Molotov, he still had hopes of recouping his losses. This he proved, before abandoning the attempt.

It is undeniable that Roosevelt had succeeded in inspiring this 'man of steel,' whose nervous strength had won the admiration of Lenin, with feelings of genuine enthusiasm. In the course of a discussion of Chinese affairs, Churchill, listening to Roosevelt's improvisations, had lost patience.

Roosevelt entered upon a long explanation. 'You see, Winston, there is something here that you are not capable of understanding. You have in your veins the blood of tens of generations of people accustomed to conquering. . . . We are here at Yalta to build up a new world which will know neither injustice nor violence, a world of justice and equity. We have proclaimed with you, in the Atlantic Charter, the principles of the organization of this world; and freedom of possession is among these principles. . . .'

Stalin, to the surprise of all, rose to his feet, sincerely moved, and going up to Roosevelt he clasped his hand, and said, as he held it in his own: 'What you have just announced here is as important in the

AA

history of the world as all the revolutions there have ever been. You
are laying the foundation-stone of a new world, and you are acting
in sincerity. Your efforts will be understood by all!'[1]

The disappearance of the man who had greater power in the
United States than he in the U.S.S.R. made a painful impression on
Stalin. His temperament has always impelled him toward policies in
which the psychological motive plays a preponderant rôle. Roosevelt
appeared to him the guarantee that an anti-Russian coalition, in
which, according to the Leninist theory, the United States would
inevitably take the lead, was out of the question.[2]

With his colleagues of the Politburo, who, after adopting
Bulganin's theories, asked that they should be put into practice, he
could no longer refer to his relations with Roosevelt and the possibility of a real compromise. What Eden and Harriman called 'the
anti-American party of the Politburo' was now free to impose and
develop its policy.

After the end of hostilities, on the 9 May, an American decision
gave Molotov and his group an effective weapon. Despite the fact
that the U.S.S.R. had undertaken at Yalta to enter into war with
Japan three months after the conclusion of hostilities in Europe, the
end of 'Lend-Lease' was officially announced. This order was the
result of a 'blunder' on the part of the bureaux dealing with the
matter. Stettinius tells us that he got into touch with President Truman, who annulled the order. But the moral results of the gesture
persisted. The U.S.S.R. found in the incident an obvious proof that
the U.S.A. wanted to start a serious quarrel. The comments and
revelations of the Turkish press confirmed these suspicions. They
announced the affair under large headlines: 'Warning to Sovietic
Imperialism.' To Russian eyes this was 'a renaissance of anti-Soviet-
ism of the Munich type.'[3] The attitude of the American enemies of

[1] This sudden effusion was unprecedented; it was never repeated. It would, of
course, be difficult to find in all Stalin's actions a trace of such idealism. But one
cannot refrain from recording, as a human phenomenon, this sudden and certainly
sincere enthusiasm, which, in a slightly romantic spirit, might be compared to the
nostalgia of Heaven in one who has been, and still is, in exile.

[2] Goebbels was of the same opinion. At the news of Roosevelt's death he telephoned to Hitler, already shut into his shelter in the Chancellery, to inform him that
'the Tzarina is dead'; in this way alluding to the death of Elizabeth II, which had
saved Frederick the Great. Champagne was drunk to celebrate the occasion.

[3] *Troud*, 12 May, 1945.

Roosevelt, who greeted the demise of the author of the New Deal with relief, and rather discourteous comments, increased the distrust of the Russians. The intransigent members of the Politburo seized this opportunity of attempting to impose their point of view on San Francisco, being quite ready to break off the negotiations relating to the drafting of the statute of the U.N.O. President Truman then commissioned Harry Hopkins, already a dying man, to proceed to Moscow, and there, if possible, to revive the memory of the atmosphere of Yalta. Hopkins left on the 23 May, with instructions to inform Stalin that Roosevelt's death had brought no change to the American policy of co-operation with the U.S.S.R. But the intransigent members of the Politburo called Hopkins 'the representative of a dead man, himself a dying man, seeking to bring about the revival of a dead policy.' They would not at any price believe in conciliation.

'One of the reasons why I thought the American attitude toward the U.S.S.R. had become cooler, and had ceased to be that of Roosevelt, was the way in which Lend-Lease was first annulled, and then, although it was restored, reduced. If the United States had foreseen that they would no longer be capable of delivering goods to the Soviet Union, that would have been another matter. But their mode of procedure was brutal and inadmissible. . . . If you wanted to bring pressure to bear on the U.S.S.R. you made a fundamental mistake, and I think it my duty to warn you. If you had approached us in a frank and friendly manner, as Roosevelt did, much might have been done. But reprisals, under whatever form, produce an effect precisely the contrary of their aim. . . .'[1]

Once more, however, Stalin took it upon himself to prevent the aggressive action of Molotov in the question of the U.N.O. Gromyko had declared, at San Francisco, that Molotov had given him instructions to repeat the Soviet demand for the right of veto concerning the questions to be inscribed on the order of the day. Once already, in the Conference of Yalta, Stalin had compelled him to abandon this demand. Now he repeated it.

On the 6 June, on the occasion of a farewell visit, Hopkins recalled the situation, in the presence of Harriman and Molotov, and emphasized the danger of a rupture. He warned Stalin that the

[1]Stettinius.

United States 'would not join the world organization if the veto on the order of the day were to figure in it.' This interview was unique as a revelation of the relations between Stalin and his collaborators. After listening to Hopkins, he turned to Molotov with a malicious wink:

'Well, Monsieur[1] the Minister for Foreign Affairs, what do you say to that? You see your hope of getting the better of your foreign colleagues is not realized. . . .'

Molotov, stammering, as he often did in moments of embarrassment, tried to persuade Hopkins and Harriman that his instructions to Gromyko 'were merely a logical expansion of the principles accepted at Yalta. . . .' He spoke in this sense for a quarter of an hour, when Stalin stopped him:

'I've already told you once that this proposition is ridiculous. With all your talents as a logician you will never succeed in proving that the right of veto on the order of the day is acceptable. I accept your proposal,' he said, addressing Hopkins and Harriman. 'Monsieur Molotov, Gromyko will be advised of this today.'

This was his last act of homage to the memory of the great President, before whom he had accepted the liberty of discussion in the Security Council of the U.N.O. From this moment he once more became a prisoner of the aggressive obstinacy of his colleagues of the Politburo, who in the vertigo of victory thought they could impose their conceptions on the whole world.

At Teheran, Stalin had reached the culminating point of his political life. He remained at this height until Yalta, where he again took decisions which were contrary to the advice of the majority of the Politburo and its famous Permanent Committee. Between Yalta and Potsdam he could no longer act with the same authority and independence. Fatigued by the immense effort which he had put forth during the war, and which had affected his health, he could struggle no longer, especially after Roosevelt's death, against the 'vertigo of victory' of the other people in the Kremlin.

At Potsdam, which, from the outside, has the appearance of his

[1]Monsieur and not Comrade: in the U.S.S.R. the use of the former word can be extremely ironical.

'international apotheosis,' he was obliged to abandon the rôle of active negotiator, confining himself rather to that of the great representative figure. A lofty semi-retirement, to be sure, but one that removed him from the permanent direct control of affairs.

CHAPTER L

POTSDAM

AT the Potsdam Conference Stalin figured, for the outside world, as the great conqueror. It was he who received Truman and Churchill in the ancient palace of the Crown Prince, which gave a twofold significance to his triumph —a victory at once over Hitlerian Germany and Imperial Germany. Extraordinary precautions were taken to ensure his safety. In order to reach Berlin, Stalin travelled in a train of eleven carriages among which were four carriages which had belonged to the Tsar's train; carriages which Trotzky had used during the Civil War, and which since then had been kept in a museum. The itinerary was so designed as to avoid Warsaw and follow the Lithuanian route. Poland, with its anti-German insurgents, which had already become anti-Russian during the last months of the war, did not seem sufficiently safe to Béria, Khroulov and Abbakerumov, who were responsible for the security of the master.

Thousands of soldiers, wearing the peaked cap with the green rim of the Frontier Guards, occupied Potsdam and all the road leading to the city. The British and Americans also had sent protective detachments. But this did not lessen the effect of the violent shock experienced by the representatives of the West when they found that the Red Army was installed in full control in the centre of Europe. Stalin received the Westerners as guests amidst the deployment of these forces, and this gave them the impression that something extremely dangerous had been accomplished. A feeling of dread not unlike that which for decades had been inspired in the Soviets by Germany now seized upon these representatives of the Western world. It was due to the material presence of the powerful army which had chased the Germans for more than 1,200 miles, and which comprised, in addition to the Russians, representatives of a number of Asiatic peoples. Its mentality was a mystery to the British and

Americans, who instinctively feared an enterprise whose purpose they did not understand.

Nevertheless, the Potsdam interview ended in the signing of fresh agreements. But the psychological atmosphere was curiously like that of another interview which had taken place in Berlin in 1940, and which had consecrated the political divorce between the Third Reich and the U.S.S.R.; the interview between Molotov and Hitler. Officially, however, the similarity of the situations was ignored; the East and the West continued to sign agreements as though a solidarity of interests was still a fact. But behind this screen of optimism men were acting without conviction.

In the midst of all this deployment of Soviet forces, Stalin appeared affable but reserved. Matters were assuming a new aspect. He had resigned himself to refraining from taking the initiative. The events of the last few months had induced him to return to the attitude of reserve and prudence which compelled others to assume, not only the formal responsibility for political actions, but also the actual responsibility. He, at any cost, must retain intact his reputation for infallibility.

The intransigent members of the Politburo had asserted their point of view. The situation had enabled them to propound their theory that the Allies were preparing to break with the U.S.S.R., and that the U.S.S.R. should be the first to act, in order to obtain the maximum of concessions. They could, for example, make much of the affair of the German troops from Schleswig-Holstein, which, under the command of Admiral Doenitz, had been retained, without demobilization, by Marshal Montgomery, and after the attempts to persuade Eisenhower to make an attack upon Berlin in order to seize the German capital, contrary to the agreements, before the arrival of the Russians. They also noted that a number of German generals were hoping to undertake an immediate campaign against the U.S.S.R. Obviously this would have been absurd at that moment, but the famous complex was at work again among the Soviet rulers, who had accepted Bulganin's theories, and who now had Molotov for their leader. Stalin had been obliged to give him his head, if only to wear him out.

A great deal was made in the Red camp of the instructions, real or imaginary, which the State Department was supposed to have given to the American press, to start an anti-Russian propaganda.[1]

Despite their ungrateful task, Truman and Churchill were still keeping to the letter of the Yalta agreements. Stalin personally did the same, but his attitude was increasingly affected by the action of his assistants, intoxicated by an unprecedented victory, and in danger of allowing themselves to enter upon a fatal incline.

The practical measures which they ordered were eloquent of their intentions. The Soviets began to dismantle the German workshops, hastily, and without taking precautions to protect the machine tools from deterioration.[2] The island of Bornholm, outside the Soviet zone, was occupied.

There are few indications of direct intervention on Stalin's part; this seems to have been confined to hints to the higher officials. We know of only two cases of direct intervention. These were described by refugees of some importance; one of whom was Goulichvili. In the one case the affected person was Bulganin; in the other, Joukov; both of whom he asked to behave 'with greater prudence and circumspection in your relations with western commandants, in order to avoid needless and dangerous tension.'

Before Potsdam he had imposed a decisive measure, in compliance with the arguments advanced by Voznessensky and Andreiev, the first being in charge of the Four Years' Plan, the second, in control of agriculture. On realizing the enormous deficiency in the stocks of petrol, of which vast quantities were needed in order to restore to normality the transport, the industry and the motorized agriculture of the country, he had issued a categorical order that 90 per cent of all motorized military transport, including the officers' cars, was to return to Russia. The result was an absurd misunderstanding. Foreign journalists from the West, not seeing any heavy war material, but meeting with horse-drawn convoys, and discovering no trace of artillery or motor-cars, deduced from this that 'the Red Army has no material; it consists only of machine-gunners on bicycles, or travelling in horse-drawn vehicles. . . .'

[1] The Soviet press was already beginning to comment on this, and at a later period entered into many explanations of the matter.

[2] Soviet refugees have since then explained in the press that the Soviet command received orders from Moscow, signed by Marshal Bulganin, requiring them to act with all possible haste, and giving the very definite impression that the signatories foresaw serious complications in the near future, and even, possibly, an armed conflict.

At the very first meeting in Potsdam a psychological barrier was raised between Stalin and his two guests. Truman was a complete stranger to him, and had not as yet had time to prove that the tradition in accordance with which insignificant persons are chosen as Vice-Presidents of the United States is not always followed. Externally, all was cordiality; the Big Three listened to music, and Truman played the piano for Stalin. But the music was not very useful; especially as the relations between the Russians and the British were rapidly deteriorating.

On the 19 March Stalin had broken the pact of friendship with Turkey, and his declaration left no one in doubt as to Russia's intention to settle the question of the Straits. On the other hand, though he was in occupation of the Balkans and the Danube Valley, Stalin knew that Churchill would regard his 'gentleman's agreement' of November 1944 as lapsing at the end of hostilities. When the Labour victory in England compelled Churchill to surrender his place in the Conference to Attlee, Stalin was left face to face with new guests, who could not have the same prestige for him as Churchill and Roosevelt, and who, he believed, must be entirely dependent on their Parliaments. He began to lose all personal interest in the Conference, especially as the Politburo was increasing its pressure. There is, after all, a limit to human strength, and two attacks of cardiac trouble, one two months earlier and one during the Potsdam Conference, had compelled him to husband his energies.

The gulf which was gradually opening between the Allies was bridged, for the time being, by the American soldiers, Marshall and MacArthur. The war in the Pacific was not yet ended, and they were insisting more and more urgently that President Truman ought to persuade the Russians to intervene against Japan, as they had promised at Teheran and Yalta. They believed that an American attack upon the Japanese archipelago would cost nearly half a million American lives, and were anxious that the Soviet Army should grapple with the main Japanese armies on the continent.

A curious and unexpected thing came to pass, whose influence was to be extremely unfavourable to the development of the international situation: It was at Potsdam, at the very moment when the psychological split had already occurred, that the Western Powers had made their maximum concessions to the U.S.S.R.!

Molotov, with his traditional obstinacy, took advantage of the situation in order to revert to questions which had already been discussed. He thought he would be able to enforce certain conditions on the Allies, and thus, from the standpoint of the internal relations of the Politburo, the success which Stalin had officially achieved at Potsdam was turned against him, reinforcing the position of Molotov's and Bulganin's supporters.

Thanks to Molotov's persistence, and also to his 'Japanese blackmail,' the U.S.S.R. was able to annex a portion of East Prussia, with the city of Königsberg, which was to become Kalinin, while its western frontier would start from the Gulf of Danzig.

The western frontier of Poland was drawn in a most surprising manner. Taking advantage of a vague decision, and the negotiators' ignorance of the geography of this part of Europe, which had already enabled the Russians to obtain certain advantages from Marshal Montgomery, during a conference of the commanders-in-chief in Berlin, Molotov succeeded in securing the Western Neisse, instead of the Eastern Neisse, as the frontier between Poland and Germany. Berlin was thus about forty-eight miles from the new territorial frontier.

These two achievements of Molotov's enabled him to declare once more, this time with the proofs in his hands, that Stalin 'was allowing himself to be duped by Roosevelt.' As far as immediate advantages went, Molotov's policy was highly profitable. But it is evident that without Marshall's and MacArthur's pressure on Truman the latter would not have granted Molotov what Roosevelt had refused to Stalin.

Stalin now found it impossible to modify the atmosphere by a few 'concessions' on other points. Before the other conferences, as we have seen, he himself studied the questions on the agenda, compiling a considerable documentation of the subjects to be discussed. At Potsdam, before each meeting, Molotov gave him a note containing a summary of the decision taken on the previous day by the Permanent Committee, which had appointed a council of experts to study each problem as it arose. Physically tired, Stalin allowed this to become the established procedure. The Conference drew to a close in such a mood that no general discussion of the future was practicable.

Toward the end of the conversations Truman repeated his attempt to come to an understanding with Stalin. He informed him of the success of the atomic experiment at Los Alamos in New Mexico. But Stalin did not react to this gesture. He did not believe in the experiment—he had been too well informed! He had, in fact, been receiving information from spies, who at this stage did not believe in the success of the experiment.[1] He himself saw only a 'bluff' in this communication, which, after Hiroshima, where it had been confirmed, definitely modified the relations of East and West, and released Truman from the 'Russian mortgage' imposed on him by his generals.

The third Conference between the Big Three and their successors marked the disagreement which was presently to assume the form of the 'cold war.' As for the technical results of the Conference, the extent of the territorial concessions subscribed by Truman and Attlee might have been future repercussions which some regarded as disconcerting. As regards Stalin himself, Potsdam marked the beginning of a period of reduced activity. While retaining all his decorative and official prestige, the Master of the Kremlin began to husband his nervous energies, no longer intervening in the settlement of current affairs, but reserving himself for exceptional occasions.

[1]During the trial of the 'atomic spies,' Harry Gold and Fuchs, it appeared that Fuchs had not then believed in the immediate possibility of getting an atomic bomb to explode.

CHAPTER LI

THE ATOMIC AGE AND THE COLD WAR

THE explosion of the atomic bomb at Hiroshima—the bomb in whose existence Stalin had refused to believe at Potsdam —bewildered him. All his calculations were suddenly overthrown. The famous equilibrium which he had sought to establish was broken, to the disadvantage of the U.S.S.R., which emerged from the war bruised and economically enfeebled by the demands of reconstruction, demands which it had to meet without assistance. What Stalin had most feared had happened.

None the less, the operations in progress continued. On the date agreed upon the Soviet armies concentrated in the Far East attacked, on three sides, the Japanese army of Kwantung, whose commander had for more than ten years imposed his wishes upon the government of the Tenno.

The second atomic bomb, dropped on Nagasaki, liberated Tokio from the ascendancy of the military clans, and the Japanese capitulation finally upset all Stalin's calculations as to the future. The government of the Kremlin did its best to conceal the importance of the event from the country as a whole. But Stalin assumed the function of President of a Committee of Atomic Research, whose political direction was confided to Béria, and the scientific section to Kapitza and Ioffe. When Kapitza fell into disgrace he was replaced by Vavilov, President of the Academy of Sciences; and after Vavilov's death, by S. Kubeltzin. They were surrounded by a whole series of Russian and German scientists, the latter being 'invited' in the course of researches carried on in Berlin at the Kaiser Wilhelm Institute, on the island of Bornholm, and in the subterranean laboratory in Thuringia.

But it was difficult to 'catch up.' Military and political measures devised for the protection of the U.S.S.R. by means of the strategic glacis of satellite countries were introduced on the initiative of Molotov and Bulganin, and supported, with a vigour that was one day to turn against him, by Jdanov, and with a less spectacular but more efficacious persistence by Malenkov.

A factor of a strictly personal order, but one that assumed the force of absolute necessity, was added, at this moment, to the tactical reasons that decided Stalin to allow the majority of the Politburo to have its way. The Politburo, in its enthusiasm, could not resist the temptation exercised by its power—which, for that matter, it over-estimated—just as in the near future other statesmen and other countries would fail to resist it. Meanwhile Stalin's health, after his illness at Potsdam, was still deteriorating.

To the extreme fatigues of his eventful life, and to overwork in time of war, were added a certain mental lassitude, due to the disappointment caused by the disappearance of Roosevelt, and the loss of the prospect of deriving all sorts of advantages from an economic cohabitation with the West. The orientation of the western politicians, whom the atomic bomb had released from the necessity of taking into their reckoning the supremacy of the Soviet armies, was once more distinctly anti-Soviet; and this was a fact of capital importance.

All this aggravated the cardiac weakness from which Stalin was suffering, and provoked an attack which caused the greatest anxiety to the men of the Kremlin. They felt an absolute need of their leader, who in his person symbolized the palpable continuity of the U.S.S.R. and the political régime in the disturbed post-bellum period, when the Sovietic masses, having come into contact with the outer world, were making insistent demands for the improvement of their living conditions. In fact, since the application of the esoteric dogma and the famous principle of the deification of Stalin,[1] the country had become a quasi-theocratic State in which the Great Man figured as the supreme source of temporal power and the official inspirer of all activities. For the populations of the U.S.S.R. decency was preserved and prestige reinforced by the current designation of the Great Man as the 'military genius,' to whom the victory over Germany was attributed. The dissensions in the heart of the Politburo were carefully concealed from the public, which saw only the image of the infallible chief hovering above the Kremlin. His authority was still extended to all the domains of life, from the most

[1]See, in the first part of this book, the passages on the 'Esoteric Dogma.'

abstract questions to the breeding of rabbits or to the most rational way of sewing on the soles of shoes. A 'metaphysical incarnation,' a principle from which issues the philosophy of Marxism-Leninism-Stalinism, whose outlines were increasingly vague, Stalin, according to the official photographs, was even immune to age. But every medal has its reverse: he had become the prisoner of his own myth, and the Politburo could not dispense with his presence, even if his actual activity was 'switched off' to half power. Accordingly, serious measures were taken in the Kremlin to safeguard his health and husband his strength. He accepted them.

A medical commission recommended him to take five or six months' rest each year, and to work less strenuously. Then a commission of supervision, composed of Molotov, Béria, and Malenkov was appointed by the Politburo, to supervise the medical supervision, and to 'make Comrade Stalin a centenarian.'—The U.S.S.R. has an affection for lapidary formulae. He was recommended to avoid exposing himself to the rigours of the Muscovite autumn and winter, and to spend as much time as possible, between September and March, in the Caucasus, where the climatic conditions are those of his childhood.[1]

In the autumn of 1945 Stalin left for Sotchi. This absence was justified by the prescription of semi-retirement, and by the state of his health, and his disappointments; it coincided with a fit of exasperation with the attitude of the majority of the Politburo, which disagreed with him on a number of questions. All this enabled him to reserve his strength for the future. Once more he could refrain from accepting direct responsibility for a political régime which would inevitably make mistakes which would have to be amended and rectified.[2] The possibility of intervening as the supreme arbiter in

[1]An ex-officer of the security troops of the U.S.S.R., Captain Mirkin, who had served in the Kremlin, published in the world press details of these measures, giving descriptions of the medical record of Stalin's health kept by the three supervisors from the Politburo.

[2]On analysing the relations between Stalin and his entourage, and the indications of his lassitude since the death of Roosevelt, and the explosion of the atomic bomb, and the rupture of the equilibrium, I had concluded that the 'semi-retirement' of Stalin would soon be inevitable. My article, published in September 1945 in *Paris-Presse*, caused a considerable sensation, especially as the journal had given the article a sensational title. One result of the article was that I was interviewed twenty times in two days. Forty-eight hours after its publication its conclusions were confirmed by Stalin's departure for Sotchi, where he remained for several months. As always, the

moments of the greatest difficulty was always in reservation. On the whole, he passed his semi-retirement 'on the heights.' Without innovations, he returned to his usual tactics, which consisted in allowing those who were too energetic to wear themselves out. It was a method which he had practised with good results for thirty years.

The Soviet State was thus beginning to function under somewhat modified conditions. Behind the ornamental façade of Stalin's portrait all was stirring as usual, but in accordance with the rules of Stalinian taciturnity the public knew nothing of what was happening.

The Government of the U.S.S.R. had by now become an extremely complex organization, comprising sixty-five ministries. As each minister had several assistants, who formed the ministerial college, and had the right to be present at the Council of Ministers, a plenary assembly of the college would number nearly 400 persons. Even without counting the existence of the ministories in each of the federative republics, we are still far from Lenin's famous affirmation that 'the guidance of the proletarian State will be so simple that twelve ministries will suffice to effect it, and without any special preparation a simple cook could become a minister at a day's notice.'

Although he was no longer intervening in the expedition of current affairs, Stalin was none the less undertaking a reorganization of the power of the State. The first measure that gave a new form to the actual government of the country consisted in the creation of a Council of Presidency, which included all the Vice-Presidents of the Council. With one or two exceptions they were also members of the Politburo, which, as well as being the supreme organ of the Communist Party, constituted, from the standpoint of the State, a sort of 'Council of Regency,' which was responsible for all governmental activities both internal and external. Molotov, the first Vice-President of the Council of Ministers, became leader of the Council of Regency.

Stalin found himself once more passing through a period in

---

press and the public underestimated the real importance of this departure. It seemed to them so improbable that Stalin would not return to Moscow for the fêtes of the anniversary of the Revolution, which he had celebrated even in 1941, when the Germans were close to the capital, that the Moscow correspondent of the *United Press* sent to all parts of the world a telegram recording Stalin's arrival in the capital, 'bronzed by the southern sun and in perfect health.' In reality Stalin reappeared only very much later, to receive the Allied Ambassadors, and extend a benevolent welcome to them, but leaving the discussion of diplomatic questions to Molotov.

which he could not clearly see the best way to follow: nevertheless, he did not lose his intuition or his realistic common sense, which were his best weapons. He refused to give his unreserved approval to the aggressive frankness of the Molotov group, which believed only in its own truth, and tried to impose it, without taking into account the truth which governed the western clan, and which was no less categorical and egocentric.

In the higher spheres of Communism no secret was made of this. Thus, Jdanov once said before Diaz and two other Spanish Communists who were refugees in Moscow, in explanation of the private ideas of the group of Stalin's successors: 'The king is absolute when he does our will.' This translation of Schiller's sentence: '*Und der König ist absolut wenn er unseren Willen tut,*' shows plainly that the new bureaucratic caste which had been created in the U.S.S.R. saw in Stalin merely an external symbol of the unity of the State, and no longer a source of immediate power. The 'Supreme Arbiter' was relegated to Sotchi for months at a time, and remained in the background, while others ruled the country in his name and under his authority. Stalin's superior astuteness consisted in accepting this 'diminution' as though it were imposed upon him, whereas it was actually precisely what he desired. From time to time he would strike a terrible blow. Jdanov, before his death, was relieved of most of his important functions for failing to restrain the vigour with which he dealt with the affairs of the Balkans.

While he let his epigoni have their way, Stalin, who was growing old, never ceased to consider what would happen to the U.S.S.R. after his death. To replace the *personal* continuity which he represented he wanted to ensure the existence of a *constitutional continuity*: thereby creating a precedent.

On the 15 March, 1946, at the time of the first meeting of the Supreme Council after the war, a sensational item of news was broadcast throughout the world. Stalin had presented his resignation, and that of his entire ministry. But a few hours later he was restored to office; and the brief excitement of the foreign commentators abated. Actually, the incident was one of the greatest importance. From the moment when Stalin, endowed with unequalled prestige, had insisted on investiture by the Supreme Council, an organ which was created by universal suffrage—carried out, it is needless to say, in accordance with the rules of Soviet democracy—every new President of the Council would be obliged, in future, to follow the same procedure, and would have to be appointed by the Supreme Council. Constitutional continuity, quite independent of party questions, was thereby established.

This did not in any way diminish the practical influence of the Politburo, since the Council of Regency was composed of its members, and the decisions of its majority were still obligatory: even for Stalin.

Harold Laski, who went to Moscow in 1947, and who had the advantage of being able to speak Russian, explained in the Labour press that 'Stalin is not a true personal dictator, since he is obliged to obey the majority of the Politburo.' Some westerners at least were beginning to acquire a fairly definite notion of the special form of the power exercised by the master of the Kremlin.

Under the new mode of procedure Stalin's direct interventions were rare. One of them, moreover, at the beginning of the new era, was not crowned with success. At Sotchi he negotiated directly with the President of the Iranian Council, Ghavam es Saltane,[1] and signed an agreement with him which gave the U.S.S.R. a petroleum concession in Iranian Azerbeidjan. After this he personally ordered the evacuation of the Soviet troops, despite the objections of the Moscow Minister for Foreign Affairs. The Iranian Parliament rejected the agreement. The affair was thus a personal defeat, which he had to accept *in order to avoid the danger of a general conflagration.*

But matters were so arranged that his personal prestige did not suffer. Moreover, on the 23 February, 1946, he was solemnly invested with the title of Generalissimo, a purely honorary title which did not correspond to any actual function, but which, throughout the whole history of Russia, had been borne only by the three most glorious of his predecessors—Suvorov, Kutuzov, and the Grand Duke Nicholas Nicolaevitch the elder, who was commander-in-chief in the victorious war against Turkey.

Despite his remoteness, which increased after the Iranian affair, Stalin still retained the practical possibility of intervening in the domain of international politics without brutally imposing his authority and without running the risk of seeing his opinions re-

[1]He had told Roosevelt of his intention.

jected by a majority vote of the Politburo. We know that the Politburo had several consultative organs—its famous commissions.[1]

Stalin, exercising the right conferred upon him by his quality of Secretary-General of the Party—a right which he had exercised in the past in order to confirm his personal power—had reports of all the sessions of the commission sent to him even during his visits to Sotchi. The Statutes of the Party enabled him to suspend any decision of a commission, though he could also suspend the divisions of the Politburo. This distinction is important.

Thus, at the time of the Berlin blockade, in respect of which all arrangements were made by the Military Commission of the Politburo, with Bulganin as President, and Vorochilov, Béria, Kaganovitch and Malenkov among its members, Stalin intervened several times, asking the commission to reconsider the methods applied and even compelling the commission to submit the question of the blockade to the Politburo. The latter met in plenary session, which, by exception, was convoked in his villa at Sotchi. It was on this occasion that the diplomatic measures were debated which ended in the raising of the blockade. It is true that in this case Stalin dragged Molotov out of an impasse in which he had been dangerously floundering.[2]

He also kept an eye on the Commission for the Far East, founded in 1924, at the time of the first wave of the Red Revolution in China. After 1933 Molotov was its president, and its members now included Vorochilov, Chvernik, Malenkov and Mikoyan. This commission was thoroughly acquainted with all questions relating to the situation in China, including questions of Korean politics. Only two members of the commission were in agreement with Stalin's ideas; Malenkov and Molotov were opposed to them. Vorochilov was a waverer. We have no data which enable us to define Stalin's attitude in respect of the outbreak of the war in Korea.

In a general fashion, certain tendencies of the non-Soviet world press did a great deal to strengthen Molotov's position from 1945 onwards. It had become quite the fashion to speak of the manner in which the U.S.S.R. could be attacked and defeated, and even to dis-

[1] See the previous chapters for Stalin's ascent to power through his control of the commissions attached to the Politburo.
[2] This is fully confirmed by the members of the 'Nauheim circle.'

cuss, with the assistance of various maps, whether the atomic bomb should be dropped in Russia as a preventive measure. In the U.N.O. there was an overwhelming majority against the U.S.S.R. Molotov, in a cold rage, reacted vigorously. Gromyko's vetoes became systematic. The Conferences of Paris, London, and Moscow effected no appeasement; the Soviet troops were permanently installed in the satellite countries. To the Marshall Plan the Soviet Government replied by the Molotov Plan,[1] which was followed by a monetary reform in the U.S.S.R., and the introduction of the gold rouble, which was to be 'the gold dollar of the Eastern zone.'[2] Czechoslovakia came under Soviet rule.

Inevitably, pressure was met by counter-pressure. In consequence of the diplomatic blunders of the U.S.S.R., which were partly due to its incomprehension of western realities, the theoretical menace of encirclement became a fact. At the same time, Stalin's semi-retirement from power had inevitable repercussions inside the dictatorial shell.

The members of the Politburo, Vice-Presidents of the Council of Regency, were at the same time active ministers; they quarrelled in respect of questions concerning their ministries, and owing to their position in the Party the Supreme Council found it difficult to control or criticize the administration of the ministries.

From his pedestal, Stalin, who was trying to ensure the harmonious functioning of his heritage, and wanted the complicated machinery of the Government, with its innumerable wheels within wheels, to be 'run in' *during his lifetime*, intervened from time to time. He obtained from the Politburo a decision to the effect that its members could no longer fill active ministerial posts. They would have to confine themselves to supervising the functioning of the Ministries. The decision, as always in the U.S.S.R., was neither announced officially nor commented upon for a considerable time. The mysterious disappearances of Ministers which ensued roused the curiosity of the world press, which looked in vain for motives, and spoke of fresh

[1] In 1947, having analysed them, I described the first measures taken in this direction as the 'Molotov Plan.' The existence of the plan was denied for some months, and it was only when the measures foreseen were introduced one by one that the term 'Molotov Plan' was unanimously adopted.

[2] The measure was announced, more than a year after its application, in the form of a commentary, by the journal *Bolchevik*.

purges and dismissals; which, however, were not confirmed. It is true that in imposing this measure Stalin deprived Molotov of the control of foreign affairs, in which his famous obstinacy, and his lack of pliability, even in ordinary conversation, made any manœuvring out of the question.

While yielding to Stalin's decision the Politburo also decided on the indefinite adjournment of the Party Congress, which was to have been adjourned until 'the re-establishment of the economic situation in the U.S.S.R.' Thus, the Politburo continued to function as a sort of 'Long Parliament.' It is true that the Central Committee had the right to change the composition of the Politburo, but it also had been elected in 1939, and had lost all authority.

Thus, the Politburo, as now constituted, became a *stabilized organ*, a sort of institution, with a majority grouped about Molotov. Stalin, of course, who had been promised a hundred years of life by the medical commission of the Politburo, could impose his point of view whenever he was absolutely determined to do so. He did impose it at critical moments; as, for example, when he forbade Bulganin to close the air corridor during the blockade of Berlin, and to provoke an aerial war with the pursuit planes of General Lucius Clay. Further, through the Military Commission of the Politburo he forbade Molotov and Jdanov to liquidate Tito's régime by military action. This would have presented no technical difficulty in 1948, but it might very soon have provoked a generalized military conflict. Tito, at that moment, realized this as clearly as Stalin.

Consequently, there have been fresh uncertainties in the foreign policy of the U.S.S.R., and sometimes a surprising duality.

A section of the Politburo believes that the United States want, and are preparing for, the 'inevitable war,' and that it would be better to fight this war in Stalin's lifetime, since his presence renders the U.S.S.R. less vulnerable by assuring its internal cohesion. Thus, certain initiatives of the intransigent members of the Politburo corresponded with the activities of the partisans of a preventive war in the Western camp, and are tending to create a situation which might automatically provoke a generalized military conflict.

But when the situation becomes altogether too tense, Stalin wards off the disaster by public interventions. These are always directed toward appeasement, toward a peaceful cohabitation, and they always lay the principal emphasis on the economic domain, which ought, according to him, to constitute the bridge between the two worlds. Such is the usual content of the statements to the press, and to foreign visitors—as, for example, the Republican deputy Stassen.[1]

But he refused to give deliberate orders—which indeed he could not have done without creating a clash, by forcing his colleagues the Soviet Government to follow a prescribed course. This would have been too contrary to the tradition of the Kremlin, and his own habits, and might have provoked incalculable eddies in the minds of the 'dictatorial shell,' which regards its power as firmly established.

However, there are those who hold the opinion, based on a study of the Soviet press, and the controversies on economic questions developed in its pages, that Stalin would be inclined to let the intransigents of the Politburo have their way, up to a certain point, in order that the West should rearm with the same rapidity. He is thought to believe—according to Voznessensky—that the economic crisis, adjourned by the United States, by a process of rearmament on a scale never yet attempted, a policy which the other members of the Atlantic Pact will end by accepting, will occur about 1953 in so extreme a form that the fabric of the capitalist States will be seriously shaken, unless indeed the war should actually break out.

But no one can positively assert that this specious argument has really been accepted by Stalin, who, in the evening of life, and prudent as ever, does not—as he has shown often enough—appear to harbour the least desire to risk a world conflagration. This would destroy a great part of his life's work—which has so greatly exceeded anything that could have been foreseen, more than fifty years ago, by the 'spoiled priest' expelled in 1898 at age 19 to throw himself into the revolutionary hurly-burly.

Stalin's personal attitude is still dominated by certain complexes which it will be as well to remember. As formerly, he still attributes a particular importance to Germany. While his lieutenants are dealing with the details of current politics, he continues, indefatigably, to consider the best way of dealing with this country. He is always

[1]During the visit of the Quakers Malik was instructed by Stalin to express the atter's opinions in this connection.

preoccupied by his dread of the consequences that may follow from the political programme which this country may adopt.

The annexation of East Prussia by Russia, and the tracing of the western frontiers of Poland, were decided upon at a time when it was decided that Germany ought to be permanently dismembered, and that she would never again be a strong Power. As matters stood these annexations could only have the effect of placing the whole of Western Germany among the enemies of the U.S.S.R. Stalin, according to certain statements of his, appears to have realized that a serious political mistake had been committed.

At all events, he persistently tried to modify the situation by offering Germany advantages of an economic order. Under different conditions the attempt that was made before 1939 was repeated. This idea was constantly emerging in that portion of the political press which served, in an indirect manner, to diffuse Stalin's ideas.

He persevered. The attempts to establish favourable relations with military circles in Germany—with von Paulus and von Seydlitz— yielded no results. The flight of Bismarck's great-grand-nephew, von Ensiedler, Political Councillor of the Committee of Free Germany, proved that no serious hopes could be entertained of results in that direction. Having realized this, Stalin turned resolutely toward the Christian-Democrat circles of Eastern Germany, with Otto Nuschke and Dertinger. These two visited the U.S.S.R., and Stalin kept Nuschke for more than a month as a guest in his villa at Sotchi.

To Nuschke he unfolded his theory of the absolute necessity for Germany of allying herself economically with the U.S.S.R., in order to open a vast outlet into the countries of the Sovietic zone, and China. Nuschke suggested to Stalin the possibility of creating the circle of Nauheim, with Professor Noak at its head, who, as a leader of the academic movement, would always be useful in Germany, as a champion of Russo-German economic collaboration. All these theories were, of course, no novelty.

It was to Stalin himself that Nuschke presented a memorandum in which he expounded the principles of economic collaboration and proposed the application of a preferential tariff on merchandise arriving from Western Germany, such as had existed between Germany and Russia until 1913.

It was evidently under Stalin's encouragement—for otherwise he would never have wasted his time—that Dertinger, during a visit of four months to the U.S.S.R., when he was several times received by Stalin, elaborated a political supplement to his proposal—which was, however, immediately rejected by Molotov. It should be noted, nevertheless, that Stalin did not express his opinion, and that his silences are always significant.[1]

Stalin always likes to retain an 'emergency exit'; so it would not surprise those who know him if he had considered the possibility of some such combination.

If he really saw the gulf of another war opening under his feet he might very well take the world by surprise again and attempt to bring about a reversal of existing alliances, by providing the Germany of Bonn with the decisive argument for the restitution of the territories taken from her in the East. While conversing on this subject in a circle of his intimates at Sotchi, he suggested that without a radical change in the territorial allocations after the war, Western Germany was doomed to become a focus of irredentism and revengeful feelings, for which the U.S.S.R. might have to pay the whole cost.[2]

On the other hand, we should be lacking in a sense of reality if we were to believe that in a period which may end in a war Stalin, who has always avoided being trapped in an impasse, would not be calculating all the possibilities of contriving a way out against the day when he would have no other chance of extricating himself.

[1] There were echoes of the incident in the Austrian press, and we have heard people speak of 'the outskirts of Nauheim.'
[2] Recorded by Goulichvili.

CHAPTER LII

THE U.S.S.R. AND STALIN AS TIME HAS CHANGED THEM

Wఆ HAT is this U.S.S.R., if we examine it objectively, and for other reasons than those that inspire the Marxists of different shades, or the inveterate enemies who see it only as a modern Pandora's box?

It emerges clearly enough that the modern Stalin's State is as remote from the Socialist ideal that Lenin unfolded before the eyes of the revolutionary masses as Stalin himself is today from the revolutionary and incendiary of old.

Today, Stalin still calls the U.S.S.R. a Socialist State. This it is, in the sense that the State, after absolutely abolishing all private property, has ended by appropriating, as its exclusive property, the factories, the subsoil, the means of transport, the mechanism of commerce, the land, and all that the Marxists, in their jargon, call 'the means of production.' But on analysing the situation we arrive at conclusions which appear to destroy for ever any justification for any future Socialist revolution.

Here we can only give a summary picture, revealing the new distribution of power. As a matter of fact, Stalin no longer finds himself confronted with a 'social vacuum,' as was the case with Lenin in 1918 and 1919, after the Revolution and the Civil War which had destroyed the organization of the old Russia, and had spread over the vast territory of the ancient Empire of the Tsars a chaos in which the vaguely formed embryos of future social strata were struggling.[1]

The social classes, as they exist in other countries, do not exist in the U.S.S.R. The stable and precise social formations which are distinguished by the *amount* of property (Ford$=$X millions of dollars; an artisan $\dfrac{X}{10,000}$ dollars) are replaced in the cities of the U.S.S.R. by

[1]A detailed examination would need a whole volume. Here we are concerned only with Stalin personally.

a single social formation—that of the officials with varying salaries. In the country districts the social formation is that of the peasants of the kolkhoses, working for salaries and having a very limited possibility of trading in the products of their individual allotment of land. In this State, in which men are occupied in industry, transport, distribution, and production, all are really functionaries.

But the top and the bottom of the scale of salaries are so far apart that the grouping of these functionaries according to the salaries they receive creates a number of superimposed social groups. The salary of a sweeper in a factory is 500 roubles; that of a director of the factory may be as much as 15,000 to 30,000 roubles, without counting the percentage quotas to which he may have a right. It must not be forgotten that in the U.S.S.R. every undertaking, although it definitely belongs to the State, is exploited as a separate economic entity.

Under these conditions the privileged stratum of this bureaucratic society does not differ in any way, in its acquired mentality, from the Western *bourgeoisie*. Its way of life is much the same as theirs, since its members often own one or sometimes two motorcars, and sometimes a yacht, and a house, and employ two or three domestic workers.

In order to guard against the danger of a restoration of capitalism, some of whose external aspects have reappeared, Stalin maintains the principle according to which the Communist Party represents 'the Order of professional revolutionaries.' Their function is not, as formerly, to overthrow a system of government, but to assure it of perpetuity. Its members have to hold the control levers, at the top of the salary scale as well as at the bottom, and they must live in close contact with the less favoured strata of the population in order to explain to them the new dogma, modified to suit the needs of the cause, of 'a State which is building Socialism without waiting for a world revolution.'

This dogma is stuffed with promises, which are used as the dispenser uses a protective coating which enables the patient to swallow a bitter pill.

'In Socialism established on a world scale the general principle will be this: from each according to his capacity, to each according to his needs. With us, in the meantime,' says Stalin, 'the principle is this: each must give according to his capacity, and each will receive according to his utility to the country.'

Unlike the Christian religion, which promises felicity in the heavens, Marxism promises felicity on earth. But having made the promise, it continues to postpone the date when this felicity will be assured. Thus, the extremist and revolutionary who is the pupil and successor of Lenin, the apostle of absolute equality, ends by returning to the most commonplace utilitarianism of the bourgeois ideologists of the nineteenth century. In order that the populations of the U.S.S.R. should believe that the actual situation is only temporary, and that it will be changed, thanks to the Communist Party, three million adult members of the Party, constituting the militants of the higher ranks, and eight millions of the Communist Youth, live under the same economic conditions, being placed, with the ordinary run of functionaries—workers or peasants—at the bottom of the salary scale.

Stalin, on the other hand, makes considerable sacrifices in order to 'buy his *clercs*.' Among these are nearly a million *Verkhi* (Party officials) and nearly the same number of technical functionaries, all well paid and living under enviable conditions. The pay of the Soviet generals and lesser officers, considering the purchasing power of the rouble in the military co-operatives, is three or four times as great as the pay of French officers, and is equal to the pay of United States officers! Many Russian engineers are more highly paid than the engineers of capitalist countries. And if we take into account the average coefficient, which, in comparison to the salaries at the bottom of the scale, is from eighteen to twenty, we find that the 2,000,000 bureaucrats draw from the State the same amount in salaries as the 40,000,000 functionaries who rank as workers. What more could they ask? Stalin has been compelled to apply to this privileged stratum of the population a system of taxes on income which is strangely like the progressive income-tax of the capitalist countries, though it is not as drastic, but is more difficult to escape.

Yet another result has been obtained which is diametrically opposed to the notions of justice held by theoretical Socialism. The higher officials of the Party, including those of the Central Committee of the Politburo, and the local committees, paid, like all functionaries, were by statute eligible every third year. But since Stalin had practically amalgamated the Politburo and the Council of

Regency, the Soviet bureaucracy had dug itself in, refusing to risk further elections. The privileged class was created.

It may be that Stalin was anxious to restrict the danger of this 'social degeneration,' foreseen by those of his adversaries who had disappeared into the cellars of the N.K.V.D., and who, above all things, had feared the emergence of a *bourgeois* State. But even if this desire existed, it was condemned to remain inactive. The creator of this super-bureaucratic State was already to a great extent its prisoner, and the prisoner of the officials whom he had purchased, and who formed the backbone of the Soviet Russia of 1951.

Here Stalin's own terminology might be applied. According to this the second world war was 'merely a struggle of the Anglo-Saxon capitalist cliques against the Germanic and Fascist clique of capitalists for social privileges and profits.'

Now, at the present time there is in the U.S.S.R. 'a privileged Soviet clique' ready to fight for its recently acquired privileges and profits. And if it had not been restrained by Stalin, who could see other historical perspectives than the mere interests of the new clan of privileged persons, and who had espoused the cause of national Russian continuity, it is impossible to say what might have happened to the world by now. . . .

However, the crystallization of the internal situation tended to counterbalance the influence of the privileged. The egalitarian tendencies of the people, encouraged by the propaganda of the Government itself, might easily shatter the ramparts of the bureaucratic State. But there were two elements which helped to reinforce it. These elements were, on the one hand, the improvement of the living conditions of the salaried workers with modest incomes, which had become very perceptible since 1949, owing to the increase in the quantity of articles of current consumption and the periodical reducing of prices. On the other hand, the existence of an enormous system of political police, devoting themselves in actual fact to the defence of the new caste, which was profiting by the peculiar structure of the State. This police force was expected, above all, to defend this structure, with its 'Socialist' framework, against individualistic and egalitarian tendencies. Nevertheless, it is highly improbable that any suggestions of foreign agencies could have been accepted even by the less well-paid officials, since access to the more generously remunerated posts was open to them, and depended only on their own capacity and their individual efforts—provided, of course, they kept within the rigid framework of Soviet legality. Many refractory elements had been eliminated by adding them to the contingents of displaced persons, and this 'purge outwards' only increased the social cohesion inside the U.S.S.R.

On the whole, the former destructive revolutionary had succeeded in creating a form of State which, while in practice it was a negation of Socialist idealism, appeared to be the only possible form in a country which, on rejecting capitalism with its political expression, which was liberalism, had ended in creating a State capitalism which was far more exacting and more dictatorial than any other social and economic organization.

The profits of all production, and all trade—the dividends of the proprietary State—are indirectly placed at the regulated disposition of the community. But as the management of the system is purely bureaucratic, the profits are always less than those of private enterprises. On the other hand, in the liberal countries a great proportion of the profits of private enterprises is confiscated by the State in the form of ever-increasing taxes and duties, and is returned to the active community in the form of social insurance, free medical attention, strike pay, and old age pensions. Thus, the advantages which a so-called Communist country offers the workers are singularly reduced. Does the difference, which becomes more and more illusory, in their economic system, justify the rigid police control which in the U.S.S.R. defends the Marxist principles, while the liberal countries are still maintaining the principles of liberty?[1]

While the internal régime of the U.S.S.R., as it travelled farther and farther away from the abstract and unrealizable construction of Marxism, represented a compromise between the doctrinal bases and the realities of life, the international policy of the U.S.S.R. is the resultant of the aggressive pugnacity of the Molotov group and the intermediary corrections of Stalin.

[1]It is important for the West, in its struggle against Communist influence, not to sacrifice its political liberalism nor its individual liberties, nor the free expression of thought, to the methods borrowed from totalitarian countries; a tendency which is unhappily revealing itself in the United States. Attacks upon political liberalism and liberty of opinion are liable, by reaction, to effect dangerous modifications in the character of economic liberalism. Any exaggeration in this direction reminds us of the Latin proverb: *propter vitam vivendi perdere causae.*

In his official declarations as to his desire for a compromise with the liberal world, is Stalin sincere? Opinions on this subject are divided. But that is not the question. Two things are certain. He knows perfectly well that the social system which he has established is far removed from the Marxist dogma, which he has distorted to such an extent that he finds himself obliged to assert 'the non-existence of any dogma in Marxism.'[1] On the other hand, as he no longer has to defend a theoretical position, he can adopt the theory of peaceful cohabitation, in so far as he judges it opportune for the U.S.S.R., and considers that it might endanger the very existence of the country if he were to steer it in another direction.

By accentuating the economic aspect of historical developments, he is proceeding to realize a vast plan of climatic transformation in various regions. The huge hydro-electric systems on the Volga and the Don, in the Crimea and the Caucasus, and to the east of the Caspian Sea, will by 1956 or thereabouts place at the disposal of agriculture, which will be completely electrified in these regions, and also of stock-raising territories which have hitherto been useless, owing to the absence of water, but which cover a total area of nearly 115,000 sq. miles. By 1957 the two hydro-electrical centres of Stalingrad and Kuibichev alone will be producing 20,000,000,000 kilowatt-hours per annum. Stalin is thus providing, for the coming years, an enormous mass of labour, and raw materials, and foodstuffs, these latter being far in excess of the actual needs of the U.S.S.R., which are already very generously satisfied. In Asia his ideological declamations have become very much discreeter. He remains more or less in the shadow, in order to avoid any interference with the purely Asiatic form of transformation which evolution is tending to assume in this part of the world. Keeping well in the background, he allows China to fill the stage, being himself content to keep pace with the accomplishments of Asiatic evolution . . . being always prepared to make use of the tremendous stocks which will be at his disposal in a few years' time, and which he appears to regard as an effectual and decisive weapon in the realization of his future plans.

[1] Cf. a letter published in No. 8 of the review *Questions d'Histoire*.

Destiny, which made him an exceptional personality, also made him a victim of its irony, compelling him to demonstrate the unsoundness of the Marxist ideas as they were taught to him by his master Lenin, in whose footsteps he followed with such enthusiasm.

Now, in 1952, Stalin is an old, white-haired man. The necessity of constantly watching over his health, and above all his heart, compels him to take unending precautions. His words and his movements have become more and more deliberate; it is evident that he is a tired man. His figure is still erect when he appears in public in the uniform of the Commander-in-Chief. But now this uniform seems too large and too heavy for him. This impression is due to the emaciation of his face. Its features are more prominent than of old: so are its wrinkles.

His smile, which used to inspire a certain discomfort, so out of place did it seem on the features of a man who had only to close his eyes, after a simple allusion or a significant silence, in order to bring about sanguinary purges or compulsory migrations, has become the pitiful smile of an old man who is not feeling very well; who knows that he must husband his energies, because he will still have to face great dangers; so that after fifty years of public life—adventurous, ardent and ruthless—his personal continuity still imposes a difficult task and a heavy responsibility.

His private life is quiet and modest. Luxury, sumptuous dwellings, adorned with works of art, brilliant receptions and recherché dinners, have no attraction for him. In Moscow he is still living in the same small house, in the courtyard of the Kremlin, in which he received Matsuoka in 1941 and Churchill in 1942.

He sees very few friends; he devotes as much time as his doctors will permit to the study of reports and memoranda prepared for him by the chief of his secretariat, Puskrebychev. He is more taciturn than ever, and is often absorbed in thought.

At Sotchi, when he walks in his garden, where he sometimes helps his gardener to tend the flower-beds or prune the fruit trees, he knows hours of solitary meditation.[1]

[1]Those who, like Mirkin, an ex-officer of security troops who has published his memoirs in the press, have seen Stalin as he lives, compare him to 'an old horse, grown grey in harness, dreaming motionless, with unseeing eyes, in a corner of the pasture. . . .'

But there is nothing idyllic in this new phase of his life. Destiny is not generous to those it brings out of the shadows in order to entrust them with great historic rôles. And it has not yet finished with Stalin. The task of this man who has never allowed himself to be distracted from his sole occupation is not yet completed.

His understanding of human psychology, which has rendered him so 'efficacious' in respect of the internal affairs of the U.S.S.R., has been reinforced—a little late in life, it is true—by an adequate realization of Western values—of the robustness of the Western powers, and the strength of their spiritual and economic defences.

It is in the light of this new knowledge that he sees the U.S.S.R. and the liberal world approaching the most perilous cross-roads of their history. But no one knows what are the latest stipulations inscribed in the book of faith which he has wrested from the hands of Providence. And even if history has changed his very nature—even though the revolutionary, now a conservative, the architect of a new social and economic order, may be really meditating a pacification—nearly all the Western rulers regard him as a symbol of evil, of discord and menace, rendered still more dangerous by the economic success reported from beyond the frontiers of the U.S.S.R., and by the solidity of which the structure of the new State gave evidence during the war. In their eyes, all their anxieties are justified.

The mere *presence* of Stalin suffices, by a kind of virulent osmosis, to reduce and weaken the liberalism of the capitalist governments.

And they remember many things. They remember the limitless cruelty displayed during the conquest of power, and erected into a rule of conduct. They remember the victims of rural collectivization. They remember the purges, and the people sacrificed at every change of the ruler's versatile policy. They remember the labour camps. They have watched, from a distance, the 'socialist transformation' forced upon Roumania, Bulgaria and Czechoslovakia, and which ended in the liquidation of the *bourgeois* classes.

For his part, Stalin confines himself to pacificatory phrases, placing the accent on material necessities of enlarging the economic gangway which exists between the East and the West. His semi-effacement before the effective rulers of the U.S.S.R. does not mean that he may not intervene directly at a decisive moment, eventually getting rid once more of those who would oppose his way.

On the 25 August, 1952, Stalin, abandoning his reserve, appended his signature in *Pravda* to the announcement of a great Party reform. This was one of those actions which have compelled him to employ the full weight of his authority. The ex-terrorist, a member of the Order of Professional Revolutionaries, had decided to destroy with his own hands the chief weapon of the Revolution—the Politburo. In his own lifetime he completed the revolutionary cycle, by liberating the Party from the magic circle traced by 'the maniac of denial,' Lenin.

He thus abolished the weapon, secretly forged in 1912, which had enabled Lenin's tiny party to seize power over the immense Russian State, since when all the ideological conflicts—the struggle for power, the decisions relating to the purges and exterminations of the various oppositions, and collectivization, had taken place, being decided upon, in the heart of this collective dictatorship, on every occasion by a vote of the majority; a vote which, as we have seen, was sometimes, after the end of the war, given in opposition to Stalin's own ideas, for as regards the outer world the Politburo was nothing less than the supreme authority, the Holy See of Communist thought, the infallible interpreter of dogma. Once it was appointed by the General Committee, after the election of the latter by the Congress, it became the absolute master of the Communist Party and the Communist world, controlling, by virtue of the accepted subterfuge, the Council of Vice-Presidents of the governmental activity of the State. On the whole, the militants of the Party behaved in the fashion of the frogs in La Fontaine's fable, who chose as their king a stork with an insatiable appetite.

In modifying the Party statutes, Stalin was acceding to the demands of the younger members of the Party, who refused to accept, as they had formerly done, the dictatorship of the 'bonzes,' fifteen or so in number, who had been in supreme power. He was thereby effecting a *normalization* of the Party, which, while it still remained the *only* Party, became, in respect of its internal functions, an ordinary political party. The presiding committee at its head was no longer a sacrosanct institution acting in secrecy and obscurity, and enjoying a semi-mystical authority. The modern "Pandora's Box" disappeared, liberating from intimidation the "clercs" on whom Stalin had built up the structure of the U.S.S.R. The weapon disappeared, in token of the end of the class conflict, which ended because there was no one left to fight. In the scheme of the new State the vast apolitical and technical organization was expected to function without being threatened with divergences in the interior of a 'dictatorial shell.'

The question of Stalin's successor was obviously settled. A preponderant authority could no longer base itself on the claim that it formed part of a supreme organization founded by Lenin—which had been eradicated by a mere stroke of the pen from Stalin. Even the word 'Bolshevik' was suppressed in the official designation of the Communist Party of Russia.

This important reform, which Stalin had succeeded in enforcing, despite all difficulties, and the opposition of interested parties, by exerting, for once, his full authority, is also an indication that the technical conditions facilitating normal relations with the outer world had been established. In the interior of the U.S.S.R. this important reform of Stalin's had caused a great sensation, and was followed by innumerable consequences. Obviously, moreover, it could not fail to influence international relations.

But if he was really seeking to crown his labour by appeasement, thus freeing the world of its present distress, then his goodwill would have to be very persuasive. Creator of a new, robust order, the reformer of the dogma and thereby the very destroyer of the Marxist bait, who has climbed by the means we know to those heights where the fate of humanity is being settled, he has before him a barrier of distrust and hate built up by his activities of more than thirty years. A unilateral desire, even the most sincere, is no longer enough to open the way to the peaceful cohabitation which the former revolutionary has so often evoked.

THE END

APPENDIX

BIBLIOGRAPHY

Memoirs (in Russian): by Iremachvili, a friend of Stalin's youth.

Memoirs (in Russian): by Gogokhia, a fellow-student of Stalin's in the seminary.

Memoirs (in Georgian): by Marakhvili, a Communist.

The Journal of the Revolution (in Russian): by Ter-Mikhailov, an Armenian Communist.

My Memories (in Russian): by Mahakradzé. (Confiscated in the U.S.S.R.)

My Diary (in Russian): by Ienoukidzé, a friend of Stalin's; executed in 1938.

My Deportation (in Russian): by Jacob Sverdlov, first President of the Soviet Russian Republic (very rare; published in 1924 by Gossizdat).

In Siberia (in Russian): by Lev Kamenev, executed in 1936. Published 1924 by Gossizdat. Confiscated after Kamenev's execution.

Recollections (in Russian): by Pestkovsky, Stalin's secretary.

The Civil War (in Russian): by Vorochilov.

At Tzaritzin (in Russian): by Minin.

Letters: Stalin, 1927 edition, published Gossizdat.

Bolchevik: The journal of the Central Committee of the Russian Communist Party for the years 1922–34.

My Life (in Russian): by Trotzky.

Stalin (in Russian): by Trotzky.

On the Roads to Thermidor (in Russian): by Gregor Bessedovsky, *ex-charge d'affaires* of the U.S.S.R. in Paris, Tokio and Warsaw. Russian edition, published Povolotzky, Paris.

Stalin, homme d'acier (in French): by Alexis Redier. Published by the *Revue française.*

Stalin, der Lebensweg des roten Tzaren: by Bessedovsky. German translation, published in Munich 1933.

My Life (in Russian): by Kalinin. Published Gossizdat, 1933; out of print.

The Days of the Past (in Russian): by Allilouev, Stalin's father-in-law.

On the Fronts of the Civil War (in Russian): by Sokolnikov. Published Gossizdat, 1923.

A series of articles in the *Soviet Encyclopaedia*, first edition, 1926–27; now confiscated in the U.S.S.R.

A Book: by Boris Bajanov, ex-secretary of the Politburo and the Orgburo, chief of Stalin's secretariat; also a series of articles in Russian in the journal *Renaissance*, Paris.

The War Against the Traitors and its Lessons (in Russian): published Gossizdat, 1939.

Stalin-Kinto: by Lado Brakhelachvili, Georgian edition, Berlin, 1927.

The Volga in Flames (in Russian): Kamensky's diary of the Civil War. Published Gossizdat of the U.S.S.R., 1926.

Lenin in Emigration (in Russian): by Krupskaia, Lenin's wife. Published Gossizdat of the U.S.S.R., 1926 and 1932.

With Ilyitch at Gorki (in Russian): the diary of Lenin's sister, Marie Ilyinitchna Oulianova (in Russian).

In Petrograd, Besieged and Blockaded: by Larissa Reissner, wife of Raskolnikov, Ambassador of the U.S.S.R. in Kabul and Sofia; who took refuge in France and died under tragic circumstances at Grasse.

With Stalin at Rostov on the Don and Kharkov (in Russian): by Malakhovsky, a Russian journalist with the armies, published Gossizdat, 1926.

My Diary of the October Revolution (in Russian): by Bontch-Brouévitch, first secretary of Lenin's *Sovnarkom*.

How I Saved Ilyitch (in Russian): a pamphlet by Pridvorov (Démian Biédny), the Soviet poet.

The Lessons of October (in Russian): by Trotzky; published Gossizdat, 1924; now confiscated in the U.S.S.R.

The Philosophy of Our Epoch (in Russian): by Zinoviev; published Gossizdat, 1924. Out of print.

The Economy of the Transitional Period (in Russian): by Bukharin; published Gossizdat, 1929.

The Class Struggle in the U.S.S.R. (in Russian): by Reingold, Vice-Commissary of Finances, executed in 1936.

Stalin and the Bolshevik Party (in Russian): by Lavrenti Béria; published Gossizdat, 1932.

My Diary (in Russian): by Karl Radek; published Gossizdat, 1923. Destroyed.

With Lenin in the Sealed Carriage (in Russian). Recollections of Alexandre Lekikh, First Commissary of Supplies in Petrograd after the October Revolution. Took refuge in France in 1930 and committed suicide in 1947, throwing himself into the Seine.

Stalin: by Dmitrievsky, ex-Soviet diplomatist, who took refuge in Sweden in 1930.

SUPPLEMENTARY BIBLIOGRAPHY

The G.P.U. Recollections of a Tchekist (in Russian): by Agabekov.

The U.S.S.R. at War with the Third Reich (in Russian): by Alexandrov; published Gossizdat.

Articles in *Agriculture in the U.S.S.R.*, the journal of the Central Committee of the Communist Party: by Andréiev.

In the Service of the Soviets: by Barmine.

The Soviet People at War (in Georgian): by Béria; published Tbilissi, 1947.

Stalin: des Lebensweg der roten Tsaren: by Bessedovsky.

Cards on the Table: by James Byrnes.

Our Strategy: by Marshal Bulganin.

Moscow Date-Line: by Cassidy.

Rencontres et Conversations en Allemagne (in preparation): by Yves Delbars.

Recollections in the review *The 20th Century:* by Geoffrey Frazer.

Preliminaries to the War in the East and *The Last Days of Europe* (in Russian): by Grigori Gafenco.

Interview in *France-Soir* and articles in the Munich *Zaria*; also statements and conversations: by General Goulichvili.

Ambassador on Special Mission: by Sir Samuel Hoare.

Izvestia of Tambov, Saratov, Koubychev and Stalingrad (lent by a refugee).

Lectures on the Foreign Policy of the U.S.S.R.: by Professor Koroirn; published Gossizdat.

I Chose Liberty: by J. Kravtchenko.

Recollections of a Soviet Spy: by Krévitzki; published Washington.

A series of articles in the Russian periodical *Dni:* by Krévitzki.

Recollections of a War Correspondent: by Korolev.

Les Relations Germano-Britanniques: from secret archives of the Wilhelm-strasse; published Gossizdat, 1949.

Articles in *Empire News* and *Weltwoche:* by Mirkin.

Electoral speeches of March 1950, in *Molotov:* by Molotov; published Moscow.

Articles in Russian Press: by Oumansky.

My Embassy to Bulgaria and articles in *Dni:* by Raskolnikov; Paris.

On the Way to Teheran: by Foster Rey.

Recollections: by James Roosevelt.

Yalta: by Stettinius.

Znamia: Soviet newspaper.

In addition to these books the author had at his disposal a number of notes and references in Russian, prepared by another ex-member of Stalin's secretariat, who took refuge abroad shortly before the war, and who died in 1940. He was engaged in writing a book under the pseudonym of Dmitri Kaskov. His notes included details of the greatest interest relating to conversations with his colleagues on the secretariat, and especially with Mekhliss.

In addition to the above works, many of which it is now almost impossible to obtain, the author has obtained material (after cross-checking) from many private conversations, and from unpublished documents which he has had the opportunity of consulting; and he now expresses his thanks to those who placed them at his disposal, and particularly to M. Bessedovsky, who helped in finding the necessary documents.

INDEX

A

Abreks, 15, 16, 51; Stalin as an, 31, 32
Africa, North, landing in, 329, 330, 334, 335
Agabekov, 56
Agriculture, 116, 118, 147-8, 150, 155, 161-3, 189, 360-1, 413; *see also* Collectivization.
Alexander Nevsky, film, 217
Alexander the Great, 12
Alexander, Tsar, 15; Stalin compared to, 256-7
Alexandrov, Gregor, 330, 336-7, 345*n*., 381*n*.
Alexeiev, General, 96
Aliocha, *see* Djaparidzé.
Allilouev, 33, 44, 61, 62, 69, 90-1
Alliloueva, Nadiejda, 33, 90-1, 105, 107, 112, 170, 222
Amilakhvari, Prince, 14, 20-1
Ammen-Em-Phta, 11
Anarchists, 87
Anders, General, 314
Andréev, 150, 172, 193, 219, 360, 381, 392
Angarsky, 28, 81
Anschluss, 343
Anti-Comintern pact, 239, 244
Anton, Patriarch, 15
Antonov, General, 365, 369, 371
Antonov-Ovseensko, 101
Arabalian, 34
Arakhvelidzé, 38
Arcos, British raid on, 150
Arctic Ocean convoys, 306
Aremachvili, Sosso, 34
Armenian Catholics, 18
Army, and Bolsheviks, 86-8; *see also* Red Army.
Artem, 93
Artenzov, 202
Artusov, 157
Assine, 87
Astakhov, 215, 225, 229-30, 231, 235, 237-9, 241

Astrakhan, 14
Astronomy, and Stalin, 31
Atlantic Charter, 306
Atom bomb, race to make, 352-3; explosions of, 396; at Los Alamos, 395
Attila, 278
Attlee, 393
Aurore, cruiser, 101
Avilov, 82
Axelrod, 31
Azerbeidjans, 51

B

Badoviev, 64
Bagratioun, General, 100
Bagratov, General, 228*n*.
Bajanov, Boris, 122, 123, 138
Bakaiev, 180, 182
Bakhtadzé, family, 16
Baku, 46, 48-9, 50, 51, 56-9
Balagan, 41, 42, 44
Balitsky, 176, 177
Balkans, 255, 258, 336, 393; Russo-German struggle for, 261-4; Stalin's fear of British post-war influence in, 306-7; Stalin seeks Allies' recognition of Russian interest in, 312-13; Stalin's fear of British landing in, 355; entry of Red Army into, 358-9; British and Russian disagreement over, 370
Baltic provinces, 239, 240, 247, 254
Balzac, his *Comédie Humaine*, 25
Barsky, 67
Barthou, Louis, 205
Bassov, 157
Batoum, general strike and demonstration at, 37-8
Bauer, 65
Beaverbrook, 306
Beck, Colonel, 205, 221, 225, 230, 237
Belgium, invasion of, 249
Benès, 186, 214, 215, 219
Benkendorf, Count, 314

Béria, 76n., 172, 183, 193, 268, 294, 303, 319, 369, 398, 402; and atomic research, 396; demands end of purges, 187; becomes head of N.K.V.D., 188
Berlin blockade, 402
Berzine, General, 93, 202, 205, 214, 215, 227
Besochvili, Boudou, 52
Bessarabia, 239, 254
Bessedovsky, 159, 199
Bielienki, 153
Bielietzky, 67
Blucher, Marshal, 115; suicide of, 187
Blum, Léon, 229
Blumkin, Sacha, 165-6
Bock, Marshal von, 309, 318, 321
Bodnareanu, 382
Bogdanov, 89
Bogomolov, Alexander, 251
Bohlen, Charles, 204
Bolcheviki, 41
Bolsheviks, origin of, 41; Central Committee, Lenin's emphasis on, 40-1; and the Duma, 51, 63; in Baku, 57-8; living abroad, 59-60; their journals, 63; as small unknown group, 66; and Lenin's Theses and Manifesto, 69-71; as too weak, 74; and decision to remain in Soviet, 76-7; Seventh Pan-Russian Conference of, 81-3; and the army, 86-8; and riot of 3 July, 1917, 87-9; reviled in Russia, 89; Kerensky's treason charge against, 90; Sixth Congress of, 92-3; Central Committee of, for October Revolution, 93; and October Revolution, 95-101; surprised and uncertain after victory, 102-3; psychology of, 110; 'old guard' of, 138-9, 151-2, 170-1, 177-8; *see also* Communist Party and Social Democrats.
Bormann, Martin, 229
Bornholm, Russian occupation of, 392
Borodaievsky, 112
Boudou, Father, 29
Boutilsky, 19
Bradley, General Follet, 325
Bratman-Brodovsky, 200
Brdzola, 28-9
Brest-Litovsk, 92n., 105, 106
Brioukhanov, 93
Britain, and Arcos raid, 150; Arctic convoys of, 306; accused of treachery, 328, 329; and France, guarantees to

Poland, Roumania, and Greece, 230; and Poland, 367, 370; and Ribbentrop, 244, 269; and Russo-German pact, 277; and Germany, 214; Stalin's fear of agreement between, 202-3; and U.S.S.R., proposed loan to, 159; mission to, 1939, 235; treaty with, 318-19; and Persian oil, 213-14; and Mediterranean bases, 350; and 'world imperialism,' 331
Bubnov, 82, 93, 99
Budienny, 115, 296
Buffer States, 247
Buguslavsky, 152
Bukharin, Nicholas Ivanovitch, 65, 93, 111, 117, 126, 127, 134, 150, 155; and Lenin's Testament, 124; as member of Septet, 136; and Stalin's new dogma, 140-3; opposed to Stalin, 157-60; arrested by Iéjov, 183; trial of, 184
Bukovina, 254, 255, 271-2
Bulanov, 184
Bulganin, Marshal, 193, 369, 392, 404; as new theorist, 379
Bulgaria, 254-5, 273, 275, 277, 278, 280, 281-3; signs Tripartite Pact, 283; Russians enter, 358
Bureau of the Seven, 99
Bureaucracy, in U.S.S.R., 167, 409, 410-11
Busch, General von, 316
Byzantium, 12

                             C

Cadbury, Sir Laurence, 297
Cambay, Gulf of, 13
Capitalism, and state capitalism, 412
Carol, King, of Roumania, 214
Cassidy, 330
Catholic Church, and Orthodox Church, 363n.
Caucasus, cooking in, 64, 150; peasants in, 83; and Russia, 14-15, 34; separatism in, 322, 332
Cave of the Dead Mule, 126
Centralist Democrats, 117
Chakhty, trial of, 164
Chamberlain, Neville, 203, 207, 219, 220, 224, 230, 249; and Hitler, faked gramophone records of, 229
Chaoumian (Stiopa), 53-4, 56, 93, 94

Chapochnikov, 227, 228, 296, 297, 315, 321, 331, 340
Cheboldaiev, 161-2
Cherbakov, 172-3
China, 254, 357, 380, 381, 413
Chioumiatzky, 78
Chirinkin, 51, 56
Chliapnikov, 73, 108, 117
Christian Socialism, 26
Chtcherbakov, 219, 308
Church, see Orthodox Church.
Churchill, Winston, 195, 196, 247, 249, 251; and attack in Balkans, 355; and Bohemian-Moravian quadrilateral, 224-5; sends Cripps to Russia, 257-9; and Franco, 335; and Hitler, 202-3; at Kremlin banquet, 305; to Moscow, 1944, 258-9; and Ribbentrop, 269; and Roosevelt on Stalin, 385; Russian suspicion of, 214; at Teheran, 350-3; at Yalta, 368, 371-3, 375, 376, 377; and Stalin, 354; meeting with, 1942, 323-4; mutual incomprehension, 317; quarrel over Second Front, 328, 330; his understanding of, 229n.
Chvernik, 193, 303, 402
Chwartzev, 260, 269
Cities, renaming of, 127-8
Civil War, 107-9, 114-15
Clausewitz, 84, 228, 331
Collective security, 204
Collectivization, 157, 189, 360; first Five-year plan, 161-3; in wartime, 322
Collier, Air Vice-Marshal, 297
Comédie Humaine (Balzac), 25
Comintern, 125, 134, 150, 208, 303; dissolution of, 338-9
Commission for Circulars, 137-8, 145
Commissions, creation of, by Stalin, 137-8, 402
Committee of Safety of the Nation and the Revolution, 102
Communism, adaptation of, to Russia's national needs, 182
Communist Party, birth of, 79-80; title assumed, 107; threat of split, 1921, 116; resolution on unity, 118; exclusion of opposition members from, 152; living standard of members of, 169; change of membership basis of, 180; Stalin's definition of role of, in U.S.S.R., 189-90; in U.S.S.R., today, 409-10. Congresses: Eighth, 111; Tenth, 124-5; Thirteenth, 134; Four-

teenth, 145-6; Sixteenth, 160, 163; Seventeenth, 172; Eighteenth, 193, 230, 233; see also Bolsheviks and Social Democrats.
Communists, the complexes of, 149; French, 206
Confessions, need for, 177, 179, 180, 181, 188; Iagoda's extraction of, 167-8
Constituent Assembly, 102, 103, 104
Cossacks, in German forces, 322, 332
Cot, Pierre, 251
Cripps, Sir Stafford, 258, 276, 280, 282n., 291
Curzon line, 366-7
Cyrenaica, 350
Czechoslovakia, partition of, 214-21, 230, 233, 403

D

Daladier, Edouard, 219, 249
Danubian Commission, 262
Dardanelles, 305n.; see also Straits.
Defence Committee, 110
De Gaulle, 370-1
Deitsch, 174
Dekanozov, 219, 269, 290
Delevska, Vera, 304
Denikin, 114
Derbent, Treaty of, 14-15
Dernières Nouvelles, Les, 73n.
Dertinger, 406-7
Deviations, 41, 142
Didi-Lilo, 16
Dietl, General, 356
Dill, Sir John, 280
Dimitrov, George, 179
Divorce, 192
Djaparidzé (Aliocha), 56, 93, 94
Djibladzé, Silvester, 28, 35-6, 39
Djugachvili, etymology of, 13-14
Djugachvili, Ivan, 16
Djugachvili, Jossif, see Stalin.
Djugachvili, Vissarion-Bezo, 16-17, 21
Dnieper, barrage on, 163
Dobrudja, 254-5
Dodecanese, 350
Doenitz, Admiral, 391
Doriot, Jacques, 206
Dragonov, 238
Drobniss, 117, 152
Dubovitch, Major, 181

Dugadov, 157
Duma, formation of, 49, 63; Bolshevik deputies to, 61, 64; Committee of, 96; decision to boycott, 49-50; and Liberals, 51
Dumbarton Oaks, 358
Dybenko, 101, 103
Dzerjinski, 82, 93, 99, 108, 111, 117, 120, 126, 136, 146, 148

E

Eden, Anthony, 196, 203, 280, 358, 370; his wartime visit to Moscow, 312-14; and Stalin, 359
Egypt, and Georgia, 11
Eichenwald, 157
Eidemann, 186
Eisenhower, 371, 384, 391
Eismont, 157
Elizarov, Anna, 80
Emelianov, 90
Encirclement, Russian fears of capitalist, 141, 345, 380, 402-3
Ensiedler, 406
Epstein, 114, 157
Equality of pay, abandonment of, 142-3, 169, 193, 409-10
Esoteric dogma, of Stalin, 170-1, 193-4, 397
Esperanto, 57
European Commission, 254
Evdokinov, 126, 127, 180
Ewest, 238
Exile, nature of, 42, 57
Expropriations, for revolutionary funds, 53, 58

F

Fabricius, 231
Fabrikant, 99n.
Fascism, according to Molotov, 209
Fälz, Rittmeister von, 229
Family, re-instatement of, 192
Fédorov, 82
Feodor, Tsar, 14
Feuerbach, 28
Finkelstein, 54

Finland, 270, 271, 272, 277, 278; Mannerheim's defence of, 356; post-war independence of, 249
Five-year plans, 169-70, 284
Flandin, Etienne, 220
Foch, Marshal, 261
Food shortages, 108, 147
Foreign affairs, Stalin's extreme caution in, 197-8
Forty-six, group of the, 132
Fountikov, 94
France, and the Big Three, 345, 358, 370-1; and Britain, guarantees to Poland, Roumania and Greece, 230; and efforts at collective security, 205, 206; and Russia, 1940, 250-3; Stalin's opinion of her army, 244
Franco, and a separate peace, 334-7
Fraser, Admiral, 247
Fraser, Geoffrey, 251-2
French Committee of National Liberation, 345
Fuchs, 395n.
Frunzé, Michel, during Civil War, 114, 115; appointed to War Commissariat, 144; and partisans, 316; his death, 145

G

Gafenko, Gregor, 202, 231, 267, 274n., 275, 282n.
Galimbatovsky, 58
Galitzin, Prince, 15
Ganietzky, 77, 90
Gatchina, 101
Gavrilovitch, Milan, 282, 283
Genghis Khan, 13, 278
George VI, 329n.
George IV, of Georgia, 12
George XII, of Georgia, 15
Georgia, history of, vii, 11-15; danger of revolt in, 303; and Russia, 78
Georgian Orthodox Church, 363
Georgian and Russian languages, 19
German army, see Wehrmacht.
Germans, in U.S.S.R. in wartime, 298
Germany, her hopes of atom bomb, 352; and Bulganin's theses, 380; Control Commission in, 384; and expansion, 213; hopes of Russo-British clash, 358; Lenin's journey through, 77; mobilizes, 227; National Committee

of Free, 342; post-war future of, and Morgenthau, 350-1; and Russian hopes of revolution in, 106, 125-6, 133, 140, 200; Social Democracy in, 142; Stalin's pre-occupation with, 197, 201-3, 405-7; Stalin forsees danger of war with, 169; and Tripartite pact, 263; and Poland, treaty with, 204-6; partition of, 246-7; drawing of frontier with, 394; and Russia, balance between, 271; treaty with, 245; illusion of collaboration with, 267, 273-4, 275; start of war with, 292; removal of machinery from, 392

Ghavan-es-Saltane, 353, 401
Gibraltar, 335-6
Gibson, expelled by Russians from Bulgaria, 358
Glébov, 82
Goebbels, 340, 358, 366, 386
Goering, 205, 260, 304n.
Goglidzé, 56
Gogoberidzé, 37
Golochtchekin, 63
Golz, General von der, 230
Gori, 11, 13, 15-16, 18, 34, 46; theological college of, 20, 21, 22
Gorki, 119, 125
Gorki, Maxim, 133
Gotz, 95-6
Goudonov, Boris, 14
Goulichvili, General, 303n., 373, 392
Gourov, 56
Govorov, General, 363
G.P.U., foundation of, 118; and confessions, 167-8; as an integral part of Soviet State, 168; and Nepmen, 168; purge of officials of, 184; Stalin's statement over use of, for internal conflict, 151-2; see also N.K.V.D., and Tcheka.
Gramophone records, faked, 229
Greece, as remaining in British zone of influence, 359; and E.L.A., 359; discussed at Yalta, 377
Grey, Edward, 314
Grimm, Robert, 71
Grinko, 157; trial of, 184
Gromyko, 370, 387, 388
Gronov, 67
Grosovska, Lydia, 212
Grozea, 382
Guéladzé, Catherine Guéorguicona, 17, 18, 19, 21, 22, 34

Guerde, 70
Gulistan, Treaty of, 15
Gustave Le Bon, 201, 217

H

Halifax, Lord, 207, 220, 370
Harriman, Averell, 306, 323, 370, 387, 388
Haushofer, Karl, 213
Henlein, 214, 220
Heraclius II, 15
Herbette, Jean, 199
Hess, Rudolph, 213, 328
Hitler, 213, 227, 230, 243, 291; and hopes of atom bomb, 352; and Chamberlain, faked gramophone records of, 229; and Churchill, 202-3; concealment of his intentions, 278-9; confident about conquest of Russia, 288n.; and biggest German offensive, 341; and hesitations of 1940, 259-60, 261; his Mein Kampf, 231; and Molotov, 270-3; and a separate peace, 337; and Pilsudsky, 204, 205; and start of Russian war, 197-8; and Stalin, and the Balkans, 262-6; and Stalin, differences between, 248; Stalin's toast to, 245; his obstinacy at Stalingrad, 331
Hoare, Sir Samuel, 207, 335
Hodja, 220
Holland, invasion of, 249
Holy Place, 363
Hoo, Victor, 196
Hopkins, Harry, 303-4, 305-6, 387
Horne, Sir Robert, 159
Hugenberg, 203
Hull, Cordell, 336, 343, 346, 351
Hungary, 275, 279
Hydro-electric schemes, 413

I

Iablokov, André, 35
Iagoda, 129, 145, 153, 154, 158, 166, 171, 179; a careerist, 120; and 'confessions,' 167-8; Stalin's doubtful confidence in him, 173; and Kirov, 175, 176, 177; falls into disgrace, 181; arrest of, 184

Iakovlev, 93, 147, 150
Ibn Melek, 12
Iéjov, Nicolas, 101n., 109, 112n., 172, 223, 268; start of his career of purging, 176; his career as head of G.P.U., 182-8
Iénukidzé, 112; shooting of, 184-5
Ignatieva, Moussia, 112, 138
Ignatiev, Count, 363
Ilmen, Lake, 316
Iman Chamil, 15
Industrialization, 161, 163-5, 172; start of, 148, 150; and war, 155, 284-6, 340
Inequality of pay, 142-3, 169, 193, 409-10
I.N.O., 203, 205, 220, 224, 229, 248
Inonu, Ismet, 280, 349
International, revolutionary, proposed by Lenin, 82
International Court of Justice, 358
Internationale, 268
Iran, 11, 14, 313-14, 401; petrol concessions in, 353
Iremachvili, 52
Irkutsk, 43, 44
Iskra, 31, 35, 39, 48
Italy, 343; surrender of German army in, 384; red network in, 248; and Tripartite pact, 263; and U.S.S.R., 244
Ivan the Terrible (Ivan IV), 14
Ivanov, Michel, 148, 251
Ivanovitch, Joseph, 46
Izvestia, 13

J

Janin, General, 109
Japan, 278; and Germany and U.S.S.R., 243; defeat by Joukov, 239; and North Saghalie, 277; 'Red Dragon' in, 248; reluctance of U.S.S.R., to be drawn into war against, 330n., 346, 393; and Ribbentrop, 269; Russian attack on, 396; Russian pact with, 286-8; and Tripartite pact, 263; Tsar's war with, 43, 45; and war in Outer Mongolia, 192-3
Jdanov, 172, 193, 228, 236, 303, 397, 400, 404; and Finland, 248-9; and world socialism, 356-7
Jet aircraft, German, 351
Jews, of Portugal, 13-14

Jodl, General, 289, 351n.
Joffé, 93, 94, 152
Jordana, Count, 334, 336
Joukov, Marshal, 227, 263, 308, 339, 341, 356, 365, 366, 392; his campaign against Japanese, 239; his 'mud offensive,' 354; and Stalingrad, 327, 331; and war in Outer Mongolia, 192-3
Joukovsky, 67
Journal de Genève, 212n., 267n., 290n.

K

Kaburov, 157
Kaganovitch, Lazar, 153, 172, 183, 193, 297, 303, 402
Kaganovitch, Rosa, 222-3
Kalinin, Michel, 33, 63, 117, 126, 136, 146, 150, 155, 172, 183, 193, 376n., 381
Kalinin, city of, 308
Kamanev (Rosenfeld), 33, 45, 46, 64-5, 73, 74, 75, 76, 77, 78, 79, 80, 93, 97, 98, 105, 111, 117, 119, 125, 126, 149; warns Stalin against Lenin, 81; and Lenin, 82; his arrest, 89; his release, 95; and October Revolution, 99; and Lenin's Testament, 124; and Lenin's death, 131; and Trotzky's Lessons of October, 133; as member of Septet, 136; in opposition to Stalin, 144-6, 158, 159; excluded from party, 152, 153-4; sentenced to imprisonment, 174; sent to Yakutsk prison, 177; final trial and execution, 178-81
Kamchatka, 287
Kandeliaki, 37
Kanner, Gricha, 112, 122, 128, 129, 130n., 151, 157, 158, 168
Kapanadzé, 20, 131
Kapital, Das (Marx), 28
Kapitza, 396
Karakhan, 184, 211
Karanov, 145
Karganov, 68
Karlik, Oldrich, 122, 123
Karpinsky, 69
Karpov, 362
Karvazine, 56
Kasbek, Mount, 18
Kathov, 331
Katioushka, 286n.

Katochvili, 20-1
Katyn murders, 354-5
Katzenelbaum, 157
Kautsky, 70
Kazakov, Dr., 120
Kazan, 14
Kchesinskaia, 79
Kchessinska Palace, 83
Kerdag, 12
Kerensky, 92, 103; his offensive in the war, 86-8; his treason charge against Bolsheviks, 90; and Bolshevik coup, 95-6, 100-1
Kerr, Sir Archibald, 329
Ketschkoyeli, 31
Kharkov, Russian defeat at, 318-19
Khimki, 311
Khintchouk, 207
Khmarovka, 63
Khondiskov, Air Marshal, 369
Khronstalev-Nossar, 48
Khroustchev, 193
Kikichvili, 34
Kikinadzé, 34
Kirov, Serge, 146, 171, 172, 174; a favourite of Stalin's, 153; and Iagoda's dossier on him, 175; assassination of, 175-6
Kislovodsk, 126
Kissel, 93
Kletskaia, 322
Klugge, Von, 341
Knatchbull-Hugessen, Sir Hugh, 277
Knight in the Panther's Skin, The (Roustaveli), 20
Koba, *see* Stalin.
Koliantz, Anastasius, 18
Kolkhozes, 162, 163, 167, 169, 409; wartime 'emancipation' of, 360-1
Kollontaï, Alexandra, 93, 94, 117, 252, 336-7
Kolobov, 158
Kolotov, 43
Kolpatchevo, 63
Kolpov, 61
Koltchak, Admiral, 109
Komorovsky, General Bor, 367
Koniev, 311
Königsberg, 394
Korea, 402
Kork, 186
Kornilov, General, 96
Koslovsky, 248
Kossiguin, 193, 233, 303

Kostino, 68
Kotschkoveli, 30, 39
Koudriavtzev, 381n.
Kouratchi, 18
Kournatovsky, Victor, 31, 32, 35, 39
Koussiki, Prince, 15
Koutaïss, dictatorship of, by Stalin, 51
Kozmine, 89
Kraft und Stoff (Burchener), 28
Krantz-Vientzov, 185, 186
Krassevsky, Col., 369
Krassin, Leonid, 35, 49, 53, 54, 110, 150; demands abolition of State control, 116
Krassnoiarsk, 71
Krassnov, General, 101, 109
Krebs, 288n.
Kremlin, fearful, and as source of fear, 204; banquets, 305, 324; Stalin's residence in, 112
Krestinsky, 93, 111, 116; arrested by Iéjov, 183; trial of, 184
Krivitzky, General, 186n., 202, 205; assassination of, 212
Kronstadt, 74; revolt at, 117
Kroutikov, 289
Krumin, 136-7
Krupskaia, 64, 84, 99, 129, 130, 149; Stalin's rudeness to her, 123; and Lenin's Testament, 132-3
Krymov, 96
Kuban, 108, 322
Kubeltzin, S., 396
Kuibchev, city of, 325
Kuibychev, 148, 150, 172
Kulaks, 136, 143, 161-2, 294
Kurdiani, 25
Kureika, 68
Kvali, 30

L

Labour camps, 191
Lachévitch, 126
Laptakinsky, 30
Laski, Harold, 401
Latvia, 239
Laurent, Ferdnand, 252
Laval, Pierre, 206, 352n.
Lavrov, Captain, 38-9
Lazarev, 71, 149
Leipa, 112

Leipzig Fair, 210
Lend-lease, 298, 303, 339; end of, 386
Lenin, and Marx and Labour movement, 30-1; his conception of Professional Revolutionaries, 32; in London, 39-41; in Switzerland, 48; in Finland, 51; and need for money for revolution, 53; and clandestine Politburo, 62; and *Lumpenproletariat*, 59; in Poronino, 63-5, 67; his 'Theses' and 'Manifesto,' 69-71; his return to Russia, 77, 78-9; his theses of 4 April, 1917, 80-3; as a speaker, 83-4; and Trotzky, 53, 84-5, and riot of 3 July, 1917, 88-90; and Bolshevik coup of October 1917, 97-8, 99; his early uncertainty, 102-3, and Brest-Litovsk, 106; and dangers of party split, 1921, 116-17; his illness, 119-20; and question of successor, 122-3; his Testament, 124, 132-3; his death, 129-30; his funeral, 131-2; deification of, 134, 147; his name as touchstone, 158-9; and government of proletarian state, 399;
  and Stalin, his opinion of, 16, 57, 60; Stalin's staunch support of, 30-2, 46; and 'the miraculous Georgian,' 35, 46; and riot at Batoum, 38; first letter to, 42-3; and Stalin's articles, 48; first meeting with, 49-50; letter from, 52; comparison with, 61; meeting with, 1912, 63-5; congratulates Stalin and Molotov on *Pravda*, 66
Leningrad, 356
Leninism, abandonment of, 142
Leontiev, 381n.
Lepa, 174
Lialin, 57
Liberalism, danger of loss of, in West, 412n., 415
Liberty, diverging views on, 306
Lielioushenko, General, 311
Lifchitz, 152
Life of the Nationalites, The, 107
Lithuania, 239, 247
Litvinov, 233, 322; and Tiflis robbery, 54; and collective security, 206, 208, 231; and Czechoslovakia, 225, 226; and Molotov, their conflicting policies, 1938, 213-17, 218; displaced by Molotov, 235, 240n.; return of, 298; as Ambassador to U.S.A., 317, 346

Lobov, 64
Loika, Stanislas, 332
Loiko, Ivan Stepanovitch, 67
Lomadzé, 37
Lomakin, 294
Lomov, 93
Lukasievitch, 226
Lumpenproletariat, and Stalin, 59
Lutovinov, 117
Lvov, Prince, 73, 75

M

Mabelski, Captain, 51
MacArthur, General, 393
MacFarlane, Lieutenant-General Mason, 297
Magaliantz, 37
Maïsky, 214, 233, 234, 304, 317, 348
Makarov, Ivan, 68
Makarovka, 44
Makrou, Tatar general, 13
Malenkov, Stepan, 38, 112, 113, 193, 219, 303, 369, 397, 398, 402; his emergence into prominence, 233, 236, 241
Malik, Jacob, 286, 357n.
Malinovsky, 64
Maltchikov, 158
Manifesto (Lenin), 69
Mannerheim, Marshal, 272n., 356
Mannstein, General von, 322, 331, 332, 341, 342
Manouilsky, Dimitri, 143, 150
Mardalian, 15
Maretzky, 157
Markov, 31
Markovitch, 282
Marranos, 13-14
Marshall, General, 371, 393
Marshall Plan, 403
Martov, 76, 104, 149
Martynov, Colonel, 56, 61, 62
Marx, Karl, 28, 30-1; his name as touchstone, 158-9; and social equality, 142
Marxism, Post-war resuscitation of, 379-81; Stalin's abandonment of, 382n., 412, 413, 414
Maslov, Colonel, 224, 334, 335
Matsuoka, 286-8
Mauriac, François, 218n.
Maximalists, 51

Mdivani, Prince, 33, 152
Medvied, 171
Medveviev, 117
Mekhliss, 112, 122, 123, 127, 132, 135, 140, 150, 151, 153, 154, 155, 177, 178, 179, 228; and deification of Stalin, 170
Memel, 271
Menjinsky, 150, 166, 167; and party discipline, 153-4; his death, 173
Mensheviks, 48, 51, 54, 61, 63, 76, 78, 89, 104, 109, 137
Merekalov, 215, 218, 234, 235
Meretzkov, 296
Merkoulov, 319
Mexico, red network in, 248
Miasnedov, 117
Michael, of Roumania, 382
Miedviedev, 64
Miejlaouk, Ivan, shot by Iéjov, 184
Mikhailov, 112
Mikoyan, 153, 172, 183, 193, 250, 279, 289, 297, 303, 336, 337, 369, 402
Miliutin, 82, 93
Military caste, creation of in U.S.S.R., 342
Miliukov, 73; his attack on Empress, 217
Mins, Admiral, 297
Mirbach, Von, 165
Mirinov, 157
Mirkin, Captain, 398n., 414n.
Mithridates VI, King, 12
Mokadzé, 34
Molotchkov, 45
Molotov, Viatcheslav Skriabin, 73, 76, 119, 122, 134, 145, 150, 172, 193, 255, 259, 279, 280, 287, 313, 323, 391, 398, 399; start of his career, 66, 67; and Stalin, early alliance of, 74-5; and Twelfth Congress, 125; as member of Septet, 136; appointment as Foreign Commissar, 198; and 'the third phase of world capitalism,' 208-9, 277; and Litvinov, their conflicting policies, 1938, 213-17, 218; and partition of Czechoslovakia, 230; displaces Litvinov, 235; and Germany, 231-2, 233, 237, 240, 241-3; and partition of Poland, 246; and Swedish neutrality, 250; and the Balkans, 261-6; in Berlin, 267-74; popular dislike of his policy, 281; and outbreak of war, 293-4; as Stalin's Harry Hopkins, 303; his visit to London, 1942, 317-18; and ratification of the treaty with Britain,

319; and Italy, 343; and Stalin, differences between, 354, 388; in Warsaw, 357n.; and Yalta, 369, 370, 374, 375, 376, 377, 379; and Poland, 382-3; and U.N.O., 387, 403; at Potsdam, 394; and Berlin blockade, 402; and Post-War Politburo, 404
Molotov Plan, 403
Mongols, 13
Montgomery, Field Marshal, 391, 394
Montreux Convention, 255, 349
Morgenthau, his plan for Germany, 350-1
Moscow, as inheritor of Byzantium, 14; Bolshevik Government transferred to, 107; food shortage in, 108; first offensive against, 308; second attack on, 310-11
Mossadeq, 353n.
Mosslov, Lieut., 58
Motpulk system, 321
Moukha, 63
Mouradiantz, see Stalin.
Mouravieff brothers, 25-6, 27
Mratchkovsky, 180
Muralov, 93
Mussolini, 244

N

Napoleon, 84, 304
Narofominsk, 310
Nationalities, Commissariat of, 105, 107-8
Nationalities, Stalin on, 65, 69
Nauheim circle, 406-7
Naumann, Friedrich, 213
Nazeretian, 138n., 151
N.E.P. (New Economic Policy), 117
Nepmen, and G.P.U., 168
New Life, The, 46
New Times, The, 46
New Year celebrations, 64
Nicholas II, Tsar, 22, 49, 79
Nicolaev, 176
Nicoll, 229
Nijeradzé, David, 43
Nikitin, General, 279
N.K.V.D., 411; and army, 362; formation of, 183; as partisans, 316; see also G.P.U., and Tcheka.

Noak, Prof., 406
Noguin, 82, 93
Norway, 249
Novaia-Ouda, 41, 42
Novorossisk, 322
Nuschke, Otto, 406
Nystad, Treaty of, 14

O

Ockanozov, 326
Ogpu, *see* G.P.U.
Oktiabrsky, 268
Olminsky, 142
Oltramare, Georges, 229
Ordjonikidzé, 62, 91, 126, 127, 150, 157,
    172; and the purges, 177-8; his
    suicide, 178
Ordjonikidzé, town of, 322
Orgburo, Stalin's representatives on,
    122; and Politburo, 127
Orlov, 67
Orthodox Church, Stalin's knowledge
    of, 28; Stalin drops campaign against,
    169, 192; in wartime, 299-300; post-
    war liberal attitude toward, 362-3, 381
Orthodox Georgian Church, 14, 15, 17,
    22, 52
Ossetes, 13, 15, 22, 68
Ouborévitch, 186
Ouglanov, 153
Oulitzkaia, Rosa, 112
Oumansky, 248, 325, 326, 368
Ouritzky, 93, 99
Our Life, 46
Oussor-Te-Sen I, 11

P

Pacificism, 70
Paltchinsky, execution of, 164
Pan-Russian Congress of Soviets, and
    Bolshevik coup, 104
Panslavism, 363-4
Panteliev, 46
'Papalists,' 30-1
Papen, von, 349
Papi-Sineh, 11
Partisans, first use of Russian, and
    strategy of use of, 316

Pastukhov, 173
Paul, Prince Regent of Yugoslavia, 282
Paul I, Tsar, 15
Paulus, General von, 318, 406; surrender
    of, 331, 332
Pavlov, 227, 248, 373, 374
Payot, René, 267n.
Peasants, 116, 118
People's Commissars, title suggested by
    Stalin, 105
Persia, *see* Iran.
Pestkovsky, 87, 105, 107-8, 113, 116
Peter the Great, 14
Peterson, 173
Petlura, 114
Petrograd, 77; food shortage in, 108;
    threatened by White Russians, 113-14
Petrograd Soviet, 74, 75, 76, 80, 96, 102
Petrossian, 33, 54
Petrovsky, 64, 125, 153, 155, 172, 183,
    187
Pharmavaz, King, 11, 12
Phil, Commander Paul, 326
Piatakov, 93, 129, 132, 142, 146, 148;
    and Lenin's Testament, 124; excluded
    from party, 152; arrested by Iéjov,
    183; trial of, 184
Piatnitzky, 150
Pick, Wilhelm, 342
Pikel, 180
Pilar von Pilschau, 176-7
Pilsudski, 114, 204-5
Plekhanov, 31, 70
Ploesti oilfields, 376
Pobiedonoszev, 331
Poison, and the Georgian court, 12;
    Lenin's, 125, 129-30; Stalin's interest
    in, 120
Poland, war against Russia, 114-15; and
    Germany, treaty between, 204-6; pro-
    posed partition of, 237; partition of,
    246-7; Anders' Legion, 314; and hatred
    of U.S.S.R., 314n.; and Katyn mur-
    ders, 354-5; formation of Provisional
    National Committee, 355; and Rus-
    sian frontier, 366-7, 394; and Col.
    Krassevsky, 369-70; Yalta discussion
    of, 372, 373-4; and Yalta decisions,
    382-4
Polietaiev, 64
Politburo, formation of clandestine,
    62-3; founding of, 82; after October
    revolution, 107; 1919, 111; and Org-
    buro, 127; Stalin's representatives on,

122; opposition to Stalin's control of, 127-8; and Frunzé, 144; 1925, 146; 1927, 153; 1934, 172; 1939, 193; and Stalin, post-war divergence of, 315, 357, 369, 379, 383, 398, 402; and Yalta, 368-9, 379; and Bulganin's theses, 381, 386; and Harry Hopkins, 387; post-war intransigence of, 391; decision that members may not be ministers, 403-4; abolition of, 416-17

Politics, and war, 84

Polkolnikov, Colonel, 100

Polovtzev, General, 89

Pompey, 12

Popov, 112

Popular Front, first exposition of, 125

Poronino, 64, 67

Poskrebychev, General, 112, 228, 369, 414

Potemkin, mutiny on, 48

Potemkin, Vladimir, 219, 224, 225

Potsdam Conference, 388-9, 390-5

Prague Conference, 1911, 62

Pravda, 63, 67, 74, 80, 110, 116, 140, 143, 151, 170, 328, 329, 332; Molotov's work for, 66; Stalin as editor of, 65

Pravdin, 82

Pre-parliament, 98, 100

Preiss, 220

Préobrajensky, 93, 116, 146; excluded from party, 152; trial of, 184

Printing-presses, secret, 37, 58

Proletarian, 97

Provisional Government, 73, 75, 80, 87, 89; end of, 100-1

Prussia, 350; East, 394

Purges, 174, 176, 179, 183-8; early cases of, in Georgia, 11; the first, 118

Pushkin, 40

Putna, 186

Q

Quebec, Conference of, 345-6

R

Radek, Karl, 106, 143, 146; excluded from party, 152; and the G.P.U., 153-4; and Trotzky's letter, 165; and Stalin's deification, 170; arrested by

Iéjov, 183; trial of, 184, 185; betrays Tutkatchevsky, 186

Radescu, 382

Rado, Rudolph, 248n., 335n.

Radovsky, 146

Rakovsky, 71; excluded from party, 152; arrested by Iéjov, 183; trial of, 184

Ramzin, trial of, 164

Raskolnikov, 198-9

Ratner, 96

Razvedoupr, 202, 205, 210, 220, 248

Red Army, 263, 301, 302, 310, 316, 321, 322, 371; formation of, 107; modernization of, 151, 155, 156; as a national one, 191; and war with Japan in Outer Mongolia, 192-3; strategy of, 327; assumption of offensive, 341-2; final superiority of, 351; restoration of degree of liberalism in, 362; morale in, 365; Stalin's direct contact with, 369

Redenss, 112, 173, 184

Red networks, creation of, 248

Red Orchestra, 248, 280-1, 291, 308, 321, 352

Red Sailors, salon of, 112, 138

Reiss, Ignace, 210, 212

Renner, Karl, 65

Reparations, 375, 377; Stalin's ideas on, 348

Revolution, Russian, and Tiflis students, 24; Lenin's early conception of, 32; planning of, in London, 40-1; general desire for, in Russia, 45; gradual advance of, 48; dying down of, 50-1; start of, 71-2; social vacuum after, 408

Revolutionaries, Order of Professional, 169; Lenin's concept of, 32; and 'deviation,' 41; as organizers of revolutionary dictatorship, 47; at home and abroad, 61; task of today, 409

Revolutionary Council of War, 106-7

Revolutionary hymn, 34

Revolutionary Military Committee, 86, 100

Revolutionary movement, Georgian, 30

Revolutionary Socialist Party, 89, 97, 104n., 109

Reynaud, Paul, 249, 250-2

Riabko, 20

Riga, capture of, by Germans, 96; Treaty of, 115

Ribbentrop, 198, 202, 203, 237, 241, 264,

279, 291; conversations with Stalin, 243-5; tries to tempt Stalin, 253-4; protests to Russia, 260; his stupidity, 261; and Molotov, 269-70, 273-4; and Matsuoka, 287-8; and a separate peace, 337; in Finland, 356
Rodimtzer, General, 188
Rodzianko, General, 113
Rokossovsky, Marshal, 188, 367
Romanoffs, 217
Rommel, his Afrika Corps, 323
Roosevelt, 195, 196; and Churchill, 368; and colonial régimes, 353; as mediator between Churchill and Stalin, 325; and Poland, 366n., 383; and Stalin's demand for a second front, 318, 323, 326; and Stalin, 338-9, 343, 344, 346-50, 353, 358, 384-6; and U.S.S.R.'s reluctance to war against Japan, 346; at Yalta, 368, 372, 373-5, 376, 377; his death, 385
Rosenfeld, Leon, 33; see also Kamenev.
Rosenfeld, Moïse, 173-4
Rostoptchin, 138n.
Rostov on the Don, 322
Roubtzova, Lera, 112, 138
Roumania, 214, 259, 261, 262, 275, 382; importance of her petrol to Germany, 224, 231, 260; German military mission to, 264-5
Roustaveli, Chota, 20
Rozmirovitch, 64
Rudzutak, 119, 136
Runciman, 218
Russia, and Caucasus, 14-15, 34; annexation of Georgia, 15; granting of Constitution by Nicholas II, 49; and Japan, 43, 45; as traditionally Germanophobe, 217; stirring of revolution in, 35; see also U.S.S.R.
Russian and Georgian languages, 19
Russians, innate suspiciousness of, 368
Rybeieff, 25
Rykov, 82, 93, 134, 144, 150, 159, 160; his opinion of Stalin, 52; as member of Septet, 136; arrested by Iéjov, 183; trial of, 184

S

Saghalien, 277, 286, 287
Salski, 157
Samirlov, 67

Sanders, General Liman von, 230
San Francisco, 387
Sapronov, 117, 152
Saradjoglou, 230
Sarkiss, 152
Scandinavia, 356
Schmidt, Hitler's interpreter, 272n.
Schmidt, W., 157
Schnurre, 239, 241, 250, 279
Schulenburg, 237, 240, 241, 246, 259, 261, 275, 277, 280, 290, 291
Scobie, General, 359
Scorched earth policy, 299
Second front, beginning of misunderstanding over, 297; lack of, as a deliberate intrigue, 330n.; demanded by Stalin, 305-6, 312, 317-18, 319, 322-6, 328-30, 351-2; launching of, 355
Secret weapons, 285; German, 351-2
Seidlitz, General von, 342, 406
Semenova, 211
Serebriakov, 111, 116, 183
Sestrorietzk, 90
Sheridan, Claire, 126-7
Siberia, nature of exile to, 42-3, 63
Siedov, Léon, 173, 210, 212
Simon, Sir John, 207
Simonov, I., 180
Singapore, 288
Sinilov, General, his conspiracy against Stalin, 185, 186
Skoda works, 234, 235, 279, 291
Skriabin, Viatcheslav, see Molotov.
Skrypnik, 93, 94, 176
Slavs, and Teutons, historic conflict of, 201
Slepkov, 157
Slovakia, 275
Smeliansky, 157
Smilga, 82, 93, 152
Smirnov, L., 111, 117, 152, 180
Smirnov, V., 152
Smolensk, 302
Smolny Institute, 104
Smutny, Colonel, 185
Social Democracy, 78-9
Social Democrats, 31, 32, 34, 37, 38, 39, 40; Congresses, 1903, 401; 1905, 47; 1907, 53; 1908, 51; see also Bolsheviks and Communist Party.
Socialism, in one country, 141-3
Sokolnikov, 93, 94, 99, 111, 183, 184
Sokolovsky, 302

Soloytchegodsk, 57, 59
Soong, T. V., 196
Sorge, his Red Dragon, 248
Sousslov, 112
Soviets, first formation of, 48
Soviet system, 117
Spain, and a separate peace, 334-5
Spandarian, 63, 68, 69, 71
Stakhanovism, 167, 284
Stalin, Jossif Djugachvili, Koba, David Nizeradzé, Bars (Leopard), Joseph Ivanovitch, Boudou Besochvili, David Tchijikov, Oganess Vastanovitch, Totomiantz, Mouradiantz, Lado Doumbadzé, Papadjanian, Stepan Papadopoulos, Piotr Galkine, the individual and the legend, v-vi; his historic task, vii, 415; birth, 11, 17; origin of his clan, 13-14; his home, 18-19; his early learning of Russian, 19; his appearance and physique, 19, 21-2, 28, 42; early experience of social injustice, 20-21; his fondness of singing, 15-16, 21, 22, 113; as pupil of theological college, 21-2; adopts name of Koba, 22, 28-9; at Tiflis seminary, 24-9; development of his character, 27; decision to become a revolutionary, 27; as organizer of clandestine group, 28-9; at Tiflis observatory, 30-3; early example of his intractability, 36; his first marriage, 46; Stalin first suggested as pseudonym, 50; as dictator of Koutaïss, 51; death of his first wife, 52-3; arrest and imprisonment in Baku, 56-9; as a journalist, 48, 63, 65, 97; arrest and deportation, 63; as a cook, 64, 150; as a drinker, 65; adoption of name Stalin, 65; arrest in St. Petersburg, 67-8; in exile, 68-72; and riot of 3 July, 1917, 88-9, 92; his second marriage, 90-1, 112; his hesitations, 75, 95; and coup of October 1917, 98-100; obscurity of his activities after coup, 103; becomes Commissar for Nationalities, 105, 107-8; at Tsaritzin, 108-9; becomes Commissar for State Control, 111; and attack on Petrograd, 113-14; and Polish war, 114-15; as head of N.E.P., 118-19; elected Secretary-General, 119; taps telephones, 122-3; is rude to Krupskaia, 123; his Commission for the Circulars, 137-8; and economic difficulties, 1926, 147-8; the peculiar character of his dictatorship, 161; as 'Little Father,' 163; his warning to engineers, 164; his address on his fifty-fourth birthday, 168-9; his letter to the Komsomolietz Ivanov, 170-1; his ruthlessness, 172; tries to justify purges to Ordjonikidzé, 177-8; stops purge, 188; at sixty, 191; his sixth sense, 193, 194, 196; his intransigence, 196-7; his traditional ideas on women, and his third marriage, 222-3; his aloofness from events, 231-2, 236, 237; distrustful of West, 233; compared with Tsar Alexander I, 256-7; and approach of war, 266; his 'Juridical' methods, 278; appoints himself supreme executive, 290; and outbreak of war, 292-302; his excellent memory, 304; as an actor, a negotiator, and host, 304-5; his anniversary speech, 1941, 309-10; and use of partisans, 316; sends his daughter to U.S.A., 317; as a catalysing agent, 327; and safeguarding equilibrium, 345; and economic changes, 1943, 360; and deterioration of his health, 393, 397, 398, 414; his semi-retirement, 398-400; made Generalissimo, 401; and Berlin blockade, 402; his interventions in direction of peace, 404-5; and peaceful cohabitation, 413, 417; as he is today, 414-15;
and atom bomb, 395, 396
and Bolsheviks, abroad, 59-60; and 'old guard, 138-9, 151-4
and Britain, opinion of, 244; fear of influence of, in Balkans, 306-7; and treaty with, 319-20
and the Church, 28; drops campaign against, 192;
and Churchill, compared with, 195; mutual incomprehension of, 317; meeting with, 1942, 323-4; quarrel with, over Second Front, 328, 330; at Yalta, 371-2, 375, 377;
deification of, beginning of, 170-1; apotheosis of, 193-4;
and Eden, 312-14, 359;
and Finland, 249;
and foreign affairs, study of, 196-7, 198-200; his method in, 223-4, 226-7, 235;
and France, 206-7, 250-3;

and Ghavan-es-Saltane, 353n., 401;
and Germany, preoccupation with, 197-8, 200-3, 405-7; and German-Poland treaty, 204-6; and treaty with Germany, 236-45; and German temptations to act in East, 254; deceived by, 291-2;
and Hitler, and the Balkans, 262-6; differences between, 248;
and Harry Hopkins, 303-4, 305-6;
and industry, 164, 284-6;
and Japan, 286-8;
and Kerensky, 90;
and Lenin, first letter from, 43; as staunch supporter of, 46; first meeting with, 49-50; Lenin's opinion of him, 57; first hint of challenge to leadership, 60; meeting with, 1912, 63-5; supports Theses and Manifesto, 70-1; and Theses of 4 April, 1917, 80-1; Kamenev warns him against, 81; his alliance with, 81; as his personal assistant, 116-17; and his Testament, 124, 132-4; and his poison, 125; and his death, 129-30; and his funeral, 131-2, 134-5; difference between, 190;
and Litvinov, 1938, 208-9, 213-21;
and Lumpenproletariat, 59
and military strategy, study of, 228-9, 302-3; personal command at Moscow, 310-11; assumes supreme command, 315, 332; and war strategy, 321-2, 339-40, 354, 365-6;
and Molotov, 66, 74-5, 208-9, 213-21, 388, 394;
and Poland, 246-7
and Politburo, early opposition to him on, 127-9; 157-60, 165, 173-4; and later split over foreign affairs, 357, 368-9, 379, 383-4, 388-9, 398
and Ribbentrop, 243-5;
and Roosevelt, 326, 338-9, 343, 344, 346-50, 353, 372, 373-5, 376, 384-6;
and Rykov, 52
and socialism in one country, 140-3;
and Trotzky, first impressions of, 53-4, 84-5; first quarrel with, 86; feud and struggle with, 97, 99-100, 110-11, 148-54, 210-11, 212n.;
and U.S.A., awareness of strength of, 276-7
and U.S.S.R., definition of Communist Party's rôle in, 189-90; his theory of government of, 167; his

theory of unity of leadership, military and civil, 228, 302; and post-war changes in government, 399-401, 403-404;
and Zinoviev, 144-5, 148-54
Stalin, Basil, 369
Stalingrad, naming of, 127; Battle of, 327-8, 331
Staritza, 316
Stassen, 405
Stassova, 85, 93, 111
State Control, Stalin becomes Commissar for, 111
Steklov-Nakhamkes, 76
Stettinius, 196, 370, 373n., 374, 386; on Stalin, 383
Stetzki, 157
Stiopa, see Chaoumian.
Stockholm, Unification Congress, 1908, 51
Stolypin, 59
Stoyadinovitch, 282
St. Petersburg, Stalin at, 66-72
Straits, Bosphorus, Dardanelles, 258, 273, 277, 349, 393
Strikes, and revolution, 30, 32
Sukhum, 131
Suner, Serrano, 334
Suritz, 233
Svanidzé, Catherine, 33, 46, 52-3
Sverdlov, 63, 65, 68, 74, 76, 82, 87, 90, 93, 99, 105, 110, 112, 117, 120
Svetlana, Stalin's daughter, 317, 338
Sweden, 14, 249
Switzerland, Lenin in, 45; red network in, 248, 334, 335n.; see also Red Orchestra.
Syrtzov, 132, 133

T

Tabakov, 174
Tamerlane, 13
Tammersfors, 49-50
Tanner, 90
Tatars, 13
Tauber, Peter, 248n.
Taurid Palace, 88, 89, 104n.
Taxation, 410
Tchaadaieff, 26, 27, 190
Tcheidze, 73, 78, 79, 88, 96-7
Tcheka, 63, 108, 118, 148, 182; see also G.P.U. and N.K.V.D.

Tcherbakov, 193
Tchijikov, David, 54
Tchoubar, 153, 172, 183, 187
Technical achievement, 285-6
Teheran Conference, 287n., 243-53, 388
Telephones, Stalin's tapping of first, 122
Telescope, 25, 26
Teniani, 50
Ter-Vaganian, 180
Teschen, 221
Testament, of Lenin, 124, 132-3
Theodorovitch, 82
Thermal bomb, 332
Theses (Lenin), 69
Third International, 119
Tiflis, 22, 35, 46; seminary at, 23, 24-9;
    Observatory at, 30, 31; May Day
    demonstration, 1901, 32-4; Stalin's
    return to, 45; treasury robbery of, 54
Tiger tanks, 340, 341
Tigg-Johns, Capt., 94
Tikhomirova, 325
Times, The, Bolshevik organ, 46
Timoshenko, 109, 227, 263, 267-8, 281,
    283, 294, 296, 308, 318, 326, 339, 341,
    369
Tioutchev, 331
Tippelskirch, 263
Tito, 358-9, 378, 404
Tolboukhin, Marshal, 363
Tomsky, 128, 134, 136, 144, 155, 159,
    160, 183
Torstukha, 145
Totomiantz, Oganess Vartanovitch, 55
Toula, 108, 308
Toustoukha, 112, 122, 216
Transylvania, 261
Trials, 180, 184
Tripartite Pact, 263, 269, 275, 276
Troglodytes, Conference of, 126; Third
    Conference of, 178
Trotzky, 46, 48, 150n.; his opinion of
    Lenin, 53; and fate of Central Com-
    mittee members, 83; joins the Bol-
    sheviks, 84-5; his arrest, 89; and
    Kerenzky's treason charge against
    Bolsheviks, 90; and Sixth Congress,
    93; his release, and election as president
    of Petrograd Soviet, 97; and October
    Revolution, 98-100, 104, 106; be-
    comes Commissar for Foreign Affairs,
    105; appointed Commissar for De-
    fence, 107; and the Kronstad revolt,
    117; his 'Tzektrauss,' 117; and Lenin's

illness, 119; his hopes of revolution in
    Germany, 125-6; and Lenin's Testa-
    ment, 124, 133-4; and Lenin's funeral,
    131; his The Lessons of October, 133;
    his policy of world revolution con-
    demned, 134-5; 'a Menshevik' accord-
    ing to Stalin, 140-1; and the new
    dogma, 142, 143, 146; removed from
    War Commissariat, 143-4; excluded
    from party, 152; and the G.P.U., 153-
    4; exile of, 160; labelled 'Judas,'
    185; and the West, 196; assassination
    of, 93, 212; and Stalin, 65, 109, 110-
    11; Stalin's first impressions of him,
    53-4; and Stalin's support of Lenin,
    82; first quarrel between, 86; and
    Stalin's attitude to Lumpenproletariat,
    59; and Stalin's control of the Polit-
    buro, 127-9; and Stalin's treatment of
    'Old Bolsheviks,' 139; alliance with
    Zinoviev against Stalin, 148-50; and
    opposition to Stalin, 158, 165-6, 173;
    and Stalin's 'betrayal of the Revolu-
    tion,' 182-3; and fresh campaign
    against Stalin, 210-11; and Stalin's
    first marriage, 222
Troud, 245, 247
Troyanovsky, 64, 65
Truman, 386, 393, 395
Tsaritzin, 108, 109, 127
Tserétéli, 88
Tsouloukidzé, Sasha, 28, 30, 31
Tukhatchevsky, 114, 115, 151, 158,
    185-6
Tuponidzé, 41
Turkey, 244, 270, 273, 277-8, 349; aban-
    dons Bulgaria, 280; impressed by
    Germany, 355; red network in, 248;
    and Russia, 393
Tzektrauss, 117
Tzvertkovich, 282

U

Uglanov, 157
Ukraine, separatism in, 374
Ulitzkaia, Rosa, 138
Unconditional surrender, 343
United Nations Organization, 403; early
    Russian interest in, 345; and Dumbar-
    ton Oaks, 358; Stalin's support of,
    378; and veto question, 373, 375, 376,
    387, 388

Ural, conspiracy in, 174
United States of America, 271; impatient at Russian intransigence, 197; Baltic population in, 240; Stalin's awareness of its strength, 276-7; and Russian demand for second front, 317; aid to Russia, 334*n.*; increasing friendliness to, of U.S.S.R., 338; as Russian ideal of technical accomplishment, 344; Poles in, 372; and U.S.S.R., possibility of war between, 404
U.S.S.R., distortion of early history of, v-vi; foundation of, 120-1; proportion of public and private sections of economy, 136-7; and outside world, 150-1; and proposed loan from Britain, 159; and danger of war with Germany, 169; new constitution of, 1936, 180; consolidation of the State, 189; pessimism of, about Germany, 203; fear of capitalist alliance against, 203, 204, 205; signing of treaty with Germany, 245; anti-German feeling in, 246; and France, 1940, 250-3; and Germany, illusion of collaboration, 267, 273-4, 275; and Germany, balance between, 271; budget for 1941, 284-5; pact with Japan, 286-8; start of war with Germany, 292; patriotic nature of the war, 298-9; and impact of war, 301; and Poland, 314*n.*; treaty with Britain, 318-19; reluctance to be drawn into the war against Japan, 346; and Poland, and Katyn murders, 354-5; wartime relaxation of authoritarianism, 360; gifts of peasants to State, 361; frontiers of, 312-13, 350, 366, 374; demand of masses for higher standard of living, 375-6, 397; and anti-American policy, 386; and Turkey, 393; and atomic research, 396; monetary reform in, 403; and possibility of war with U.S.A., 404; post-war state of government of, and changes in, 399-401, 403-4; present international policy of, 412; today, 408

V

VI, and V2, weapons, 352*n.*
Vandenburg, Senator, 162*n.*
Vendervelde, 70

Vessilevsky, 32, 327, 339, 341
Vatican, 380
Vavilov, 396
Vazov, 66
Verba, 157
Viazma, 308
Viburg, 61, 74
Victory banquet, 296*n.*, 299
Vienna, 65
Violence, Lenin's justification of, 70
Vishinsky, Andrei, 46, 262, 344*n.*; as public prosecutor, 178, 211; and Roumania, 382; at Yalta, 373
Vlassov, General, 311
Voikov, assassination of, 151
Voldarskaia, Ida, 112, 138
Voroneje, 322
Voronov, 331, 340, 341
Voroshilov, Klementi, 51, 108, 109, 110, 126, 127, 146, 150, 151, 158, 172, 186, 187, 193, 219, 223, 227, 236, 240, 241, 296, 303, 326, 369, 402
Voroshilovsk, 322
Voznossensky, 172, 193, 233, 284, 360, 381, 392, 405

W

War, and politics, 84
War criminals, 328, 343
Wassilevsky, 365, 369
Wavell, 305*n.*
Wehrmacht, 308, 310, 311, 341; first defeat of, 302; as inferior to Red Army, 351; 'reconditioning' of, 351*n.*
Weizsäcker, Baron, 234, 237, 238, 290
Welles, Sumner, 351
Weygand, 115, 205, 206, 253
White Russians, 108, 113-14
Wiedemann, Capt., 220
Wiehl, 234
Wilkie, Wendell, 325-6
Willoughby, General, 248*n.*
Witte, 49
Woermann, 238
Women, in U.S.S.R., 192
World War I, outbreak of, 69; Kerensky's offensive in, 86-8
World War II, start of Russian campaign, 295
Wrangel, 114

Y

Yakir, and conspiracy against Stalin, 185, 186
Yalta Conference, 367-79, 388
Ybarnagary, 252
Yogi, 69
Youreniev, 210-11
Yudenitch, 113
Yugoslavia, 280, 282-3, 358-9

Z

Zakopani, 64
Zakovsky, 182, 184, 188
Zaloutzky, 73
Zavarzine, 33
Zelim-Khan, 16

Zimmerwald Conference, 90
Zinoviev, 64, 82, 90, 93, 97, 99, 105, 111, 113, 117, 125, 134; and Stalin, 60; and Trotzky, 84-5; and Lenin's illness, 119; and Lenin's Testament, 124; and Cave of the Dead Mule, 126-7; and Lenin's death, 131; as member of Septet, 136; and Trotzky's 'Lessons of October,' 133; and Kamenev, their attempt to oppose Stalin, 144-6; and Trotzky, their alliance against Stalin, 148-50; excluded from party, 152; and the G.P.U., 153-4; sentenced to imprisonment, 174; sent to Yakutsk prison, 177; final trial and execution of, 178-81
Zozoula, 114
Zuckermann, 184, 211
Zurich, 77
Zviezda, 63

Printed in Great Britain
by Amazon

83683734R00251